HISTORY
OF RUSSIA

Sergei Mikhailovich Soloviev

The
Academic International Press
Edition
of
Sergei M. Soloviev

History of Russia From Earliest Times

G. EDWARD ORCHARD
General Editor

Contributing Editors

HUGH F. GRAHAM

JOHN D. WINDHAUSEN

ALEXANDER V. MULLER

K.A. PAPMEHL

RICHARD HANTULA

WALTER J. GLEASON, JR.

WILLIAM H. HILL

G. EDWARD ORCHARD

LINDSEY A.J. HUGHES

NICKOLAS LUPININ

GEORGE E. MUNRO

DANIEL L. SCHLAFLY, JR.

ANTHONY L.H. RHINELANDER

SERGEI M. SOLOVIEV

History of Russia

Volume 17
Michael Romanov

The Last Years, 1634-1645

Edited and Translated
By

G. Edward Orchard

Academic International Press
1996

The Academic International Press Edition of S.M. Soloviev's
History of Russia From Earliest Times in fifty volumes.

Volume 17. *Michael Romanov. The Last Years, 1634-1645.*
Unabridged translation of the text of Chapters IV and V of Volume
9 of S.M. Soloviev's *Istoriia Rossii s drevneishikh vremen* as found
in Volume V of this work published in Moscow in 1965, with
added annotation by G. Edward Orchard.

ISBN: 0-87569-149-8

Composition by Sharon Lackey

Printed in the United States of America

A list of Academic International Press publications is found at
the end of this volume.

ACADEMIC INTERNATIONAL PRESS
Box 1111 • Gulf Breeze FL 32562-1111 • USA

CONTENTS

Urged to Accept Orthodoxy—Correspondence with Patriarch—
Valdemar Attempts to Escape—Marselis Converses with
Valdemar—The Basistov Affair—Valdemar Writes to Tsar and
Stempkowski—News of Pretender in Turkey—Prince Lvov's
Mission to Poland—Two Pretenders in Poland—Fatal Illness of
Tsar Michael.

WEIGHTS AND MEASURES

Linear and Surface Measures

Arshin: 16 vershoks, 28 in (diuims) 72.12 cm
Chetvert (quarter): 1/4 arshin, 1/2 desiatine, 1.35
    acre (sometimes 1.5 desiatinas or ca 4.1 acres)
Desiatina: 2,400 square sazhens, 2.7 acres, 1.025
    hectares
Diuim: 1 inch, 2.54 cm
Fut: 12 diuims, 1 foot, 30.48 cm
Obza (areal): c. 10 chetverts, 13–15 acres

Osmina: 1/4 desiatina, 600 sq. sazhens, .256
    hectare
Sazhen: 3 arshins, 7 feet, 2.133 m
Vershok: 1.75 in, 4.445 cm, 1/16 arshin
Verst: 500 sazhens, 1,166 yards and 2 feet, .663
    miles, 1.0668 km
Voloka (plowland): 19 desiatinas, 20 hectares, 49
    acres

Liquid Measures

Bochka (barrel): 40 vedros, 121 gallons, 492 liters
Chetvert (quarter): 1.4 bochkas, 32.5 gallons
Kufa: 30 stofy

Stof: Kruzhka (cup), 1/10 vedro, c. 1.3 quarts, 1.23
    liters
Vedro (pail): 3.25 gallons, 12.3 liters, 10 stofy

Weights

Berkovets: 361 lbs, 10 puds
Bezmen: c. 1 kg., 2.2 lbs
Chetverik (grain measure dating from 16th century):
    1/8 chetvert, 15.8 lbs
Chetvert (grain measure): 1/4 rad, 3.5 puds, 126.39
    lbs, c. 8 bushels
Funt: 96 zolotniks, .903 lbs, 14.4 ozs, 408.24 kg
Grivenka: 205 grams
Kad: 4 chetverts, 14 puds, 505.56 lbs
Kamen (stone): 32 funt

Korob (basket): 7 puds, 252 lbs
Osmina (eighth): 2 osmina to a chetvert (dry
    measure)
Polbezmen: c. 500 g, 1 lb
Polosmina (sixteenth): 1/2 osmina
Pud: 40 funts, 36.113 lbs (US), 40 lbs (Russian),
    16.38 kg
Rad: 14 puds, 505.58 lb
Zolotnik: 1/96 lbs, 4.26 grams

Money

Altyn: 6 Muscovite dengas, 3 copecks
Chervonets (chervonny): gold coin of first half of
    18th century worth c. 3 rubles
Chetvertak: silver coin equal to 25 copecks or 1/4
    ruble (18–19th centuries)
Copeck: two Muscovite dengas
Denga: 1/2 copeck
Grivna: 20 Muscovite dengas, 100 grivnas equals 1
    ruble, 10 copecks
Grosh: 10 peniaz
Grosh litovsky (Lithuanian grosh): 5 silver copecks
Kopa grosh: 60 groshas, one Muscovite poltina, 1/2
    ruble
Moskovka: 1/2 copeck
Muscovite Denga: 200 equals 1 ruble
Novgorod Denga: 100 equals 1 ruble

Novgorodka: 1 copeck
Peniaz: 10 equals one grosh (Lithuania)
Poltina (poltinnik): 50 copecks, 100 dengas, 1
    ruble
Poltora: 1 1/2 rubles
Polupoltina (-nik): 25 copecks, 50 dengas
Ruble: 100 copecks, 200 dengas
Shiroky grosh (large silver coin): 20 Muscovite
    copecks.

Foreign Denominations

Chervonnyi: c. 3 rubles
Ducat: c. 3 rubles
Efimok: c. 1 ruble, 1 chervonets or chervonnyi
Levok: Dutch silver lion dollar
Thaler (Joachimsthaler): c. 1 ruble, 1 chervonets
    or chervonnyi

Note: Weights and measures often changed values over time and sometimes held more than one
value at the same time. For details consult Sergei G. Pushkarev, *Dictionary of Russian Historical
Terms from the Eleventh Century to 1917* (Yale, 1970).

PREFACE

This book is an unabridged translation of Volume 9, Chapters 4-5, of the Soviet edition of Soloviev's *Istoriia Rossii s drevneishikh vremen* (History of Russia from Earliest Times) republished in Moscow in 1959-1966. In the Moscow edition it is found in Book V, pages 186-354.

We have divided the original two chapters into six. Soloviev's first chapter, in the original pp. 186-255, is divided into three. Our first chapter covers pp. 186-201 in the original, and deals with relations with Russia's immediate western neighbors, Poland and Sweden, in the period immediately following the War of Smolensk. The second chapter, pp. 201-229 in the original, deals with Russo-Turkish relations from the conclusion of Turkey's war with Poland (1622) to the Muscovite decision not to accept Azov from the hands of the Don and Zaporozhian Cossacks (1643). The third chapter, pp. 229-255 in the original, deals with the abortive attempts to secure a match between the tsar's daughter Irina and the Danish prince Valdemar, and ends with the tsar's death in 1645.

The second of Soloviev's chapters is likewise divided into three. The first, in the original pp. 256-283, is largely a retrospective treatment of the reign of Michael, and of the earlier part of the seventeenth century in general. Chapter V, corresponding to pp. 283-311 in the original, is largely taken up with the rather dismal picture presented by the urban population during this period. Chapter VI, pp. 311-354 in the Soviet edition, presents an ill-assorted mélange of material, which I have labelled "Exploration, Religion and Culture."

Soloviev's pages are featureless and interminable, one long and complex sentence treading Indian file after another. To make the text easier to follow, long paragraphs and sentences have been broken into shorter ones. The main consideration has been to make his history as readable as possible consistent with accuracy. An effort has been made to find English-language equivalents for all the technical terms that Soloviev employs (ranks, offices, titles, legal, administrative, and so on) in order to smooth the flow of the narrative for the general reader and to avoid cluttering the pages with untranslated words. The exception involves Russian words which have become common in English—boyar, tsar, cossack, khan. The translator remains acutely aware of the shortcomings of this approach.

Most of the subtitles are based on the descriptive topic headings clustered at the beginnings of the chapters in the Russian edition. These headings have been moved into the body of the text as subtitles to mark the transition from one subject to another. In some cases new subtitles have been added, but Soloviev's arrangement of the material has not been altered.

Remarks in parentheses in the text are Soloviev's, as well as the italicization of words or phrases for emphasis. Explanatory or interpretive information has been supplied by the translator in footnotes placed at the end of the book. Where it appears in the text of the translation, it is enclosed in brackets. The general policy followed in annotating has been to identify prominent personalities at first mention and to give explanations and elucidations of obscure or uncommon terms and passages, assuming that the usual reader will have relatively little familiarity with Russian history. Most of Soloviev's own notes are not included; their highly specialized archival, documentary, and bibliographic nature would only be of value to specialists who would prefer to consult the original Russian text. Similarly, most of the notes added by the editors of the Soviet edition also have been excluded since they too are technical in nature, primarily supplying fuller bibliographic citations than Soloviev's notes. When the author's notes and those of the Soviet editors are included, they are so designated. All other notes are those of the present editor. In the notes the reader frequently is referred to entries in the *Modern Encyclopedia of Russian, Soviet and Eurasian History* (MERSH) and its *Supplement,* a reliable and up-to-date reference source readily available in most university libraries.

Russian personal names are preserved in their Russian form except for Alexander, Alexis, Michael, Nicholas, Catherine, and Peter, which English usage has made familiar with respect to Russian historical figures. The names of important ecclesiastics have been recast into Latin or Greek equivalents, especially for the earlier period of Russian history. This applies to prominent individuals; less prominent figures get their Russian forms. Certain other names and terms have been anglicized for the sake of clarity and because they are used widely, such as Casimir, Sophia, Danzig, boyar, rubles, versts, and Dnieper.

The editors of the edition published in the USSR frequently added patronymics and other names, and these have been retained without brackets; patronymics appearing in the original edition also have been kept. Plural forms for names and terms which might be confusing have been anglicized—Vologdians rather than Vologzhane, Voguls and not Vogulichi, the Dolgorukys not Dolgorukie, and so on; in a few cases the Russian plural form is used when it is common. The final "-iia" in feminine personal names has been shortened to "-ia" — "Maria" and "Evdokia" instead of "Mariia" and "Evdokiia." Most Slavic surnames show gender, and this has been preserved. An "-a" at the end of a word usually signifies a female. For example, Golovkin's wife or daughter would be Golovkina.

Non-Russian names, locations, terms, ranks and so on are spelled according to the language native to the person or particular to the city, region or culture where this can be determined. Confusion arises at times because the text is not clear about nationalities. An example is Lithuania where at least three languages intermingle. In such cases the context rules; the Russian rendering is the last resort. Individuals whose names were once non-Russian but were in Russian service for generations are named by the original spelling of the family name. Turkish, Tatar, Persian, and other names and terms are usually spelled in the original according to accepted forms in scholarly books. In some instances, if not otherwise ascertainable, they are translated from the Russian as given by Soloviev. The names of geographical locations conform to commonly accepted English usage—Podolia, Moscow, Copenhagen, Saxony, and so on.

With respect to transliteration, the translation follows a modified version of the Library of Congress system, omitting diacritical marks and ligatures, and rendering an initial "Ia-" and "Iu-" as "Ya-" and "Yu-" ("Yasnaia" and "Yury") and occasionally the initial "E-" as "ye" (Yermak, Yevlev); the suffix "-yi" or "-ii" as "y" ("Dmitry Poliansky" instead of "Dmitrii Polianskii"); and the form "-oi" has been replaced by "-oy" ("Donskoy" instead of "Donskoi"). The soft sign, indicated by an apostrophe in some transliteration systems, is usually dropped altogether ("tsar" instead of "tsar'"), although in some cases an "i" has been inserted in place of a hard or a soft sign: "Soloviev" instead of "Solov'ev."

All dates, as in Soloviev's original text, except where otherwise specified, are according to the Julian calendar, in use in most of Western Europe in the sixteenth century until 1582; this in spite of the fact that the Russians themselves at the time figured dates from the creation of the world (which they reckoned to be 5508 BC), though in the seventeenth century some Russian authors were beginning to compute dates from the birth of Christ.

A table of weights and measures is included at the front of this volume for the convenience of the reader. The source of illustrations in each case is as noted.

This volume was translated intermittently while editing other segments of this history. In the main it was occupational therapy in order to keep my hand in as a translator and to see if I can practice what I preach; sometimes a change is as good as a rest. It also enabled me to round off the work I did in translating the preceding three volumes, prior to becoming General Editor. Since no man is competent to judge his own cause, I am grateful to Lindsey Hughes, of the School of Slavonic and East European Studies, University of London, for agreeing to a reversal of customary roles in editing the text, making many helpful suggestions and curbing some of my wilder guesses. Needless to say, responsibility for any errors that remain are mine.

G. Edward Orchard

INTRODUCTION

The previous volume ended with the death of Patriarch Filaret and the conclusion of the Russo-Polish War of 1632-1634. Under the terms of the Truce of Polianovka, Muscovy did somewhat better than may have been expected, given its dismal performance in the war. While Smolensk, the main objective, was unattained and the Swedish alliance had collapsed with the death in battle of King Gustav Adolf, the truce fulfilled the classic demand of diplomacy, namely that both parties left the conference table with some degree of satisfaction. Russia retained Serpeisk, and a number of boundary commissions were appointed, some of which subsequently found in Moscow's favor. Wladyslaw IV, but newly elected to the throne and short of cash, was delighted to pocket the indemnity paid to him personally for renunciation of his pretensions to the Muscovite tsardom; besides, it was more than doubtful that his overmighty subjects would foot the bill for yet another campaign.

Apart from the War of Smolensk, Michael's reign after the Truce of Deulino (1618) was without any major external conflict. The main reason was that in Russia war and peace tended to be anticyclical to what was going on elsewhere in Europe. The determining factor was the mercenary market. While the Western powers were embroiled in the Thirty Years War mercenaries commanded for their services a high price, which Muscovy could not afford. From Soloviev's account, moreover, it is apparent that those who did find their way into Russian service were not of very high quality. After the Treaty of Westphalia, on the other hand, things changed, and Tsar Alexis was able to recruit seasoned veterans at bargain prices to lead his "regiments of the new formation" during the Thirteen Years War against Poland. Consequently the Russians and Poles for the last eleven years of Michael's reign were not very serious in their mutual belligerency, even though a state of war still existed, mitigated only by a long truce. Their exchanges were confined to quibbles over protocol, minor border provocations, trade disputes and allegations of smuggling brandy and tobacco.

A constant irritant in international relations was posed by the cossacks. The Zaporozhian Cossacks technically were subjects of the Polish king, the Don Cossacks of the Muscovite tsar. In practical terms they were subject to neither, and there was much coming and going between them, nor was it easy to distinguish between the two hosts. This factor was convenient when either government wished to disavow the cossacks' actions, but could also prove embarrassing when Moscow wished to preserve correct relations with either Poland or Turkey.

With Sweden relations had been amicable since the Peace of Stolbovo (1617). Michael and Gustav Adolf even were allies in 1632. At the king's death the scepter passed to his six-year-old daughter Kristina, under the able tutelage of Chancellor Axel Oxenstierna, who continued most of the policies of the previous reign. During the Thirty Years War grain frequently was sold at cost by Russia to Sweden, for re-export at a profit to the Netherlands; thus Russia indirectly was subsidizing the Protestant cause.

It was with Sweden that Russia first exchanged permanent diplomatic representatives or "resident agents." Even in Western Europe this practice was barely a century old, and both Russia and Sweden were novices at international diplomacy, so neither really knew how such exchanges should be handled. Should the resident's costs be borne by his own government, or by the host country? What redress was appropriate for injury or dishonor to the ambassador or members of his suite? Conversely, how was misconduct by members of the embassy to be dealt with? At what point did gathering of information for dispatches become tantamount to espionage? It became evident that the Muscovite government was less than enthusiastic about the innovation, considering it to be more trouble than it was worth. In 1642 the Muscovite resident Dmitry Frantsbekov was recalled from Stockholm, though the Swedish resident Krusbjorn remained in Moscow until the end of the reign.

The Muscovite government repeatedly encountered demands from representatives of Western governments for transit facilities for the purpose of trade with Persia. This was one of the main objectives of the English Muscovy Company in the sixteenth century, and of the Dutch early in the seventeenth. Neither had been successful, and Patriarch Filaret in particular had set his face against any further concessions to foreign merchants. Now that Filaret was dead, another such request received a more sympathetic ear, especially as it was accompanied by a promise of six hundred thousand reichsthalers annually for the tsar's treasury. This proposal came not from England or Holland, but from a consortium of Holstein merchants backed by Duke Friedrich I, represented by Philip Crusius and Otto Brüggemann. Secretary to the embassy was Adam Ölschläger, who wrote under the name Olearius, to whom we shall return later.

It soon became apparent that both parties to the deal were over-optimistic. The ready cash was not forthcoming, while Russian merchants and boyars accused the Holsteiners, in the case of Brüggemann with ample justification, of dishonesty. The expedition lost two of its ships, not on the high seas, but on inland waterways supposedly under the tar's sovereignty. The Persians proved to be less than cooperative in the venture. The enterprise dissolved amid mutual recriminations between duke and tsar, and Brüggemann paid for the failure with his head.

Soloviev then turns to a discussion of Turkish affairs, from the end of the Polish-Turkish war of 1620-1621 to the abandonment of Azov in 1643. The war was provoked by the action of Sigismund III in 1618, when he sent troops to Vienna to aid his brother-in-law Ferdinand II against the Transylvanian prince Bethlen Gabor, a Turkish vassal. Bethlen then intrigued with Osman II to attack the Poles. In September 1620 the Ottoman armies under Iskender-Pasha inflicted a crushing defeat on the Poles at Cecora. Hetman Sahaidachny was taken prisoner and Hetman Zolkiewski was slain. The decision was reversed the following year when the defenders of Chocim made a desperate sortie and defeated the Turks, who were commanded by the sultan in person and had a three-to-one superiority. The conflict thus ended in a draw, both sides considering further hostilities pointless. The Polish Sejm, having exacted a record eight-fold land tax to meet the expenses of the war, warned the king off any further military adventures, whether against Muscovy or Turkey, or intervention in what was to become the Thirty Years War.

By the time the Turkish ambassador Thomas Cantacuzene reached Moscow the issue of an anti-Polish alliance was dead, though each side accused the other of bad faith in making a separate peace. Further complications were posed by the cossacks and the Crimeans, both of whom raided their respective borderlands even as Russian and Turkish emissaries were talking peace and alliance, leaving the diplomats with much explaining to do and exposing them to much hostility and danger along the way. Matters almost came to a head when in 1637 the cossacks first murdered Cantacuzene and then proceeded to capture Azov, which they then offered to Tsar Michael.

The offer was very tempting, and an Assembly of the Land was called to deliberate the matter. Soloviev gives a very detailed description of the Assembly's proceedings. Sober counsels eventually prevailed. To annex territory was one thing; to defend and administer it was another, and Moscow could not afford a war, whether against the Turks or anyone else. Reluctantly in 1642 the tsar ordered the cossacks to evacuate Azov, which they did, leaving the city an uninhabitable pile of rubble.

There follows a narration of the Prince Valdemar affair. Tsar Michael was anxious to find a suitable match for his daughter Irina. After the Danish-born translator Ivan Fomin was sent to his native land to sound out the situation, the candidate chosen was Prince Valdemar, a son of King Christian IV by a morganatic marriage. In 1641 the prince came to Moscow in the capacity of an ambassador, giving the Muscovite officials a good chance to observe him. A return embassy was sent but the ambassadors, much to the annoyance of the tsar and boyars, came back without fulfilling their mission. The project was rescued by another Dane resident in Moscow, Peter Marselis, who was sent to Denmark to offer a generous settlement to the prince, whom he also gave to understand that he would be under no compulsion to convert from Lutheranism to Orthodoxy.

This assurance proved to be misleading since once in Moscow Valdemar found himself subjected to intense pressure from tsar, boyars and patriarch to change his religion. He even was prepared to have any children born of the marriage raised as Orthodox, but could not bring himself to make the change. Even when he refused outright and asked to be sent home, he was detained by force, and vainly tried to fight his way out. Despite Marselis's efforts to smooth the matter over, an international scandal ensued, and Prince Shakhovskoy almost lost his head over the matter. Valdemar's dispatch homewards was the first piece of unfinished business taken care of after the accession of Tsar Alexis.

Another international scandal was the appearance in Poland of two pretenders, one claiming to be a fictitious son of Tsar Vasily Shuisky. The other, more serious, was Luba, touted as Marina Mniszech's son, executed in 1614, but for whom it was alleged that another child was substituted. Luba actually was brought to Moscow under safe conduct and interrogated, and then sent back after swearing he would renounce his imposture.

The Prince Valdemar affair and the Luba investigation were still pending when Michael died on July 12, 1645. His was one of the most unremarkable reigns in Russian history, despite its thirty-two years' duration. Very little is written about it, in comparison with what preceded and followed it. Michael himself had a very bland personality and was of very limited intelligence, marred by a disturbed childhood and chronically poor health. On the positive side it may be said that for most of his reign Russia stayed clear of international complications, giving the land time to recover from the trauma of the Time of Troubles, a breathing space which likely made possible the expansion and reorganization of Tsar Alexis's reign and eventually the reforms of Peter the Great.

The remainder of this volume is of a retrospective nature. As before, the events of the Time of Troubles are rehashed. Social relations, severely shaken by Ivan the Terrible's reign of terror, were thrown further into turmoil by the Troubles. Yet neither the oprichnina nor the Troubles destroyed the old boyar aristocracy. "We were in disgrace under previous sovereigns, but they did not take the government away from us." What domestic upheaval and war had failed to do was achieved by attrition. "The Romanovs came to the throne, the Godunovs were banished, the Shuiskys became extinct, followed by the Mstislavskys and Vorotynskys, while the most important and energetic Golitsyns perished." Even the younger branch of the Romanovs faded out of the picture. Michael's uncle Ivan Nikitich, rather than have to take part in a number of undignified precedence disputes, even though for the most part he won them, absented himself from court, preferring the comfort of his Probrazhenskoe estate. His only surviving son Nikita was a lifelong bachelor.

The ancient boyar aristocracy was increasingly under pressure from the service gentry, which successive governments in their stumbling fashion sought to protect through ensuring the viability of their landholdings by restricting the movement of peasants. Very soon the outcry against lowborn favorites was heard and a tedious succession of precedence suits was launched, recorded by Soloviev, not for the first time, in agonizing detail. When the reader reaches Volume 25 of this series he doubtless will be as relieved as contemporaries were in 1682 when it was proclaimed "May this Code of Precedence, hateful to God, creating enmity, hateful to brotherhood and destructive of love, perish in the flames and nevermore be recalled for all times!"

Another antagonism, which Soloviev points out here and expands upon in the next chapter, was that between the nobility and the urban population. The townsmen, along with the service gentry, had played a major role in the liberation of the country, with little to show for their efforts. "Shattered during the Troubles, their businesses ruined, oppressed by the exaction of fifths which were so vital to the reconstruction of the realm...the townsmen had no sympathy for the aspirations of that class from which their governors were drawn."

Above it all stood the tsar. "His weakness, good nature and purity of life produced an impression upon the people which was very favorable for the supreme authority." Anything evil must of necessity have proceeded from his underlings without his knowledge. The tsar could do no wrong. Indeed, this particular tsar could not do much of anything. On being commissioned to write an encyclopedia entry about him,[1] I was hard put to it to compile a four-page biographical sketch, such a nonentity does he appear to have been. Apart from two very slim volumes by V. Berkh, published in 1832,[2] there does not exist a full-length biography of him. Perhaps the earlier and latter parts of his reign, before the return and after the death of Filaret, lend credence to the theory that government worked best when the monarch was a figurehead, what we would call a rubber stamp, being trundled out for ceremonial occasions, but for the most part leaving the running of affairs to "natural advisers" as embodied in the boyar council and its attendant corps of bureaucrats in the prikaz (bureau) system. Particularly after the death of Filaret there seems to have been no real power behind the throne, though by the end of the reign the star of Boris Morozov was patently in the ascendant; yet somehow things continued to function fairly normally.

The next section follows the subsequent careers of individuals and families prominent during the Time of Troubles. Some of the Godunovs returned to service, but none of course enjoyed their former prominence. The same may be said for the Nagoys, whether as relatives of the true or false Dmitry. Boris Godunov's tragic daughter Xenia finally was laid to rest in 1622 alongside her parents and brother in the forecourt of the Trinity-St. Sergius monastery. The last of the Shuiskys, Prince Ivan Ivanovich, returned from Polish captivity, played no further significant part in public affairs. Prince Dmitry Timofeevich Trubetskoy, one of the "triumvirs" of 1612, subsequently had a rather undistinguished military record before being shunted off into semi-honorific exile as governor of Tobolsk. Even Minin and Pozharsky, the undoubted heroes of the liberation, were consigned to relative obscurity, although their services did not go unrewarded. The careers of the conciliar secretaries Tomila Lugovskoy, who remained steadfast, and Ivan Gramotin, the archetypal timeserver, also are traced.

Following this we are given a very good idea of why Michael's Muscovy did well to stay out of armed conflict. For a start, any military appointments made entailed the inevitable precedence disputes, hopelessly scrambling the chain of command. Next there was the problem that many whose names were on the muster roll failed to report for service, and so more time was wasted rounding up defaulters. Frequently those who did turn up were inadequately equipped. Some pleading poverty did so legitimately, and some interim provision had to be made so that they could report for service. Even the official figures given later in the chapter were not such as to inspire confidence in the event of hostilities. As far as the mercenary market was concerned, Michael's recruiting agents evidently were scraping the bottom of the barrel, while cossack and Tatar auxiliaries were often more trouble than they were worth.

Soloviev then expands on the unsatisfactory state of the urban communities. Even the tsar's tax collectors, men not noted for their compassion, reported back that the townsmen were destitute and unable to pay more. Some abandoned their homes and businesses in order to evade excessive taxation. Tax assessments were unrealistic, taking no account of the devastations of the Troubles or the number of abandoned habitations. Other townsmen fled their communities for the protection of ecclesiastical and secular landlords. Decrees called for their return to the town quarter, but to judge from the frequency of their repetition these injunctions had little effect. In borderland towns the artisan class was virtually nonexistent, and local governors turned a blind eye to unofficial activities by the musketeers of the garrison, whose pay in any case was likely in arrears.

Another problem, to which the central government was not entirely insensitive, was that of the malfeasance of local officials, whether appointed or elected. During Ivan IV's reign the tendency was for the vicegerents, representatives of the central government, to be replaced with locally elected magistrates, the so-called guba elders. Difficulty in finding men willing or competent to shoulder such onerous and unpopular responsibilities led once again to the appointment of representatives of central authority, this time taking the form of town governors or voevodas, a practice formerly limited to towns close to the military frontier. Although Soloviev does not comment on the phenomenon, it is evident that in the early seventeenth century town governors and elected magistrates existed uneasily alongside each other.

Complaints about the rapacity and venality of local officials were legion. In some places the communities themselves asked for elected officials to be replaced by governors. Soloviev cites the case of Shuia in detail. It is not known how far this community was typical, but the townsmen petitioned the tsar against their local officials no less than five times in twenty-eight years. Sometimes governors, usually appointed in pairs, paralyzed all business by refusing to speak to each other. In Yakutsk differences between followers of the two hostile governors actually came to a pitched battle. If the community concerned was relatively close to Moscow, it was possible to petition the tsar for redress; further away the local inhabitants were forced to take the law into their own hands. In Yeniseisk the residents of the town and district virtually staged a strike against a governor who illegally demanded transportation duties.

Special provision was made for Novgorod, which had been under Swedish occupation for six years. The inhabitants were given tax exemption for three years, and attempts were made to revive commerce. Foreign merchants were restricted except for the Swedes, who benefitted from the free trade provisions of the Peace of Stolbovo. Other foreigners had to be licensed by the tsar's officials, and measures were taken against interlopers. Non-Russians were prohibited from entering the citadel, which was placed in a posture of ready defence. The Novgorod mint, which in the past set the standard for the whole of Russia, soon resumed production.

While Russians looked askance at foreigners they still needed experts from abroad, especially metallurgists. During Michael's reign the armament manufactories in the vicinity of Tula developed, thanks to the expertise and organizing ability of the Dutch entrepreneurs Vinius and Akema. The merchant Peter Marselis, already known to us in connection

with the Prince Valdemar affair, established a mercantile dynasty in
Muscovy.[3]
The exploration and conquest of Siberia proceeded under its own
momentum. Yeniseisk was founded in 1619, Krasnoiarsk in 1628, Ilimsk
and Bratsk in 1630, Verkholensk in 1642, while cossack winter quarters
appeared along the Upper and Lower Kolyma rivers. Although after the
conquest of the Siberian khanate towards the end of the preceding century
there was little in the way of organized political units to resist the Russian
advance, the process was far from peaceful. Force and fraud were used to
extract both tribute and information from the natives. The government and
church were aware of this problem, but to little avail, since the natives had
no Bartolomé de las Casas to advocate their cause. Besides, as in South
America, the government and church were at cross purposes. Moscow was
primarily concerned with tapping the wealth of the new lands and discour-
aged attempts at conversion to Christianity, which might make the native
tribes less willing to accept Russian protection. At Tobolsk, on the other
hand, there was established a missionary archbishopric which carried on
vigorous proselytizing activities. Patriarch Filaret nevertheless seemed
more concerned with the morals of the European population, especially the
contracting of unlicensed marriages with native women, often with the
connivance of the local clergy, and the influx of prostitutes into the new
settlements.

Not only in Siberia but also elsewhere in Russia the state of the Orthodox church was lamentable. Discipline even within the leading religious foundation was nonexistent. Archimandrite Dionisy of the Trinity-St.
Sergius monastery, who during the Troubles distinguished himself by his
physical courage and civic leadership, within his own community allowed
himself to be bullied by two monastic thugs, "idle chatterers" such as the
precentor Login and the subprecentor Filaret. Then, much against his
better judgement, he accepted the task of revising the service books, which
as Soloviev quickly points out was to lead to the schism nearly half a century later. Since the patriarchal see during the vacancy caused by the
absence of Filaret Nikitich was administered by the obscurantist Metropolitan Jonas of Krutitsa, Dionisy quickly got into trouble, being deposed,
imprisoned, humiliated, accused of heresy and banished to the New Savior
monastery. Fortunately for him Filaret soon returned, assumed the patriarchal throne, dismissed Jonas and reinstated Dionisy.

If discipline had slipped so far even within the Trinity monastery, what
could be said of the lesser foundations? Soloviev cites a whole series of

cases of laxness and corruption. Respect for the clergy was at a low ebb. Priests and deacons were subjected to physical violence, and even venerable bishops were known to engage in undignified fisticuffs. The same malaise also affected secular affairs. The government's only response seems to have been to increase the harshness of penalities, but the problem was that of apprehending malefactors, since there were many interstices in the system of law enforcement where the tsar's writ simply did not run.[4]

Soloviev then turns to the intellectual and cultural history of the reign. The case of Prince Ivan Khvorostinin, a Westernizer *avant la lettre,* must have been of particular interest to Soloviev, who intellectually was firmly with the Westernizers in their controversy with the Slavophiles, but did not share the Catholicizing tendency of Chaadaev and Pecherin or the secular outlook of Belinsky and Herzen, remaining devoutly Orthodox. Soloviev perceives that in the seventeenth century there was an inability to distinguish between form and substance. "They did not see that Orthodoxy was not a matter of beards, not eating veal and so forth. Changing their external and immutable for another external and immutable was regarded as changing the basic, the substantial, the religious, and therefore a heresy and a sin." Neither, Soloviev argues, could the dissidents themselves make this distinction. "A Russian who went abroad dressed in foreign garb, accepted foreign customs and thus changed his ancestral faith, since he had no proper understanding of that faith, it being in his consciousness bound up with the customs and superficialities he renounced. Consequently by renouncing the one he could not help renouncing the other."

Such is the explanation he advances to explain the popular attitude to False Dmitry, but these observations could apply equally to Khvorostinin. Even though he never physically left Russia, his was a mental emigration which was equally abhorrent. The same dread of foreign ideas is found in the interrogation of Lavrenty Zizany concerning his catechism. Incidentally, Soloviev does not tell us in the text or explain in his note that Zizany was an immigrant from Lithuania.[5]

Soloviev then turns to the chronicle literature of the period, again harking back to the Time of Troubles. First he deals with The *Manuscript of Filaret, Patriarch of Moscow,* a recension of the official chronicle, and discovers there some interesting emendations. In particular the account of Vasily Shuisky's election as tsar is rewritten in more fulsome terms, and a passage attributing Skopin's death to the tsar's jealousy is deleted. In another chronicle the role of Avraamy Palitsyn in rallying the troops before Moscow is attributed entirely to Minin. The cellarer of the Trinity monastery is ignored completely, while in yet another account even Pozharsky is written out!

Early seventeenth-century accounts of the Troubles, rather than give just a bald factual narrative, also make an attempt to analyze events and apportion blame. "Thus in the historical literature of the seventeenth century there were three contrasting views concerning the Time of Troubles; the view that the population was punished for its sins, without singling out any culprits who were especially sinful; the same view but simultaneously pointing the finger at a specific individual [Boris Godunov or Grishka Otrepiev]; third and last, limiting the causes of the Troubles to personal relationships between Godunov and the aristocrats."

Apart from the main actors in the historical drama, who are depicted in a sometimes lurid light, the secondary actors such as Skopin, Hermogen, Minin and Pozharsky are presented in a very two-dimensional fashion. Eulogies of these heroes, as well as battle scenes, evidently are copied from chronicle or epic descriptions of other heroes and battles, often themselves derivative. Soloviev then contrasts the two chronicles from Pskov, written respectively from the point of view of the "better" and "lesser" people, letting the two accounts speak for themselves with very little commentary.

Supplementing the historical accounts, Soloviev then cites three popular ballads, one concerning the fall of False Dmitry and two concerning the death of Skopin, both of which show the boyars in an unfavorable light; in one they plot the hero's death, in the other they rejoice at it.

Amid all this pessimism regarding the spiritual desert that was Muscovy there appears an oasis of lay piety in the biography of Yuliana Lazarevskaia, written by her son Kallistrat Druzhina Osoryin. As Serge Zenkovsky remarks, "Yuliana was neither a nun who spent her life in a convent, nor a princess whose Christian charity and works gave her the halo of a saintly protectress. She spent all her life with her family, and her biography is filled with the every-day events. While her life was one of prayer and Christian piety, the fact that she remained all her life with her husband and children as a devoted wife, mother and daughter-in-law distinguishes this *vita* from the usual hagiographies dealing with heroes who performed miraculous deeds or defended the Orthodox Faith, and who were usually either hermits, church leaders of pious rulers. With this *vita* there began to appear in Russia a realistic, secular biography."[6] Indeed, the combination we find here of piety and common sense reminds us of her namesake of Norwich, or even St. Theresa of Avila.

Travel literature always has been a popular genre in Russia, the most famous being that of Afanasy Nikitin (1469-1472). For the early seventeenth century we have the voyage to Persia of the Moscow merchant Rodion Kotov, and that of Vasily Gogara to Palestine and Egypt. Soloviev concludes with yet another travel account, this time of foreign origin. Although the final goal of his travels was Persia, the Holstein scholar Adam Olearius left a detailed description of the Russian leg of his travels. The expedition set off from Holstein in 1633, visited Persia in 1634 and 1636, and finally returned to Gottorp in 1639. Olearius visited Moscow again in 1643. Despite the difficulties which beset Russo-Holstein relations, Tsar Michael was sufficiently impressed with Olearius to offer him employment on two separate occasions.

Olearius published two editions of his work, the first in 1647, and an augmented version in 1656, though it is curious that Soloviev evidently preferred to use the earlier edition. Olearius provides us with the most detailed foreign account of Muscovy since that of the imperial ambassador Sigismund von Herberstein, who visited Muscovy in 1517 and 1526. Later commentators on Muscovy cribbed shamelessly from both.

Indeed Soloviev was fortunate in having so many primary sources readily at his disposal. The reign of Nicholas I was perhaps not the most conducive to scholarly enquiry, but in mitigation it must be said that a number of vast projects were undertaken to collect and publish original documents. The trail was blazed in the previous reign by the *Collection of State Documents and Treaties Preserved in the State College of Foreign Affairs.*[7] Other collections of primary sources used include *Letters of Russian Sovereigns and Other Members of the Ruling Family,*[8] the third volumes, respectively, of *Historical Acts Collected and Published by the Archeographical Commission*[9] and the *Acts Collected in the Libraries and Archives of the Russian Empire by the Archeographical Expedition of the Academy of Sciences,* the first two volumes of *Supplements to the Historical Acts Collected by the Archeographical Commission,*[10] and the service records contained in the *Court Records of Military Service* and the *Military Service Books.*[11] A couple of collections of Polish primary sources were also available in print.[12]

Among the secondary sources used were J. Hammer, *History of the Ottoman Empire,*[13] Kobierzycki's *History of Wladyslaw, Prince of Poland and Sweden,*[14] while some local color is provided by V.A. Borisov's *Description of the Town of Shuia and its Surroundings*[15] and Iosif Gamel's *Description of the Tula Armament Factory in its Historical and Technical Aspects.*[16]

For the official chronicle of this period, Soloviev relied upon a 1792 edition, though a much better version was subsequently published,[17] as well as the *Chronicle of Many Rebellions.*[18] Another source used extensively, though still not available in printed form, was the *Obolensky Chronograph.*[19] The Pskov chronicles were available to Soloviev in printed form, though they too have been republished in more recent critical editions.[20]

Of unpublished manuscript sources used by Soloviev, the most important were those contained in the Archive of the Ministry of Foreign Affairs, now deposited in the Central State Archive of Ancient Acts in Moscow.[21]

As indicated earlier, there is very little literature in any language specifically on Michael's reign. In English the most detailed account apart from this translation is George Vernadsky, *The Tsardom of Moscow, 1547-1682* (Yale, 1969), especially Chapter 3. Translation of the relevant sections of V.O. Kliuchevsky's *Course of Russian History* is available in two versions.[22] Paul Dukes, *The Making of Russian Absolutism, 1613-1801* (London, 1982), the fourth volume in the *Longman History of Russia,* provides a brief overview in the opening chapters.

Particular aspects are covered in Michael Hittle, *The Service City* (Harvard, 1979), especially the first three chapters; Walter McKenzie Pintner and Don Karl Rowney, *Russian Officialdom* (Chapel Hill, 1980), again particularly the first three chapters, and Robert O. Crummey, *Aristocrats and Servitors. The Boyar Elite in Russia, 1613-1689* (Princeton, 1983) is a painstaking and readable account of the Russian aristocracy during the last pre-Petrine century. For a survey of the literature of the period, the reader would do well to consult N.K. Gudzy, *History of Early Russian Literature,* translated by Susan Wilbur Jones (New York, 1970) or J.L.I. Fennell and Anthony Stokes, *Early Russian Literature* (London, 1974).

I

POLISH AND SWEDISH RELATIONS, 1634-1640

Thus ended the wars initiated by the Time of Troubles. Shuisky's remains were placed solemnly among those of other Muscovite tsars,[1] but the Godunovs' resting place remained within the Trinity monastery[2] since Dmitry's tomb barred their way into the Archangel cathedral.[3] The moral and political pacification of the Russian people, which Shuisky had wished to impose by external force, now was consummated over his coffin, brought from Poland. Everything went on as before, except that Smolensk, Dorogobuzh and the Severian towns were occupied by Polish troops, while the Swedes held the Izhora land. King Wladyslaw sincerely wanted peace and goodwill with his recent adversary the Muscovite tsar, but the tsar incessantly sent embassies with complaints against Wladyslaw's subjects.

EMBASSY OF PESOCZYNSKI AND SAPIEHA TO MOSCOW

Even as in Warsaw the Muscovite ambassador Prince Lvov[4] and his companions were witnessing the king's oath to observe the Peace of Polianovka,[5] the Polish ambassadors Pesoczynski, castellan of Kamenets, and Sapieha, son of the famous Leo,[6] witnessed the tsar's kissing of the cross in Moscow. At the Polianovka conference several articles demanded by the Polish commissioners were omitted until such time as the Polish emissaries came to Moscow. Accordingly Pesoczynski presented to the boyars a demand that not only the tsar, but also the boyars and the inhabitants of the borderland towns kiss the cross not to violate the peace. Receiving a refusal, they then demanded that in the event that one or the other sovereign died, the oath must be renewed by his successor. This demand also was rejected, as was the demand that the king be allowed to recruit soldiers within the Muscovite realm.

"This is an unprecedented demand," the boyars replied. "Nothing of the kind ever was done before. None of the great sovereign's subjects ever went to serve in any neighboring country, for they are Orthodox Christians of the Greek dispensation. Should they go to serve in foreign lands without any Russian priests accompanying them, they will stop going to church and die unshriven."

The request for free access for service, residence or marriage for subjects on either side likewise was refused. "Our great sovereign," was the reply, "will resist all his foes with his own people, and if at the time it seems appropriate, he may add foreign recruits. But now the sovereign is in brotherly love with your ruler, and so he has dismissed the foreigners in his employ, having paid them in full for their loyal service. If his majesty needs soldiers then, according to his means and if there is good reason, he will hire them; but for now to hire soldiers and keep them idle would be an unnecessary expense. Poles and Lithuanians in Muscovy never before married Russian women because the Russian realm is of the Orthodox faith, while even in Poland and Lithuania people of differing faiths cannot marry."

BORDER DISPUTES

The first complication giving rise to an exchange of notes and complaints was the fixing of the new borders. In 1635 the emissary Yury Telepnev was dispatched to the king to complain about the Polish boundary commissioners encroaching upon Russian territory in the region of Briansk. "In order to induce the boundary commissioners," the instructions read, "in accordance with the treaty to give up the land everywhere and evacuate all the territories seized, we have sent with Telepnev five hundred rubles' worth of sables. He is to assess the local situation and decide which of the lords has greatest influence with the king, and he is to bribe him with the sables." The sables did not help. The boundary disputes dragged on, much to the Muscovite sovereign's displeasure.

DIMINUTION OF THE TSAR'S TITLE

Another grievance was added, the diminution of the tsar's title. In February 1637 Prince Semeon Shakhovskoy[7] was sent to Poland to secure the punishment of the Polish borderland governors for not according the tsar his proper title, as well as to discuss border disputes and the exchange of prisoners. Concerning the transgression of the borderland governors, the lords of the council made the excuse that the governors were military men, not courtiers, and could not write. Moreover the tsar's titles were so extensive that they could not remember them all.

"How is it," the Muscovite emissaries objected, "that nothing is done improperly on our part? When did we ever diminish the king's title? For when perpetual peace was concluded we distributed formularies to all our borderland governors, so they would know how to inscribe the king's title, and they were commanded to adhere to this formula under threat of severe punishment. Yet how did you go about it? Marcin Kalinowski and his companions, instead of writing 'autocrat' wrote merely 'ruler' of All Russia.[8] The intention is clear. Not only Kalinowski and his companions, but anyone who can hear can grasp the implication. Therefore the king should order them to be punished without mercy, and so lift the burden of sin from the soul of your king."

"Marcin Kalinowski and Lukasz Zolkiewski,"[9] the lords replied, "wrote the sovereign's title improperly, and for that they were called before the Senate and reprimanded by the whole Commonwealth, being called simpletons and ignoramuses. For them this was sufficient humiliation and punishment. To punish them any more severely is impossible, since they acted out of ignorance. Furthermore even God does not punish instantly, but is merciful. Your sovereign is great, Christian, pious, merciful and just, and also cannot desire their execution. Moreover our king cannot punish a member of the free gentry except according to statute and with the consent of the whole Commonwealth. The knout as wielded in the Muscovite realm is unknown here, neither was it ever used within our realm. Let us drop the matter, and discuss the boundary."

"We cannot drop the principal matter," protested Shakhovskoy. "Ask something else. The matter of the boundary is the last item on the agenda. Our principal task is to protect our sovereign's honor. If any of you senators are addressed not by your proper title, you would rush to defend your honor, and go to any lengths." "If anyone addresses us improperly, out of malice," the lords answered, "why should we not avenge the insult?"

Shakhovskoy. You, my lords, want to defend your honor, yet out of malice you corrupt our sovereign's title, calling him Mikhail Filaretovich or Fedor Mikhailovich. When you can say that such offenses should go unpunished, where is your justice?

The lords. Such things should not be punished because they were done by mistake, not out of malice. If anyone does this in future, he will be punished.

Finally the lords accepted the ambassadors' demand in writing, and promised to report on it to the king.

"Since the errors in the title," read the reply, "were committed not out of malice but out of foolishness. The tsar should refer these innocent mistakes to the king, who will assume the blame. Now that it has been established between us how our rulers are to be styled, his majesty the king and we, lords of the council, will command that the tsar's title be printed in Polish and distributed to all the borderland towns. In this way there will be no errors. If after November 1 any error appears it will be punished mercilessly, and the king will discuss the matter with all of us, the lords of his council and regional deputies, as to how we shall punish any future errors in inscribing the tsar's title. Whatever the Sejm decides will be written in the form of a constitution, to be printed and distributed to all the borderland towns."

MORE BORDER DISPUTES

Once this matter was settled disputes arose over the border in the regions of Chernigov and Putivl. On this matter, among other things, the lords asserted "In the ancient chronicles it is written that Grand Prince Michael of Chernigov,[10] coming from Algirdas and being subject to Lithuania, died an exile in Moscow." "This is false," replied the ambassadors. "Michael of Chernigov was martyred at the Horde. These chroniclers are not to be believed, since they do not follow the canon.[11] They wrote as they wished, but the chronicler did not follow other chronicles, neither did he observe the canon of the holy fathers."

The lords of the council took leave of the ambassadors. "Our great sovereign and his brother," they said, "wish to be in firm amity and love such as exists with the ambassadors' hereditary sovereign and the king's friend. Our sovereign wishes him and his children all the best, as also between the tsar's children and their own descendants they firmly desire continued brotherhood, amity and unity, so that the subjects of both sovereigns may dwell in peace and tranquillity, and the pagan Muslim nations, seeing their friendship and love, will be intimidated and leave Christian nations unmolested.

"We lords of the council and regional deputies, on behalf of our great sovereign and the whole Commonwealth, promise under oath to seek with all our hearts and true diligence that between our sovereigns brotherly love and affection multiply and not diminish, and that quarrels and enmity not arise on the king's part. Also we ask of you emissaries of his majesty the tsar that you report this to his majesty and our brothers his boyars and councillors. Urge them earnestly to induce the sovereign to be in unshakable brotherly love and amity with his brother our great sovereign."

BOYARS' REACTION

As proof of the sincerity of these wishes in July 1637 the Polish emissaries Jan Oborski and Prince Samuel Sokolinski arrived in Moscow, announcing his majesty's intention of marrying Cecilia Renata, the emperor's sister.[12] Having announced this to the tsar, the emissaries stated "It would be appreciated were his majesty the tsar pleased to send his ambassadors to this great and honorable event and joyful marriage, thereby showing to all the world that by acknowledging these festivities the king's gracious brother is gratified and rejoices. If his majesty the tsar is pleased to comply, not only will the heart of his grace the king be confirmed in fraternity and love towards him, but also the nations subject to the tsar will rejoice in the hope of concord and love and so, God grant, will there be perpetual and unshakable peace and tranquillity. The king our sovereign also will be able to demonstrate to all the world his immutable brotherly love and firm perpetual friendship."

The emissaries were told that the tsar was gratified to receive this news, and were asked when the wedding was to take place. The emissaries answered that it would be on September 6. The boyars pointed out that this was short notice, since an ambassador would not have time to travel from Moscow to Warsaw. The emissaries replied that the king would postpone the event and await the ambassadors. The tsar then ordered all the boyars to consider the matter.

"His majesty the tsar is amazed," was the boyars' answer, "that you emissaries arrived so tardily, for now the sovereign cannot send his ambassador to his royal majesty in time. The autumn season is upon us and the roads are bad, for there will be mud, rain and potholes, making it impossible to dispatch an embassy post haste. Even though his majesty offered to wait, we cannot rush an ambassador to the king's nuptials. But for the sake of friendship and love the great sovereign will send an ambassador to congratulate him as soon as the roads are frozen over."

Accordingly as soon as the winter roads were open the lord-in-waiting Stepan Proestev[13] and the crown secretary Leontiev were dispatched to Warsaw. They brought the newlyweds rich gifts. The king received a golden goblet with a lid, inlaid with sapphires, rubies, emeralds and gems, valued at two thousand rubles; four times forty[14] sable furs, worth fifteen hundred rubles, and two live sables. The queen was given a golden binding with precious stones, worth six hundred rubles; three times forty sables, worth 935 rubles, and two live sables.

The ambassadors' instructions were as follows. "If the king receives their credentials, and tells them that the queen also will be present, they are to say that they are prepared to discharge their embassy, but they must add that when the great sovereign's ambassadors are received by the king the queen should not be present, since never before has this been the practice. Having said that, they are to proceed with their mission. If they are invited for an audience with the queen, they must go, show the presents and then kiss her hand. If the queen speaks to them, they are to compose a reply and speak in a manner befitting the name and dignity of the sovereign, and conducive to the exaltation and expansion of the realm. If the king invites them to dine, they must order the nobles and members of the ambassadorial suite to seat themselves in proper order of rank and carefully, not to get drunk or exchange quarrelsome words. Middle-ranking or lesser members of the suite are not to be brought into the dining hall, lest there be any drunkenness or insubordination. They are not to take carousers or drunkards into the king's palace."

Proestev and Leontiev were sent not just to exchange civilities, or to demonstrate the tsar's friendship and love towards his majesty. They were ordered to reopen the question of punishing those writing the tsar's title incorrectly. "Speak of this to the lords of the council," they were directed, "and express yourselves forcibly and at length with protracted speeches. If the lords say that the town secretary of Dorogobuzh has been ordered to correct his missives, or that the governor Poplonski has been dismissed, tell them that you are tired of hearing of so great an offense receiving such a trifling penalty. Such punishment befits dishonor committed against simple people, not against rulers. Once you have been with the king and have raised the subject according to the sovereign's instruction, say that this is a serious matter, and on behalf of the sovereign demand to appear before the Sejm of the whole Commonwealth to name those who wrote documents in which the tsar's title is belittled. Demand that the lords of the council and all the Commonwealth sentence the offenders to condign punishment, some with the death penalty, others with severe punishment. If such men are not punished, how will disputes arising from such slights ever cease?

"Concerning boundary disputes, declare to the Sejm that these are dragging on in clear violation of the ambassadors' treaty, by reason of the intractability and obstinacy of the king's boundary commissioners. To the Putivl frontier the king has sent as boundary commissioner the bishop of Kiev, who is an interested party and does as he pleases, entering the tsar's lands unlawfully and indulging the inhabitants of Kiev and Chernigov who have settled there. Say that many prisoners yet have to be released, that the king's emissaries on their way back from Moscow hired Russians in Dorogobuzh and tried to abduct from Moscow the master printer Nikita Nesterov, who had to be rescued by the bailiff.

"Complain about Lithuanian merchants. According to the treaty of eternal peace, Polish and Lithuanian merchants were to be allowed to trade in borderland towns, but not to come to Moscow or the surrounding towns, except in ambassadorial suites. Similarly Muscovite merchants may come to Wilno or Cracow only with ambassadors; but Polish merchants, in violation of the treaty, came to the Muscovite towns along the forest roads bringing brandy[15] and tobacco. Those Lithuanian merchants remaining behind after the emissaries' departure apparently were not expelled, while others remained behind ostensibly to seek out prisoners of war. These merchants broke the law, selling brandy and tobacco and causing much disorder amongst the population. Brigands took tobacco from the people and burned it before them, so that shortly afterwards the merchants might come and sell them brandy and tobacco. Lithuanian merchants arriving in the Oskol region illegally with brandy and tobacco were set upon by the governor Konstantin Pushchin, who took from them their goods. The sovereign ordered him executed for this offense, while his son and twenty-five other offenders were punished severely in the presence of the Lithuanian officials sent to investigate this matter, and the seized goods were returned.

"Our sovereign, on account of some common Lithuanian bootleggers, spared not even his governor and many of his followers, yet his majesty the king and you, lords of the council, refuse to execute anyone committing so grave a crime as the slighting of the tsar's majesty.

"In Tver there arrived two Lithuanian merchants, one from Wilno, the other from Smolensk, with brandy and tobacco. They were turned back at Tver, and a bailiff was assigned to them for their protection. Yet five versts from Tver they chased the bailiff away and proceeded illegally to Yaroslavl, committing crimes in many towns. When they arrived at Yaroslavl they were expelled, but then they sold brandy and tobacco around the countryside. For this offense they were imprisoned at Yaroslavl. Later they were released, but the barrel of contraband was broken and the tobacco burned."

LITTLE RUSSIAN COSSACKS CROSS OVER TO MUSCOVY
The emissaries were to declare to the lords of the council that the Crimean khan Bogadyr-Girey sent his brother Nur-ed-Din[16] against the Muscovite borderlands because the Don Cossacks captured Azov. Nur-ed-Din in his

missive stated that he would be accompanied by the Dnieper Cossacks. His majesty the tsar did not believe the Crimean document where it said that his majesty the king allowed the Zaporozhian Cossacks to aid the Crimean khan. If the lords of the council said that the king restrained the cossacks but they evaded punishment and were fleeing to the tsar's side, the emissaries were to answer "In the ambassadors' treaty it was not prohibited to receive refugees, and it is useless to discuss what was not written in the ambassadors' treaty."

If asked whether his majesty were in correspondence with the Roman Pope, they were to reply "His majesty the tsar never has been in correspondence with the Roman Pope, for he has nothing about which to write. The Roman territory is far from the Muscovite realm, there are many intervening realms and lands, and there is nothing to discuss."

Finally the emissaries were ordered to find a master engraver who could inscribe portraits of Tsar Vasily Ivanovich Shuisky, Patriarch Filaret, King Wladyslaw and his queen.

Proestev and Leontiev had an audience with the king and presented their gifts, which Wladyslaw ordered them to place before him on the ground, on top of the carpet. The ambassadors said that it was not meet to place his majesty the tsar's gifts on the ground, but to receive them with respect. The king ordered his entourage to take the gifts. After their audience with the king, the emissaries went to pay their respects to the queen.

The king then summoned them to the palace to attend a comedy and a Russian-style entertainment. The ambassadors replied that they were prepared to attend the comedy, provided that no other ambassadors or emissaries were present. The bailiff assured them that there would not be any, but when they arrived at the palace they learned that the papal legate would be there. "The legate resides in Warsaw," the lords assured them, "for spiritual and not for political reasons. In all lands he is placed at the king's right hand, and you ambassadors must treat him with respect." "Only if we are placed at the king's right hand along with the papal legate," retorted the ambassadors, "will we come to see the comedy."

The ambassadors' words were reported to the king, who sent them word that the king's brother Bishop Karol of Breslau[17] would be seated to the king's right, and to the left the king's sister Katarzyna. The ambassadors would be assigned to the right hand position corresponding with that of Princess Katarzyna on the left. The ambassadors agreed, and the protocol recorded that the papal legate sat on the left next to the princess, while the ambassadors sat to the right about half a sazhen from the queen and prince, and on the same level as the princes' seats.

In response to the ambassadors' points concerning disrespect to the sovereign, answer was given that the lords guilty of diminishing the tsar's title had been reprimanded. Concerning the scribes, it was resolved that if the culprit were a noble he would be imprisoned for six months, and if a commoner he would be knouted. Concerning the boundary disputes, the answer was that the Polish side was entirely in the right. Concerning prisoners, it was pointed out that there still were many prisoners being held in Muscovy.

As for the merchants, it was pointed out that Muscovite borderland governors were taking bribes and gifts from Lithuanian merchants to grant passports, while in other towns merchants were being imprisoned even though their papers were in order. Concerning the cossacks, Nur-ed-Din was lying, since Zaporozhians never were enrolled in the Turkish army.

When Proestev brought this reply to Moscow the tsar sent him to Tula to ask the boyars and princes on frontier service, namely Prince Ivan Borisovich Cherkassky[18] and his companions. "We, your slaves," the principal commander Cherkassky answered the sovereign, "wrote to your boyars and lords-in-waiting and distributed an extract from the reply given by the lords of the council, a separate copy to each, so that they might consider the matter and submit their opinions in writing. So I, your slave Ivashka, and my companions took counsel regarding the first and most important matter, concerning the sovereign's title and how Potocki and his scribe were punished. The lords wrote falsely, in contradiction to the resolution adopted at the last Sejm. When the king's emissaries were with you, they tabled before the boyars the printed proceedings of their Sejm, in which it was written that whoever in future writes your majesty's title in diminished form shall be executed. Now they have altered it to a minor punishment." Prince Prozorovsky[19]wrote that the tsar's honor must be defended. "As the sovereign pleases," wrote Ivan Sheremetev,[20] "so will he do. Concerning the sovereign's great matter, I am not now in the tsar's presence, neither can I take counsel with my brethren. All the same it is clear to me that we must all risk our lives for the sovereign's honor."

"As for the Lithuanian towns, villages and trading settlements established on the sovereign's territory around Putivl," wrote Prince Ivan Andreevich Golitsyn,[21] "it is not befitting to call them to mind. I am unaware of any transgression on our part. I do not feel competent to give my opinion on such a great matter of state, but as for what they write concerning the sovereign's honor, about the title, is a matter for us, the tsar's slaves, to avenge. Neither do we need a Polish alliance against the Crimeans. It seems to me that there is no way our Russian troops can serve alongside the king's, despite all their blandishments. For if they send Cherkass, these also will be accompanied by Poles. If they remain in service for one summer, by the next summer more than half of the Russians will be gone, except for those boyar servitors who are too old or do not wish to serve, while not one poor man will remain."

Prince Dmitry Pozharsky[22] wrote to Cherkassky, "Prince Ivan Borisovich, how can I express my opinion? First of all we must protect the tsar's title. The matter of heralds and merchants is regulated by treaty, and that concerning boundary disputes and scribes is according to what the sovereign decides and the boyars resolve. It would be well if God saw fit to end the boundary dispute in a satisfactory manner and without grief to the sovereign, so that Orthodox Christendom might live in peace and tranquillity."

Having heard the boyars' replies, the tsar ordered a herald to be sent to King Wladyslaw with a written proposal that the disputed lands be surveyed and divided equally. Furthermore the tsar demanded that the king be so good as to seek out Russian prisoners still held in Lithuania. "They may say," the herald was instructed, "that the Cherkass disobeyed the king, who ordered them to be pacified and punished for their offenses. Many of them proceeded to the towns of his majesty the tsar, who by receiving such brigands and lawbreakers displayed hostility towards his brother the king. You may be asked whether, if the king writes about this matter to his majesty the tsar, the sovereign will have them extradited. You are to answer 'You yourselves know that nothing was written in the treaty concerning the extradition of refugees. As for how many Cherkass came over, nothing has been written in any reports from the towns, and it is rumored that the Cherkass dispersed to many places other than the tsar's towns.' If they don't ask, don't bring up the subject."

The king replied that he could not consent to equal partition of the disputed territories. After several insignificant items of correspondence, in February 1640 the king's emissaries Strachowski and Rajecki came to Moscow. On the occasion of their arrival the tax office received a memorandum stating "It has come to the sovereign's attention that Lithuanian merchants now arriving with the emissaries have brought brandy and tobacco for sale. They sell illegally to all manner of people, causing dissension among them. The tsar strictly forbids everyone to buy any, under pain of death."

The emissaries declared that those who incorrectly inscribed the tsar's title were punished mercilessly according to the statute. After this announcement they delivered a complicated article concerning the Zaporozhian Cossacks. "Routed by the king's forces, more than twenty thousand cossacks fled from various towns and places, taking with them many captives, whom they sold in various places. Among these captives were the daughters of Lord Dulski and many others, whom they either sold or gave away to the Putivl governor Nikifor Yurievich Pleshcheev. We sought to recover them from him, but he is detaining them in his Moscow residence. These traitorous cossacks have settled in the tsar's new trading settlements in the steppes, namely along the Userd river and around Livny, Yablonnovo, Novosil, Mtsensk, Oskol, Valuiki, Voronezh, Gremiachy, Dudinsk, Rylsk, Kursk, Putivl, Sevsk and other of the ancient towns belonging to his majesty the tsar.

"His majesty heard a rumor that the greatest traitors and ringleaders of this multitude, Yatsko Ostrenitsa and Andriushka Gunia, were settled and living in Azov, with many of their elders. All these traitors fled to the Muscovite towns with their wives and children, while the tsar was rewarding them and giving them employment. It would be fitting if, according to the judgment of God and by the decree of his majesty the king, they were rotting on the stakes on which they ought to have been impaled. In the definitive treaties it was written that whoever is the king's enemy will also be the tsar's, but rebellious subjects are worse than any foreign enemy. Accordingly the tsar should extradite immediately those twenty thousand cossacks with their leaders Yatsko Ostrenitsa and Andriushka Gunia lest the king voice his complaint before all the world, and the tsar incur the censure of all Christian realms."

The tsar answered Wladyslaw in his letter that he was disappointed by his decision concerning those guilty of diminishing his title. "You, our brother, did not execute or punish these offenders. Without interrogating them you personally condoned their crime, excusing them in violation of all justice on the ground that they were ignorant of Russian writing or speech." The tsar as before demanded the execution of the culprits.

Concerning the cossacks he replied, "Only a few of them arrived, not twenty thousand. There is nothing in the definitive treaty about the extradition of refugees, and it is useless to reopen discussion of what it not written in the treaties." Thus apart from dissatisfaction at the diminution of the title and definition of the frontier, from the direction of Little Russia there appeared a storm cloud threatening to unleash a renewal of fearful hostilities.

RELATIONS WITH SWEDEN

With Sweden there was no dispute, whether concerning titles, frontiers or Zaporozhian Cossacks, and so throughout the reigns of Gustav Adolf[23] and Kristina[24] amicable relations were maintained. After conclusion of the Peace of Polianovka the sole interest of the Swedish government with regard to Moscow consisted of the question whether the tsar would permit Swedes to buy grain at cost. For this purpose Queen Kristina in 1634 sent the tsar a gift of ten cannon with all the necessary munitions, and two thousand muskets, to the total value of 9,034 rubles. Succeeding Meller, the Swedish resident in Moscow was Krusbjorn, to whom the tsar ordered for his maintenance thirty-five rubles a month.

FIRST MUSCOVITE RESIDENT IN STOCKHOLM

The first Russian resident, or *resident agent,*[25] was sent to Stockholm in 1635. He was Dmitry Frantsbekov (Fahrensbach),[26] a baptized foreigner, to whom the queen ordered the same sum to be given as Krusbjorn received in Moscow. She also wrote to the tsar that in other realms it was not customary to give subsistence allowances to foreign agents, because this might lead to inequities and disputes. For this reason the queen proposed to his majesty the tsar whether, for the sake of good neighborly and amicable relations, it would not be better for residents to receive subsistence from their own rather than from their host government.

Frantsbekov complained that even while he was under way to take up his post his servants were assaulted and his baggage stolen. When he reached Stockholm he was lodged outside town in a tavern. Drunken Swedes came up to the tavern keeper and insulted the resident, who complained to the queen's councillors, but they ignored him. Finally on April 25, 1635 some Swedes came at night and attacked his servants with knives, stabbing two of them. Once again the Swedish councillors gave him no satisfaction except to evict the tavern keeper. Frantsbekov also complained that in Stockholm he and his companions were given only seventy efimoks a month, but that bread and all other supplies cost ten times as much as in Moscow. He mentioned this to the councillors but they replied that the Swedish resident in Moscow was receiving only thirty-five

Queen Kristina of Sweden (1645)
Portrait probably by Jacob Elbfas. Stadhus-
expeditionen, Stockholm. By kind permission.

efimoks a month, and he had to be sent from the queen's treasury a supplementary grant of two thousand.

The queen in turn complained to the tsar that Frantsbekov's servants beat a Swede so severely in his home that shortly afterwards he died. "Previously," the tsar wrote to the queen, "Johan Meller[27] resided in Moscow for four years, receiving food and drink monthly, and you never complained that he was being given insufficient subsistence. Yet we sent our agent to you a little over six months ago, and you are demanding that ambassadors serve at their own expense. You write that our agent's servants fatally wounded one of your subjects, but it was your man who started the quarrel, wounding our man in the face with a sword. We have set aside comfortable lodgings for your merchants, while our traders in Stockholm have yet to be provided with any kind of lodging."

The sovereign wrote to Frantsbekov to behave more circumspectly, to petition the queen concerning any grievances, and not take the law into his own hands. "It is shameful to write about the disgraceful deed you have committed in a foreign country. To take the law into your own hands and use force against a man is unbefitting."

It was resolved that the agents of both countries live at their own expense, but Frantsbekov did not remain much longer in Stockholm. In April 1636 he was recalled to Moscow. "According to our decree," read the tsar's missive, "you were to have been in Sweden to gather all kinds of intelligence and communicate it frequently to us in Moscow. You have been in Sweden for some considerable time, but have not sent us any reports, and when you did write, it was about some trifling matter. Therefore we order you to travel back from Sweden to Moscow."

MUSCOVITE ATTITUDE TO RESIDENTS

Krusbjorn, on the other hand, remained in Moscow and continued to give the Chancellery for Foreign Affairs reports about the successes of Swedish arms in Germany during the Thirty Years War. For the sake of friendship and amity the tsar ordered him to be given the loan of three thousand puds of saltpeter, and also against a promissory note signed by Queen Kristina a cash loan of a thousand rubles.

Moscow nevertheless continued to have trouble over residents, as is apparent from the tsar's missive of 1642 to the governor of Pskov, who informed him of the arrival of Peter Loffelt, who was to replace Krusbjorn in Moscow. "There was no mention in the peace treaty of any agents or residents. In former years there came to us from King Gustav Adolf of glorious memory the herald Johan Meller as an agent for the conduct of various business. He remained in Moscow for a year or two, and when he died the agent Peter Krusbjorn was sent to replace him. To represent us in Stockholm Dmitry Frantsbekov was sent as our agent, to gather intelligence concerning Poland and Lithuania, for at that time we were at war with King Wladyslaw of Poland. Now eternal peace has been concluded between us and King Wladyslaw, and we are at peace also with other neighboring realms. We have recalled our agent Dmitry Frantsbekov to Moscow, for there is no point in him remaining in Stockholm, neither will we maintain agents any longer, since they serve no purpose. As for the Swedish agent now residing in Moscow, he no longer has any important state business to conduct. Consequently there is no point in allowing the new agent Peter Loffelt to enter our realm of Russia. There is nothing written in the ambassadors' treaties to say that there should be residents or agents permanently stationed in each other's realm, nor is it befitting to exceed the terms of the treaty, lest anything arise which is contrary to the treaty." Krusbjorn nevertheless remained in Moscow for the remainder of the reign.

THE HOLSTEIN COMPANY AND PERSIAN TRADE

While Filaret Nikitch was alive neither the English nor the French nor the Dutch were allowed transit facilities to Persia. When Filaret died the attitude changed, and in December 1634 a treaty was concluded with the Holstein ambassadors Philip Crusius[28] and Otto Brüggemann,[29] permitting a consortium of Holstein merchants to trade with Persia and India by way of the Muscovite realm for a period of ten years.

The company undertook to pay annually into the tsar's treasury six hundred thousand reichsthalers, in exchange for which they would pay no duty. They undertook to provide the Chancellery for Foreign Affairs a manifest for their goods, and if any of these were needed for the tsar's treasury, they were to surrender them on the spot in exchange for the current market price. The Holsteiners were to buy in Persia all manner of goods; raw silk, precious stones, dyestuffs and all other major goods in which Russian merchants did not trade. They were not to sell raw silk or dyestuffs in Persia, neither were they to encroach on the Russian merchants' trade in finished silk. They then were given a list of prohibited merchandise, consisting mostly of textiles, dyestuffs and munitions.[30]

The Holsteiners were not to trade in Russia in any of the goods they brought from Persia, but carry them directly to their own land.[31] "If the

Duke Friedrich III and the Holstein Embassy

Phillip Crusius

Friedrich III

Otto Brüggemann

Adam Olearius

John Albert Mandelslo

Frontispiece, Olearius, *Travels* (1669). By permission of the British Library.

Holsteiners buy in Persia or in India any madder or soft dye, they are not to transport it except through the Russian realm, but they must give the tsar's treasury annually four thousand puds of madder should the tsar's majesty have need of it. If he needs less, as much as needed shall be given, in exchange for payment from the treasury of fifteen rubles a pud, for in India it can be purchased for two, and in Persia for seven. The Holsteiners each are obliged to pay as revenue into the treasury thirty puds of madder and an equal amount of indigo root, to be distributed to Russian traders at the same price the Holsteiners paid for it in Persia. If the Holsteiners sell their goods in Russia, they must pay duty. The Holstein Company is to consist of thirty men from the various towns of the duchy, and non-Holsteiners are to be excluded. For the defense of its vessels the company must send four hundred men-at-arms, forty assigned to each of ten ships. The craft may be armed with medium and small cannon and also handguns. None of these weapons are to be left in Persia, neither is any bronze to be exported there.

"If on the way they are plundered by Russians or foreigners, the Holsteiners will have no recourse to his majesty the tsar. If they need additional troops or workers, they may be hired on a voluntary basis from the free population. Fugitive peasants may not be conveyed on company vessels.

"Ships may be built within the tsar's realm, and timber may be purchased freely from the tsar's subjects. Carpenters and casual workers may be hired from among the tsar's subjects, and the secrets of the shipbuilding trade must not be concealed from these carpenters. Have nothing to do with brigands, and wish no harm to the sovereign. If you hear of anything bad, report it. Churches[32] of your own faith may not be built in any of the lands given to you; religious services may be held privately in your quarters. You will not bring any priests or teachers of the popish faith, nor anyone of the Latin faith into the Russian realm, neither may you keep any secretly with you, on pain of death.

"If the company in any given year fails to pay the agreed sum, it subsequently must pay double. Should the company's business become unprofitable for the tsar, he reserves the right, after waiting for two or three years, or at the most five, to dismiss the company, and Duke Friedrich[33] is not to hold any grudge against the tsar on this account."

The proposal was accepted and the Holstein ambassadors set out for Persia. They received permission from the shah, and it was agreed that the ten-year term should start from the day of their return from Persia to

Moscow, January 2, 1639. At the expiry of seven months from that date, namely August 2, 1639, they undertook to deposit half the agreed sum into the tsar's treasury, even if by that time their merchandise did not arrive at Yaroslavl.

When this agreement was concluded, the Holstein ambassadors complained that the merchant extraordinary Vasily Shorin[34] went to see the boyars and uttered all kinds of slanderous remarks about the Holsteiners, alleging that the duke did not have sufficient money to pay the required amount into the tsar's treasury, and was borrowing from both Russians and Germans just for food.

The boyars answered Shorin and his companions that they were telling a pack of lies, and they would write down all he said and bring it to the tsar's attention. The ambassadors replied that the words uttered by Shorin and his companions dishonored both the duke of Holstein and his ambassadors, who could not be silent, but demanded that Shorin be punished. Apart from Shorin, the ambassadors complained about the crown secretary Nazar Chistov, who told the ambassadors that the tsar decided nothing concerning the Persian trade without his advice. The ambassadors gave him a bribe of two thousand efimoks, which the foreign merchants Peter Marselis[35] and Andreas von Ringen guaranteed, giving a precious pendant as security. When Marselis brought him the two thousand efimoks to redeem the pendant, Chistov demanded three thousand. When the ambassadors refused he threatened them, kept the pendant, and together with Shorin conspired against the Holsteiners, writing false and slanderous petitions. Chistov denied that he took the pendant, and the ambassadors left without any satisfaction.

After the ambassadors left the Holstein agent appeared before the boyars, declaring that the duke was requesting transit facilities for the Holstein embassy to proceed to Persia with eighty wagons loaded with goods, for which the company would pay into the tsar's treasury twenty-five thousand reichsthalers and a similar amount would be paid when they returned to Moscow with goods from Persia.

The boyars replied that it was improper, considering that the agreed sum was not yet paid, to conclude any side deal. The agent should declare what manner of goods were contained in the eighty wagons coming from Holstein, what sort of transit duty they were prepared to pay, and whether the agreed sum of three hundred thousand efimoks would be paid, since the period of grace had expired, and the money had yet to be paid. Without payment it would be improper to allow transit, nor could the Holsteiners be trusted again.

The agent replied that the cargo consisted of cloth, silver coins and other goods, but he did not know what. The agreed sum would be paid as soon as the present ambassadors reached agreement with the shah. The boyars demanded a hundred thousand efimoks transit duty, promising in return to provide transportation as far as Moscow, and from Moscow to Astrakhan ships and oarsmen were to be provided. The agent offered only sixty thousand, the boyars agreed and the tsar sent a letter in March 1640 informing the duke of this arrangement, with the reservation that the efimoks be paid into the treasury in accordance with the earlier agreement. In the same document Michael complained about the Holstein ambassadors. "What kind of honesty is displayed by your ambassadors in bribing Nazar Chistov, giving him a pendant as a pledge for three thousand efimoks? All the while they appeared before me in proper diplomatic form they were doing business with some of our common subjects, completely bypassing our boyars and councillors. Such things are highly irregular, and I place the blame upon you, Prince Friedrich, for the misdeeds of your ambassadors and the disrespect to our boyars and councillors."

In September Peter Marselis, a native of Hamburg, handed to the Chancellery for Foreign Affairs a letter from the duke of Holstein to the tsar. The duke wrote that his ambassador Otto Brüggemann concluded the agreement without the duke's approval or written instructions, and concealed it from his colleague, for which offense he was executed, and the treaty in no way could be ratified by the duke. Also false was the latest proposal of eighty wagons of cargo initiated by the agent De Mucheron at the secret written instigation of Brüggemann. Since then De Mucheron had died, and was replaced by the Danish chancellery official Peter Marselis, to whom he gave explicit orders with regard to the Persian trade.

"Prince Friedrich," replied the tsar, "how can you be trusted? You confirmed the dealings of your ambassadors. Letters of agreement bore your own signature and seal. Your principal ambassador was Philip Crusius, while Brüggemann was only his colleague. The ambassadors' treaty was confirmed by your own princely hand and seal, and now you want to break it, contrary to justice! It is unheard of that a treaty agreed and confirmed by both parties be revoked. If you cannot hold firm on such a great matter, how can you be trusted any longer, or how can any kind of agreement be reached with you? We, the great sovereign, will not yield on any of the conditions of this agreement."

The duke replied that he knew very well how to conduct himself with Christian rulers who were in amity and kinship with him; therefore let the tsar refrain from writing to him any more such letters. Doubtless every ruler has faithless servants who abuse their trust, and the ruler cannot be held responsible. Concerning the Persian business, the duke was willing to postpone it to a later and more opportune time. With this the matter ended.

II

TURKISH AFFAIRS, 1622-1643

EMBASSY OF KONDYREV AND BORMOSOV

With Poland and Sweden there was definitive peace, of which no breach was expected in the near future. Russia also tried to avoid a quarrel with the dreaded Turks. We left off our discussion of Turkish affairs just as Sultan Osman[1] was dispatching Thomas Cantacuzene[2] with the proposal for an anti-Polish alliance.

In 1622, together with the Turkish emissaries, the sovereign dispatched to Constantinople his emissaries Ivan Kondyrev[3] and the crown secretary Bormosov. As they approached the Don, the emissaries sent a dispatch to Moscow. "We expect to be delayed for some considerable time on the Don," they wrote, "because the Don ataman Epikha Radilov came up to us and said 'I was summoned before the boyars in Moscow, and the boyars came to me with loud complaints, telling falsehoods and heaping slanders upon me and my host. We are free men in this host and will not endure any kind of servitude. Now that you emissaries have arrived at the Don, we will do with you as we please.'"

The emissaries reported that there were at that time on the Don some Zaporozhian Cherkass, just returned from the Black Sea. In the cossack towns the emissaries encountered also the renegade Volga Cossacks, Bogdan Chernushkin and his companions, altogether about fifty men, who were wandering around in taffeta shirts, with velvet and satin caftans. They had been at sea and committed piracy against Persian ships. The Don ataman Epikha Radilov invited them to come from downstream, and when the emissaries told him he should not recruit such brigands, he replied "If we do not accept them, they will take up service in some foreign land." When the emissaries arrived at the cossack encampment they found it almost empty, and even the remaining cossacks set out with Ataman Epikha Radilov, before the emissaries' very eyes.

The cossacks nevertheless did not want to lose the tsar's pay, and therefore Ataman Isay Martemianov sent word to Kondyrev that they would wait by the estuary and ambush Turkish caravans in order to prevent them from reaching Azov, but soon they would be in Monastyrsky Gorodok where the emissaries were staying, and until then they were not to distribute the tsar's pay.

The cossacks did in fact return to Monastyrsky Gorodok, but when the emissaries announced to the cossack circle the tsar's usual demands, that they live in peace with the inhabitants of Azov, the cossacks replied that they were grateful for the sovereign's grant but they were not finished with the inhabitants of Azov, neither could they make peace with them. For this reason they could not allow the emissaries to proceed for a while.

Having given this answer, the cossacks took from the emissaries the tsar's grant, consisting of money, cloth, grain, munitions and wine, together with the ships on which this treasury was brought. They unloaded the vessels, placed the provisions beneath the clock tower in the middle of the square, and beached the ships on the river bank.

The emissaries urged them to pile the stores elsewhere, not in the middle of the square where the Turks could see; neither should they appropriate the vessels. The cossacks replied that there was nowhere else to pile the stores, neither did they allow any ships to pass downstream beyond the Don.

Having spent only one day at Monastyrsky Gorodok, the cossacks again put to sea on fifty rafts, each with a crew of thirty or forty. With them were new arrivals from Belgorod, Kursk, Oskol, Putivl, Livny and Elets and also Muscovite traders who had come to the Don with their wares. At the Don estuary the cossacks encountered Turkish caravans making for Azov. They fought them, captured a ship and two barges,[4] and with their booty returned to Monastyrsky Gorodok. They paraded past the lodging of the Turkish emissaries and, being armed to the teeth, menaced them by firing their muskets. In vain did the Muscovite emissaries tell them to make peace with Azov. "If the men of Azov sue for peace," they answered, "perhaps we will be amenable, but the first move will not come from us. You can deal with them if you want, but leave us out of it."

The emissaries dispatched to Azov a junior boyar to announce their arrival. The messenger came back with the news that the inhabitants approached him very noisily, saying "Let the emissaries come to Azov. We will know how to deal with them!" The civic leaders, however, sent word to the emissaries that the previous envoys proceeding to Constantinople were able to make peace between the cossacks and the people of Azov. Did the cossacks want peace this time? The emissaries addressed this question to the cossacks, who replied that they would make peace and let the emissaries proceed as soon as their comrades came back, for presently there were more than a thousand of them at sea.

Soon afterwards, on August 8, the Don and Zaporozhian Cossacks came back from sea. There were seven hundred of them on twenty-five rafts, commanded by the Zaporozhian ataman Shilo. They reported that they had crossed the sea, about thirty-six hours' voyage from Constantinople. They raided villages and hamlets in the vicinity of Constantinople and slaughtered many inhabitants, but then some galleys were sent from Constantinople, and the Turks killed about four hundred of their men.

Thereafter the cossacks sent the envoys to Azov. When he reached Kaffa, Kondyrev gave the pasha the usual assurance that if the cossacks again took to the sea the tsar, out of friendship to the sultan, would not intercede for them. "Every year," replied the pasha, "our men slaughter many Don Cossacks, but we cannot kill them all, for as many as we kill, yet more arrive from Russia. If there were no new arrivals from Russia on the Don, we would have dealt with them long ago and driven them from the Don."

In Constantinople the emissaries encountered great disorder. Sultan Osman had been killed by the janissaries, and his uncle Mustafa[5] was enthroned in his place. In Baghdad there was an uprising against the janissaries in reaction to this, and they were butchered. Hearing of the fate of their brethren in Asia, the Constantinople janissaries rose in rebellion. The pashas abruptly told the emissaries they had no time for them now.

Worse was yet to come. A mob of janissaries appeared before the foreign ministry complaining that the cossacks had raided their ship laden with goods, and demanded that the emissaries compensate them for the damage. The emissaries would not receive them, so the janissaries made a great tumult and uttered abuse. "We won't let you get away with this," they cried. "You come here to deceive us and tell a pack of lies. You send cossacks out to sea and order them to raid our ships. You go slave raiding around Constantinople. For this we will cut off your noses and ears." The janissaries burst into the ambassadors' lodging, went searching for slaves, rifled their baggage, and finding nothing they wanted, went away noisily.

The emissaries lodged a complaint with the vizier about the enormity of the insult. "I've no time now for ambassadors," he replied, "they want to get rid of me." The vizier was in fact replaced. The new vizier Husayn first of all demanded that the emissaries give him a robe of black fox fur and some good sables to make another robe. The emissaries had no robes, but they sent a few sables. The vizier was incensed and greeted them with reproaches about the cossacks. The emissaries complained that they had received no subsistence for five weeks. "Even without subsistence," the vizier replied, "you have enough and some to spare. You have many sables, but do not send me any. Sables are bred in Moscow, and from there are exported to all lands. Sables are not bred in Lithuania, yet the Lithuanian ambassador sent me more than fifty. If you're wise you will buy for me twenty times forty sables, or even more."

The emissaries replied that they had no sables, they had given all they had to the previous vizier and the sultan's privy councilors. If he, the vizier, was prepared to do business, they would see that he got two or three times forty sables. The vizier promised to conduct official business. The emissaries sent him three times forty sables, but he became angry and refused them. "You haven't been in Constantinople very long," he said. "When you have been here two or three years, perhaps you will honor me by giving as much as the Lithuanian ambassador."

The emissaries added yet five times forty sables, valued at two hundred rubles, and sent gifts to the vizier's majordomo. The vizier was satisfied, and the emissaries were dismissed with the answer that Sultan Mustafa had made peace with the Lithuanian king. He wanted to be at peace also with the Muscovite sovereign, and to forbid the inhabitants of Azov from attacking the Muscovite borderlands. If the Lithuanians violated the treaty, if even one Zaporozhian raft put to sea, the sultan immediately would declare war on the king and inform Moscow. The French emissary Césy[6] was delighted that Kondyrev was sent away empty handed.

The conduct of that particular emissary presents an interesting phenomenon in the history of European diplomacy. At this time the most Christian king,[7] locked in a struggle with the Protestants within his own country, had no scruples about allying with the Protestant powers of Northern Europe in order to counteract the growing strength of the House of Habsburg, so perilous for France. The Polish king was in alliance with that house. As a result the French emissary in Constantinople was obliged to act against Poland.

Césy, however, was a fanatical Catholic. He was horrified at the prospect that the Turks, in alliance with Moscow and Bethlen Gabor of Transylvania,[8] might overwhelm Poland; that the Polish Protestants might take advantage of the situation and proclaim the Protestant Bethlen Gabor as their king. That is why he strove to assure his government that France had nothing to fear about an alliance between Poland and Austria, to which the Polish people felt a strong aversion, and so there was no need to incite Turkey against Poland.

On the other hand Césy was agitating for the overthrow of Patriarch Cyril,[9] in whom he saw an active opponent of Catholicism. He reported to Louis XIII that Cyril was a dangerous heretic, a Calvinist who only had one aim, the destruction of Catholicism and the spread of Calvinism in Greece and all the East; that Cyril was designating as his successor one of his relatives, who had learned Calvinism in England.

In 1623 Césy managed to overthrow Cyril but several months later Cyril managed to make a comeback, and Césy continued hostile propaganda against him. According to Césy's denunciation, Cyril had printed in Wittenberg, under the name of his pupil Zacharias, a tract containing all manner of Calvinist and Lutheran ideas, which he caused to be distributed throughout the East.

Misfortune awaited the emissaries in Kaffa, where news arrived that the Don Cossacks had put to sea. For this reason the emissaries were detained. The Kaffa population threatened to kill them but news of the cossacks was not confirmed, and the emissaries were allowed to leave.

When they reached Kerch about a thousand Don Cossacks on rafts appeared before the city and attacked it, capturing a ship. There was an uprising in the city and the emissaries were snatched from their boat, brought into the city and imprisoned in a tower, where they were threatened with death. Kondyrev sent word to the cossacks that they should return immediately up the Don otherwise they, the emissaries, would be killed. The cossacks replied that they could not return upriver without any booty, so they sailed past Kerch to the Black Sea, making for Kaffa.

The emissaries were released from the tower and were told to proceed by way of the steppe, on the Cherkass[10] side. Near the Cherkass town of Temriuk they were set upon by some Zaporozhians who clamored that the Don Cossacks, bypassing Temriuk, had seized the son of the Taman governor and held him for ransom in the amount of two thousand ducats. The emissaries were told immediately to hand over the required sum, otherwise they would be killed. The Turkish emissary and the Azov governor, who were escorting the emissaries, wanted to intercede for them, but the cossacks turned them both back to Kaffa, while Kondyrev and his colleague were detained in Temriuk and imprisoned in a tower. Then the governor and the emissary brought the cossacks some gifts, barely persuading them to let everyone proceed from Temriuk to Azov. Then in the steppe they had to fight off the Nogay, and the brother of the second emissary Bormosov was captured. The Nogay clamored that in the springtime the Don Cossacks attacked their encampments, seizing their wives, children, horses and livestock. If the cossacks gave back all they captured, the Nogay would let the prisoner[11] go. The governor of Azov and the Turkish emissary persuaded them to release him.

After all these adventures the emissaries at last reached Azov; but they were not out of the woods yet. They were barely settled in their lodging when some of the citizens burst in with cries and threats. They clamored that the emissaries should be killed, while the rest of their suite should have their ears and noses cut off and sent home along the Don, since the Don Cossacks would not desist from brigandage, for now they were lying in ambush at the estuary, awaiting a caravan from Kaffa. The emissaries wrote to the Don, urging the cossacks to make peace with Azov and recall their rafts from the estuary, otherwise the emissaries would be killed. The cossacks complied with this demand, sent peace overtures, but could not agree on terms. When it was known in Azov that the cossacks would not make peace, the emissaries' windows were showered with sticks and stones. Finally the cossacks agreed to make peace, and the emissaries were allowed to leave Azov.

THOMAS CANTACUZENE'S SECOND EMBASSY TO MOSCOW
In the fall of 1627 the Greek Thomas Cantacuzene arrived in Moscow for the second time as an ambassador from Sultan Murad IV.[12] "You should call to mind our former love and affection," wrote the sultan to the tsar, "and follow attentively the precedents set by your forbears. You should write to us directly expressing your heartfelt affection, and send us your ambassadors without any interruption, and if you need any kind of help, we will come to your aid."

Cantacuzene, who could speak Russian without an interpreter, declared to Filaret Nikitich that Sultan Murad wanted to have the tsar, Michael Fedorovich, as a brother, and to have his holiness the patriarch as a father. "The two sovereigns[13] will be as brothers and you, great sovereign, will be their father, and nobody will be able to put asunder their brotherly love.

The aim of this brotherly love will be as before, to make war in concert against the land of King Sigismund."

"Between my son," replied Filaret, "and Sultans Ahmed,[14] Osman and Mustafa there was uninterrupted correspondence concerning friendship, and there was no hindrance to this friendship. There has not been any correspondence between my son and Sultan Murad since this has been prevented by the lawlessness of the Crimean heir apparent Shan-Girey, who attacked our ambassadors proceeding to Sultan Mustafa. Hearing of Murad's accession, our son wished to send his congratulations, but he did not, because he did not know where to send them. It is dangerous to send anyone to Azov, lest Shan-Girey treat our ambassadors as others were treated before. We could not send them by sea because all the German states are embroiled in war. Yet our son wishes amity and friendship with Sultan Murad more than ever before. Shan-Girey when he assaulted our ambassadors also assaulted some Turks, sending to the shah whatever he took from their treasury. Our son did not blame Sultan Murad for this, for this was none of his ordering, but on account of his crimes our son can in no way be in peace and friendship with King Sigismund without first avenging these wrongs."

"When I visited you the first time," continued Cantacuzene, "the subject of our conversation became known immediately to the Polish king. Someone or other wrote to him from Moscow, this we know for sure, but we do not know who it was."

Filaret, without answering, changed the subject to the incorrect wording of the title in which Michael Fedorovich was addressed as "king" rather than "tsar." The ambassador concluded with a request that the sovereign forbid the Don Cossacks to attack Turkish people and lands. Filaret made the usual excuse that the inhabitants of the Don were brigands over whom the sovereign had no control.

At the end of the audience Filaret asked Cantacuzene how long it was since Murad's accession, how old he was, how tall and of what faith, of what faith were his pashas. Cantacuzene answered that this was the fourth year of Murad's reign, he was seventeen years old, fully grown and intelligent. He was of the Greek faith, since his mother was formerly a priest's wife.[15] She was very intelligent and had much influence over her son. The vizier Hassan-Pasha was of the Greek faith, the sultan listened to him and favored him, and the second-ranking vizier Rezep-Pasha was also of the Greek faith.

EMBASSY OF YAKOVLEV AND YEVDOKIMOV

Accompanying Cantacuzene in 1628 back to Constantinople were the tsar's ambassadors, the noble Yakovlev and the crown secretary Yevdokimov, taking with them as was customary the grant for the Don Cossacks, consisting of two thousand rubles cash, cloth and various supplies. As before the ambassadors learned when they reached the Don that the cossacks, led by Ataman Ivan Katorzhny, were at sea attacking the Turks, and that the cossacks were not at peace with Azov. As usual the ambassadors demanded of the cossacks that they make peace with Azov and recall their comrades from the sea.

"We will make peace," the cossacks replied, "and stop plundering Turkish ships, villages and hamlets, provided we have no further strife with the men of Azov, who must stop attacking the sovereign's border-lands and destroying his towns, taking our fathers, mothers, brothers, sisters and wives captive to sell as slaves. If the men of Azov trouble us, let it be as God and the tsar will, but we shall not tolerate it, and will defend our fathers, mothers, brothers and sisters. Apparently it is also the will of God and the sovereign that we cossacks are forced by need and poverty to take to the sea in order to subsist.[16] This occurred before you came, for we did not know of the tsar's decree or his bounty, and there is no way we can get word to them, for they are constantly on the move."

Katorzhny arrived back from sea and announced that the Turks had routed him near Trebizond. Having made peace between the cossacks and the people of Azov, the ambassadors set off for Constantinople. They were received very graciously, but then news came from the Crimea that the Don Cossacks were attacking, and had taken the two towns of Karasa and Minkup. The attitude towards the ambassadors changed, and as they took their leave the vizier told them "You may leave safely, but you don't deserve to, on account of your people. Call off the cossacks, and inform the sovereign that he too should call them off. If he doesn't, nothing good can come of it." "If the sultan allows us to leave safely," the ambassadors replied, "he will have done a good deed, but if on account of the cossacks he orders some kind of harm done us, he will do himself a great dishonor. We have suffered much harm and many privations, but we don't know why. If we are suffering privation on account of the cossacks, we are being oppressed and starved for no good reason. If indeed the cossacks are committing piracy, write about it to our great sovereign, who will restrain them; but there is no reason in victimizing and starving us."

CANTACUZENE'S THIRD EMBASSY

In May 1630 Thomas Cantacuzene came to Moscow a third time, with an announcement that the sultan had sent his troops against the Dnieper Cossacks, asking that for his part the tsar attack the Polish king. The sultan also requested that the tsar send his army against Persia, there to join up with Turkish troops. Finally he asked the tsar to restrain the Don Cossacks.

Filaret answered the ambassador that the tsar's army would be ready to move against Poland, for his son the sovereign would not await the expiry of the truce with the Polish king. The ambassador declared that the sultan's serdar[17] was at the Uza river in full readiness, waiting for the Muscovite courier to bring the message to begin. As soon as the courier gave the message, the serdar would attack the Polish king in spring, as soon as the grass grew.

Filaret pointed out one unfortunate circumstance. The Swedish king Gustav Adolf had concluded a truce with the Polish king.[18] On the other hand, added the patriarch, the Poles were involved in an intense religious dispute with the Cherkass, whom the Poles wanted to convert to the popish faith, but the Cherkass were refusing to forsake their Christian religion, and over this a major conflict was arising. Gustav Adolf of Sweden had declared war on the Holy Roman emperor, and the Swedish king had as allies the kings of England, Denmark and France, as well as the Dutch States. The Polish king wanted to help the emperor, so the truce between Sweden and Poland inevitably would be of short duration.

Cantacuzene replied that the wrongs committed by the Poles were known to all nations, and many Poles favored Sultan Murad, while from Kiev some Orthodox[19] and Calvinists were writing to the sultan, saying that as soon as Turkish troops invaded Lithuania they were ready to rise up against the Poles.

Filaret then asked the ambassadors about the Don Cossacks. Cantacuzene replied that a few years ago, in 1626, the Don Cossacks and some Zaporozhians plundered the monastery of St. John the Baptist on the coast, about two hundred versts from Constantinople, and taken much treasure.[20] The sultan sent his commanders to pursue them, and they captured seven rafts and brought them to Constantinople. The sultan ordered the prisoners interrogated. They were asked on whose orders they raided that locality. They replied that they were following their own initiative, not any order from the tsar. The sultan ordered them executed. The ambassador added that his people were very angry at the tsar on account of the Don Cossacks, but the chief admiral[21] favored him, and even proposed that both sides,

Muscovy and Turkey, give subsidies to the Don Cossacks, so that there would be no further quarrels between the two countries. The Don Cossacks could even be resettled along the Sea of Marmora.

SOVIN AND ALFIMOV DISPATCHED TO CONSTANTINOPLE

In July of the same year the ambassador Andrei Sovin and the crown secretary Alfimov[22] were dispatched to Constantinople. Sovin carried a letter to the Don Cossacks ordering them to attack the Polish king in conjunction with the Turkish troops stationed on the Uza river. "It was never the practice of former sovereigns," the cossacks protested after reading the letter, "that we cossacks were dispatched by ourselves to foreign lands without the tsar's commanders. We atamans and cossacks never have served any foreign ruler, only the Muscovite tsar. Nobody is so distasteful to the Turks as the Don Cossacks; how can we serve alongside them? They hate us even worse than they do the Lithuanians. If the sovereign orders us to attack the Polish king without the Turkish pashas, but under the leadership of the sovereign's commanders, we are ready to do his bidding. The Zaporozhian Cherkass take to the sea, but we Don Cossacks have not been going to sea, as the men of Azov allege out of hostility, trying to get us into trouble. Even if we do take to the sea, it is because we have no other way of feeding ourselves, since the tsar's bounty has not been sent to us for a long time, neither is any being sent now."

KARAMYSHEV MURDERED BY DON COSSACKS

Accompanying the ambassadors was the commander Ivan Karamyshev. From Moscow and Valuiki to the Don came rumors that Karamyshev had volunteered for this assignment in order to flog and hang the cossacks. Acting on this rumor the cossacks rushed at the commander with muskets and spears, drew blood, dragged him from the raft and brought him to their camp. The ambassadors intervened, telling the cossacks not to kill the commander, not to believe slanderous rumors, but to write about it to the sovereign in Moscow. The cossacks replied with abuse and threats. "This is none of your business," they shouted at the ambassadors. "Go back to your quarters, otherwise we will do the same to you." Karamyshev was dragged into the circle, beaten with the flats of their swords, poked with spears, and then was dragged by his feet to the Don, where he was thrown in still alive. The ambassadors, however, were allowed to proceed to Azov without further incident.

AMBASSADORS' FURTHER MISADVENTURES

The Muscovite ambassadors arrived at Constantinople, but not before the Polish ambassadors there concluded peace with the Turks.[23] Moreover the Persians were gaining the upper hand over the Turks in Asia. Worse still, the Crimean khan sent news that in the spring the Don Cossacks, in conjunction with the Cherkass, were preparing to set sail on the Black Sea. Therefore the vizier told Sovin and Alfimov, "Now we are at odds not only with the Poles, but also with enemies on all sides. It is not opportune at this time for us to seek vengeance for the wrongs committed by the Poles." The sultan in his missive answered the tsar in the very same terms, though much more politely.

The ambassadors set off for home but before they reached Kaffa they encountered some Don Cossacks who did them violence. They met with a very grim reception in Kaffa. The people noisily rushed at the ambassadors' ship and stormed it, wishing to kill Sovin and Alfimov in revenge for the depredations of the Don Cossacks. They were called off only by use of considerable force. On one hand news came to Kaffa that the Don Cossacks had attacked Sinope and the surrounding villages and hamlets, then proceeded towards Constantinople and attacked places within a hundred versts of the capital. On the other hand there came from Azov to Kaffa two boatloads of Russian captives, whom the men of Azov had taken from the Muscovite border towns of Voronezh, Valuiki, Oskol, Belgorod, Elets and Kursk.

In Kerch the ambassadors received much the same reception as in Kaffa, while in Azov they found a missive from the tsar forbidding them to proceed along the Don until further notice, because the Don Cossacks wanted to kill them. In fact a yurt Tatar[24] from Astrakhan, arriving at the Don, told the ambassadors that after the murder of Karamyshev and the dispatch of the ambassadors to Azov, the seaborne cossacks and all those from the towns gathered in a general meeting of the host and shouted at Ataman Volokita Frolov "Let the ambassadors go! We already have committed one crime, so we'd might as well kill them all. When they come back from Constantinople, let's kill all of them. It makes no difference, since now all our service to the tsar is in vain. He wants to hand us over to our enemies the Turks. Even though a hundred thousand are sent against us from Moscow, we shall not be afraid. They will not capture us without a struggle. We will gather together in a single town and fight to the death. If the tsar concludes an agreement with the Turkish sultan and the Crimean khan, and soldiers come against us from all sides, we will go to the Cherkass in Zaporozhia. They never will betray us." Accordingly they sent word to the Dnieper Cossacks that if the Muscovite army came after them the Dnieper Cossacks should never hand them over but give them immediate help. The Don Cossacks themselves agreed to gather from every town, since they feared the tsar's army would come after them.

At that time some traders came to the Don to buy up the booty the cossacks brought from beyond the sea, and to these traders the cossacks uttered many threats against the ambassadors. "They came to us once and we let them go; if they come again they will never leave alive." They also had spies in all the borderland towns. Finally the wretched ambassadors were rescued from Azov by Muscovite regular troops sent to the Don under the command of Prince Boriatinsky.

FURTHER EMBASSIES TO CONSTANTINOPLE

In 1632 the Don Cossacks did not take to the Black Sea but instead proceeded to the Yaik river, and together with local cossacks sailed on to the Caspian Sea and raided the Persian regions along its shores. In the summer of that year, as Shein was making preparations for the Smolensk campaign, the noble Afanasy Pronchishchev[25] and the crown secretary Bormosov were sent as ambassadors to Constantinople, where they were received with great honor. The ambassadors declared that in the year 1632 the cossacks were not taking to the sea, neither were they plundering Crimean territories, but rather attacking the sultan's foe the king of Poland, and they were at peace with the inhabitants of Azov. Yet the men of Azov were attacking the tsar's borderlands, and therefore many Crimeans joined in these attacks.

The ambassadors declared also that his majesty the tsar had sent his troops against the Polish king, therefore Sultan Murad should write to the Poles urging them to enthrone as their king the tsar's friend King Gustav Adolf of Sweden,[26] on account of his honesty and love for the sovereign tsar.

"I don't think," replied the vizier, "the Swedish king himself wants to rule the Lithuanian kingdom. Moreover the Swedish ambassador was here when news came that the Polish king Sigismund was dead. I told the ambassador, and asked whether his king was interested in the Polish throne. The ambassador thought for a long time, then said 'Maybe earlier the king would have sought the Polish throne, but now I don't think so, because God has raised the king's hand high above his enemies.'

"As for us," continued the vizier, "we have received reliable news that Prince Wladyslaw has been elected to rule over the Lithuanian kingdom." "If this is the case," answered the ambassador, "Sultan Murad can expect no honest dealing from him in anything, for like his father he will commit all manner of deceit. Now Wladyslaw will send his ambassadors to announce to the sultan his election, and as before the Lithuanian ambassadors will promise much and dangle many bribes, but give nothing, so don't believe anything they say, as they always tell lies."

"We are only too aware of the dishonesty and cunning of the Lithuanians," replied the vizier, "and if the Lithuanian ambassadors while they are here try any subterfuge, we will be wise to them." Finally the ambassadors proposed that the sultan send ambassadors to Persia to make peace between the shah and the sultan. Then the sultan could make common cause with his majesty the tsar against the Polish king. On this matter the vizier kept his own counsel.

Pronchishchev and Bormosov spent all winter in Constantinople. In the spring the vizier announced to them that he would persuade the sultan to send troops from the adjoining places into Lithuanian territory the following summer. As they were given their leave, the ambassadors were told that the sultan had ordered the Crimean khan and Cantemir-Murza to attack Lithuania from Belgorod, using Crimean and Nogay troops. Captives taken in Russia during the year 1632 were to be released. Furthermore Abaza-Pasha, with his Turkish, Moldavian, Wallachian and Bukhara Tatar forces, was ordered to make ready to invade Lithuanian territory.

No sooner were Pronchishchev and Bormosov on board their ship than news came to Constantinople that the Don Cossacks had put to sea on twenty-five rafts, attacked villages and hamlets around Kaffa, and captured two ships at sea. The ambassadors somehow managed to evade the vizier's queries, but when their ship was driven by storm into Sinope, the inhabitants came noisily to them on their ship, crying out that ten days previously some Don Cossacks came to the city of Konya, capturing it and setting it on fire, killing and capturing much of the population. Consequently the inhabitants of all Anatolia converged on Constantinople, petitioning the sultan that on account of the Don Cossacks they no longer could live in those places, since they were attacked every year. Their towns were captured, their villages and hamlets burned, even though Muscovite ambassadors incessantly came to Constantinople. They ostensibly came for a good purpose, but in reality for espionage, to spy out the fortifications of the cities and then inform the cossacks, which was indeed why the cossacks forever were putting out to sea.

The ambassadors answered the inhabitants of Sinope that these could not have been Don Cossacks but Zaporozhian Cherkass. The men of Sinope replied that they knew the difference between Don Cossacks and the Cherkass, and that the Muscovite ambassadors were up to no good. In Kaffa the ambassadors almost were killed on account of the cossacks' exploits.

The Muscovite ambassadors who replaced Pronchishchev and Bormosov were the noble Dashkov and the crown secretary Somov.[27] They arrived at Constantinople in the summer of 1633. They opened their embassy with a complaint that the Crimean khan Janibek-Girey had violated his treaty and in the past year sent his troops against the Muscovite borderlands. They, the ambassadors, encountered in the steppe eight thousand troops, from Azov and the Nogay horde, who were attacking the sovereign's borderlands and even assaulted the ambassadors, attacking their leaguer for two days and two nights. It was known for sure that the Crimean khan wanted to go in person or send his son on campaign against the sovereign's borderlands, at Lithuanian instigation. Therefore the ambassadors demanded that the sultan give orders to replace the Crimean khan.

Next the ambassadors received from Moscow a dispatch to the effect that in July 1633 the Crimean crown prince with seventeen murzas attacked the Muscovite borderlands, crossed the Oka and advanced on Serpukhov. When they received this dispatch the ambassadors even more emphatically demanded that the khan be replaced. The vizier replied that the khan was sent orders immediately to attack Lithuania with all his horde, despite the winter weather. If the khan did not reply immediately, the vizier would urge the sultan to replace him, so that in spring the Crimean troops would invade Lithuania.

Dashkov and Somov feared the arrival of Polish ambassadors, who could turn the tables on them. Indeed in 1634 Polish ambassadors came with the news that Wladyslaw had defeated the Muscovites and relieved Smolensk. It was very important for the Muscovite ambassadors to find out what answer the sultan sent the king's letter, and they managed to obtain a translation of this reply. The sultan said that he was prepared to keep peace with the king, provided that the Poles dismantle all the towns and bytowns they constructed near the Turkish borderlands and forbid the cossacks to sail upon the Black Sea. They were also to send the Crimean khan the same tribute as previously, and make peace with the Muscovite sovereign.

Not even waiting for the return of Dashkov and Somov from Constantinople, yet two more ambassadors were dispatched in the spring of

1634. These were the noble Korobyin[28] and the crown secretary Matveev. The vizier greeted these ambassadors with the following words. "In previous letters from your sovereign which were handed to Sultan Murad it was urged that the sultan and your sovereign make common cause against the Polish king. In accordance with your sovereign's earlier letters his majesty the sultan has sent many of his troops against the Polish king; but now rumor has it that your sovereign made peace with the Polish king without informing Sultan Murad. The sultan would like us to ascertain from you whether, when you left Moscow, your sovereign was making peace overtures, and whether you think that by now he has made peace with the Polish king."

"We were given no instructions by our sovereign concerning this matter," replied the ambassadors. "We only know that there was fighting between our sovereign and the Polish king, that the sovereign's troops attacked many Lithuanian towns and slew Lithuanian troops in many places. As we left Moscow we heard on the way that the Polish king Wladyslaw sent our sovereign an earnest plea to leave off contention and desist from the shedding of Christian blood while he, the Polish king, would amend all his former faults. The great sovereign, according to his merciful disposition, sent his high ambassadors to a conference, but we do not know what they agreed with the Lithuanian delegates. We are sure the great sovereign will inform his majesty the sultan."

The vizier dropped the subject and raised that of the Don Cossacks who, despite the tsar's assurances that he forbade them to attack Turkish possessions, that summer raided Turkish ships on the Black Sea and devastated coastal villages. The ambassadors replied that the cossacks were out of their control. "The sovereign sent the boyar Karamyshev to them," they pleaded, "to bring them to order and punish them for having sailed the Black Sea in violation of the tsar's prohibition, but the brigands slew this commander. Let the sultan send his own troops against them, and the tsar will have no objection."

During a later interview the vizier told the ambassadors "The sultan has reliable information that your sovereign has made peace with the Polish king even though earlier he promised he would not do so without consulting the sultan. The sultan is vexed that your sovereign has made peace with the Polish king." "If indeed," the ambassadors replied, "the sovereign made peace with the Polish king, we think that the Crimean khan Janibek-Girey is to blame, since he attacked the sovereign's borderlands. The soldiers from these places, learning that their fathers, mothers, wives and children were either being killed or taken captive, deserted the tsar's service. Therefore the tsar's military effort was hindered greatly." "Perhaps this was so," replied the vizier. "The sultan now has ordered the Crimean khan no longer to attack your borderlands, so now your sovereign must call off the Don Cossacks."

On that note Korobyin and Matveev were dismissed but on November 2, as they were about to board their vessel, the vizier informed them that the Don Cossacks and Zaporozhian Cherkass had advanced on Azov, bombarded it with their artillery, damaged the town in many places and almost captured it. "This is not the first time," the ambassadors sent reply, "that the Don Cossacks without the tsar's knowledge, and the men of Azov without the sultan's knowledge, have quarreled and made up." Nevertheless the ambassadors must have guessed what was in store for them. In Balaklava and Kaffa they were kept without food in unheated quarters and were subjected to indignities. They barely bought their freedom from the pasha of Kaffa with a gift of ten times forty sables. It was the fall of 1635 by the time they got back to Moscow.

TSAR'S LETTER TO THE SULTAN

The Eternal Peace with Poland, as far as the Muscovite government was concerned, removed the urgency from Turkish relations. This time Moscow did not send ambassadors or even emissaries, but merely the interpreter Bukolov, who early in 1636 left Moscow with a letter for the sultan. "You our brother," wrote the tsar, "should not be angry at us over our peace with Poland. We were compelled to conclude it, because help from you was slow in coming, and we were involved in a major war with the Crimean khan." The tsar promised to call off the Don Cossacks but added, "You know very well that those living on the Don are renegade cossacks who hardly ever heed our sovereign decrees. Whatever you decide to do about them, we will not come to their defense." In conclusion the tsar complained about the yearly attacks by the men of Azov.

CANTACUZENE ARRIVES ON THE DON

When Bukolov left Constantinople, Cantacuzene was dispatched along with him. He was going on personal business, but in the guise of an emissary. Arriving on the Don, Thomas sent word to the cossacks that the sultan sent them his bounty, four caftans. "Previously," replied the cossacks, "emissaries were sent frequently from the sultan to the great sovereign, but they never brought anything for us cossacks. Clearly you,

Thomas, are doing this on your own initiative, and the caftans are from your own stock. We receive plentiful bounty from the tsar, so we don't need your gifts." The caftans, however, were attractive, so the cossacks after some hesitation accepted them from Cantacuzene.

ATAMAN KATORZHNY'S MISSION TO MOSCOW

At that time the cossacks considered an important undertaking to deal with Azov, but they had few munitions, so they dispatched Ataman Ivan Katorzhny to Moscow with a letter for the tsar. "For the past many years," it read, "your majesty was gracious to us your slaves, and sent us money, cloth and all manner of supplies. Yet in the past year, 1636, there was no such bounty, and we are starving, naked, barefoot and hungry, for we have no other resource save your majesty's bounty. Many hordes exult over us, come to make war on our cossack settlements and destroy our downriver towns, while we have no lead, cannonballs or powder. In former years our atamans and cossacks have gone to the tsar with lists of troops, and on leaving Moscow received transportation as far as Voronezh, where they were supplied with ships and oarsmen for the journey downriver. Now we are deprived of transportation and ships, neither are there any oarsmen. Also from the Don come atamans and cossacks who in fulfillment of vows want to come on pilgrimage to monasteries. When they have made their pilgrimage and given money to the monastery for the salvation of their souls, they also buy supplies or sell some of their own goods. Whenever they do so, the tax collector swoops on them and imposes an intolerable amount of duty. Merciful sovereign tsar, have pity on us your slaves, and favor us with your bounty."

The sovereign acceded to their request, ordered their demands to be fulfilled and dispatched Stepan Chirikov to accompany the supplies. He was also to meet with the Turkish ambassador Thomas Cantacuzene.

COSSACKS GATHER BEFORE AZOV

Having dispatched Katorzhny to Moscow, the cossacks began to gather for the campaign. They sent to the towns upriver and along all the tributaries, ordering them to assemble at Nizhny Gorodok. Those in the host were to forgive each other any offenses. Coming together from all the encampments, the cossacks decided to proceed in mass array to Azov and finally settle accounts with its inhabitants. At the same time there arrived along the steppe about a thousand mounted Zaporozhian Cherkass, thinking that the Don Cossacks were going by sea. These Cherkass also decided to join the Azov campaign. In 1637, during the second week after Easter, on Wednesday April 21 the allies, numbering about four thousand four hundred men, set off on campaign to Azov.

CANTACUZENE MURDERED

Cantacuzene was left at Yar in the barracks, under heavy guard. The Muscovite interpreter Bukolov, a witness to these events, overheard cossack conversations. "If the tsar favors us, he will allow those in Azov to be joined by auxiliary troops and all manner of freemen, and we will never leave Azov, but take up residence there."

A week later the cossacks captured two of Cantacuzene's servants on a skiff along the Aksay channel. The cossacks came to Cantacuzene accusing him of sending his servants along the river without permission, without informing the cossacks, with the aim of sending messages to the defenders of Azov while the cossacks were besieging it. Cantacuzene replied that he sent his servants to catch fish, but the cossacks found no fishing nets in their possession, and informed the host at Azov of this incident.

From Moscow two weeks before the St. Peter's fast[29] Stepan Chirikov came, accompanied by Ivan Katorzhny, who set off for Azov. On the last evening before the fast Katorzhny returned, and on the next day, the Monday of the first week of St. Peter's fast, he announced to Cantacuzene that the cossacks were letting him proceed to the tsar, and wished to entrust him to the care of Stepan Chirikov. Let him board the raft with all his suite. Thomas emerged from the barracks to embark upon the raft, but then he was greeted by another messenger. The atamans invited him into their circle in order to say farewell. Thomas entered the circle, in which the cossacks stood all armed. Two atamans stepped forward and spoke to Thomas. "Previously," they said, "you went to the great sovereign on behalf of the sultan. You were corrupted, for many times you sowed dissension between the sovereigns, inciting quarrels, and so caused great losses and aggravation to the great sovereign. You boasted that you would ruin us Don Cossacks and drive us from the Don. From Azov you wrote denouncing Ataman Ivan Katorzhny, saying he should be hanged in Moscow. For such crimes the Don atamans and cossacks have ordered your execution."

Sentence was carried out immediately. Cantacuzene's servants and the monks traveling with him to Moscow also were killed. The cossacks ran amok, also wishing to kill the Muscovite interpreter Bukolov, but he hid in the clock tower. Afterwards Bukolov heard from the Don Cossacks that they had killed Cantacuzene for sending his servants with messages to Azov, urging the inhabitants to sit tight, for the cossacks were running out of supplies.

AZOV CAPTURED BY COSSACKS

After Cantacuzene's murder the cossacks besieged Azov for two weeks. Some yurt Tatars[30] came to their aid from Astrakhan, and on June 18 Azov was captured. They slaughtered all the inhabitants except for the Greeks, and freed all the Christian captives. The victors then occupied the city.

On July 30 there arrived in Moscow ambassadors from the cossacks with news that they had killed the Turkish ambassador. "You atamans and cossacks," answered the tsar, "acted wrongly in killing the Turkish ambassador out of hand, with all his suite. Nowhere is it permitted to kill ambassadors for, even if there is war between rulers, ambassadors are permitted to perform their function, and nobody harms them. You captured Azov without any authorization from us, neither did you send any properly accredited atamans or cossacks to ask what is to be done now."

The killing of the Turkish ambassador was embarrassing for the Muscovite government, but it rejoiced over the capture of the important Azov stronghold from the Muslims. Nevertheless it did not wish to get mixed up in the affair, lest it involve a quarrel with Turkey.

In 1637 the tsar sent a letter to the sultan that the cossacks had captured Azov illegally, that the tsar's noble Chirikov was being held by them in close confinement. He was not allowed to go anywhere, and the cossacks were thinking of killing him too. The sovereign once before wrote to the sultan, and now was reiterating, that the Don Cossacks were renegades from way back, runaway slaves who did not heed the tsar's commands, and it was impossible to send the army after them, since they lived in distant places. "You our brother should not be angry or hold a grudge against us that the cossacks killed your emissary and seized Azov. They did these things without our command and illegally, and we shall not defend these brigands, neither do we wish to have any quarrel with you on their account, even though you order all of these brigands to be killed within a single hour. We want to be in great friendship and brotherly love with your majesty the sultan."

Needless to say it was difficult to avoid disputes with the Turks. In September the Crimeans devastated the Muscovite borderlands, and Khan Bogadyr-Girey wrote to Moscow that this attack was ordered by the sultan in revenge for the capture of Azov by the cossacks, and that in spring even more Tatars would attack the Muscovite realm. These threats, however, amounted to no more than a desultory war against the cossacks, who remained undisturbed in Azov while the sultan was preoccupied with the Persian war.

COSSACKS DEFEND AZOV AGAINST TURKS

This war ended in 1639, and Sultan Murad made preparations for a campaign against Azov, but he died. Only in 1640 did his successor Ibrahim I[31] move against Azov with 240,000 troops and over a hundred siege cannon. The cossacks within the city amounted to 5,637 men and eight hundred women, who deserve to be numbered among the active defenders, since they enthusiastically aided their menfolk in the defense. According to other accounts the defenders numbered fourteen thousand men and eight hundred women. Considering the possibility that cossacks arrived at Azov from all sides, and also taking into account intelligence that Ostranitsa and Gunia also had sought refuge in Azov, the latter estimate cannot be discounted.

Whatever the case may be, the defenders withstood twenty-four assaults with desperate courage. Not one deserter reached the Turkish lines; not one prisoner, no matter how severely tortured, revealed the number of Azov's defenders. Having lost twenty thousand of their men, on September 26 the Turks lifted the siege, which failed because of the lack of skilled engineers, dissension among the commanders, and lack of food supplies and munitions.[32]

The cossacks sent news of their triumph to Moscow but also requested help, begging the sovereign to accept Azov from them. "We are naked, barefoot and hungry," they wrote, "we have no supplies, powder or lead, on account of which many cossacks want to disperse, while many are severely wounded."

"We graciously commend you," wrote the tsar, "for this your service, solicitude, effort and fortitude. You write that you are naked, barefoot and hungry, there are no supplies, many cossacks want to disperse, and there are many severely wounded. We, the tsar, have sent you five thousand rubles cash. Concerning what you have petitioned and ordered to be written to us about the city of Azov, we have ordered our noble and our crown secretary to survey Azov, to write down their findings and submit their estimates. You, atamans and cossacks, on account of the service you have rendered, your nobility, valor and fortitude, must not besmirch your honor and fame, but continue strongly to defend the true Orthodox faith and us your great sovereign, and unswervingly rely upon our favor and bounty."

ASSEMBLY IN MOSCOW

Yet while urging the cossacks to be steadfast the tsar saw that matters could not rest there, that either Azov be taken under Muscovite authority and defended against the Turks, or surrendered. A month after the foregoing letter was sent to the Don, on January 3, 1642, Michael summoned an assembly, for which "delegates must be chosen from all ranks, greater, middle and lesser. Honest and wise men must be chosen, with whom we can discuss this matter. From the major categories between seven and twenty delegates should be chosen, from the less numerous between two and five. The names of those selected must be sent here, with full details."[33]

It was announced that the men of the Don wrote from Azov asking the Muscovites to accept the city from them. Meanwhile news came that in the spring the grand vizier in person would arrive before Azov, and if he did not capture the town quickly he would besiege it firmly and send Turkish and Crimean troops against Muscovy. "Should the sovereign tsar break with the Turkish sultan and Crimean khan by accepting Azov from the Don Cossacks? If we accept it and break with the Turks and Crimeans, we shall need to send many troops to Azov, to the towns of the steppe and borderlands, and those along the Volga. Much money will be needed for fortification works in Azov and to pay soldiers. We will need grain, munitions and supplies, not just for one year, for we will be fighting the Turks for longer. How are we to gather so much money and so many supplies? All of you—table attendants, Moscow gentry and crown secretaries, captains and company commanders of musketeers, provincial gentry and junior boyars, leading merchants, members of the Merchants' and Cloth Merchants' Hundreds,[34] hundreds of free taxpaying traders, all servicemen and residents—are to consider this matter carefully and submit your opinions in writing, in order that we may be fully informed."

"The matter of reviewing the tsar's military situation," the clergy replied, "and that of the sovereign's boyars and councilors, is one to which we are not accustomed. If, O sovereign, at this time your majesty is pleased to muster an army, we your clergy will be pleased to do all in our power to help."

The table attendants replied that the matter of whether or not to take Azov and break with the Turks was entirely up to the tsar. In their opinion the tsar should order the Don atamans and cossacks to hold on. If the tsar wished to send reinforcements, he should dispatch some auxiliaries and volunteers. The tsar was free to order the muster of troops and the gathering of supplies, and they, the table attendants, were ready to serve wherever the tsar commanded.

The gentry also did not wish to serve alongside the cossacks in the defense of Azov, but in order not to offend them, they added a special consideration. "The sovereign should order the defenders of Azov to use the tsar's cash bounty to recruit auxiliaries from the borderland towns. Many from these towns have been on the Don and are familiar with that country."

Nikita Beklemishev and Timofey Zheliabuzhsky expressed their opinions somewhat more explicitly. They said that the injustices of the Turkish sultan and the Crimean khan were well known to the sovereign. The khan in particular constantly swore oaths and then violated them. None of the money sent from Moscow to the Crimea was to any avail; better to send the money to be used to pay our own troops. "We must hold on to Azov, because as soon as we secure it the wars with the Tatars will cease. Volunteer auxiliaries should be sent to reinforce the cossacks, and these volunteers should remain in Azov under the ataman's overall command. Muscovite governors should not be sent to Azov, for the cossacks are a lawless people. For the collection of money to pay the troops, let the tsar order all ranks to choose two or three honest men to assess and collect the money, taking into account the difference between rich and poor. Let him order money to be gathered from the large towns, from monasteries and from well-endowed individuals possessing many service tenures and patrimonies. Those who have lands in excess of their service entitlements are to be assigned to governorships, neither let the poor be required to serve alongside the well endowed." Beklemishev and Zheliabuzhsky closed their submission by saying "If Azov belongs to the sovereign, the Great Nogay, the encampments of the Kazy and Cantemir, the Mountain Cherkass, the Temriuk, Kzhen, Besleneev and Adin tribes all will serve the sovereign, and every last Nogay will wander off from Astrakhan to the neighborhood of Azov."

The musketeer captains and company commanders replied that the tsar must do as he pleased but they, his slaves, were ready and willing to serve wherever he commanded. The Vladimir gentry and junior boyars gave the same answer, but added, "The poverty of our town is known to the sovereign and his boyars." The inhabitants of the towns of Nizhny

Novgorod, Murom and Lukh gave a like answer, but without additionally pleading poverty. "If it is to the sovereign's advantage, he will order that Azov be accepted; if not, he will order that it not be accepted. It is up to the tsar to decide how to get troops to Azov and raise the necessary money, but it is the boyars who always have been the tsar's advisers in such matters." The inhabitants of Suzdal, Yuriev, Pereiaslavl, Belaia, Kostroma, Smolensk, Galich, Arzamas, Great Novgorod, Rzhev, Zubtsov, Toropets, Rostov, Poshekhonie, Novy Torzhok and Gorokhovets, on the other hand, said "You, pious sovereign, should pray for the grace of the All-merciful God and order the acceptance of Azov from the Don Cossacks, and break with the Turkish sultan and Crimean tsar on account of the injustices you have suffered from them. If you do not see fit to command the acceptance of Azov, it will belong to the infidel, and so will the icon of St. John the Baptist.[35] Do not, O sovereign, bring down upon the All-Russian realm the wrath of God and the great luminaries St. John the Baptist and St. Nicholas, for God has entrusted to you this distant borderland town without any expenditure from your treasury or any great levy of troops. For these luminaries were steadfast, giving their favor and intercession to so few warriors."

The gentry of the aforesaid towns urged that auxiliaries be levied from the estates of those who were rich or had many lands, and also that money be exacted from their possessions. The same measures should be applied to ecclesiastical landowners, and evasion must be punished.

Finally they had a word to say about crown secretaries. "Sovereign," they said, "your secretaries and clerks have been favored by you with salaries, service tenures and patrimonies. Being continuously about your service, they have enriched themselves greatly by corruption. They have bought many patrimonies, built many houses, even stone palaces, in a manner that it is not fitting to relate. Under previous sovereigns of blessed memory even aristocrats did not have such houses, even though their birth entitled them to live in such dwellings.

"We, your slaves, are devoted to the house of the Immaculate Mother of God, the Moscow miracle workers, the true Orthodox faith and you, O pious tsar, for your great kindness to us. We are ready to risk our lives and souls to resist attacks by the hateful infidel on your majesty's lands but we your slaves are poor, destitute and helpless. We have no service tenures, or else our estates are either ruined or too small. Sovereign, in your kindness seek out and reward us with estates and money as God will show you the way, so that we may perform service for you. Order a survey to be taken, O sovereign, of all the patrimonies and service tenures throughout the land. Survey the lands of all the table attendants, crown agents, Moscow gentry, Moscow residents and us, your slaves, and men of all ranks, including crown secretaries and clerks, to determine how many peasants they have. Let them respond to the sovereign's inquest and kiss the cross to you. If anyone conceals peasants, let these be ascribed to you irrevocably. Order it to be proclaimed how many peasants from each estate are to serve the tsar without pay. Take money from whoever has surplus peasants in the amount the tsar decrees, to be paid into the treasury for the maintenance of troops. Take also as much money and grain supplies as are needed for such troops.

"If, O sovereign, you need a war chest in a hurry, order the seizure of the patriarch's treasury, those of the archbishops and bishops, and the money on safe deposit in the monasteries. Also gather into your treasury money from your leading merchants, and all traders and free peasants who come to market, carry on manufacturing or other business, as much as God wills, and your treasury will fill up.

"Also, O sovereign, order your chancellery officials, crown secretaries and customs collectors in Moscow and the other towns to keep accurate accounts, lest the state treasury be exhausted without your knowledge, and you have no money left to pay the troops. Order the leading merchants and the officials of the tax office to collect money for your majesty's treasury. Order whoever is serving in your towns as governor or chancellery official to come to your service against the hateful infidel with a large following. Thus your land, O sovereign, will be ready to meet the ferocious infidel attacks. This is the opinion and resolution of us, your slaves, the gentry and junior boyars and the various towns."

The same sentiments were expressed by the gentry and junior boyars of the southern towns, except that they added "Even if we surrender Azov, the Muslims will not be satisfied or appeased. War and bloodshed on the part of the Crimean and other pagan infidels will not ease off, and the Turkish infidels will be all the more aggressive on account of such a surrender. Better, O sovereign, to accept Azov for yourself and all the land, and defend it valiantly. Order money and all manner of supplies to be collected from all ranks, according to how many peasant households they have, not according to the cadastral surveys. We, your slaves, with all our followers and all our retinues, are ready to report for crown service against your enemies wherever you command. Yet we suffer greater destitution than we ever did from the Turkish and Crimean Muslims on account of Muscovite rules and delays, injustices and corrupt judges."

The leading merchants and traders said "We, your slaves, your leading merchants, members of the Merchants' and Cloth Merchants' Hundreds, and provincial traders, are suffering in the towns on account of the exactions of your officials, neither do we have any service tenures or patrimonies.

We are continually on your majesty's service every year in Moscow and the other towns on account of which, and also of the collection of fifths[36] which we gave you to subsidize the soldiers and servicemen taking part in the Smolensk campaign, many of us are destitute and utterly impoverished. While we were on your service in Moscow and other towns we collected money for your treasury as sworn officials, and very profitably. Where under previous sovereigns and in the earlier years of your reign the tax yield was only five or six hundred rubles we managed to exact from all the land five or six thousand and even more. Yet at the same time our own business has suffered, for much of our trade in Moscow and other cities was taken away by foreign interlopers, Germans and Persians who came to Moscow and other towns with their large inventory to sell all manner of goods. Also in many of the towns much of the population is impoverished and utterly ruined through the rapacity of the sovereign's governors, for traders who go from town to town to trade suffer detention and violence as they arrive, and their goods are despoiled. Under previous sovereigns elected magistrates had authority, and townsmen settled their own disputes. There were no governors in the towns, except in the borderlands, where they were sent to command troops for defense against Turks, Crimeans and Nogay Tatars."

The raising of taxes for the present war was referred by the traders to the tsar's will. They said they were willing to lay down their lives in the tsar's service, to die for the tsar's safety and the Orthodox faith. "Such is the resolution of us traders, leading merchants and members of the Merchants' and Cloth Merchants' Hundreds."

Elders of the free tax-paying communities, the hundredmen and elders of the settlements said the same, pleading impoverishment through fires, the fifths, levies for auxiliaries and cartage dues exacted for the Smolensk campaign; from market fees, fortification works, heavy taxes and service as sworn officials. "On account of this great poverty," they said, "many taxpayers have left the settlement and abandoned their houses."

Thus the gentry and junior boyars expressed their readiness to go to war, indicating the necessity of accepting Azov, expressing that failing to do so would bring celestial wrath down upon the Russian tsardom. At the same time for the success of this venture they demanded strong measures and curtailment of deep-rooted abuses. Traders clearly pointed out their ruined state. Loud voices were raised against those in whose hands the decision lay. It is interesting to note that in the summaries made of the speeches, presumably for the tsar, there is no mention of official wrongdoing. It was easy to find cogent arguments against the war. In March there came to Moscow the Turkish emissary Mustafa-Chelibey. The Moldavian hospodar Lupul pointed out to the tsar what misfortunes lay in store for the Russian army before Azov in the event of the slightest reverse. The cossacks could not be relied upon, for they were a perfidious and inconstant people, as was better known in Moscow even than in Moldavia. Finally the hospodar pointed out that in the event of war the sultan vowed to exterminate all Orthodox Christians in his domains. According to the survey made of Azov, it appeared that the city was heavily damaged and almost razed to the ground. It could not possibly be refortified at short notice, neither could it be defended against an army.

Accordingly on April 30 the tsar sent the cossacks the order to abandon Azov. The cossacks evacuated the city, leaving not one stone standing upon another. The huge Turkish army which came to renew the siege found only heaps of rubble.

EMBASSY OF MILOSLAVSKY AND LAZAREVSKY

Ambassadors were dispatched from Moscow to Constantinople, namely the noble Ilia Danilovich Miloslavsky[37] and the crown secretary Leonty Lazarevsky, declaring that the great sovereign was, and wished to remain, in firm fraternal friendship, brotherly love and communication with his brother His Majesty Sultan Ibrahim, more than with any other great sovereign. On this his word was immutable for all time, and would never change.

The ambassadors traveled by the winter road as far as Voronezh, and from there by boat along the Don, which was in full flood. They brought the Don Cossacks the tsar's grant in the amount of two thousand rubles cash, not counting cloth, wine and other supplies, but they had to pretend that this money, cloth and wine was their own. The members of the suite were strictly forbidden to tell anyone that they were bringing any grant to the Don Cossacks, lest it become known in Azov. They were to tell the cossacks not to talk among themselves about the tsar's bounty, lest the ambassadors suffer harm or be detained while within Turkish territory. If the secret of the tsar's bounty got out to Azov, the ambassadors were to say "A small grant from the tsar to the cossacks was dispatched with us so that they would obey the sovereign and evacuate Azov. It was not sent for any other purpose."

If the Don Cossacks said that the grant was small, that they were serving the sovereign and they were doing no harm, the ambassadors were to answer that the grant was small because the ambassadors had to travel light and set off quickly. This was in order that they receive the grant and serve the sovereign, not abandon him, for much already was sent, and even more would be sent later, and so no further harm was to be expected from the Turks. Concerning this his majesty the tsar wrote to the sultan confirming that they no longer would put out to sea to raid Turkish towns and villages. The cossacks must cause no more trouble which might embroil the tsar in quarrels with the sultan and cause the ambassadors losses, harm or detention.

In Constantinople the ambassadors first of all were to meet with the translator Zelfikar-Aga, give him the tsar's letter and the sables the tsar granted him, and consult with him how best to handle the local situation. They were to tell the grand vizier Mustafa-Pasha that his service and favor to the great sovereign were well known, remembered and never would be forgotten. For his service and favor to his majesty the tsar granted him ten times forty sables, and would send him more, in keeping with the service rendered. Furthermore the ambassadors were to consult with Patriarch Parthenios of Constantinople[38] what gifts from the sovereign to give the grand vizier, and upon which of the other pashas and chancellery officials might the tsar place his reliance on account of their devotion and honesty.

Should the vizier or the sultan's other privy councilors bring up the subject of Azov, alleging that the Don Cossacks took it at the tsar's instigation, and that the sovereign sent aid to them, the ambassadors were to answer. "You know very well that the Don Cossacks are brigands from way back, fugitive slaves living on the Don, escaping execution. They do not heed any of the tsar's decrees, and they captured Azov without the tsar's orders. His majesty the tsar sent them no aid, neither now will he defend or aid them since he wishes to have no quarrel on their account. If your sovereign Sultan Ibrahim were to order these bandits executed within a single hour, his majesty the tsar would not be vexed, because they are brigands and fugitives who live in distant places in lawless and nomad fashion. Many times before did the tsar write to them, urging them to leave off brigandage, not to put to sea, not to cause harm to Turkish or Crimean towns. Some years ago, in 1632, the tsar sent his commander Karamyshev to pacify them, but they beat him to death."

"They may say 'How can you assert that the Don Cossacks do not obey your sovereign? When after the capture of Azov they came to request aid, why did the tsar not order the emissaries executed? Or when the tsar sent orders to them to evacuate Azov, did they do so? Your sovereign himself wrote to our sultan that he ordered the execution of those cossacks who came to him after the capture of Azov.' In that case you are to answer 'The sovereign never did write to the sultan about that matter. Out of friendship to the sultan the sovereign several times wrote to the cossacks, urging them to evacuate Azov, gave them a small grant to induce them to obey, and by the same token sent them another grant after they left Azov.'"

The vizier and the pashas might say "When the sultan's emissaries were sent from Valuiki back to the Crimea they were escorted back only as far as the Northern Donets, not as far as the Tor river, where they were despoiled by Zaporozhian Cherkass, one of whom, being taken prisoner, said they did this at the instigation of a monk from Mount Athos." The ambassadors were to answer "The tsar ordered the execution of those soldiers who failed to escort the emissaries further than the Northern Donets. The Cherkass molest not only Turkish emissaries, but also the tsar's, as well as servitors of the Polish king. They do not heed the tsar's com-mands. Neither should you have believed that Cherkass brigand. He told this tale about the Mount Athos monk to avoid being killed, in order to excuse his banditry and instigate a quarrel between great sovereigns."

The ambassadors were to hand Patriarch Parthenios the tsar's letter and five times forty sables, worth two hundred and fifty rubles. These were to be handed over secretly, so that the Turkish officials would not find out. Should the vizier and the pashas detain them, subjecting them to dishonor or harm, they were to consult on everything with Patriarch Parthenios and follow his counsel. "Tell the patriarch," continued the instructions, "to use his good offices on the tsar's behalf, and incline the vizier, pashas and the sultan's privy counselors to favor the tsar, and go to the patriarch frequently to obtain his blessing on your undertaking. If Parthenios dies, do not go to see the new patriarch very often, and do not take him into your confidence. Give the sables sent for Parthenios to the new patriarch if he is pious and not a heretic; if not, give him nothing and do not go to receive his blessing. The patriarchs of Alexandria and Jerusalem each have been sent four times forty sables, worth a hundred and fifty rubles. Gifts have been sent to various holy places in the amount of twenty times forty sables. Apart from that, for supplies for the ambassadorial suite, for disbursement for state affairs and ransom of prisoners, we have sent furs worth fifteen hundred rubles, and for general expenses three thousand. They must be distributed according to local circumstances, and nobody is to be given any for nothing. Give ransom for prisoners; for nobles and junior boyars twenty to fifty rubles; for lesser men, musketeers, cossacks or commoners ten to twenty." Finally the ambassadors must insist that the sultan inscribe the tsar's title properly, not as king, "for never have we had kings in the Muscovite realm."

Arriving at the Don, the ambassadors discovered that the Turks had captured and burned cossack settlements such as Manych, Yar and Cherkask, killing or taking captive their inhabitants. The remaining atamans and cossacks fled to the small town on the Upper Razdor. They settled there and elected Ivan Katorzhny as their senior ataman. The ambassadors proceeded to Razdory, handed the cossacks the tsar's letter and read them the prepared speech.

The cossacks replied that they were grateful for the tsar's bounty, but they could in no way make peace with the inhabitants of Azov because the Turks utterly ruined their people. On the second day after the ambassadors' arrival at Razdory, on June 6, the town was besieged by Turks and Tatars but they fled after a fierce battle with the cossacks, who made peace with Azov, whither the ambassadors proceeded. From there they traveled to Constantinople.

Here the ambassadors were received with honor. The chancellery officials of the Moldavian hospodar Basil sent them mutton, chicken and vegetables on twenty dishes. The grand vizier sent them two hundred and fifty dishes of locally grown vegetables and a hundred barley loaves. In order not to vex the vizier, the ambassadors paid their respects to him before being presented to the sultan. The translator Zelfikar-Aga informed them that the vizier was unyielding and that they should send presents to his favorite Rezep-Aga. The ambassadors sent Rezep-Aga four times forty sables, worth 215 rubles, and matters proceeded smoothly. The vizier sent word to Rezep-Aga that he would resolve diplomatic matters entirely in favor of the tsar's ambassadors. The vizier was sent ten times forty sables, worth two thousand rubles, and he gave his word that the sultan would write the tsar's title in full and in proper form.

As they were dismissed the sultan said to the ambassadors "Tell the great sovereign that for the sake of mutual brotherly love and affection he should send his command to the Don Cossacks forbidding them to sail on the Black Sea, attack my villages and hamlets, kill my people or take them captive, and I shall send my command to the Crimean khan, the pasha of

Kaffa and the prince of Azov, neither themselves to make war against your majesty's borderlands, nor to send their troops there."

After they took their leave the translator Zelfikar-Aga approached the ambassadors, telling them that the grand vizier had conducted diplomatic business entirely in their favor and he, Zelfikar-Aga, thought that the vizier would like some small token of esteem, so perhaps they should send him a small gift. The ambassadors, thanking Zelfikar-Aga for his services and good offices, sent the vizier from their stores four times forty sables, valued at 345 rubles. The vizier on receiving this gift replied that he was glad to have been of service to his majesty the tsar and to have furthered his cause. The vizier also was rewarded richly by the Moldavian hospodar Basil for his conduct of the Muscovite affair.

The ambassadors, suspecting nothing, said openly that Basil wrote to the tsar urging him not to break with the Turks on account of Azov. The vizier was very displeased at this direct correspondence between a vassal of the sultan and his coreligionist the Muscovite tsar. Hearing this from the ambassadors, he *pondered* and was silent for a while, and then the ambassadors learned that the hospodar was deposed and another put in his place although Basil had a protector, Kasim-Aga, said to be the vizier's father. Kasim's request was backed by fifteen thousand efimoks brought to him by chancellery officials of the Moldavian governor, so Basil remained as hospodar.

The sables from the ambassadors' stores also produced an effect. The vizier declared to the ambassadors that the letter from the sultan to the tsar already was written with the full title, more exalted than previously. Letters also were written to the Crimean khan, the pasha of Kaffa and the prince of Azov that they should not dare attack the Muscovite borderlands, that the Crimean khan release all Russian captives without ransom, and that he punish those brigands who went to attack the Muscovite towns.

The ambassadors were very pleased, but then became tormented by uneasiness. Was the vizier telling the truth? Was the chief and most important condition being observed, the correct inscription of the tsar's title on the letter? They sent for the translator Zelfikar; could they see the draft copy? He replied that the secretary to the council must have it. They sent to the secretary, promising him gifts. The secretary to the council replied that the document was with the vizier. Again they asked Zelfikar, giving him considerable gifts, whether it would be possible to obtain the document from the vizier. Zelfikar promised to bribe those close to the vizier, but returned with the answer that there was no way of obtaining the document. All the same, the ambassadors should not worry, since he would ask the secretary to the council directly, and he would verify whether the tsar's title was written in full. The ambassadors were not reassured, but rushed to the patriarch, calling upon him to show his loyalty and favor; could not the draft copy be inspected? "We cannot gain access to these documents," the patriarch replied, "but the ambassadors can rest assured that the title was written in proper form, since the vizier is an honest man, and is as good as his word."

Finally Araslan-Aga, named ambassador to Moscow, showed Miloslavsky the form of address on the sultan's document. "To Michael Fedorovich, according to the law of Jesus sovereign of Muscovy, exalted above all other great sovereigns, tsar and possessor of All Russia, the sultan's beloved friend." The same Araslan was to carry to the Crimea, Kaffa and Azov the prohibition against attacking Muscovite territories.

As far as the cossacks were concerned, the ambassadors in accordance with their instructions repeated to the vizier "Even if your sovereign ordered all these brigands killed within a single hour, his majesty the tsar would not be vexed." "If your sovereign would not be vexed," replied the vizier, "our sovereign certainly will deal with them." Then he said "Could not your sovereign send his troops after these brigands to restrain them from their depredations?" "Until these brigands are ruined," replied the ambassadors, "our tsar cannot send his troops against them, for these brigands, men from many countries who call themselves Don Cossacks, have inhabited distant places, living the life of bandits and nomads, moving from one place to another. Presently and for some time to come there is no way we can send troops after anybody because this spring your troops came to their encampments, devastating them until nothing remained. We assure you that the ruination of these brigands by your warriors causes our sovereign no vexation whatsoever."

DISCONTENTED DON COSSACKS PROPOSE MOVE TO THE YAIK

The cossacks knew that, in its correspondence with the Turkish government, Muscovy characterized them as brigands. "Always when they write about us," they complained, "we are called brigands, yet we have performed many services for the tsar. We cannot make a living on the Don. Let us wait for our brothers to return from the sea, and if they return safely we will continue to live on the Don. If only a few return, there is no point in us remaining on the Don, so let us move elsewhere. A town has been established at the mouth of the Yaik. We will build the town up, go to live on the Yaik and take to the sea from there." When he found out about their intentions the tsar commanded the Astrakhan governors that if the Don Cossacks made for the Yaik soldiers were to be sent against them, and they were to be dealt with by every possible means.

PERSIA AND GEORGIA

The cossacks also got mixed up in Moscow's relations with Persia. As early as July 1621 the Astrakhan governors informed Moscow that the cossacks were committing piracy on the Caspian Sea, plundering servicemen, traders and all manner of people. Their ataman was Trenka-Us.

In 1641 the ambassador of Abbas's successor Shah Safi[39] sent a petition to the tsar. "From your side of the sea all manner of vagabond propertyless fugitives have assembled, attacked places surrounding Gilian[40] and Mazanderan. They make war, kill people, plunder and take captives. They treat in like manner seafaring traders. Our sovereign will make common cause with your against these vagabond cossacks, and we will keep each other informed."

At the same time the ambassador complained about Russian governors oppressing Persian merchants. Yet it was not merely the governors who oppressed them. "Previous Persian ambassadors," read the petition, "were allowed to trade, sell and buy. Their gates were always open, people of all ranks came and traded without fear, but now we sit in close confinement, and nobody is allowed access to us. Grigory Nikitnikov ordered us to trade with him alone, and we have not been able to make a single altyn[41] from the tsar's goods, for everyone is too afraid to come to us."

The ambassador received a reply to his complaint against the cossacks, to the effect that orders long since were sent to the governors to send troops in pursuit of the cossacks, to kill them and execute all prisoners. If in his land the shah apprehended and killed these brigands, the great sovereign would not intercede for them. As for the wrongs committed by the governors, the great sovereign had no knowledge of the nature of their offenses. In what towns did they occur, and what were the names of the governors? Give the names, and the sovereign would order an investigation. Russian merchants in Persia also suffered great violence from the shah's governors and chancellery officials. Regarding the third complaint, the leading merchant Nikitnikov was indeed authorized to trade with the Persian ambassadors, but freely. "You were under no compulsion. You saw Nikitnikov's wares and showed him yours, but you did not do any business. We do not know why you wanted to drag your heels in this manner."

The Persians could not understand the concept of "free trade" with a single client. "I spoke with the escort many times previously, and now I repeat, I do not wish to do business with Grigory Nikitnikov. He put too high a price on his goods, and I don't want to sell the shah's goods at giveaway prices and risk being shorter by a head." The ambassador stood his ground and won the right to trade with all comers, provided he set up shop in the ambassadors' courtyard and not in the street.

We have seen that the tsar in his capacity as nominal suzerain of Georgia demanded of Shah Abbas that he not lay waste that unfortunate country. The shah replied that he was prepared to cede Georgia to the Muscovite sovereign and return to the Georgian ruler Teimuraz[42] his family, provided that he forsake the Turkish alliance. Michael ordered that the message be conveyed to Teimuraz's ambassador, who at that time (1624) was in Moscow, adding that his majesty the tsar could not break with the shah or help Teimuraz financially because the treasury was exhausted by the Polish war.

In 1637 there arrived in Moscow from Georgia one Nicephoros, a chief emissary[43] and archimandrite, who declared that Teimuraz was prepared to become the sovereign's vassal. Consequently, after long deliberation and gathering of information, in the spring of 1637 Prince Fedor Volkonsky,[44] the crown secretary Artemy Khvatov and five clergy were dispatched to Georgia to administer the oath of allegiance to Teimuraz. Along with the emissaries there went two icon painters and a joiner, with materials, iron and paints.

On their arrival in Georgia Volkonsky found the country in a most piteous condition. After the recent devastation by the Persians, only Kakhetia still remained in Teimuraz's hands. The aim of the mission was achieved. Teimuraz kissed the cross to Tsar Michael, and the ambassador managed to avoid Michael undertaking any obligations in return. Teimuraz asked that the tsar order the building of a fortress in the mountains in order to restrain the Kumyks[45] from attacking Georgia. He also requested the dispatch of a physician and an ore assayer.

The answer came in 1641 with Prince Efim Myshetsky, who was obliged to tell Teimuraz that at present it was impossible to build the fortress. In Moscow the sad fate of the Russian army in the mountains during Godunov's reign was remembered all too well.[46] A physician was on his way. As far as the assayer was concerned, Myshetsky suggested that first Teimuraz send to Moscow samples of minerals discovered in his country. Finally Myshetsky was entrusted to hand over twenty thousand efimoks, as well as some sables.

III

PRINCE VALDEMAR, 1640-1645

DANISH GROOM PROPOSED FOR TSAREVNA IRINA

During the final years of his life Tsar Michael was preoccupied with two weighty matters relating to Denmark and Poland. We have seen that previous relations with Denmark came to nothing over the dispute regarding the placing of the king's name. Early in 1637 the courier Holmer arrived in Moscow with letters from Christian IV requesting the transportation to Denmark of the remains of Prince Johan. This request was granted.[1]

Several years later in Moscow it was decided to follow Godunov's example and invite a Danish prince to become the bridegroom of the tsar's eldest daughter, Irina Mikhailovna. On June 9, 1640 the Danish king's chancellery official Peter Marselis[2] was summoned to the Chancellery for Foreign Affairs and asked how many children the Danish king had, and what age they were. Marselis replied that Christian IV had two sons by his first marriage. One of them, the heir to the throne, already was married, and the second was engaged to be married. There remained a third son, Valdemar, from another lawfully wedded wife, Countess Kristina Munk, to whom the king was married morganatically.[3] This prince was twenty-two years old. The king did not live with the prince's mother since it was alleged she had a bad influence on him, but the king loved his son Valdemar.

FOMIN SENT TO INVESTIGATE

In November a courier was sent to Denmark, the foreign translator Ivan Fomin,[4] with a complaint against the prince of Holstein, who was not fulfilling the terms of the treaty concerning trade with Persia.[5] This Fomin was to find out reliable information secretly about how many children the king had in wedlock with wives of equal status, from queens, and how many not from such wives, and what rank they held. He was to find out particularly all he could about Prince Valdemar; how old was he, was he healthy, of what stature, posture, countenance, eyes, hair color, what was his education, was he literate, and could he understand foreign languages?

What were his disposition and manners, and was he free of any sickness or deformity? Was he already engaged to be married, and whose daughter was his mother? Was she still alive, and in what condition did she live? Fomin was to make sure to see the prince himself and sketch his likeness on a piece of paper or tablet, without attribution. He was to obtain the services of a portrait artist, even though he might have to remain in Denmark for an extra week or two, feigning illness if necessary. He was to strive to find out all he could, sparing no expenses, but for the sake of decency and to conceal the aim of his mission, he was to order portraits of King Christian and all his sons.

When he returned from Denmark Ivan Fomin reported that Prince Valdemar was twenty years old, with reddish hair and medium stature. He was thin, had grey eyes, was handsome, fair of countenance, healthy and wise. He could speak Danish and Italian, and could understand High German. He also was skilled in military arts, for Fomin himself had observed the prince at gunnery practice. His mother Kristina was in poor health. Her father was a great aristocrat and knight whose name was Ludvik Munk, and her mother was similarly of high rank.

With regard to the portraits Fomin reported, "Ulfeldt, governor of Copenhagen, summoned me and said 'Rumor has come to me that you are paying money to obtain original portraits of the king and princes, without any attribution. But you yourself know that this is an impossible undertaking because the portrait artist would have to stand before the king and princes for a long time and observe them. Our king, on the other hand, has consented to sit with his sons for a portrait to be sent to your sovereign.'"

Later Ulfeldt asked, "Why does your sovereign need these portraits?" "The sovereign's thoughts are in God's hands," replied Fomin, "I do not know." Then the king's secretary repeated the same question, but added, "If your sovereign wants Prince Valdemar to serve him in a military capacity, the king would be glad to release him to his majesty the tsar."

PRINCE VALDEMAR'S EMBASSY TO MOSCOW

In the summer of 1641 it was announced in Moscow that an embassy extraordinary was coming to the sovereign from Denmark. Prince Valdemar of Schleswig-Holstein would be the chief ambassador, while the second ambassador would be Gregor Krabbe. Special arrangements were made to honor the ambassadors. In all the towns governors came out to greet Count Valdemar and bowed low. In Moscow the ambassadors were lodged in the house of the conciliar secretary Ivan Gramotin,[6] in the Kitay Quarter. For this purpose the halls, kitchen, all the apartments and the stable were surveyed, swept clean and any dilapidations repaired. Tables, benches and window seats were placed in all the rooms. All sawdust and manure was removed from the floors, which were sprinkled with fresh sand. Iron gates were placed on the central hall and, since there was no bridge or stairway, it was ordered to make a bridge with railings and a staircase. The well was cleaned out, while in the halls and in the rear apartments the tables and benches were upholstered with silken cloth. In the hall and in the chamber where the count was to lodge one table was covered by a tapestry, the other three with purple silk.

The bailiffs were given orders to the effect that they diligently observe by whatever means they could, and find out discreetly from the nobles and embassy staff, how they and Ambassador Krabbe regarded Count Valdemar, whether as royalty or as a commoner. The bailiffs answered that sometimes Krabbe removed his hat in the count's presence, but while traveling spoke to him with his hat on, and sat with him at mealtimes. The councilors and nobles respected the count, spoke to him with their hats removed, and addressed him as prince, not as ambassador, regarding him as royalty.

The embassy was received in the usual fashion since in the protocol Valdemar was inscribed as ambassador, not as prince. Valdemar's request that he be allowed to present himself wearing his sword was refused, even though he asserted that on this account he would suffer lasting dishonor. In his audience with the boyars Valdemar demanded preferential trade for Danish merchants throughout the Muscovite realm.

The boyars replied that the Danish merchants could come in groups of five or six and could trade wholesale, not retail, paying the regular duties. Valdemar requested permission to build a cordage factory. The boyars replied that such a factory could not be run without pitch. A monopoly in pitch had been granted in 1635, but when the monopoly ended the sovereign would grant the Danes the monopoly for a specified period.

Valdemar asked permission for the Danes to build houses and churches. He received the reply that the Danes already had houses in Moscow, and they could buy houses and erect them in the trading quarters of Novgorod, Pskov and Archangel, but could not build Protestant churches.[7] Russian merchants likewise should be permitted to own houses in Denmark. Valdemar demanded that the Danes be permitted to maintain agents and officials in Moscow, and were permitted a single agent.

The Danes demanded that the cargo be recovered from shipwrecked vessels and returned to their owners, and the transfer be peaceful and without payment of the tenth.[8] This condition was agreed, with the observation that the tenth never was collected previously. Valdemar demanded that a company of Danish merchants be formed with a monopoly in hides and Russia leather, and the company would pay extra duty. Previously they paid four percent duty, now they would pay seven. The boyars replied that this kind of preferential trade was inconvenient, since the tsar's subjects would suffer loss.

Valdemar demanded that the Danes be allowed to purchase annually a thousand shiploads of grain, and a similar amount for Norway. They were told that the Russian realm had suffered harvest failure two years in a row, and their own people did not have enough to eat. If there was a good harvest, permission would be granted.

Following these negotiations the ambassadors wanted a definitive agreement drawn up, but this also met with insuperable obstacles. Valdemar demanded that in the Danish copy the king's name be inscribed before the tsar's. The boyars refused, and as before the ambassadors went away empty-handed.

PROESTEV AND PATRIKEEV FAIL TO CONCLUDE MATCH

In October 1641 the Danish ambassadors departed and in April 1642 it was realized in Moscow that an embassy must be sent to Denmark to conclude this important business. Stepan Matveevich Proestev, already known to us,[9] and the crown secretary Ivan Patrikeev, were sent to conclude the treaty and present gifts to Prince Valdemar. For their stores they were given sables worth two thousand rubles. They were to make rounds and assess the local situation, and determine what was essential for the successful conclusion of their business. The principal matter of state consisted of proposing a match between Prince Valdemar and Tsarevna Irina Mikhailovna. Secret instructions given to the ambassadors on this matter read "If they ask whether you have a portrait of the tsarevna, you are to reply, 'For the sake of the security of the realm it is not the custom for our great sovereigns to allow portraits of the tsar's daughters to be taken out of the country. Also in the Muscovite realm the tsar's daughters are not seen by any except the privy boyars. Other boyars, or officials of whatever rank, are not allowed to view them."

The ambassadors were not received in Denmark very graciously. When they were presented to the king they conveyed the tsar's respects and asked after the king's health, saying that his brother the tsar was in good health the last time they saw him. The king remained silent, did not ask after the tsar's health, and did not rise. The ambassadors, without handing over the tsar's letter, stood silent for a long time, waiting for the king to rise and ask after their sovereign's health. Finally Proestev said that they awaited the customary response, whereupon the king ordered the chancellor to say that he was glad to hear that his brother was in good health. The ambassadors answered that the tsar personally had asked after the king's health, and stood up. "When our ambassadors were with your sovereign," asked the king, "how did he conduct himself?" "When your ambassadors were with our sovereign," Proestev replied, "he did not slight his majesty's honor, but we see things are done differently here." The king rose, removed his hat and personally inquired after the sovereign's health.

Negotiations opened with the question whose name should be inscribed first on the documents. "This matter cannot be resolved according to your wishes," said the chancellor. "Our sovereign is second to none in respect throughout Europe, and does not wish to purchase affection at that price from any ruler." So once again the matter of concluding a treaty came to nothing.

The other question was broached. The ambassadors spoke of high matters of state, saying that the great sovereign wished to be in amity, firm friendship, love and unity with his royal majesty, more than with any other great sovereign. He therefore ordered them to declare to his majesty that the time was come for his daughter Tsarevna Irina Mikhailovna to be married, and that he, the great sovereign, was aware that King Christian had a noble and high-born son, Prince Valdemar Christian, duke of Schleswig-Holstein. If his royal majesty wished to be in perpetual brotherly friendship with the great sovereign, let him permit his son to take the sovereign's daughter as his lawful wedded wife.

"In what degree will Count Valdemar be related to him," the king's privy councilors asked, "and what honor will they accord him? More specifically, how many towns and villages will he grant him for his support?" The ambassadors replied that they were given no instructions on that matter. Concerning religion, they said that Valdemar must be baptized into the Orthodox faith of the Greek dispensation. This demand met with refusal, and the ambassadors were dismissed without achieving either of the desired ends.

Valdemar at that time was not in Copenhagen. The ambassadors sent him the tsar's gift of five times forty sables. After they were dismissed, Valdemar arrived in Copenhagen and came to pay his respects to them for the tsar's gift. "Now," he said, "I see your sovereign's unforgettable kindness towards me, because he has showered me with his sovereign bounty." The ambassadors did obeisance to the prince and invited him to sit, but the prince said "When you ambassadors are seated, I will sit down with you." "You are a king's son," the ambassadors replied, "and we are instructed to treat you with proper respect, so you must sit down first, and we will sit with you." The prince sat at the middle of the table, not at the end. Concerning the betrothal he said, "My father told me everything about it. I am not supposed to discuss it with you or say anything except that I shall follow my father's wishes completely."

Proestev and Patrikeev received a grim reception in Moscow. They were accused of not following their instructions, in which they were told to be diligent and give presents wherever necessary. Yet the ambassadors on the first refusal came running home without bargaining with the king. They were dispatched with a treasury to promote crown business yet they gave out the sables for their own honor and not for the tsar's business. They spoke to the king's privy councilors only a few words, which were irrelevant, leaving out many pertinent matters, and many points were left unanswered.

PETER MARSELIS RESCUES PROPOSAL

Proestev and Patrikeev arrived in Moscow in September. In December the sovereign sent the Danish commissioner Peter Marselis to Denmark, "having full confidence in him, because your father Gabriel and you, Peter, previously have given loyal service to the great sovereign. When the sovereign's father was imprisoned in Poland and Lithuania, Gabriel Marselis diligently strove to obtain his release, and you both performed many other valuable services for the sovereign."

Marselis was to declare to the king that the previous ambassadors Proestev and Patrikeev did not speak according to the tsar's instructions, neither were they authorized to raise with the king's privy councilors the matter of the prince's conversion. They spoke and acted negligently. They were supposed to send dispatches to the tsar from Copenhagen should they encounter any difficulty, but they did not write about anything and set off for home without accomplishment. For this the sovereign placed them in great disfavor.

The great sovereign would hold the king's son in great esteem and high honor, as a prince of the blood and as his son-in-law. His privy councilors and all officials of the Russian realm would treat him with great honor, and he would be endowed with all he wanted. Towns, villages and money would be given to him in plenty. The sovereign commanded he be given the major towns of Suzdal and Yaroslavl with their districts, and all the towns and villages he needed. The prince would be under no religious constraint, for baptism into the Orthodox Christian faith of the Greek dispensation is a gift of God for all people, which God gives to whoever is led to it, but God's will is above all in the thoughts and deeds of men. The tsar's kindness would extend to all privy councilors or courtiers who accompanied the prince and wanted to serve in his court, and none would be under any constraint.

Marselis was obliged to sort out all kinds of difficulty, smooth out all kinds of objections, but he was diligent and used every means possible. Thus many in Denmark said "How can the prince go to Moscow, to a savage people, there forever to be enslaved? For they do not perform what they promise. Can he therefore live there on his father's charity?" So spoke those who wished that Valdemar marry a daughter of the king of Bohemia, the unfortunate Friedrich.[10] "If the people in Moscow were savage," answered Marselis, "I would not have lived there many years, neither would I seek to live there any longer. It would be good if there were in Denmark such order as in Moscow. Nobody can prove that the tsar will not do as he promised, for he strictly keeps his word not only to Christian, but also to Muslim rulers."

"In Moscow," said the king's privy counselors, "many boyars do not wish the tsar to give his daughters to princes of the blood, since they themselves want to be in kinship with the tsar." "The Muscovite sovereign is an autocrat," Marselis replied, "and does as he pleases. Moreover the great privy boyars are fully conversant with this great matter." "At first the prince will be shown great honor in Moscow," insisted the Swedes and Dutch, "in order to seduce him from the Lutheran faith, and if he refuses they will cease to honor him." Marselis replied that the Swedes and Dutch were saying this in order to frustrate this momentous matter. It was initiated in good faith and would be brought to a favorable conclusion.

Finally Valdemar, who brought back unpleasant memories from his first journey to Moscow, displayed a strong reluctance to go a second time as a suitor, and only went out of fear of angering his father the king. He questioned Marselis whether all this was being done in good faith. Marselis answered that everything would be fine. "If things go badly for you, they will also go badly for me, as I will have to answer for it with my head." "What use," the prince retorted, "will your head be to me if I have a bad time there?"

"Evidently God has willed this," he added, "since the king and his councilors have decided. I have led a wandering life for many years, and have learned to accommodate myself to others, some of them malevolent, so how can I fail to please such a good natured ruler?"

TERMS OF ENGAGEMENT

The king announced to Marselis the conditions in which the preliminary answer to Moscow should be couched. (1) The prince should suffer no compulsion with regard to religion, and a church must be established for him according to his faith. In Moscow the reply was that the prince and his court would suffer no religious pressure. Concerning the granting of a site for a Protestant church, there would be an agreement with the king's ambassadors accompanying Count Valdemar to Moscow. (2) That the prince be honored by all, high and low, clergy and laymen, as the tsar's son-in-law, so that nobody but the tsar and his son the tsarevich outrank him; to them will he defer as his sovereigns, and nobody else. This condition was agreed. (3) The lands granted to the prince and his direct successors were to be theirs unconditionally. If Valdemar died without issue, Irina would inherit those towns for the remainder of her life. If the great sovereign in addition to the towns and lands gave her a cash dowry, that would be all the more honorable and magnanimous. This condition was agreed with the addition "If Valdemar is survived by heirs, the count's possessions in Denmark shall go to Irina and his successors. Also we the great sovereign have been pleased to grant all manner of chattels and money to the value of three hundred thousand rubles. (4) Apart from the towns, the prince should be given an allowance to support his court since the income from the towns was unknown. Answer: the designated towns yield plenty of revenue; if it is insufficient we can add more towns and villages. (5) The prince can dress his courtiers as he pleases. He also must be free to bring servants from Denmark and send them home. This was agreed, with the stipulation that the prince's suite in Moscow be limited to three hundred servants.

VALDEMAR ARRIVES IN MOSCOW

When Marselis set off to Moscow with the king's conditions and returned with satisfactory replies under the sovereign's seal, Valdemar with two ambassadors, Olaf Passbjorg and Stren Villen, sailed from

Copenhagen to Danzig in order to reach Moscow by way of Polish rather than Swedish territory. In Wilno he was received very graciously and honorably by King Wladyslaw, and amazed the Polish courtiers with his knowledge of French and Italian.

In December 1643 Valdemar crossed the Russian frontier, and was met near Pskov by the boyar Prince Yury Sitsky[11] and the crown secretary Shipulin. In Pskov the governors greeted him. The leading merchants and townsmen met him with gifts of loaves, sables and golden coins, twice forty sables and a hundred ducats. At first Valdemar did not want to accept the presents, but when the crown secretary Shipulin, following the tsar's instructions, pointed out that otherwise he would offend the inhabitants of Pskov, he accepted them.

"Take good care of Valdemar son of Christian," Sitsky was told, "and accord him every mark of honor. Make sure he is not bothered by Russians or any kind of people." Yet it was impossible, to protect him completely from unpleasantness. In Opochka his carriage overturned, and the velvet was torn from the door.

In Novgorod the prince received the same kind of reception as in Pskov. In Moscow, which the prince entered on January 21, 1644, he was brought bread and gifts by Muscovite, Dutch and English merchants and traders, whom Valdemar invited to approach.

PRESENTED TO SOVEREIGN

When on January 28 the prince arrived at the palace, in the middle of the Palace of Facets,[12] in front of the pillar, he was greeted by Tsarevich Alexis Mikhailovich, who was introduced to Valdemar by the boyar Prince Lvov. The tsarevich inquired after his guest's health, took his hand and walked to the right of the prince. The same Prince Lvov introduced the prince to the tsar, who rose from his seat, took the prince's hand and inquired after his health. The prince begged the tsar's favor and on behalf of his father the king bowed first to the sovereign then to the tsarevich, Alexis Mikhailovich.

The king's ambassadors pronounced the following speech. "His majesty the king, in the name of the Holy Trinity, sent his beloved son Count Valdemar Christian to your majesty the tsar, so that he may according to your majesty's desire and request enter into marriage with her highness the tsar's daughter, Grand Princess Irina Mikhailovna. The king requests that his majesty the tsar be so good, for the sake of greater trust and to seal the marriage contract, as to give his solemn oath in the presence of the king's ambassadors and to give his written promise, that he will honor the king's son as he would his own son, for the king has given strict orders to his son to honor your majesty the tsar as a father, to accord him befitting respect and render him appropriate service."[13] On behalf of the tsar a conciliar secretary replied "We desire that Almighty God bring this matter, which has been well begun, to a favorable conclusion. We wish to be in firm friendship and love with our brother his majesty the king, and wish to have his son Valdemar Christian in close kinship, good friendship and respect, and accord him the honor befitting the tsar's son and son-in-law."

DANISH EMISSARIES PRESENT ARTICLES TO BOYARS

On February 3 the Danish envoys were in conference with the boyars, Prince Nikita Ivanovich Odoevsky,[14] Prince Yury Andreevich Sitsky, the lord-in-waiting Vasily Ivanovich Streshnev[15] and the crown secretaries Grigory Lvov and Mikhaila Voloshenin. The ambassadors spoke of a definitive agreement containing the following terms. (1) Confirmation of former treaties concerning peace, unity and free trade. (2) Danish and Norwegian merchants were to be allowed to trade in all places within the Muscovite realm, and to manufacture cordage. (3) The Danes were to be permitted to have their own churches and residences. (4) They were to appoint agents and officials in whichever towns were suitable. (5) In case of shipwreck, goods were to be returned to their owner without payment of duty, while those who recovered them were to be given a modest fee for safe keeping. (6) The king's subjects were to be free to purchase in Russia a thousand shiploads of grain, more or less, and a similar amount could be exported to Norway. (7) Since there were border disputes between the great sovereign and the Polish king, the Danish king was prepared to act as an intermediary. (8) Concerning the clergy officiating at the wedding of the prince and the tsarevna, the ambassadors hoped that everything would be ordered that was conducive to the honor of the All-High God. (9) The ambassadors hoped that all the conditions negotiated with Peter Marselis would be confirmed. (10) They wanted to know the site of the church to be built for the prince. Where would his court be, and where would his court personnel be housed? (11) The king ordered them to ascertain how much revenue the towns of Suzdal and Yaroslavl yielded. Could this income support the court expenses of the prince and his successors? If not, would the tsar keep his promise and supplement these revenues? (12) How are the prince and his successors to inscribe these towns and lands in his title, coat of arms and seal? (13) What would happen should the prince or his wife die? (14) In the king's copy of the documents the name of King Christian should be written ahead of that of the tsar.

PRINCE CONVERSES WITH THE SOVEREIGN

On February 4 the tsar visited the prince, who complained to him about the wrongs committed by the Swedes, in that they encroached upon Holstein in violation of treaty obligations. "Therefore," said Valdemar, "all rulers should know how untrustworthy the Swedes are, and be on their guard against them. His majesty the tsar should exercise particular vigilance. I, the prince, remind you of this because I have come to contract a marriage alliance with you, and wish you and all the Russian realm well, because what benefits you benefits me also."

"It is true," replied Michael Fedorovich, "that the Swedes are perfidious and cannot be trusted, but they have not yet caused me any trouble, and I have concluded a definitive peace with the Swedish king." "What evil they did the Muscovite realm!" rejoined the prince. "They were called upon by Tsar Vasily for help, yet they turned out to be evil foes."[16]

PRINCE URGED TO ACCEPT ORTHODOXY

On February 8, on orders from the tsar, Patriarch Joseph,[17] who succeeded Joasaph,[18] sent to the prince the former resident in Sweden, Dmitry Frantsbekov, to deliver the following speech. "His holiness and all the consecrated assembly greatly rejoice that God has brought you, a prince of the blood, to our great sovereign to contract a marriage with Tsarevna Irina Mikhailovna. So you, a king's son, should join in faith with our great sovereign, the tsaritsa, their highborn children and us who pray for you."

The prince replied that he could not accept the faith of the Greek dispensation, neither would he do anything not covered in the agreement concluded by Peter Marselis. "If Marselis agreed verbally with the tsar that the prince would change his religion, he did not say anything about it to the king and the prince, and was deceiving you, since he did not represent the thoughts either of the king or the prince." Had the prince known that the religious question would come up, he would not have left home. Furthermore unless the tsar ordered everything to follow the terms of the Marselis agreement, the prince should be given leave honorably, to go back to his father King Christian."

Frantsbekov replied that Marselis was not authorized to speak or resolve on matters of religion. It would not be dishonorable for the prince to travel back home, neither would anyone be offended, but he wondered whether it would not be advantageous to discuss the faith from scripture with the clergy. "I am more literate than any priest," replied the prince, "I have read the bible five times from cover to cover, and remember it all. If the tsar and patriarch want to debate from scripture, I am willing to speak and listen."

On February 13 the prince had a private audience with the tsar, who addressed to him the following words. "The king's ambassadors while they were here said that the king commanded you to respect my sovereign wishes, to obey me and follow all my commands. It would be pleasing to me if you accepted the Orthodox faith."

"I would be pleased to follow your sovereign will and obey you," the prince replied. "Gladly would I shed my blood for you, but I cannot change my faith, for fear of transgressing my father's oath. Moreover in our land it is possible for the husband to be of one faith and the wife of another. If your majesty the tsar does not wish to abide by the agreement, send me back to my father."

Tsar. Out of affection for you, for the sake of our close kinship, I accorded you a suitable great honor, such as was never given before. In order to enjoy our great love and affection, you should defer to my will and join our faith. For such a good deed you will enjoy God's supreme favor, my love and affection and the respect of all men. If you do not join me in faith, you cannot marry my daughter, for with us it is impossible for husband and wife to be of different faiths. Peter Marselis has been in the Muscovite realm for some time and must know that, not only among the ruling family, but also commoners, this is not permitted. To send you back would be embarrassing and dishonorable. We would be shamed before neighboring nations should you leave us without achieving the good purpose for which you came. You should reflect upon and fulfill my request, and also consider your reasons for not joining the Orthodox faith of the Greek dispensation. Do you not know that Our Lord Jesus Christ showed all Orthodox Christians the way of salvation by being immersed three times?

Prince. We also formerly practiced immersion in the Lutheran faith, but ceased to do so thirty years ago. I have nothing against immersion, but I cannot be baptized into another faith, for fear of violating my father's oath. Moreover during the reign of Ivan Vasilicvich one of the tsar's nieces was married to our Prince Magnus.[19]

Tsar. Tsar Ivan Vasilievich did that because he had no care or affection for his niece, but I wish to be in the same faith with you, because I love you as my own son.

The prince asked that he be allowed to consult with his father, and discuss with the sovereign the matter of faith some other time.

On February 16 the prince sent the tsar a letter with the following articles. "(1) Perhaps it is unknown to your majesty the tsar that for two years the high ambassadors were being sent to my father concerning the match, and when they demanded that I change my religion, they met with flat refusal. (2) Does your majesty still adhere to the condition stipulated when you sent Peter Marselis to my father, under which according to your decree I should be subjected to no compulsion or hindrance in religious matters? (3) In your majesty the tsar's letter, sent under your seal, does not the first article speak of freedom of religion? Surely we cannot believe that your majesty the tsar, a sovereign everywhere glorified and famous, listened to evil counselors who told you to violate your promise and agreement? This would cause not only my father, but also all other rulers to wonder, and will cast reproaches in your majesty's face."

"Now we declare to you," replied the tsar, "that you are under no religious compulsion, but we encourage and urge you to join with us in one Christian Orthodox faith, for you cannot marry our daughter and remain in a different faith. In our reply sent with Peter Marselis to your father, nowhere is it stated that you could marry our daughter and remain in your own faith, neither was it written anywhere that we could not try to convert you to our faith. We, the great sovereign, wish to conclude this matter in a way pleasing to God and our dignity, and to that end we urge, pray and implore you to seek your own salvation and physical health, and join with us in faith. We do not heed the counsel of malicious men, neither is it befitting for his majesty the king, other Christian rulers or you to impute anything contrary to truth or justice. There will not be any reproaches cast in my face, neither should you believe those wishing to set us at variance."

On February 26 the prince sent his response. "We perceive from your reply," he wrote, "that your majesty the tsar does not express himself in plain language, as is the practice among great Christian rulers throughout Europe, but insists upon his own interpretation and understanding of this matter. Never was there any such agreement in which our father his majesty the king changed the terms to suit his own interpretation, turning plain words into another meaning, as apparently happens in this country." In conclusion the prince asked to be allowed to return to Denmark.

He was not allowed to return. On March 21 the prince invited Fedor Ivanovich Sheremetev[20] and asked him to obtain his release. "I know," said the prince, "that you are the leading boyar in the tsardom, close to the tsar, just and great, and therefore I beg you to aid me, so that the tsar will let the king's ambassadors and me go home." "It would be well," replied Sheremetev, "if you would join his majesty the tsar in the faith, for it is inconvenient for you to travel back such a long way." "I cannot stay here," the prince answered, "and if his majesty will let me leave with honor, I will sing his praises loudly." Sheremetev agreed to convey the prince's wishes to the tsar. Consequently on March 25 the guard around the prince's residence was reinforced.

On March 29 the boyars declared to the Danish ambassadors that the prince could not marry the tsarevna without changing his religion, and that the ambassadors should persuade Valdemar to accept Orthodoxy. The ambassadors replied that they had no instructions to do this, and that if they even mentioned a word about it to the king, they would all be shorter by a head. "Even if," continued the ambassadors, "the prince were to accept the faith of his majesty the tsar, what about the other matters, such as fasting, dietary requirements and dress? We now clearly see that the principal matter of our embassy cannot be accomplished. The prince will not change his religion, so nothing more can be said. May it please his majesty the tsar to give us leave to go?"

CORRESPONDENCE WITH PATRIARCH

On April 21 a messenger with a letter from the patriarch appeared before Valdemar and addressed him as follows. "Lord Prince Valdemar, son of Christian! I have been sent by the sovereign's father and intercessor, the most holy Joseph, patriarch of Moscow and All Russia. He has ordered me to inquire how Christ in His mercy is preserving you, and told me to find out why, lord prince, you sent to the tsar asking to be allowed to go home without achieving with the tsar's majesty the mission of love for which you came. Thus the most holy father Joseph has sent you this letter containing his counsel under his own seal, asking you to be so good as to read it through and send your gracious reply."

In his letter the patriarch wrote, "Accept, O Valdemar son of Christian, this letter and read through it, meditate in love, do not be obstinate. The lord tsar is solicitous for you and wishes you well, both in this life and the next. Do not frustrate by your obstinacy the good, great and loving relationship with his majesty the tsar, but do everything according to his will and listen to God, Who does not chase you away but wants you for His own. Also your father King Christian revealed his counsel to his majesty the tsar, and wanted to enter into kinship through you his beloved son, whom he sent to his majesty to marry his daughter. Also to his ambassadors he ordered that when he dispatched you he commanded you to be subject in everything to the will of his majesty the tsar. Therefore you should heed his majesty the tsar and join us in the Orthodox Christian faith. We know that you call yourselves Christians, but you are deficient in some of the articles of the faith, and in many respects you have deviated from us…. So you, prince, should accept holy baptism by threefold immersion, in this way leaving no doubt that you are baptized. Baptism according to your faith is deficient, it needs to be performed in full, and so there will be one baptism according to the one holy, ecumenical and apostolic faith, and not a second, for with us there is no second baptism."

The prince replied the next day with the following letter. "We are aware that you have much influence with the tsar, so we petition you that he allow me and the lord ambassadors to return to Denmark with the same honor as that with which he received us. You accuse us of obstinacy, but you cannot call our constancy in the Christian faith obstinacy. In matters pertaining to salvation we must listen to God rather than man. We appeal to Christian rulers to judge whether we can be called obstinate. Perhaps with you a change in faith is a small matter, when you demand of me that I change my religion in order to please his majesty the tsar, but with us it is considered an extremely serious matter, and those who change their faith for temporal benefits are considered frivolous and apostate. Consider how, if we are faithless to our own God, can we be faithful to his majesty the tsar. We have no instructions from our father to dispute concerning political or religious matters. His majesty the tsar assured us that neither we nor our servants would be subjected to any constraint in matters of religion. We wish to conduct ourselves before the tsar as a son before a father, we wish to obey his will in all things that do not anger God, cause vexation to my father or violate our conscience, and wish for nothing better than the conclusion of the marriage contract, but we will never renounce our faith in order to achieve it. You command us to join with you, telling us that if we see in this a sin, you, O patriarch, and all the consecrated assembly will take this upon yourselves. To this we answer that each is responsible for his own sins. If you are convinced that on account of your humility and sanctity you can take upon yourselves the sins of others, then be so kind as to take upon yourselves the sins of Tsarevna Irina Mikhailovna and let her marry me."

VALDEMAR ATTEMPTS TO ESCAPE

All of April was taken up with admonitions. According to Danish accounts the boyars spoke to the prince. Perhaps he did not think that Tsarevna Irina was fair of countenance; it would be well if he were content with her beauty. He should not think that Tsarevna Irina was like other Muscovite women, who like to drink themselves into a stupor. She was a prudent and modest maiden who never in her life was drunk.

On May 7 the ambassadors definitively asked to be given leave, and named the day on which they would like to have a farewell audience with the tsar. They asked that the prince be allowed to accompany them. The sovereign replied that this request was improperly written, as though it were a command. This was not how ambassadors plenipotentiary should write to great sovereigns. As far as the prince was concerned, they the ambassadors brought him to the sovereign and entrusted him entirely to the sovereign's will. Therefore he would not be dismissed along with the ambassadors, but when the time was appropriate the ambassadors would be sent by themselves back to King Christian. "If by your obstinacy," concluded the reply, "you do anything dishonorable or harmful, you and your servants will be held responsible. The ambassadors will not set off without being given leave."

On May 9, at the third hour of the morning, fifteen of the prince's infantrymen left his lodging, approached a musketeer sergeant who was standing on guard, and asked for some musketeers to accompany them beyond the White Quarter and the Tver gates. The sergeant conveyed this request to the captain, who refused, whereupon the Danes attacked the musketeers with their swords, severely wounding many of them. At the same time about thirty Danes, both mounted and on foot, surprised the musketeers on guard at the Tver gates, which they tried to break down. The musketeers prevented them, so the Danes fired their pistols, attacked them with their swords and broke down the gates. When the sentries gave the alarm, other musketeers came and forced the Danes back from the gates. One of them was taken prisoner, but when the musketeers brought him to the Kremlin, just as they were passing the St. Nicholas of Gostun cathedral, some Danes rushed out of the prince's lodging and attacked the musketeers with swords, killing one of them and wounding six, and snatched the prisoner from them.

MARSELIS CONVERSES WITH VALDEMAR

On May 11 Peter Marselis came to see the prince and said "The night before last a serious incident occurred. It is a pity, since nothing good will come of it." "My followers should not be held in such confinement," replied the prince, "they are tired of living here without being allowed to go anywhere. I would be very glad if I and they broke a few necks." "You should have patience," urged Marselis, "and don't try anything untoward. If anyone tries to talk you into it, don't listen. What you did was harmful."

> *Prince.* That's all very well for you to talk! You live in your own home, neither is your heart aching like mine. They want to dismiss the ambassadors, but his majesty the tsar refuses to let me go.

As Marselis was leaving Valdemar's lodging the prince's cupbearer met him and took him aside into the garden. "Did you hear," he said, "the misfortune which occurred the night before last? The prince tried to escape from Moscow and was at the Tver gates. Only his valet and I knew about this; the ambassadors didn't. The prince took valuable pendants and as many gold coins as he thought he would need. They were stopped at the Tver gates, and then tried to turn back and try to get through some other gates, but the musketeers seized the prince and his valet. They tore the prince's sword from his hand and were beating him with their fists and holding the bridle of his horse when the prince drew his dagger, cut the bridle and escaped from the musketeers, for the horse he was riding is well trained and responds without a bridle. Arriving at the door the prince told him his plan had miscarried, his valet was seized and the musketeers would not release him.

Marselis, having heard the cupbearer's story, returned to the prince and told him he had acted foolishly. Had the prince managed to escape from Moscow he, Marselis, would have perished through the tsar's disfavor, should he be suspected of any prior knowledge of the escape. "I would be a great fool," replied the prince, "were I to have told you or anyone else about it, except those I was taking with me."

Marselis. What will his majesty the tsar think when he finds out that you perpetrated such an insolent deed?

Prince. I told his majesty the tsar that I would do this, and kill anyone who tried to restrain or stop me. I will continue to contrive ways to get out of Moscow. If I fail, that will be another story.

Marselis concluded from the prince's last words that he was thinking of doing something desperate, perhaps even taking poison. Hearing of such a plan Marselis could not fail to inform his majesty, in order to avert his displeasure.

On May 12 the prince declared to the boyar Sitsky that he had tried to get out through the Tver gates, and that he killed a musketeer. The tsar, hearing of this admission, sent word to the royal ambassadors that such a thing was not permitted even to common men. To hear of it was shameful, and even more shameful for the tsar to hear of it, and a dishonor to King Christian. The ambassadors replied that they should be permitted to leave together with the prince openly, in broad daylight and all together. If this incident occurred, it was not the ambassadors' fault but that of those who detained them. If the prince wished to go about alone at night, what business was it of theirs?

On May 13 the prince sent the tsar a fresh request to be allowed to leave, vowing that never would he change his religion, so therefore there was no point in his remaining. The tsar answered with a reproach, asking how could Valdemar recompense the love and favor he was shown with such a shameful deed, about which the ambassadors soon would have some explaining to do before the boyars.

The ambassadors were summoned and it was demanded that they, together with the prince, give a letter under their own signatures and seal and kiss the cross, saying that the matter of the prince's marriage was referred by both sides to the will of God, and that the tsar would be in perpetual and unshakable friendship, love and correspondence with the king, after which the prince and the ambassadors were free to return to Denmark. The definitive treaty would be on the same terms as the treaty concluded between Tsar Ivan and King Frederik.[21]

"If the principal matter," the ambassadors replied, "that of the prince's marriage, is no longer under discussion, we have no other business, for we cannot transact or conclude any matter without the king's instruction, even if we have to stay here in Moscow for ten years."

Thereafter several requests to be given leave were answered by the assertion that the ambassadors could not be dismissed unless there were an exchange of letters with King Christian, "and when the king writes, we the great sovereign, having perused his letters, will decide how to deal with you, as the occasion demands." The prince wrote that neighboring rulers, those of Poland and Sweden, were concerned about his distress, and would not regard his captivity with equanimity. "We the great sovereign," read the reply, "have accorded you great honors of state from the time of your arrival to the present, and it is unbefitting for you to write alleging that you are in captivity. We never promised to release you, because your father sent you to us to be entirely subject to our will. So how can you leave without fulfilling the task for which you came?"

May, June and half of July went by with vain requests to let the prince and the ambassadors leave, in vain exhortations for the prince to be baptized into the Orthodox faith, in fruitless religious disputes by the king's chaplain with Russian and Greek divines.

THE BASISTOV AFFAIR

On July 19 Prince Pronsky, governor of Viazma, dispatched to Moscow the priest Grigory from the village of Bolshoe Pokrovskoe. This priest declared that on July 15 his son arrived from over the border with two fugitives named Trop and Belous, who told him that they had been in Smolensk, and that the sovereign might wish to know that Andrei Basistov,[22] a native of Smolensk, came on behalf of the Danish prince, accompanied by Mikhail Ivanov, and brought letters. For the sake of friendship Basistov read these letters to Trop and Belous. They were addressed to the governor of Smolensk, asking whether Andrei Basistov could be trusted to guide the prince into Lithuanian territory by the back roads.

Trop and Belous further stated that in their presence the leading burghers of Smolensk were questioned. They said they could vouch for Basistov's story, and he could be trusted. The governor of Smolensk wrote to the Danish prince in Moscow that Basistov was trustworthy.

When this information reached Moscow from the governor of Viazma, Father Grigory was ordered to identify Andrei Basistov secretly. To this end, so that Basistov would not recognize him, the priest was to trim his beard and shave off his whiskers on either side. On July 31 Father Grigory seized Basistov and brought him to the Chancellery for Foreign Affairs. The sovereign immediately ordered the boyar Fedor Ivanovich Sheremetev and the conciliar secretary Lvov to interrogate Basistov, put him to the torture and bring him to a confrontation with Father Grigory, Trop and Belous, in order to get to the bottom of this criminal matter.

Basistov was interrogated and tortured in the provisions yard. He said he was a native of Wilno, saw service with the cossacks, and now lived in Smolensk, where he traded with the burghers. He came to Moscow out of poverty in order to sell some tobacco, not in order to abduct the prince. He did intend to bring out the prince's huntsman who promised him fifty rubles, but he was lying and did not pay the money. He heard not a word about the prince, and had no such designs, for he was accused falsely.

He was subjected to two harsh interrogations and was given five strokes with the lash, and then he confessed. He, together with Maxim Vlasov, a native of Smolensk, intended to abduct the prince from Moscow to Smolensk. Vlasov came to Moscow a long time ago, and was trading in tobacco. They conspired with the huntsman to abduct the prince. The huntsman promised him a hundred rubles, but he never saw the prince. He waited around for more than three weeks, but the huntsman called off the deal, saying it was impossible to get the prince out of Moscow.

Concerning the tobacco, Basistov said he brought to Moscow seven puds. He sold one pud to his friends, two more to his fellow natives of Smolensk, making altogether five rubles, which he buried in a field a verst or two out of Moscow. Two puds were stolen from him, while five were hidden in the forest by the Khodynka, where he dug a pit.[23]

Musketeers were dispatched immediately to arrest the Lithuanians with the tobacco, and they rounded up five men, Basistov's friend Maxim

Vlasov from Smolensk, and four natives of Dorogobuzh. They were hiding with the tobacco in threshing barns near Butyrki, in a hamlet belonging to Prince Repnin. Under torture Vlasov confessed he heard from Basistov about the plan to abduct the prince from Moscow, but he was not party to the conspiracy. Thereupon Basistov was interrogated again. "What orders did you have from Governor Madalinski of Smolensk, and what do the king and the lords of the council know about this?" "Madalinski ordered me," Basistov replied, "that I should render the whole Commonwealth a signal service and guide the prince into Lithuania, for on account of the prince Lithuanian couriers proceeding to Moscow no longer are permitted to travel through his domains. This way no expense will be incurred by the king's treasury; also the king and lords of the council do not need to know about this." Basistov then acknowledged that he was suborned not only by the prince's huntsman, but also one of his Danes, the master glazier Zacharias and his son-in-law Daniel.

VALDEMAR WRITES TO TSAR AND STEMPKOWSKI

Nothing very much happened until the end of November. On the twenty-ninth the Danish ambassadors had an audience with the tsar, to whom they presented documents newly received from the king. King Christian demanded that the tsar fulfill all his treaty obligations as concluded by Peter Marselis, otherwise he should dismiss honorably the prince and the ambassadors. On December 29 the tsar personally declared to the prince that he could not marry Tsarevna Irina without being re baptized, neither could he be allowed to leave for Denmark, because the king gave him to the tsar to be a son.

Valdemar replied in writing on January 9, 1645. "We petition that your majesty no longer detain us," he wrote. "We are the son of a sovereign king, and our people are all freemen, not slaves. Your majesty the tsar has no right to command that we and our followers be detained, though you can keep us here by force. If your majesty indeed has such an improper intention, we freely and frankly tell you that there will be no easy way out of this predicament, and so what honor will your majesty have before all the world? There are only a few of us here, so we cannot threaten you with force, but we merely wish to say that all nations will call you to account because in violation to the treaty and all justice you did to us what even Turks and Tatars, for fear of besmirching their good name, hesitate to do. We ask you to reflect that if you seek to detain us by force, we will strive to regain our freedom, even if it costs us our lives."

Having received such a letter, the tsar sent word to the Danish ambassadors, urging them to calm the prince and restrain him from his youthful rash intention and desire. "If he pursues his intention and some misfortune occurs, it will be his own fault, not that of the sovereign or his servants." "The prince," replied the ambassadors, "takes counsel in his own house with his own followers, not with us."

The Polish ambassador Stempkowski intervened in the affair. He urged the prince to fulfill the tsar's will, fearing that otherwise the tsar would ally with Sweden against Denmark and exile the prince to distant lands.

Valdemar sent a written reply to Stempkowski, stating "I can yield only on the following conditions. (1) My children may be baptized according to the Greek rite. (2) I will try to observe the fasts, insofar as I can without endangering my health. (3) I will comply with the sovereign's wishes in the matter of dress and all else which does not violate my conscience, treaty obligations and my religion. The great sovereign can threaten as much as he likes, but may thunder and lightning strike me, let him send me to the uttermost bounds of his tsardom, where woefully I will end my days, before I renounce my faith, even though he crucify and put me to death. Better I die an honorable death with unstained conscience than live with an uneasy conscience. I call upon God my Savior to witness.

"Even if things go badly for my father, even if the grand prince allies with the Swedes against him, this will not be my doing, for I think the Danish and Norwegian kingdoms can get along quite well without Russian help. These kingdoms existed before the Muscovite realm arose, and are still standing firmly. I am ready for any eventuality, let them do with me as they please, only let them make haste about it."

On June 25 Peter Marselis announced that the previous day Prince Valdemar had fallen ill of a heart ailment. His heart was aching and hurt, he was bringing straight up whatever he ate or drank, and if not treated quickly he would have a stroke or a heart attack and die. On the twenty-sixth, however, the prince's chamberlain Mina Alexeev said that on the twenty-fifth the prince ate in the garden. The marshal, cupbearer, courtiers and privy counselors were all joyful, eating and drinking as usual. After supper the prince walked in the garden for a long time, while the marshal summoned to his quarters the cupbearer, nobles and privy counselors and treated them to wine and brandy, Rhenish and all kinds of drink until two in the morning. They were all quite drunk, played on the cymbals while he, Mina, did not see the doctor visit the prince's lodging.[24]

NEWS OF PRETENDER IN TURKEY

While the tsar was occupied in Moscow with the tedious affair of the prince, sinister news of pretenders came from Poland and Turkey. In October 1644 a Greek archimandrite Amphilochios sent a letter from Constantinople in which he announced that in August two Turks came with a letter to the sultan, written in Russian. The call went out for a translator and Amphilochios was summoned, but when he took the letter from them and glanced at its contents, he took it to Bursa and immediately sent it on to Moscow.

The letter was written in Little Russian and read as follows. "Most merciful and nobly born tsar! You are to me a father and a mother, for I have no recourse to anyone else. When I came from Persia to Poland I ran into some of your men who robbed me of my treasury and took me prisoner. They did not take me to you, but sold me to the Jews. If you will have pity on me, you will be like a father and mother to me, a sinner and wretched captive, a Muscovite tsarevich. If by your mercy I come to rule the Muscovite land, I will share it equally with you." The signature read, "Prince Ivan Dmitrievich, tsarevich of the Muscovite land, his powerful hand." Yet even before that, news came from Poland concerning two pretenders.

PRINCE LVOV'S MISSION TO POLAND

In 1643 ambassadors plenipotentiary were sent to Poland, Prince Alexis Mikhailovich Lvov,[25] the conciliar secretary Grigory Pushkin and the crown secretary Volosheninov, to deal with old business such as the title and the boundary survey of the Putivl region. They were given two sets of instructions, one open, the other secret. In the first it was written, among other things, that if the lords of the council brought up the matter of three Lithuanian merchants, natives of Dorogobuzh, who came to trade in Moscow but were arrested, sent to Kazan, tortured and held long in prison, and who then had their goods confiscated while they themselves were expelled across the frontier, the ambassadors were to say "These merchants were arrested in the Kazan region, on the Volga river, while carrying contraband tobacco, fifteen puds of which they were taking to the Lower Towns. First they left Dorogobuzh and sneaked past

Viazma, then skirted Moscow, taking ship upon the Oka and from there along the Volga, traveling by the back roads pretending to be traders from Moscow or peasants belonging to Prince Cherkassky or some other boyar. They sold tobacco in the villages and hamlets to all manner of people, for which they deserved to be executed.

"The tsar, out of respect for the king, did not have them put to death, but exacted only a trifling penalty, and sent them back to Dorogobuzh, neither were any of their possessions taken away from them. Subsequently there secretly appeared in the Nizhny Novgorod region and in Balakhna six Poles, bringing with them six wagons loaded with tobacco, but they were seized with their unsold tobacco, amounting to more than six puds. They themselves were sent on to Moscow, but on the way they fell on their escorts and beat them almost to death, and disappeared without a trace."

Concerning the Cherkass they were to say as they did before that in the treaty nothing was written about the extradition of refugees. The Cherkass had spent some time on his majesty the tsar's side of the Dnieper, done a lot of damage, and then left for the king's side.

TWO PRETENDERS IN POLAND

In the secret instructions they were told to say to the lords "His majesty the tsar has reliable information that in January 1639 a certain man came from the Cherkass into Poland, in the vicinity of Sambor. He was a brigand, thirty years or slightly more, who appeared before a certain priest and moved into his home, as a weekly wage laborer. The priest noticed on his back a brand of the Russian coat of arms, so he sent him on to the archimandrite of the monastery, who in turn referred him to the crown treasurer Danilowicz.[26] The treasurer examined the brand and interrogated the brigand, who declared he was Semeon Vasilievich Shuisky, son of Tsar Vasily Ivanovich, and the proof that he was the tsar's son was in the brand on his back. He was taken captive by the Cherkass while Tsar Vasily was being transported from Moscow into Lithuania, and since then he lived with the Cherkass.

"The treasurer kept him in his quarters and spoke concerning him and his distinguishing features to the nobility and all ranks. The nobility and all the Commonwealth ordered the treasurer to keep a close watch on him, to give him food and clothing and charge it to the treasury. The treasurer sent the brigand to a monastery to learn how to read, write and speak Russian, and this brigand is still in Poland.

"Also the same sovereign King Wladyslaw has maintained at Brest Litovsk, in a Jesuit convent, a thirty-year-old brigand who also has a brand on his back, between the shoulders, and claims to be the Renegade Monk's son."[27] If the lords said that the brigand who called himself Shuisky had fled to Wallachia, and the hospodar had sent his head to Moscow, the ambassadors were to reply "This is untrue, because his majesty the tsar knows very well that the brigand is with you in Poland. You, my lords, should search him out and either hand him over to the ambassadors or have him executed."

The matters concerning the title and border adjustments were settled. It was agreed in borderland correspondence to write the names of the rulers simply using the titles without mentioning the names of towns. Two disputed towns, Galich and Sarsky, were ceded to Poland, in exchange for which the Poles ceded Trubchevsk with all its region and territory, the village of Kurets in the Novgorod Seversk district, and other villages and hamlets on the left bank of the Kleven river, which flowed into the Putivl region. Also ceded to Moscow were the small towns of Nedrigailovskoe, Gorodetskoe, Kamennoe, Akhtyrskoe and Olshanskoe. The village of Oleshkovichi and its hamlets were ascribed to the Komaritsk district.

Fulfillment of the secret instructions, on the other hand, ran into insuperable complications. The lords declared that neither they nor the king knew of any pretenders, but that the king would order an investigation. Some time later the results of the investigation were announced. "It is true that a man came to the crown treasurer Danilowicz, claiming his name was Semeon Vasilievich Shuisky, but the treasurer, aware that the brigand's claim to be a sovereign's son was false, ordered him to be beaten with rods and sent away. Where this brigand subsequently hid, we have not the slightest idea.

"Concerning the other brigand, Lord Osinski told us that he does have such a man, working as one of his scribes. This man in jest was called tsarevich of Moscow, but he, hearing such words about himself, wished to become a monk. He never himself claimed to be a tsarevich, neither did his majesty the king or lords of the council ever take this idler for a tsarevich, otherwise we would not have allowed him to live with Osinski and serve him as a scribe."

"We are greatly surprised," replied the ambassadors, "that you lords of the council, mindless of the fear of God and shame before men, and ignoring the treaty concluded by the ambassadors, are concealing the brigand. We have reliable information concerning a Sejm resolution authorizing disbursement from the treasury for subsistence and an allowance for this brigand. Moreover on our way here we stopped in Brest Litovsk, where our servants saw him. He has been calling himself a sovereign's son for some time, but also in his letters he styles himself tsarevich of Moscow; a number of letters written by him are in our possession." The lords replied that the pretender had been summoned and would appear before the ambassadors.

At this time the king traveled from Cracow to Warsaw. The ambassadors followed him, and once again raised before the lords of the council the matter of the brigands, adding that some of the king's courtiers approached the ambassadors saying "If you ambassadors do not reach an agreement with the lords of the council on matters of state, we have a son of Dmitry ready to wage war at the head of the Cherkass." The crown chancellor Osolinski came to the ambassadors and said "In compliance with your requests, the lords of the council have petitioned the king to surrender to you the ruffian who calls himself a tsarevich. The king told us that for the sake of brotherly love and friendship with the Muscovite sovereign, he would not protect such a man, should such not be perceived as conducive to the prestige of the great sovereign. But this man is innocent of any evil, he is not a tsarevich, but a native of Podliashie, the son of a simple father, though he was raised by a Pole named Belinski, who called him a tsarevich, a son of Dmitry, allegedly born of Marina Mniszech.[28] This Belinski wanted to curry favor, and presented his protégé to King Sigismund, who ordered him sent to Alexander Gasiewski,[29] who in turn taught him to read and write and provided him with everything he needed to substantiate his claim to the Muscovite tsardom, for at that time there was war between the two realms. When a definitive peace was concluded this man received no more support, and no longer claimed to be a tsarevich. He wandered without any refuge, served among the gentry, where he would have been quite contented, since he no longer aspired to the Muscovite tsardom. He is a Pole, not a Russian, and wishes to become a Catholic priest in the near future. To surrender him to you would serve no purpose. The king and the lords of the council will give you whatever written guarantee you wish, but our law does not permit us to hand over an innocent man. He has been brought to Warsaw, and the king has ordered that he be made available to you for interrogation."

"We are utterly amazed," the ambassadors replied, "that such an unbefitting and evil deed was initiated on the part of your sovereign. If the king and lords of the council will not surrender this brigand, we cannot do any further business with you."

The pretender under interrogation admitted he was not, neither did he call himself, a tsarevich, but his name was Ivan Dmitrievich Luba.[30] His father Dmitry Luba was a nobleman in Podliashie, who together with his small son came to Moscow with the army during the Time of Troubles and was killed there. Belinski took the orphan and brought him back to Poland, making him out to be the son of False Dmitry and Marina. Allegedly the mother entrusted the child to him for safekeeping. When the child grew up Belinski, on the advice of other nobles, told all this to the king and the lords of the council assembled in the Sejm. Sigismund and the lords entrusted the youth to Leo Sapieha, with a grant of six thousand zlotys for his upkeep, and Sapieha in turn sent him to Abbot Afanasy of the St. Simeon monastery in Brest Litovsk, there to learn Russian, Polish and Latin. The youth spent seven years with the abbot. Then, when a truce was concluded with Moscow, the grant to Luba was reduced to a hundred zlotys a year, and when definitive peace was concluded he was forgotten completely. The wretched Luba turned to Belinski, asking whose son he really was, and why he was being called tsarevich of Moscow. Belinski replied that he was the son of the nobleman Luba, but was called tsarevich of Moscow *for numerous reasons.* When in Moscow they were about to hang Marina's son Belinski wanted to hand him over to be hanged in place of Marina's son, whom he planned to abduct; but Marina's son was hanged the next day, so he could not steal him away; therefore Luba was called tsarevich in his stead.

In response to this declaration the ambassadors said to the lords "The brigand states that he does not call himself tsarevich, but he is lying, trying to hide his crimes. We have letters written in his own hand in which he styles himself tsarevich." The ambassadors showed the lords a letter given to them in Cracow by the Brest Litovsk abbot Afanasy, Luba's former guardian. Chancellor Osolinski showed the letter to Luba, who acknowledged that it was in his hand. The chancellor, perusing the letter said "The lad wrote the letter in his own hand, but signed it 'Ivan Faustin Petrovich.' He didn't style himself tsarevich." "In this screed," replied the ambassadors, "it says it was written at dinner time at the tsarevich's house and in the tsarevich's apartments. Lords of the council, your bad faith and evil intentions are plain. You conceal what actually is written. We can see your intentions in all matters, and now your dishonesty is patent. This brigand and pauper could scarcely have written and styled himself by the lofty name of tsarevich except at the instigation of the king, the lords of the council and the whole Commonwealth."

"If he was writing and calling himself tsarevich of Moscow," argued the lords of the council, "he would not have used the Latin form of his name. Since it was written in the tsarevich's apartment or at the dinner table, it was probably a game in which the counters and pieces are called 'emperors' or 'kings.'"

> *Ambassadors.* Are you not ashamed to talk like this, to conceal and protect such a brigand?
>
> *Lords.* We do not know of any crime he has committed. We do not intend any harm against the Muscovite realm, but we cannot hand him over to you because he is a member of the Polish nobility.

The ambassadors repeated their demand. The lords said they would confirm in the Sejm and have a resolution printed that there would not be any attempt to subvert the Muscovite realm, whether by Luba or anybody else. "Although there may be no support for this brigand in either Poland or Lithuania," the ambassadors replied, "how can we be sure he will not go somewhere else and recruit lawless renegade Cherkass? Might he not go to some other land and stir up trouble?" "We will give confirmation in our own hand and under our own seal," the lords replied, "that none of this will happen."

> *Ambassadors.* We cannot believe this, because even now this criminal design stands revealed. When we were in Cracow some of the king's courtiers came and told us that if we did not conclude an agreement with you, the son of Dmitry was ready to attack the Muscovite realm at the head of his Cherkass. There the criminal conspiracy and intention was revealed.
>
> *Lords.* The king has ordered that the words uttered by these courtiers be investigated and punished.

At the next interview the lords said "You told us that Luba has a brand on his back, between the shoulders. If he has such a sign, he must be the son of a tsar. In that case we will not protect him, but hand him over to you.

Ambassadors. We don't know whether he has a brand or not. We merely heard about it from many people.

Lords. He does not have a brand on his back, neither did he ever have any.

Ambassadors. Whether he has the brand or not, he still claims to be the tsarevich, and therefore you should execute him.

Lords. God is witness that this nobleman never called himself tsarevich of Moscow. May God destroy us body and soul if we are not speaking the truth.

Ambassadors. We have our doubts. Either you should have this brigand executed, or sent to our sovereign accompanied by one of your king's nobles.

Finally it was resolved to send a courier to Moscow with a clarification. At the same time the lords urged the ambassadors to write to the sovereign exculpating Luba, who soon would be ordained priest and would be under observation. "We cannot do that," the ambassadors replied. "Even though he may be in the clerical estate he can still cause trouble if you don't surrender him. Grishka Otrepiev[31] also was tonsured. Nevertheless his majesty the tsar has no fear of brigands; nobody in the Muscovite realm would believe him. We merely wish to point out that holy orders are no cure for brigandage, only death."

"The king," the lords replied, "has ordered this Luba to be sent under guard to the strong fortress of Marienburg,[32] to be kept in the tower there for three or four years, or for however long his majesty the tsar deems necessary. When he has served his time and is ordained priest, no longer will he be able to plan any mischief, and for this we will give an undertaking over our own signatures and seals."

After these conversations there arrived the high referendary of the grand principality of Lithuania with a declaration that the king would send Luba to Moscow with his high ambassadors, provided that sovereign not execute him, but send him back with the same ambassadors. Prince Lvov demanded of the lords confirmation under their signatures and seals that the king immediately send the brigand with his ambassadors to the tsar, otherwise the recently concluded treaty and boundary agreements would be void. This confirmation was given, and the ambassadors set off for Moscow, where their conduct was viewed with satisfaction. Prince Lvov was awarded the rank of majordomo with all the perquisites, the conciliar secretary Pushkin was promoted to lord-in-waiting, and the crown secretary Volosheninov was advanced to the rank of conciliar secretary.

In November 1644 the promised high ambassador and his companions came from the king. He was Gawrila Stempkowski, castellan of Braclaw. Stempkowski was given quarters in the house belonging to Prince Peter and Ivan Pozharsky. Here in two pavilions it was ordered to line the walls and benches with silken cloth. The same was done in the log cabin adjoining the pavilions, and the table was covered with a fine cloth.

Stempkowski brought Luba. In his letter the king asked the tsar to send the wretched noble back with Stempkowski, but when negotiations opened the boyars demanded that the ambassador hand the brigand over to his majesty, who would deal with him as he saw fit. The ambassador replied that he could not hand over someone of gentry birth, because the king forbade it. The boyars repeated this answer to the tsar, who sent word to Stempkowski that unless Luba were surrendered neither he nor his boyars would do any business with the ambassador, nor would they listen to anything he had to say.

The ambassador did not surrender him, but demanded that he be allowed to send a courier for the Sejm's instructions. The sovereign agreed, and sent his own courier to the king with a letter stating that the Poles had yet to surrender Trubchevsk and the other places ceded, and that the ambassador Stempkowski refused to surrender Luba, lest we execute this brigand. Unless he is handed over he cannot be either executed or pardoned. The king should order the brigand surrendered to be dealt with according to the tsar's request, at his sovereign discretion.

The king replied he would immediately send his court officials to oversee the transfer of Trubchevsk and other places. "Concerning the noble Yan Faustich Luba, we declare that he is an innocent man, who neither has stirred up trouble nor would ever do so, since he wishes to enter the spiritual monastic state. He was not sent along with our ambassador in order to be handed over, but merely that he might demonstrate his innocence before your majesty the tsar. To you, our brother, it is known that in our great realms it is not the custom to hand over men of noble birth, though if found guilty he would be executed immediately. Luba, however, has not been convicted of anything, so you should let him leave in the custody of our ambassador, and not detain him." The courier brought news that the abbot who first exposed the brigand was himself confined in irons at Warsaw, pending the outcome of the Luba affair.

The matter dragged on without resolution for half a year. The bailiff reproached Stempkowksi for allowing the Lithuanian merchants who accompanied him to go around trading in wine and tobacco, wandering the streets late in the evening or at night completely drunk, insulting all manner of the tsar's subjects, slashing them with their sabers and stabbing them with their swords. In answer the ambassador requested that the merchants be allowed to trade in wine and tobacco because in the treaty it was written that they should be permitted to trade in all commodities. "It is disgraceful," the bailiff responded, "to call such wares commodities and to write them in the terms of the truce. The Lithuanian merchants themselves know that trading in such goods to all and sundry incurs a stiff penalty, such as the slitting of nostrils, merciless flogging with the knout and imprisonment."

"His majesty the tsar's envoys," complained the ambassador, "Prince Lvov and his companions, were well treated when they were with us. Senators honored them, invited them to banquets and gave them gifts. They lived in Poland as among brothers, who entertained them in the open air and in their homes. Yet here I, a high ambassador, encounter nothing but shame and insults. I live in confinement, not allowed to go anywhere, and my servants are not even allowed to call upon the Danish prince." The bailiffs replied that his majesty the tsar was sick, on account of which he barely emerged from his bedchamber, but when God granted his majesty relief a conciliar secretary would report to him on all matters.

FATAL ILLNESS OF TSAR MICHAEL

This relief was not forthcoming. Failure to provide for his daughter's future inflicted a heavy blow on Tsar Michael's weak constitution which even previously, in 1639,[33] had been undermined by family tragedy. In the course of three months he lost two sons, Tsareviches Ivan and Vasily Mikhailovich.

In April 1645 his doctors Vendelin Sibelista, Johan Beloy and Artman Graman analyzed his urine and found that his stomach, liver and spleen, because of an accumulation of mucous, had lost their natural warmth, and therefore gradually the blood was diluted and the patient's temperature dropped, from which there arose scurvy and other types of dropsy. They prescribed a cure of Rhenish wine laced with various herbs and roots to act as a mild purgative. They also ordered moderation in food and drink. They forbade him to take supper or consume any hot or sour beverages. Medicine did not help. On May 14 another purgative was ordered. On May 26 the doctors again examined his urine, which was colorless, because the stomach, liver and spleen ceased to function from much sitting, cold drinks and melancholy caused by personal grief. They gave him yet another purgative, after which they administered a compound of sugar and applied a balm to his abdomen. On June 5 they administered a potion for headache.

On June 12, his nameday, the feast of St. Michael Malein,[34] the tsar attended matins, but in church he fainted and immediately was carried to his apartments. Towards the evening the pain intensified. He began to groan, complaining that his insides were being torn apart. He commanded that the tsaritsa be summoned, also his son, the sixteen-year-old Alexis Mikhailovich, along with his tutor Boris Ivanovich Morozov,[35] and the patriarch. He said farewell to his wife, blessed his son with the tsardom, and then said to Morozov "To you, my boyar, I entrust my son and implore you, that even as you have served us and labored joyfully, leaving home, possessions and tranquillity, being solicitous of his health and instruction in the fear of God and all wisdom, living continuously in our house for thirteen years in order to take care of him, so also serve him now."

At two in the morning, sensing the approach of death, Michael confessed, partook of the sacred mysteries and then, just after the third hour struck, he died. Apart from his son, he was survived by three daughters, Irina, Anna and Tatiana.[36]

MICHAEL'S REIGN OBSERVED, 1613-1645

SIGNIFICANCE OF A NEW TSAR

The Time of Troubles ended with the election of a tsar, and young Michael's throne was supported because the people of the Muscovite realm *did penance,* because of the efforts of the majority, of the people of the land, to re-establish order violated by the efforts of a minority, to go back to the old ways, as things were under previous rulers. Naturally, against the efforts of the majority, those of a feeble minority in another direction were bound to fail.

There is a story that the boyars exacted from the new tsar the same kind of oath that Shuisky gave, "not to execute anyone without a fair trial in conjunction with his boyars, neither to punish relatives along with the offender."[1] Another version asserts that Michael undertook not to punish any of the magnates by death, only banishment. Shein's fate contradicts the second version, the fate of his relatives the first.[2]

If indeed such an oath was exacted evidently it was in force only at the beginning of the reign. In 1625 the tsar wrote to his governors "According to our decree a new seal has been made, larger than the old one, since on the previous seal there was not room for the tsar's full title, but now there has been added the inscription 'autocrat.'[3] Also on the old seal there were words between the eagle's heads, but now those words are not there, while over the eagle's heads there is a crown."

Concerning the relationship of the boyars to the tsar and towards the rest of the Muscovite population at the beginning of Michael's reign, the information concerning the flight and capture of the infamous Fedor Andronov[4] is of interest. On March 14, 1613 Prince Fedor Ivanovich Volkonsky, in whose house Andronov was being held, informed the boyars that on the night of the thirteenth the prisoner escaped. The boyars immediately gave orders for his arrest, and Andronov was captured by peasants and Cossacks on the Yauza near Kalinin Gulley, seven versts from Moscow. Reporting on this incident to the tsar, the boyars wrote "We the nobles, commoners, cossacks and all manner of people plead that Andronov be executed because we wrote concerning his flight to all the

MICHEL PHEDORWITZ GRAND DVC
de Moscouie de l'an 1612 il est de la religion des grecs schismatiques
Moncornet ex. *et grand Capitaine:*

Tsar Michael Fedorovich (1642)
Herzog August Bibliothek, Wolfenbüttel.
By kind permission.

towns, and later concerning this traitor we wrote letters to all the towns with news of his capture. Therefore all the towns are informed, and there is no doubt about his capture. On behalf of all the people, concerning this traitor we declare that the sovereign will mete out to him his just deserts, in accordance with the sentence passed by men of all ranks and freemen."

The Muscovite trader Grigory Fonarik also was seized, having been with Andronov while he was at large, when he went about the towns to collect money on his behalf. Grigory declared that Andronov ordered this money to be brought to him in order that he might be tonsured.[5] Through this same Grigory, Andronov urged Prince Volkonsky to persuade the boyars to let him take religious vows in the Solovetsk monastery. Prince Volkonsky replied that this was not his decision, but was up to God, the tsar and the boyars, for when he, Fedka Andronov, was despoiling Moscow he had no desire at that time to become a monk.

Thereafter we do not find, whether in any forms or expressions, any change in the concept of the great sovereign's importance. Thus we see that, as before, ambassadors contrasted the significance of the sovereign in the Muscovite realm to that of the king in Poland. Assemblies were called very frequently by Tsar Michael, but this was inevitable given the state of the country at that time. The resources of the state were exhausted during the Time of Troubles. The realm was cleansed of enemies by the extraordinary efforts of the people, but this cleansing was not complete, for neither domestic nor foreign enemies gave up their purposes. These efforts therefore had to be prolonged. The tsar explicitly demanded this as a fulfillment of the promise of support to the throne, to cooperate with the newly elected tsar in the cleansing and pacification of the realm. Thus when he was elected Michael refused to come to Moscow until the assembly fulfilled its promise to put an end to brigandage along the roads and in the towns.[6] Yet in these frequent assemblies we do not find any change in the relations between the land and the ruler. The powerful majority, it is true, regarded the significance of the tsar as previously, while the weak minority was obliged to conform to this view.

THE ARISTOCRACY

The minority was in fact weak. Of the hereditary aristocracy, the upper stratum was gone. There were merely ranks: boyar, lord-in-waiting, treasurer, conciliar secretary, table attendant, crown agent, noble and junior boyar. In the absence of a class interest family interests alone predominated, which in conjunction with the principle of ranking gave rise to precedence disputes.[7]

The complete attention of the rank holder was concentrated on not disparaging his family with regard to placing in the rank order. Understandably the tendency to support only the dignity of the family did not leave room for any class interests, for the precedence system presupposed continuous enmity, continued family feuds among rank holders. Here was the bond, such were the common interests between men who, when first appointed to attend the tsar's throne or to serve on the frontier disputed among themselves, saying that one did not wish to be lower than the other, for was not some relative of his at one time higher than some relative of his rival?

We have seen that Prince Ivan Mikhailovich Vorotynsky,[8] ordered to recite the litany of the Polish king Sigismund's crimes, was obliged to state that he appointed unworthy men to important positions in the Muscovite realm, those who were low born, and in that category he mentioned two princes. Thus in the eyes of a prince who held rank, a prince without rank was base born.

Because of precedence, at the top of the service ladder we encounter the same old surnames. "We were in disgrace under previous sovereigns," the same Vorotynsky said to the Polish commissioners, "but they did not take the government away from us." In fact Ivan the Terrible, forever suspicious, ceaselessly *disgraced* the members of his aristocracy, surrounding himself with his crown servitors,[9] but he did not deprive the boyars of the administration of the regular territories. The boyars surviving Ivan the Terrible of course were not like those who survived the disfavor of Ivan III or his son Vasily. The latter had fresh memories of the situation of princes and the retinue.[10] They remembered that even Ivan III did not treat them as harshly as his son Vasily, whose behavior for that reason appeared to them something new, even fortuitous. Ivan the Terrible's behavior removed the last hopes, dashed all pretensions, all opposition. Those who emerged from his severe trial were a different set of boyars, with a different spirit, but they still had seniority on their side. Despite disfavor, the government was not taken away from them.

It is understandable the important significance attached to names permanently associated with governmental affairs. *They ran the council,* as they themselves expressed it. In the absence of education such practice ruled everything; knowledge of customs, traditions. Given the exclusive dominance of custom and tradition such lore was the supreme governmental wisdom, and men who themselves, and whose fathers and grandfathers *ran the council,* seemed like pillars of state to the lowly and uninitiated, especially those who distinguished themselves by their wit and industry. We have seen a man of relatively humble rank at the time, the table attendant Prince Dmitry Mikhailovich Pozharsky,[11] saying of the boyar Prince Vasily Vasilievich Golitsyn[12] "If such a great pillar as Prince Vasily Vasilievich, who could by his strength support the whole earth, is willing to undertake this great task, I will not stand in his way." Why did Prince Golitsyn appear so lofty to the famous commander of the liberation forces? Golitsyn himself provides the explanation. "Nobody ever expelled us from the council. We have been in every boyar council."

Golitsyn never returned from Polish captivity, and his brother Andrei perished, defending the honor of the council defiled by the presence of Fedka Andronov and his cronies.[13] Both left the scene as a result of the Time of Troubles, which had a significant role in the fate of the ancient Muscovite aristocracy. Such a whirlwind could not pass over without uprooting many things. Especially great was the uprooting when after the death of the first False Dmitry there began the strife between two tsars. Thus was between Shuisky and the tsar of the cossack encampments, the Tushino tsar,[14] the second pretender who, in order to have a court, a boyar council and an army, turned to those who could never have been at court, in the council or in the army of the Muscovite tsar, or who at least could not have received exalted rank there. The Tushino pretender not only incited the lowest strata of the population against the highest, promising them their places, but provoked a powerful ferment also in every sphere. Everyone who wanted advancement at all cost, to obtain higher rank than under normal circumstances they could hope to attain, rushed to Tushino, beginning with princes who wanted accelerated promotion from table attendant or lord-in-waiting to boyar, commoners who wanted to become crown or conciliar secretaries, and all these wishes were granted.

After the battle of Klushino, in which all of Shuisky's resources were wiped out,[15] the boyars, in order not to be subject to a slave tsar, the second False Dmitry, proclaimed the Polish prince as tsar. Even prior to this, those who earlier deserted to Tushino now went running to the Polish king, prepared at any price to hold on to their Tushino ranks, and even swore allegiance to the king rather than the prince, promising to promote Sigismund's candidature in Moscow. Therefore the boyars who were prepared to do anything to dissociate themselves from hated Tushino saw to their horror the Tushinites forcing their way to join them in the council under Gasiewski's protection. Such men as the petty trader Fedka Andronov sat alongside Mstislavsky and Vorotynsky. This in their own words was death for the boyars, but they could do nothing since they were prisoners of the Poles. Whoever raised his voice was arrested, like Andrei Golitsyn and Vorotynsky. Meanwhile the land, being deceived by the king, rose up in the name of Orthodoxy. In the absence of their usual pillars the land had to turn to comparatively insignificant men. The leaders of the uprising were such as Liapunov,[16] one of the first to take advantage of the Troubles for personal advancement, who was hostile to the boyars and to those of aristocratic birth[17] in general. Alongside Liapunov were the Tushino boyars, Prince Trubetskoy[18] and the cossack Zarutsky.[19] "How can such men as Trubetskoy and Zarutsky," wrote the boyars in Moscow to the towns, "govern the realm? They cannot even conduct their own affairs." The Russian people concurred with the boyars in this sentiment but could not agree to remain loyal to Wladyslaw, which meant waiting for the king himself to come to Moscow with his Jesuits. They therefore raised the Second Militia Force, the leader of which was a member of a decayed princely family, a man of lowly rank, the table attendant Pozharsky, and alongside him was the butcher Minin.[20]

The Militia Force achieved its aim. The majority, exhausted by the Troubles, loudly demanded that everything be as before. Antiquity was in fact restored, but not fully, for in a historical nation no event passes without consequence, without affecting one or other part of the social organism. Among the leading families there were gaps. The Romanovs came to the throne, the Godunovs were banished, the Shuiskys became extinct, followed by the Mstislavskys and Vorotynskys, while the most important and energetic Golitsyns perished. Given the hierarchical nature of society at that time, given the restricted number of families standing at the top and preserving ancient traditions, the disappearance of the most important of these had a decisive impact.

Thus the Time of Troubles brought to a conclusion a process rooted in the primeval governmental functions at the very dawn of history, and revealed itself in the mid-fifteenth century when the Muscovite state evolved. At that time the princely and aristocratic clans surrounding the throne of the gatherer of the land, the sovereign of All Russia, did not bring with them the means to support their independence. These were not rich hereditary possessors of whole regions and towns, able to provide a livelihood for numerous retainers by giving them parcels of land, keeping them by these grants in dependence upon themselves. Former rulers of ancient principalities merely brought with them their princely names.

Their patrimonies merely consisted of their own princely private domains, subdivided more and more by the need to endow family members and by the lack of primogeniture, as well as the custom of giving lands to monasteries for the commemoration of souls.

Only the grand prince, sovereign of All Russia, had at his disposal a huge quantity of land, by the distribution of which as service tenures he could create a numerous army completely dependent upon him. The expansion and support of this army, the provision of its needs so that it always could stand on the alert, became the primary interest of the state, and we have observed the effect this interest had upon the agrarian population at the end of the sixteenth century. For servicemen, for this warrior mass, for this majority, service tenures were the exclusive interest, which the state hastened to satisfy.

Those occupying the upper ranks held different interests, and after a long and hard struggle these interests appeared to have been satisfied when Shuisky gave his famous rescript. Then the Troubles intervened. The boyars were confined to Moscow while servicemen, gentry and junior boyars, acting under leaders from their own ranks, liberated the country and expelled the cossacks. Once again they were in the forefront with their exclusive interest in service tenures, hostile to those having greater resources, and thus an unfair advantage in securing dues and labor services. This interest constantly clashed with that of the mighty, rich and highborn. Guided by this hostility, the service gentry naturally lacked sympathy for the upper class, and could not support its ambitions.

Alongside the service gentry in liberating the country stood the townsmen, who had their own interests. Shattered during the Troubles, their businesses ruined, oppressed by the exaction of fifths so vital to the eventual reconstruction of the realm, they constantly were in conflict with governors and elected magistrates, seeking protection in the authority of the tsar, who did not let any complaint go unheard. Therefore the townsmen entertained no sympathy for the aspirations of the class from which their governors were drawn. We need but read the account, ascribed to a townsman of Pskov, concerning the Time of Troubles and the reign of Michael Fedorovich, to appreciate the hostility of townsmen to the attempt of the boyars to obtain the rescript guaranteeing boyar interests.

Finally it must be noted that Tsar Michael's personality most of all was conducive to the strengthening of his authority. His weakness, good nature and purity of life produced an impression upon the people which was very favorable for the supreme authority. Such an impression induced the people to view its actions in the most favorable light. The tsar was known to be good natured, which excluded the thought that anything evil could originate with him; therefore whoever disliked this or that measure blamed it upon intermediaries between the supreme power and the people. The same Pskov narrator, who of course cannot be suspected of any official bias, particularly reflects this favorable popular view of Tsar Michael.

Prince Fedor Ivanovich Mstislavsky[21] during the first decade of Michael's reign was the ranking member of the boyar council, the nominal spokesman for the boyar class. As before, decrees were written "The boyars, Prince Mstislavsky and his colleagues...." He died in 1622. Not capable even earlier of playing a decisive leading role, naturally Mstislavsky was not highly regarded in Michael's reign. Prince Vorotynsky's energy went no further than protest against the disparagement of the Mstislavsky and Vorotynsky families. He died in 1627. Both council and court during the first years of Michael's reign were in a sorry condition, dogged by the disorder that usually follows from such a mighty tempest. The remnants of antiquity were weak, impotent, deprived of their main supports, which were overthrown by the whirlwind. Beside them were those brought in by the hurricane, a new class, not yet firmly established, having yet to assume its place. In this uncertain state of affairs, and in the absence of a strong hand to restore everything to order and put everything back in its place, it was all the easier for someone energetic, adroit, daring and unscrupulous to dominate the will of others and obtain a prominent place. Such were the Saltykovs at the start of Michael's reign, having family connections with the tsar's mother.[22] Filaret Nikitich overthrew them and during his rule they were in "irrevocable" exile, but after his death they immediately were restored to their former ranks, while in 1641 Mikhail Mikhailovich was promoted to boyar.

There is evidence that during the period of dual power Prince Boris Alexandrovich Repnin[23] in particular became more powerful. This influence gave rise to discontent among the other boyars, to whom the tsaritsa turned after the death of Filaret Nikitich. The boyars succeeded in getting Repnin banished from Moscow, appointed governor of Astrakhan under the pretext of calming disorders among the Nogay. While he was away the boyars succeeded in denigrating him before the tsar.

Concerning Boris Repnin, we only know that he was promoted from lord-in-waiting to boyar in January 1640. In May 1641 he was sent to Tver to search for gold ore, and in April 1643, as we have mentioned, was sent as far away as Astrakhan when news came of treason among the Nogay

Tatars. We also saw that during Godunov's reign Prince Boris's father Alexander Repnin was related to and a great friend of Fedor Romanov and Prince Ivan Sitsky. Therefore it is not surprising that Prince Boris, who was more energetic and able than his elder brother Peter, became quite powerful during the rule of Filaret Nikitich.

PRECEDENCE

The clan interest in the ranking principle as before was in the forefront, and therefore to understand contemporary relations among the aristocracy we must turn our attention to litigation over precedence.

In 1613, on the Feast of the Nativity of the Virgin [September 8], Prince F.I. Mstislavsky, Ivan Nikitich Romanov[24] and Prince Boris Mikhailovich Lykov[25] were invited to the tsar's table. The tsar's uncle without any dispute yielded place to Mstislavsky, but Lykov refused to concede Romanov the second place, petitioning that he not be placed lower than Ivan Nikitich. The tsar repeatedly begged and implored Prince Boris to come to table, that he could be below Ivan Nikitich. For this occasion Lykov yielded to the tsar's appeals, but later he regretted this concession. In April 1614, on Palm Sunday, once again Mstislavsky, Ivan Nikitich and Prince Lykov were invited to the tsar's table, and once again Lykov petitioned against Romanov. The sovereign reminded him that the previous year he had sat below Ivan Nikitich. Lykov replied that in no way could he be inferior to Romanov—better the tsar order his execution. Nevertheless, if the tsar ordered him to take the lower place on account of Ivan Nikitich being his uncle, he would comply.

The tsar disagreed, saying there were many other reasons besides Ivan Nikitich's kinship with the tsar why Lykov should occupy the lower place. Therefore he should stop complaining and sit below Ivan Nikitich. Lykov would not obey, refused to sit at table and went home. Twice he was sent for in vain, the emissaries being given the reply "I am ready to go to my death, but I will not sit below Ivan Nikitich." The tsar then ordered him to make his submission to Romanov.

On one occasion an embassy arrived from Persia. An escort was appointed to present the ambassadors to the tsar. The envoys started arguing over precedence, as a result of which one fled from the palace and the other pleaded sickness. The tsar was kept waiting, for there was no escort! Finally Prince Vasily Romodanovsky was appointed, and to be his associate Ivan Chepchugov,[26] he who pleaded sickness, was brought to the palace. Chepchugov petitioned the tsar that he could not serve alongside

Romodanovsky. Then Prince Dmitry Mikhailovich Pozharsky intervened in the affair on account of his kinship with Romodanovsky. In his submission he stated that Chepchugov was dishonoring the entire family since he was the son of a low-born[27] father, and his grandfather was a Tatar captain. Moreover he happened to be related to Shchelkalov,[28] though Shchelkalov would not acknowledge him. The tsar ordered that Chepchugov be beaten with rods and make his submission to Prince Romodanovsky.

Pozharsky easily could clinch the case against Chepchugov, the son of a low-born father, but his own case against the Saltykovs had a different ending. The sovereign promoted to boyar our old friend Boris Mikhailovich Saltykov,[29] and ordered Prince D.M. Pozharsky to rise and present the new boyar. Pozharsky petitioned that he could not acknowledge him as boyar, nor could he be in an inferior position to him. The case opened in the sovereign's presence. It transpired that Pozharsky's relative Prince Romodanovsky had served alongside the infamous Mikhail Glebovich Saltykov,[30] but within the family Mikhail Glebovich ranked lower than Boris Mikhailovich Saltykov. It also emerged that the Pushkins were equal to Pozharsky, but at the same time somewhat lower than Mikhail Glebovich Saltykov. When these articles were read, Pozharsky was silent and could say nothing. The sovereign ordered him to announce Saltykov's promotion, and he could occupy the lower position, but Pozharsky refused, left for his house and pleaded sickness. The conciliar secretary announced the promotion, but in the service record it was written that the announcement came from Pozharsky. Saltykov was not satisfied and petitioned the tsar concerning the dishonor, and Pozharsky was ordered to make his submission.

On June 10, 1618 the boyar Prince Pozharsky wrote to the sovereign from Kaluga, saying that he lay sick and expected to die at any hour. The tsar ordered the table attendant Yury Ignatievich Tatishchev[31] to convey to Pozharsky his good wishes and to inquire after his health. Tatishchev petitioned, saying it would be out of place for him to carry a message to Prince Pozharsky. He was told he must go, but he disobeyed the sovereign's command, fled the palace and did not show up at his home. He was lashed with the knout and sent to make his submission to Pozharsky.

In 1627 the tsar appointed to his bodyguard the table attendants Peter and Fedor, sons of Prince Dmitry Mikhailovich Pozharsky, and with them Princes Fedor and Peter Volkonsky.[32] The Volkonskys petitioned saying they were prepared to serve along with the Pozharskys, but were concerned lest there be any disparagement of their ancestors, since on one occasion

.

an action was brought against Prince Dmitry Mikhailovich Pozharsky by Gavrila Pushkin[33] and others with whom they were on a par. The sovereign sent word to them that there was no need to bring the petition, and they could serve alongside the Pozharskys without disparagement, since Gavrila Pushkin's petition was rejected and the others were punished. The Volkonskys served in the bodyguard, but Pozharsky was not content with this and petitioned they not be allowed to shame his sons, since even the Volkonskys' great-grandfather did not rank alongside his sons. In 1634 Boris Pushkin[34] was imprisoned as a result of Pozharsky's petition.

There was at that time a distinguished émigré from the Crimea in the tsar's service, Prince Yury Yansheevich Suleshov.[35] When Ivan Petrovich Sheremetev was appointed to serve in the bodyguard alongside him, he petitioned that "Prince Suleshov is a foreigner, and in our ranking order hitherto nobody was lower than him. If this is the sovereign's will, let it be as he pleases, so long as our ancestry is not disparaged."

Immediately Buturlin, Pleshcheev and Prince Troekurov petitioned against Sheremetev, saying "He petitions against Prince Suleshov, saying that previously nobody ranked alongside Prince Yury, but we previously served alongside him, and our pedigree is no worse than Ivan Sheremetev's, and so he dishonors us." Suleshov petitioned, saying "Not only Ivan Sheremetev, but even someone senior to him may serve alongside me. Tsar Vasily put Prince Mikhail Vasilievich Skopin-Shuisky on a par with me, and back in the Crimea our relatives were somewhat more exalted than the Urusovs, and this is well known to the sovereign." "The Urusov and Suleshov princes," replied Sheremetev, "are Crimean families living in the Muscovite realm. Nobody knows whose pedigree is superior to whose; this is up to the sovereign. If the sovereign wishes to accept a foreigner and make him honorable and great, he will do so, and hitherto nobody has placed any of the Sheremetevs on a par with Prince Yury." The sovereign sent word to Sheremetev that he could serve alongside Prince Yury, "counting him as a foreigner."

Even after that precedence suits still dogged Suleshov's steps. Thus the boyar Prince Grigory Romodanovsky[36] petitioned that he was misplaced by being in an inferior position to the boyar Prince Yury Suleshov. "Last year," he said, "in 1615, I was sent to a conference with the Crimean ambassadors, and one of the ambassadors at the time was Prince Yury's great-uncle Akhmet-Pasha Suleshov, who approached me during the conference, and was with me in the sovereign's pavilion." The sovereign and the patriarch told Prince Grigory, "How can you compare places with

Akhmet-Pasha? He serves the Crimean ruler, while Prince Yury serves the sovereign." Romodanovsky dropped the case.

The lord-in-waiting Nikita Vasilievich Godunov[37] petitioned that he could not serve in a lesser position than the boyar Vasily Petrovich Morozov.[38] The sovereign sentenced Godunov to imprisonment for dishonoring Morozov, despite which Godunov resubmitted his petition, citing the instance that at Kromy[39] his nephew Ivan Godunov was senior to Morozov. Then the entire Morozov and Saltykov families petitioned that at no time were the Godunovs on a par with them. In the case of Godunov's nephew which he cited against them, Boris was tsar at that time, and that was his will. Ivan owed his promotion to kinship with the tsar, and at that time nobody would challenge Tsar Boris, for even the sovereign knew how things were under that ruler. Many were killed and exiled without cause. Godunov was imprisoned and ordered to submit to Morozov.

Having won his case against Godunov, Morozov lost against the prominent Prince Dmitry Timofeevich Trubetskoy, appointed to greet Filaret closer to Moscow than Morozov, who declared he was yielding place to Trubetskoy only because the tsar declared that considerations of precedence be suspended. On account of that declaration Trubetskoy abused and humiliated him in front of the boyars, calling him a peasant. Morozov replied that in 1597 Prince Ivan Kurakin[40] petitioned concerning precedence against Dmitry's older cousin Prince Yury Trubetskoy,[41] and was not forced to serve alongside him. Prince Yury is now a traitor and is serving the [Polish] king, and the previous sovereign's ruling is that those who are in service and defect thereby deprive their kin of many places.

Michael and Filaret, having heard out the petitions of both boyars, Trubetskoy and Morozov, ordered the boyars to deliberate on the matter. It was decreed that Morozov's petition was without foundation and that he should be imprisoned but, in celebration of his father's joyful return, the sovereign released Morozov.

In 1623 on the occasion of the marriage of the Tatar tsarevich Mikhaila Kaibulovich, two members of the same family became involved in a dispute. Vasily Klepik-Buturlin petitioned that at the wedding he was ordered to sit at a lower table, while his cousin the lord-in-waiting Fedor Levontievich Voron-Buturlin[42] was seated at the high table. Therefore he could not sit at the lower table, since within the family he was many ranks higher than Fedor. Fedor petitioned that Vasily could be placed lower than himself. "They are only distant relatives of ours," he said, "they served out of Novgorod and misplaced their genealogy; but the genealogy of my grandfather, uncle and father has not been misplaced, so I beg my Novgorod cousins not be compared with us. These Novgorod relatives served alongside our grandfathers and fathers and were even ahead of them, but our grandfathers and fathers were prominent, held every state rank, were all inscribed by name in the genealogies. Where is there similar information concerning the Novgorod branch? How many descendants do they have, and who is the senior or junior brother? They themselves do not know, so how can this matter be reckoned?"

The sovereigns, having heard extracts from the service records and the genealogies, declared that the service records vindicated the cause of the lord-in-waiting Fedor Buturlin, and not that of Vasily Klepik and Ivan Matveevich Buturlin. According to the genealogy Vasily and Ivan were descended from the older brother and Fedor from the younger, but later their fathers Vasily and Ivan dropped many degrees.

At the sovereign's wedding in 1624 there was a dispute between the most exalted personages. To prevent precedence suits the tsar ordered the day of the celebration to be without considerations of precedence, and to reinforce this decision he ordered the conciliar secretaries to sign a decree and affix the state seal. Nevertheless the boyar Prince Ivan Vasilievich Golitsyn[43] declared that he could not be below Princes Ivan Ivanovich Shuisky[44] and Dmitry Timofeevich Trubetskoy, so he would not attend the wedding. To the entreaties of the tsar and patriarch he gave the usual reply. "Even though the tsar order my execution, in no way shall I sit lower than Shuisky and Trubetskoy." The sovereign referred the matter to the boyars, who replied that Prince Ivan Golitsyn acted out of treasonable intent, and was deserving of the most extreme punishment and ruination. As a result of this resolution the sovereigns decreed that, on account of his disobedience and treason, his service tenures and patrimonies were all forfeit, except for one patrimonial village in the Arzamas region, whichever was smallest, while he and his wife were to be exiled to Perm.

In 1642 a nephew of this Golitsyn, the boyar Ivan Andreevich, lost his suit against Prince Cherkassky. "The sovereign was in the Golden Chamber in the presence of foreigners," the conciliar secretary told him, "and you, Prince Ivan, wished to sit higher than the boyar Prince Dmitry Mamstriukovich Cherkassky,[45] calling him your cousin, and thereby dishonoring him. Prince Dmitry Mamstriukovich is a great man, and his honor is ancient. During the reign of Tsar Ivan Vasilievich his uncle Prince Mikhail Temriukovich[46] was held in great favor by the tsar, and was with him frequently."

We saw how Prince Lykov was fined for dishonoring Prince Cherkassky by refusing to serve alongside him. Pozharsky agreed without argument to serve as a commander subordinate to Cherkassky. In 1633 Princes Kurakin and Odoevsky, appointed to serve in conjunction with Cherkassky, petitioned that they were prepared to serve alongside him, but if in the future anyone equal or less than him refused to serve alongside them, neither they, Kurakin and Odoevsky, nor their relatives should suffer any humiliation on that account. In this connection Odoevsky cited the Lykov case. Cherkassky petitioned against Kurakin and Odoevsky, saying that Lykov petitioned against being compelled to serve in the same regiment with him on account of his harsh disposition, not on account of ancestry, and on account of his petition Lykov was fined twelve hundred rubles. There was no way Lykov could have outranked him. Under previous sovereigns Cherkassky was closely related to Prince Sheidiakov and many other great families, which outranked even such families as the Obolensky, Kurakin and Odoevsky by many degrees. The boyars sentenced Odoevsky and Kurakin to imprisonment.

As before there was scarcely a service appointment which did not give rise to precedence disputes. In 1624 Princes Ivan Golitsyn and Nikifor Meshchersky were appointed governors of Tula. Golitsyn informed the sovereign that some gentry approached him in the town meeting hall, threw down their commissions[47] and said they would not be subordinate to his colleague Prince Nikifor Meshchersky.

In 1633 the sovereign sent the governor [Grigory Andreevich] Aliabiev[48] to Starodub to assist the governor Buturlin, and he was to be accompanied by Moscow gentry, residents and palace attendants. The gentry and residents petitioned against Aliabiev, saying they could not serve in his regiment, since every single noble and resident was at least equal to him. The sovereign ordered the gentry and residents to serve under Buturlin, and only the palace attendants under Aliabiev: hearth-tax collectors, brewers, grooms, hawkers, falconers, hunters and junior boyars of the tsaritsa's suite.

Sometimes a noble petitioned that he could not serve alongside someone for reasons of precedence, but in fact he only was seeking under this pretext to evade service. Thus in 1614 Kikin petitioned against Mikhalkov, but later acknowledged that he had no precedence claim against him, since they never served together. He petitioned because he was a poor man and could not afford to take up his appointment, and thought he would be excused.

In 1618 the table attendant Bogdan Nagovo mutilated his hand in order to avoid bodyguard service alongside Prince Prozorovsky.[49] Eagerness to protect family honor sometimes led to surprising results. In 1621 Maxim Yazykov returned to Moscow after a tour of duty as governor of Bezhetsky Verkh. He presented to the chancellery his report, stating some Cherkass had attacked Bezhetsky Verkh, and also his personnel list, in which the names of his captains and company commanders were inscribed. Among those mentioned were Prince Andrei Mordkin, David Miliukov and Alexis Ushakov. Mordkin and Miliukov submitted a petition saying that Yazykov made all this up. They never served as captains under him, since such appointment was unworthy of their status, and Yazykov falsely reported this service to the sovereign. He never fought the Lithuanians, there was no attack upon the town, and Mordkin, Miliukov and Ushakov were never among his captains. The sovereign ordered Yazykov to be beaten mercilessly with rods, his salary entitlement be reduced by twenty-five rubles, and a hundred and fifty chetverts of his service tenure to be confiscated. For the dishonor to Mordkin, Miliukov and Ushakov he was to remain in prison for three days.

An attempt was made to subject to genealogical calculations not only appointments to places, but also promotions. Prince Fedor Lykov[50] petitioned against his brother the boyar Prince Boris Mikhailovich Lykov "that my younger brother Boris is among the boyars, while I languish ignominiously among the lords-in-waiting." The sovereign rejected his petition, telling him to remain among the lords-in-waiting.

The appointment of women to various ceremonial duties at court, such as banquets in the tsaritsa's apartments, led to the same kind of disputes over precedence, so much so that sometimes the women were ordered to suspend considerations of rank.

Wearied by incessant quarrels and petitions arising out of every appointment, even over the detailing of bodyguards, attempts were made to appoint men of "lesser categories" without genealogies, who could not count upon their ancestors' service. Yet even here petitions could not be avoided. For example the crown agent Larionov, appointed bodyguard alongside another crown agent Telepnev, petitioned that he, Larionov, was the son of a provincial noble, while Telepnev was the son of a clerk who rose to be a crown secretary. Let the sovereign be so good as to order an investigation. He received the reply that it was befitting for him to serve alongside Telepnev, whose father was a conciliar secretary who personally served the sovereign, while Larionov's father was only an ordinary crown secretary. Furthermore neither family had any official genealogy, so no comparisons could be made. They must serve the tsar as ordered. Despite all this, Larionov petitioned a second time. The sovereign was displeased, ordered him demoted from the rank of crown agent and removed from the list of resident Moscow nobility for having disobeyed the sovereign's decree. At the same time the conciliar secretary repeated the sovereign's words that the sovereign chose men from the lesser categories because he was weary of incessant petitions, yet these men were presenting petitions too!

This was bad enough, but then there were frequent cases of those not possessing genealogies bringing actions against those who had. This particularly vexed the boyars whose task it was to deal with precedence disputes. In the case of such petitions those possessing genealogies did not even wish to acknowledge them. Thus the Romodanovsky princes did not appear with the Levontievs, asserting that "it is not befitting for us to go to judgment with the Levontievs, because they are men without genealogy, petty junior boyars who cannot even be compared with us." The Romodanovskys also called the Levontievs horse doctors.

When in 1635 Fustov petitioned against Prince Boriatinsky on grounds that Fustov's uncle in one of Tsar Ivan's campaigns held a higher command than one of the Boriatinsky princes, the conciliar secretary said to Fustov "Your petition is frivolous. The Boriatinskys are honorable men and have a genealogy, whereas you do not. Even though some of your relatives ranked higher in the service records, you yourself can rank lower than the Boriatinskys."

The following year, in connection with Golenishchev's petition against the same Prince Boriatinsky, the petitioner was told that the Boriatinskys were princes "for a good reason." When at the same time Miasnoy petitioned against Rzhevsky, he was told "There is good reason why you are commoners and the Rzhevskys are men with a genealogy."

Men without genealogy sometimes fared badly when presenting petitions against men with genealogies. In 1617 Levontiev petitioned against Prince Gagarin, and the conciliar noble struck him about the cheeks. In 1620 Chikhachev petitioned against Prince Shakhovskoy. The boyars ordered the petitioner beaten with the knout but the conciliar secretary, the famous Tomila Lugovskoy,[51] told the boyars "We'll have to wait too long for that!" He seized a staff, laid about Chikhachev's back and legs, while the boyar Ivan Nikitich Romanov grabbed another staff and also beat him on the back and legs. Both uttered the verdict "You brought this petition frivolously. By this know your worth!'

The period of dual power also brought its share of precedence disputes. Prince Peter Repnin,[52] sent by the patriarch to entertain the Persian ambassador, petitioned that Prince Sitsky, likewise sent to entertain the ambassador, but on behalf of the tsar, boasted that thereby he ranked higher than Prince Repnin. The sovereign sent word to Repnin that both he and his father were equally sovereign, their sovereignty was indivisible, and therefore one appointment was no higher than the other. The great sovereigns did not wish to see any more such petitions, otherwise they would be angry.

In 1621 the sovereigns sent word to the boyars "Ambassadors, emissaries and couriers from among the high and provincial gentry are sent to various realms about the sovereigns' various business yet these gentry petition, saying they cannot go because formerly the duty of ambassador or emissary was not carried out by fellow-gentry who were their equals, but now they are being dispatched as ambassadors and emissaries, thus causing them dishonor and loss of place. Previously such appointments were not the subject of petitions, since the dispatch of ambassadors and emissaries is to various realms for various purposes. Neither are they sent together on the same mission. Frequently it occurs that gentry are sent as emissaries, then as ambassadors, and yet again as emissaries or couriers, depending upon the task at hand. These gentry petitions are something new, and are a hindrance to the sovereign's business. Previously petitions from the gentry only arose when the two were sent on the same mission." The boyars decreed that no further such petitions be entertained.

The government as earlier continued to accept into service and grant service tenures without paying much attention to the origins of the new servicemen. The provincial gentry and junior boyars were reluctant to admit those of lowly birth into their company. In 1639 the gentry and junior boyars of Uglich petitioned against their fellow Uglich junior boyar Ivan Shubinsky. "This Ivan was granted by the tsar a service land entitlement and a salary. Since then, although he has not performed service and is not of equal birth to us, he has been inscribed among the roll of gentry in our town, though none of the Shubinsky family was on the roll under previous sovereigns. Even during your reign, sovereign, the Shubinskys were overseers, while Ivashka's uncle was an artillery man. Gracious sovereign! Order that this Ivan be struck off our list lest we be dishonored by him, for he does not deserve to be on this list either on account of his ancestry or his service."

The same Uglich gentry petitioned against two of their confreres, Boris Morakushev and Bogdan Tretiakov. "This Boris and this Bogdan were inscribed as auxiliaries, not for regular service. They did not take part in the siege of Smolensk, neither were they wounded. We, your slaves, have served the sovereign thirty or forty years, and have not petitioned falsely concerning the muster roll. Gracious sovereign! Order them struck off the muster roll, lest we be dishonored."

Service with the sword was considered more honorable than that with the pen, and therefore it was dishonorable for a member of the gentry to serve as a crown secretary. The crown secretary Larion Lopukhin[53] petitioned that since time immemorial his ancestors served in the provinces in a military capacity, and that he before becoming a crown secretary served with the Moscow residents. Therefore he requested to be allowed to leave the bureaucracy. The tsar decreed that his fellow gentry were not to consider him dishonored or reproach him for serving as a crown secretary. He was transferred from the gentry to the bureaucracy at the tsar's express wish, not of his own volition.

How strong still was the basis of precedence, family unity, is evident from the following petition. "Your slave Stepanka Miliukov does obeisance to the lord tsar. You, O sovereign, ordered us your slaves, the whole Miliukov family, to pay Prince Sontsev-Zasekin a hundred rubles cash for his slave Vaska, for Vaska's wife and the son he had by her. The money, a hundred rubles, I alone paid, taking out an indenture. In addition I paid the interest together with the principal. The following did not pay: Matvey Ivanov, son of Old Miliukov, Andrei Klementiev son of Miliukov, Ivan Fedorov son of Miliukov, Davyd Mikhailov son of Miliukov, Andrei, Fedor, Yakov and Astafy, children of Ivan Mikhailov Miliukov, Yermolay Nazariev son of Miliukov, Moisey Yemelianov son of Miliukov and Sergei Ulianov son of Miliukov. Therefore by your decree let it be ordered that the indenture be drawn up in the name of the whole family, because we all petitioned concerning Vaska, not I alone."

VETERANS OF THE TROUBLES

Thanks to precedence disputes and appointments written in the service records we can gain some information concerning the people and families we encountered frequently in our account of the Time of Troubles.

We saw that the Godunovs had to abandon the ranking to which their position during the reign of Tsar Boris entitled them. One of them, Matvey Mikhailovich, was a boyar under Michael, and in 1620 governor of Tobolsk. In 1631 he was sent to Riazan to muster the gentry and junior boyars, and in 1632 was governor of Kazan. In court ceremonies the lord-in-waiting Nikita Vasilievich Godunov is mentioned frequently as dining at the tsar's table. Irina Nikitichna, wife of the lord-in-waiting Ivan Ivanovich Godunov, the tsar's aunt, was still alive, being mentioned in connection with the tsar's wedding in 1626. Boris's daughter Xenia, or Olga, died in 1622 at Suzdal.[54] Prior to her death she petitioned the tsar to allow her to be buried in the Trinity-St. Sergius monastery alongside her father and mother. The tsar fulfilled this request.

The last of the Shuiskys, Prince Ivan Ivanovich, returned from Poland and took his proper place among the boyars in accordance with his exalted ancestry. He is only mentioned as being active on one significant occasion, his presence at the reading of the charges against Shein prior to his execution.

The Nagoys are mentioned among the table attendants and governors. Prince Dmitry Timofeevich Trubetskoy after his disastrous campaign against the Swedes, and after his victory in the precedence dispute with Morozov, according to Lithuanian intelligence was sent to Yaroslavl in 1622 to muster gentry and junior boyars for the sovereign's service. In 1625 he was governor of Tobolsk.

Vladimir Prokopyich, son of the famous Prokopy Liapunov,[55] was mentioned in 1614 as governor of Mikhailov, then as second-in-command of the vanguard regiment at Pereiaslavl-in-Riazan. In 1625, in connection with precedence litigation, the relationship of the Liapunov family to Riazan was thrown into prominence. There this family continued to have great significance. The table attendant and boyar Peter Alexandrovich Repnin and Prince Ivan Fedorovich Chermny-Volkonsky were appointed to Pereiaslavl-in-Riazan. Prince Fedor Fedorovich Volkonsky-Merin and Ulian Semeonovich Liapunov were appointed to the vanguard regiment at Mikhailov. When these appointments were made, the Liapunovs, Vladimir and Ulian, petitioned against the Volkonskys, accusing their rivals of bastardy.

The deputy governor of Riazan, Prince Ivan Volkonsky, took fright and petitioned the sovereign that he could not serve alongside Prince Peter Repnin and his companions because they petitioned against the Liapunovs on behalf of their entire family, while Prince Peter Repnin petitioned against the Liapunovs personally. Volkonsky was married to the daughter of Zakhar Liapunov,[56] and the Liapunov family was prominent in Riazan. Volkonsky was afraid Repnin would victimize him on account of the Liapunovs.

The tsar ordered that Volkonsky be recalled and Lovchikov appointed in his place. Ulian Liapunov petitioned against Lovchikov, saying he could not serve under him. The boyars dismissed Liapunov's petition, saying that the honor of the Lovchikovs was long-standing, whereas Ulian's father enjoyed no honor, neither did he serve as governor anywhere. Then Liapunov submitted a petition against the Mikhailov commander Prince Fedor Volkonsky. Here also the boyars decreed that Liapunov's petition be rejected because the Volkonskys enjoyed honorific positions such as lord-in-waiting, table attendant and governor, whereas Liapunov served in Riazan, and he was lucky even to receive a command. Liapunov reported for service, but would have nothing to do with Volkonsky. Gagin was sent from Moscow to compel Liapunov to deal with Volkonsky, under threat of imprisonment. Liapunov refused and was placed in confinement, but Volkonsky reported that Gagin restricted him to the town hall, not placing him in the prison. Liapunov broke down the drawbridge and went from the town hall to the tower, where he lived in his own apartments rather than in the prison. Then Pushchin was sent from Moscow to deliver Liapunov from the town hall and send him on service. If he refused, he was to be put into prison along with the other jailbirds, not in the town hall. Liapunov gave way.

In 1629 Vladimir Prokofyich Liapunov was appointed second-in-command of the rearguard regiment at Krapivna but then was recalled because of the petition of the gentry and junior boyars of the local towns, who said he was "hostile" to them.

We encountered Prince Dmitry Mikhailovich Pozharsky frequently during Michael's reign, and upon important occasions, on campaigns and assisting in the collection of funds for the war chest. On September 27, 1618 Prince Dmitry Pozharsky stood before the tsar's throne and received the following citation. "You were in our service against our foe the Lithuanian king. You served us, you resisted the Poles and Lithuanians, you attempted many missions against them, ordered the building of forts, slew many Poles and Lithuanians, and after these battles sent many informants to us. You were solicitous and industrious in the affairs of our land, and covered the retreat of our boyar Prince Boris Mikhailovich Lykov from Mozhaisk to Moscow." For all these services Pozharsky received a gilded silver goblet with a lid, thirty-six gold pieces equivalent to three grivenkas, a fur robe, Turkish satin upon sables and some gilded silver buttons.

It was understandable that Pozharsky, as a consequence of Filaret Nikitich's well-known tendency to reward those who labored hard during the interregnum, had nothing to lose by Filaret's return. Immediately after Filaret's consecration in 1619 Pozharsky was given three villages and a hamlet for his valor and bravery in the recent war. In 1621 the patrimony given him by Tsar Vasily was augmented and confirmed by charter. At that time he was in charge of the Chancellery for Criminal Affairs. At the tsar's first wedding, in 1624, he occupied second place among the groomsmen, and at the tsar's second wedding in 1626 he occupied the same position. His wife Praskovia Varfolomeevna was second matron of honor on the tsaritsa's side, although in precedence petitions it continued to be written that the Pozharskys were not a service family, and that under previous sovereigns they saw service only as elected urban and rural magistrates. In 1628 Pozharsky was appointed governor of Great Novgorod, where he spent 1629 and 1630. In 1635 he was appointed to the Moscow Judicial Chancellery. Pozharsky is mentioned for the last time, at the tsar's table, on September 24, 1641. He is thought to have died in 1642.

Speaking of Prince Dmitry Mikhailovich's fate, we cannot forbear to mention the curious petition he submitted to the tsar in 1634, together with his first cousin Prince Dmitry Petrovich. From this petition the strength of kinship ties during the period under consideration is evident. The uncle had the right to beat or place a nephew in shackles or irons for unbecoming conduct. If these measures did not help, he could complain to the tsar out of fear that the nephew's misconduct might bring disfavor upon the uncle, for with the unity of the family the older members were responsible for the younger.

"Our nephew Fedka Pozharsky," the uncles petitioned, "while on service with us in Mozhaisk has misbehaved. He drinks incessantly, commits robbery, frequents the taverns, drinks his shirt away, drinks himself unconscious and does not heed us. We, your slaves, have done everything possible to bring him to his senses. We have beaten him and placed him in fetters and irons. He long ago has ruined the service tenure which the tsar granted him, he has drunk everything away, he cannot stay out of the Mozhaisk taverns, he drinks himself into a stupor, and we cannot do anything with him. Sovereign, have him recalled from Mozhaisk and sent to a monastery under supervision, so that we do not incur disfavor on account of his criminality."

Finally one more instance in which Pozharsky's name is mentioned should be pointed out. This is in connection with his conduct during the election of the tsar in 1613. This can be accepted merely as a piece of information rather than definite evidence for or against. In 1613, during the survey of the Russian-Lithuanian boundary in the Pskov region, the table attendant Vasily Romodanovsky the Elder[57] disputed with the noble

Larion Sumin and petitioned that at the surveyors' tent Sumin uttered impertinent words, saying "that he, Prince Vasily, did not rule or attain the tsardom, but his cousin Dmitry Pozharsky attained the tsardom, and it cost him twenty thousand rubles." Sumin was interrogated as to when Prince Dmitry attained the tsardom and purchased it. He denied he ever uttered such words, but witnesses confirmed that he did.

The name of Minin is linked indissolubly with that of Pozharsky. For the deed which earned Pozharsky his boyardom, Minin received the rank of conciliar secretary, together with service tenures and a patrimony. He received these "for his services, in that with the boyars, commanders and soldiers he came to the relief of Moscow and liberated the Muscovite realm."

In 1615 the tsar wrote to the governors of Nizhny Novgorod "Our conciliar secretary Kuzma Minin petitioned us that he is living with us in Moscow, but his service tenures and patrimonies are in the Nizhny Novgorod district; his brothers and son are in Nizhny Novgorod and suffer much loss on account of lawsuits and slanders brought against his peasants and servants. We are asked to grant that he, his brothers, servants and peasants not be judged in Nizhny Novgorod, but in Moscow. From the time this charter reaches you, no cases are to be heard in Nizhny Novgorod concerning Kuzma, his brothers, servants or peasants without our express permission, excepting cases of robbery with violence and brigandage."

We know nothing about Minin's activities and only once do we encounter information about him, in the aforementioned affair concerning Andronov's escape. The trader Isakov under interrogation said he was related to Andronov, and took out of Moscow Andronov's sister Afimia, wife of Vasily Bolotnikov, but she took none of her possessions with her except for one dress which Kuzma Minin gave her.

By 1616 Kuzma Minin was dead. The tsar gave his patrimony, the village of Bogoroditskoe with its hamlets, to his widow Tatiana and his son the crown agent Nefed, at the same time confirming the charter whereby Nefed, his servants and peasants could be judged only in Moscow. In 1625, on the occasion of the farewell audience of the Persian ambassador, Minin's son Nefed was listed in the eighth place among the crown agents bearing the tsar's vestments. The following year he was a torchbearer at the tsar's wedding. The last mention of him is in 1628, at the reception of the Persian ambassador. In 1632 his patrimony the village of Bogoroditskoe was granted as a service tenure to Prince Yakov Kudenetovich Cherkassky.[58] Kuzma Minin's house in Nizhny Novgorod was given to the tsar's jilted fiancée Maria Khlopova,[59] after whose death in 1633 it was given to Princes Ivan Borisovich[60] and Yakov Kudenetovich Cherkassky.

Famed for his civic courage during the interregnum, the conciliar secretary Tomila Yudich Lugovskoy[61] returned from Poland in the company of Filaret Nikitich, and we encountered him in 1620 meting out summary justice to Chikhachev, who sought to bring a precedence dispute against Prince Shakhovskoy. Such action on his part is not surprising since, given the moral state of Russian society at this time, harshness and decisiveness which constituted the greatness of the man in crucial circumstances normally is found in connection with inclination towards harsh measures on all occasions. Afterwards Lugovskoy was promoted to conciliar noble and became deputy governor of Kazan. Not surprisingly Lugovskoy, whose good side was well known to Filaret Nikitich, received promotion.

What is surprising is that the principal man of affairs in Michael's reign was another conciliar secretary, Ivan Tarasievich Gramotin[62] who, as we have seen, left behind him a very evil reputation in Pskov. Next he proceeded to Tushino, and then to the king's encampment before Smolensk. He went to Moscow and became a fanatical supporter of the king. Making a timely escape back to the king, he was sent with Mezetsky to urge Moscow to swear allegiance to Wladyslaw. Even after the heroic deed of the Second Militia Force he went back to the king.

It is unknown when he reappeared in Moscow and received back his old position of keeper of the seal. During the rule of Filaret Nikitich at last Gramotin suffered disfavor. On December 21 Yefim Telepnev was appointed secretary to the Chancellery for Foreign Affairs. "Ivan Gramotin," he was told, "was in the Chancellery for Foreign Affairs, and when conducting state business he did not heed the decrees of the tsar and his father the holy patriarch, carried on business without the tsar's decree and arbitrarily, on account of which the sovereigns were greatly angered and placed their disfavor upon him." Gramotin was sent to Alatyr, but after the death of Fedor Nikitich was recalled to Moscow and received his former rank.

MILITARY ORGANIZATION

Michael's reign was marked by difficult wars which increasingly demonstrated the inadequacy of the Russian army, consisting of gentry, junior boyars, foreigners, atamans and cossacks, granted service tenures scattered over various regions of the realm. Consequently with the opening of hostilities it was necessary to gather soldiers, and to rally these service tenure holders at a designated place under a specific commander. Then someone was named from among the Muscovite nobility or with a court rank to gather and bring the soldiers. The first obstacle would be that the official appointed, because of considerations of precedence, could not possibly bring soldiers to such-and-such a commander, who was many places inferior. The difficulty might be overcome by telling the petitioner to bring the soldiers to some commander indisputably a few grades higher. The official was pacified, set off and returned with only a few soldiers. The rest were "defaulters" who hid, being unwilling to be parted from their warm, comfortable hearth and home for a distant, arduous and dangerous campaign. Others appeared before the muster official, set off with him for the designated location, but deserted along the way. Then the muster officials were dispatched a second time with instructions to muster immediately all the gentry and junior boyars according to a list they were given. "If some junior boyars try to hide," read the instructions, "they must be sought out and beaten with the knout, after which sureties shall be gathered for them. In the event they cannot be found, go to their service tenures and patrimonies and take hostage their estate managers, servants and peasants, keeping them in jail until the serviceman is found. If junior boyars disobey the tsar's decree after giving sureties for themselves, and do not accompany the recruiter, seek out their guarantors, beat them with rods and order them to seek out those for whom they gave surety. When these are discovered, they are to be beaten with the knout, imprisoned and then compelled to go on the sovereign's service. Apart from service tenure holders known to the government, the muster officers also are to bring auxiliaries and volunteers with all manner of weapons, both firearms and bows.

Gentry, junior boyars and new recruits had to report for service with harness, armor, breastplate, plate armor, helmet and casque. Nobody was allowed to ride to war with just pistols; in addition he had to have a carbine or a regulation sized musket. Nobody could come with just a quiver; he had to have also a pistol or a carbine. If they did not bring a quiver, they at least had to bring a long musket and a good carbine. If they were too poor to afford a long musket, they were at least each to bring a boar spear or an axe.

When news came that the Crimean Tatars were advancing, commanders were sent to the borderland towns. They immediately informed the borderland, steppe and Riazan towns, ordering all governors and officials to come to a designated rallying point for the sovereign's service. They were to be accompanied by all the gentry and junior boyars from the border and Moscow region towns, atamans, cossacks, Lithuanians, Germans and all other foreigners, the Tatar princes from the Lower Towns and Meshchera, together with their murzas, Tatars, captains and company commanders, musketeers, mounted and unmounted cossacks with firearms, and many other troops to protect the sovereign's frontiers from Crimean and Nogay Tatars and Cherkass. If there were any Crimeans, Nogay or Cherkass in the towns, a list of them must be submitted immediately, and the boyar muster officers were to assign them to the command of various gentry and junior boyars.

When the gentry, junior boyars and all servicemen were assembled the commanders were to take a roll call, calling out each name individually, and then send the sovereign a list of who was present and who was absent. If any of the gentry or junior boyars of the borderland towns were absent they were to be sought out by force, beaten with rods, imprisoned for a while, and then on release were to give written sureties. Traveling expenses for the recruiters also were to be exacted. If the defaulters had thriving service tenures and patrimonies, the entire travel expenses were to be exacted. If the estates were run down the traveling expenses were to be exacted in proportion, reckoning one fee for all the estates. If junior boyars or foreigners from the towns around Moscow failed to report, inquiry was to be made among the leading gentry and junior boyars, who had to state under oath who had how much in service tenures and patrimonies, what income was derived from them, and whether these defaulters were capable of performing the sovereign's service alongside them. Concerning the defaulters, they were to inquire whether their failure to report stemmed from poverty or through deliberate intent; also the service entitlement of each must be determined. All this information was to be written down, and the assessors, gentry and boyars had to sign the report and send it on to the sovereign, who would order the decree applied to the defaulters with utmost severity.

If junior boyars from the borderland towns failed to appear for the roll call, and the officers failed to find them, several of the gentry and junior boyars from their town were asked their whereabouts, whether they were killed in action or died from natural causes, and who was in possession of their service tenures or patrimonies. Having inquired diligently, they were to send a written report to the sovereign. They were also to seek out minors who were about to reach the age for service, and order them to report for duty, sending their names on to Moscow.

As soon as news came of the enemy's approach, the commanders were to send junior boyars around the encampments and rural districts, ordering the evacuation of women and children of all boyar servitors. All widows and youths were to take refuge in the town, a list of them was to be made, and they were to be reviewed frequently. "As soon as there is reliable news concerning the Crimeans," the instructions continued, "all boyar servants and agricultural peasants must be sent into the town with their wives, children and possessions, there to await the troops. Grain must be threshed and stored in pits, while a few men are to be detailed to tend the livestock. The rural population also is to be told to keep all manner of supplies, should there be a siege. If when such news comes any junior boyars, wives, children, non-serving gentry, widows or minors fail to seek refuge in the town, and are captured by the Tatars, they will not be ransomed with funds from the sovereign's treasury. Criers are to announce these conditions for several days.

"If anyone disobeys the order to seek refuge in the town, order him to be imprisoned for a while. If a widow, take her children and servants and put them in prison. When you release them take firm surety that they arrive in town in good time. If even then they do not obey beat them with rods and put them in prison, and in the case of widows take their servants, beat them with rods and imprison them for a while.

"For every errand, to secure the encampments and entrances and gain information, send selected gentry and junior boyars, who should not sit around doing nothing. Also the senior categories of junior boyars and selected gentry should not be subordinate to those of lesser categories.

"When news is received of the enemy's approach place captains in all fortified lines and swampy places, and with them send soldiers with muskets. These captains may also muster as many of the local population as possible to man the fortifications with muskets and any other kind of weapon. Where the fortifications are in disrepair, they must be strengthened, refortified and propped up with timbers, and in other places ditches are to be dug. Around gates and towers repairs must be made and the moats cleared.

"Any disputes or disorders among the troops must be settled expeditiously. They must obtain provisions for themselves and for their horses by purchase from the local population at the going price, even if this price has increased. They must not take anything by plunder or violence. Take good care that the troops commit no brigandage, plunder, murder, robbery, banditry or any other form of violence, nor let them frequent taverns or houses of ill repute. It is forbidden to release anyone from service before his time is up. When troops no longer are needed the tsar will send a decree to his commanders to dismiss their men."

Soldiers who deserted Shein before Smolensk when they heard of the prince's approach were punished only by having their pay docked. The commander Prince Boriatinsky, who was dilatory in the advance against Lisowski, devastating villages and hamlets on the way, was imprisoned on account of his brigandage.

The basis on which soldiers were paid is evident from the following information. In December 1633 table attendants, crown agents, Moscow residents and gentry appointed to serve in the Polish campaign of Cherkassky and Pozharsky petitioned saying they had not the means to go on campaign. They had no service tenures or patrimonies or, if they had, they were ruined and unpopulated, or only had three to six peasants, which was insufficient to generate enough income to enable them to report for service. If the sovereign would grant them a salary, they would be glad to serve the sovereign. The sovereign ordered each to submit a signed statement to the chancellery stating who had no service tenure or patrimony, whose was ruined, or how many peasants he had. When the reports were submitted to the sovereign, he would grant to those who had no service tenures or patrimonies, or those whose estates were ruined twenty-five rubles, those having fewer than fifteen peasants twenty rubles, and those with fifteen peasants, nothing.

We know that according to Ivan the Terrible's law code serving junior boyars or their children could not be enslaved. Now, in 1641, gentry and junior boyars were petitioning that their brothers, nephews, sons and grandchildren, whether endowed or not, did not wish to continue enduring poverty in the sovereign's service and were entering the service of boyar houses. They were becoming indentured to boyars, lords-in-waiting, table attendants, crown agents, Moscow nobles and even to their fellow-gentry, men of all ranks.[63]

The response was that all such men, together with their wives and children, even if they married serf women and girls,[64] were to be taken out of boyar houses and put to service, and they were to be given service tenures and patrimonies in the provinces. As for unendowed junior boyars who never had served the sovereign anywhere or received any service tenures or patrimonies, let them remain in boyar households as before. Those junior boyars who according to the sovereign's decree and resolution of the boyar council were released from slavery, but to evade service entered the households of other boyars or men of other ranks, were to be returned as slaves to those they served prior to the issue of the sovereign's decree. From the date of the decree no gentry or junior boyars, neither their children, nephews or grandchildren, whether endowed or not, were to be received as slaves by anyone.

With regard to the inheritance of estates, either earned or hereditary, it was resolved not to give estates to widows of husbands who died without issue. Instead the lands would be given to collateral relatives. If the owner of a patrimony was survived by children the estate was given to the sons, while the daughters were to receive an allowance. If they had no brothers, daughters could inherit. Grandsons and great-grandsons after the death of their grandparents shared the estate with their uncles and aunts.

Concerning the inheritance of service tenures, the First Militia Force decreed in 1611 that in the event of gentry or junior boyars dying in action or from natural causes, widows and sons should not be deprived of the service tenure. In the case of gentry or boyars not survived by wife or children, the service tenure should go to a kinsman who did not have an estate, or only a small one. The service tenure was not to be given to anyone outside the family.

Tsar Michael resolved that in the case of gentry or junior boyars who were killed, taken prisoner or missing in action (not simply having died, as in the previous enactment), the service tenure must be given to his wife and children. If he left no wife or children the land was to be given as an entitlement or supplement to a family member or kinsman. It was not to be given to anyone outside the family, or to any noble or junior boyar except those pertaining to the town from which the deceased served. If a foreigner died his estate was not to be given to anyone except another foreigner. When a noble or junior boyar remained in captivity for ten, fifteen, twenty-five years or even longer, and the estates which he inherited from his father were given to others, on his return from captivity he might petition for return of the lands given away during his last ten years of captivity. Lands lost for more than ten years could not be recovered, but he would receive preferential treatment next time service tenures were distributed.

Musketeers received their captains from among the free volunteers. The office was passed on from father to son, brother to brother or uncle to nephew. They were fine brave fellows and excellent marksmen. Unfit youths, serfs, townsmen or agricultural peasants could not enroll in the musketeers. Concerning the service of cossacks, we know from a regulation dating from 1632 that those free volunteers in the towns of the

Novgorod Seversk region who enlisted for service as cossacks were to be inscribed on the roll with their patronymics and surnames. When ordered on campaign, all cossacks must be equipped with muskets. The sovereign also granted them a salary of four rubles. Nobody could be enrolled as a cossack who already was in service, was a taxpayer or a serf. The newly enrolled cossacks were to be placed under a captain chosen from the gentry, and company commanders. Great care was to be taken lest cossack regiments indulge in brigandage.

Concerning foreigners, as early as the 1614 campaign the sovereign ordered that the contingent under Ivan Izmailov be augmented by Lithuanians, Germans and other foreigners, whose names were to be inscribed in the service record and at the Chancellery for Service Foreigners. The following year, for the campaign against Lisowski, the sovereign ordered the Englishman Arthur ("Prince Artemy") Aston[65] to serve alongside the Germans.

This was the same Aston whom Merrick[66] asked the tsar to permit to return home. We saw that Merrick's request was refused, but then King James sent a personal request to the tsar to allow Aston and his family to return to England. Aston was given leave but then the tsar was told that while he was in Moscow Aston corresponded with the Polish prince, dispatched Captain Barnaby from Moscow for sinister purposes, and Barnaby entered Polish service. On the last occasion he was in Moscow, the boyars told Merrick "It is known that Prince Artemy Aston came to the Muscovite realm at the instigation of the French traitor Margeret.[67] When he left Moscow, Aston barely touched ground in England before setting off to the Polish king, and he left his wife in Poland. Then his son arrived in Poland to ask the king whether he could recruit troops to attack the Muscovite realm, concerning which he uttered many scandalous and abusive words. For this the king ought to have punished him severely. How are we to trust you people?" Merrick replied that he had no instructions concerning this matter, but he thought Artemy would receive no support from the king for such a criminal venture.

We also saw how Merrick pleaded with the boyars not to exile English servicemen to Kazan, insisting that the Englishmen and Scotsmen who came with him and with Aston, together with two who arrived at Archangel and one elderly foreigner, altogether twenty individuals, be allowed to remain in Moscow. Those foreigners who arrived from various places suffering from hunger and poverty, victims of war and brigandage, might be sent to the Lower Towns to subsist there.[68] Nevertheless the English who were left in Moscow fled to Lithuania.

Although some foreigners were in bad odor in Moscow, although some others could not bear the thought of remaining there permanently since it was extremely difficult to be given leave to go home, there nevertheless were many eager to enter the tsar's service. One captain, an Irishman by birth but in Polish service, commanded the citadel of Belaia. He surrendered it to the Russians, and with all his regiment went over to the tsar's service. The foreign explosives expert Yury Bessonov received absolute title to his service tenure as a reward for his service during Prince Wladyslaw's advance on Moscow. The charter stated that the freehold would be enjoyed by his children, grandchildren and great-grandchildren.

Some foreigners were given service tenures and supported themselves on the income, while others were given a subsistence allowance in addition to their pay. Thus in 1628 in the Great Regiment at Tula there were with Captain Roganowski some Poles and Lithuanians holding service tenures, 118 men altogether. With Captain Denis van Wissen (Fon-Vizin) there were 63 German service tenure holders. Captain Kremski had 120 Poles and Germans receiving subsistence allowance. Among those surrendering Belaia along with Thomas Hearne were ten holding service tenures and 54 receiving subsistence allowance. With Captain Wood there were Greeks, Serbs, Wallachians and Germans, eighty altogether, receiving subsistence allowance.

Although it felt a great need for foreign soldiers, and sent abroad to recruit them, the Muscovite government regarded Catholics with suspicion and refused to engage them. Thus Colonel Leslie,[69] sent abroad to recruit soldiers, received the instruction, "Hire soldiers from the Swedish and other realms, but not the French. For Frenchmen and others of the Roman faith are not to be hired."

We also have seen that apart from mercenary and service-tenured foreigners, during Michael's reign there appeared regiments of Russians who trained in foreign drills. Shein had before Smolensk many mercenary soldiers, captains of cavalry and infantry, as well as ordinary foot soldiers, but alongside these foreign colonels and captains there were Russians, junior boyars and men of various ranks, who were signed up for military instruction. Under the German colonel Samuel Charles there were cavalry soldiers, altogether 2,700 gentry and junior boyars from the various towns, and 81 Greeks, Serbs and Wallachians receiving subsistence allowance. Colonel Alexander Leslie had in his regiment 946 men, including captains, majors, officials and soldiers. Jakob Charles had 935, Colonel Fuchs 679, Colonel James Sanderson 923,[70] Colonel William Keith and George Mattheson 346 noncommissioned officers and 3,282 ordinary soldiers.

Foreigners from various countries, dispatched by the Chancellery for Foreign Affairs, numbered 180, and the total number of foreign mercenaries was 3,653. Foreign colonels commanding Russian troops, under the jurisdiction of the Chancellery for Service Foreigners, were four colonels, four lieutenant colonels, four majors (in Russian parlance "regimental guard commanders"), two quartermaster-captains (in Russian "great regimental lords-in-waiting"), two regimental quartermasters, seventeen captains, 32 lieutenants, 32 ensigns, four regimental judges and scribes, four wagon masters, four chaplains, four law clerks, four provosts, one regimental drummer, 79 sergeants, 33 ensigns, 33 recruiting sergeants, 65 German corporals, 172 Russian corporals, 20 German drummers and a piper, 32 regimental clerks, 68 Russian drummers, two German youths to act as interpreters, Russian and German soldiers in six regiments, Poles and Lithuanians in four regiments, totaling in all 14,801 men.

When Princes Cherkassky and Pozharsky were ordered to advance to the relief of Shein there were with them 162 foreigners—Greeks, Serbs, Wallachians and Moldavians—and also Colonel Alexander Gordon in command of 1,567 dragoons.

Concerning the rates of pay of foreign mercenaries, a colonel received 400 reichsthalers a month, a lieutenant colonel 200, a major 100, a quartermaster 60, the provost marshal 30, a secretary 25, the two chaplains each 30, the four surgeons each 60, the law clerk 12, a sergeant-major eight, a provost ten, an escort four, the executioner eight. For each cavalry regiment the company commanders received 150, a lieutenant 45, and ensign 35, a sergeant 14, a fusileer captain 12, wagons, scouts and scribes ten, a drummer seven, a corporal eight, a wagon master six, his assistant five, a common soldier four and a half.

Tatars as before constituted an integral part of the regular Russian forces. As part of the force under Cherkassky and Pozharsky the Kazan murzas and Tatars were ordered to advance with altogether 275 men; the Sviiazhsk murzas, Tatars and converts totaling 205; from Kurmysh 155 Tatars and Tarkhans; 508 Kasimov Tatars, 550 from Temnikov, 347 from Kadom, 359 from Alatyr and 220 from Arzamas.

Apart from Cherkass and Don Cossacks, during Michael's reign Yaik Cossacks are mentioned as forming part of the Muscovite army. With respect to artillery, there has come down to us an itemized description of the weapons used in the siege of Smolensk by Shein. For a cannon called *Unicorn* the shot weighed thirty puds, the barrel weighed 450 puds, the mounting 210 puds, and it required 64 rollers to transport it. This artillery piece had a gun carriage weighing 200 puds, requiring ten rollers. The cannon named *Stepson* had shot weighing fifteen puds, the barrel weighed 350 puds, the mounting 165 puds, and it required 52 rollers. Other guns were named *Wolf, Hawk, Achilles,* and so on.[71] In 1629 the tsar received a curious petition. Its author was the Tver priest Nester. "I inform you, O sovereign, of a great matter, and it is with great trepidation that I broach the subject, but in my fear I rely upon God, from whom I have received this great gift, such as has not been revealed to previous generations under previous sovereigns. This God has revealed to your majesty's eternal glory and for the redemption of our oppressed land, to strike fear and amazement into the heart of your enemies. I will build for you an artificial fortress called Redkodub,[72] at not much cost. It will not require many rollers to move it, and soldiers can hold out and take cover in it as in a real unmovable town."

Nester was summoned to Moscow and ordered to make a wooden model or to draw a plan of his invention. He demanded to be admitted to the tsar's presence forthwith, saying "Unless I am not admitted to the sovereign's presence, I cannot make the model, since I do not trust the boyars in this matter." Several times he was told to make the model, and then he would be presented to the sovereign, but each time he gave the same reply. Then the sovereign commanded that the priest Nester be sent to the Transfiguration monastery in Kazan, and placed under supervision there, because he had presented a petition, promised to perform great things, but did nothing. Perhaps he did this because he was disturbed, and not in his right mind.

The wretched inventor languished for three years chained up in the monastery, and during the fourth year he submitted a petition in which he described his earlier feats. In 1609, during the Time of Troubles, he went with letters to Prince Skopin in Great Novgorod, and from there back to Moscow. Then he went with letters and gunpowder through Lithuanian lines to the St. Joseph monastery of Volokolamsk. In 1611 he was sent from Liapunov's headquarters outside Moscow clear across country with letters for Metropolitan Filaret. He was seized, brought to the king, sentenced to death, but got away again. We do not know the final disposition of Nester's case, since the end of the file containing it has perished.

V

TOWNS, TRADE AND COMMERCE

We observed how careful Michael was to prevent a breach with the Crimean khan, and the reason is easy to grasp. All his attention was turned towards the West, entire the strength of the realm was pointed in that direction. Only in 1636 did the government find it possible to pay attention to the fortification of Southern Ukraine. In that year new towns were built: Chernavsk (between Elets and Livny), Kozlov, Tambov and Lomov, while Orel was reconstructed. In 1640 Khotmyshsk on the Vorskla and Volny Kurgan on the Rogozna were built. To defray the cost of this construction 13,532 rubles were disbursed. All this work of town construction was supervised by the Chancellery of Cannoneers.

Tsar Michael's first task after his accession was freeing the realm from foreign and domestic enemies, and for this an army was needed. To support the army, money was needed, but the treasury was plundered, so the burden had to fall upon the urban and rural population.

RUINOUS STATE OF TOWNS

The state of the towns at the beginning of Michael's reign is evident from the following plea. "In Uglich there are no soldiers, gentry, junior boyars or foreign troops. There are no musketeers or sentries, not a single man, only six cannoneers, and they are starving. There are no reserves of grain in the event of a siege, neither are there any supplies of grain in the countryside to be gathered from anyone. The powder magazine is low, the drawbridge in the fortress has yet to be built, and the drawbridges on the towers are in disrepair. The townsmen, because of the shortfall in tavern taxes and the current high price of gain, have deserted their wives and children. Those remaining are totally unfit for a siege, neither can we withstand any siege unless soldiers are dispatched to us in a hurry because all our defenses are utterly destroyed by the Lithuanians through fire and demolition. From the rural districts no men report to provide a siege garrison because they also are destitute and there are no grain supplies in the towns, so they flee into the forest."

As early as 1618 Andrei Obraztsov, sent to Beloozero to gather money, was reproached for his dilatoriness. In reply he wrote, "Your majesty, I have not put pressure on the townsmen, neither do I insist they meet the deadline. Before news came of the Lithuanians I exacted all of your majesty's dues without mercy, *even beating some to death,* but now, O sovereign, no more money can be exacted from the townsmen, as your majesty will appreciate. For I, your slave, in view of the Lithuanians' advance, have to remain with the townsmen day and night in the fort in order to dispatch them to man the defenses."

When Filaret Nikitich returned from Poland measures were undertaken for the reconstruction of the devastated zone. This is what the tsar's circular had to say about it. "On account of the sins of all of Orthodox Christendom, the Muscovite realm has been ruined and devastated by Poles, Lithuanians and brigands. All manner of dues are being exacted from some according to the cadastral surveys, and others according to later revisions. For some the burden is light, for others heavy. The surveyors who after the destitution of Moscow were sent throughout the towns to conduct the revision, in some places out of friendship rendered a light assessment, in other places out of enmity rendered a heavy assessment. On account of this many people in the Muscovite realm suffer extreme grief.

"From the towns of the Muscovite region and from some of the border towns many inhabitants come to Moscow without leave, seeking to evade payment of taxes in their own towns. They arrive in Moscow and other nearby towns and live with relatives and friends. From other ruined borderland towns the inhabitants and other people petition that on account of their ruination they be given relief from all taxation. Many men of the towns and the surrounding countryside also pledge themselves as bondsmen to boyars and other men of rank, and so pay no dues alongside their brothers, the inhabitants of the town and surrounding district. Others petition boyars and other men of rank to protect them from violence and wrongs committed against them by the powerful.

"The great sovereign and his father, with all the consecrated assembly, the boyars, lords-in-waiting, councilors and all the people of the Muscovite realm, should call an Assembly of the Land, so that all the estates might discuss how to put all this right and reconstruct the land. Having deliberated, they should decree that honest surveyors, having been duly sworn, be sent to those towns suffering ruin from the Lithuanians and Cherkass, to inscribe and survey all the towns without accepting any bribes.

"If any men of borderland towns are living in Moscow they must be sought out and returned to where they resided before, and given tax exemption according to the extent of their ruination. Those townsmen who pledged themselves as bondsmen to the metropolitans, any of the clergy, monasteries, boyars or men of rank are to return to where they lived before, and those who received the pledges are to be responsible for all arrears in taxes accumulated over the past years.

"Harm committed by the powerful shall be investigated, and a report shall be sent to our boyars, Prince Ivan Borisovich Cherkassky,[1] Daniel Ivanovich Mezetsky[2] and their companions. All the towns, to provide information and consider measures for reconstruction, are to send to Moscow one of the clergy, two honest and prudent men from the gentry and junior boyars, and two townsmen who can itemize the damage, violence and ruination. They are also to consider how the Muscovite realm may be made whole, the soldiers paid, and how to organize the realm so that everything is as it should be."

While on one hand care was taken that townsmen not escape the tax roll and thereby leave their fellows in the lurch, on the other hand the government transferred to Moscow the richest inhabitants of the provincial towns. Thus in 1630 it was ordered that two of the townsmen of Cherdyn be brought to Moscow with their brothers, to be enrolled in the Cloth Merchants' Hundred.[3] Moreover the governor of Cherdyn received a decree saying that should the townsmen hide, the cannoneers and muster agents were to search them out. From this it can be seen whether these transfers took place voluntarily!

CONFLICT WITH GOVERNORS AND OFFICIALS

One of the chief obstacles to the reconstruction of the towns and the prosperity of its citizens was the arbitrariness of the governors and officials. In 1620 the government was compelled to send out documents containing the following. "We are informed that in the towns our governors are disobeying our decrees, doing violence to monasteries, compelling townsmen, rural inhabitants and transients to perform service, inflicting heavy exactions and losses upon them, taking bribes and excessive subsistence fees.

"The great sovereign, taking counsel with his father and in consultation with the boyars, has resolved that governors and officials are not to take bribes, gifts or subsistence fees. They are not to buy horses, clothes or any other commodity, except for foodstuffs. They are not to make overseers, junior boyars, musketeers, cossacks, cannoneers and garrison soldiers, water carriers from the town quarter and those engaged upon fortification work mill grain, grind flour or bake for them in their homes, or in the town quarter or the settlements, neither are they to cultivate land along with the townsmen or rural inhabitants, fell timber or mow hay.

"If in any of the towns the governor disobeys our decree, and we receive a petition, we will exact double the penalty from him, and he will incur our great disfavor. Also archimandrites, abbots and all the consecrated estate, gentry, junior boyars, elders, sworn officials, townsmen and all rural residents are not to give the governors or officials any bribe, gift or subsistence fee from anywhere in the town quarter or rural district. You are not to sell them any horses, livestock or any other commodity except foodstuffs. If you give the governors bribes or gifts, and this comes to our attention, double the penalty shall be exacted from you, and you also will incur our great disfavor.

"We write to you out of compassion so that you, by God's mercy and our gracious solicitude, will be enabled to live in peace and tranquillity. May you recover from your great misfortunes and ruination, no longer suffering oppression, losses or other impositions. May you be confident of the tsar's favor."

Very curious is the naïve expression encountered in these documents clearly reflecting the separation, the particularism of the separate branches of the governmental body, and the conflict between them. In the charter to the towns it is stated that the tsar is ordering his own officials to protect the towns *from his own boyars* and all others.

Yet as before the Pskov chronicler complained bitterly against the governors, as in the entry for the year 1618. "Prince Ivan Fedorovich Troekurov[4] was in Pskov, and took the fourth sheaf[5] from the monasteries and churches for the benefit of the soldiers, and given out to boyars as service tenures were the tsar's villages which previously provided support for soldiers; but for insulting the church of God and ruining the entire community he soon came to a sticky end, for in Moscow he was poisoned by a potion given him by one of his own family, and he hemorrhaged to death."

The same chronicle mentions Prince Vasily Turenin and the crown secretary Tretiak Kopnin under the years 1627-1628. "They ascribed the estates of churches and monasteries to the crown, chased donors away, took no care of monasteries and churches, so that at patronal festivals there were no masses said."

In 1632, during the administration of Prince Nikita Mezetsky and Pimen Yushkov, "many refugees came from the Lithuanian land, all manner of Russians with their wives and children, in great distress, suffering from heavy exactions and hunger for the sake of the Orthodox faith. Mezetsky and Yushkov assigned many of these refugees against their will as peasants on the estates of junior boyars, while many went shackled around the town begging alms. Those refusing to comply were held in prison until someone came to claim them as indentured slaves. The same Mezetsky and Yushkov did not allow anyone to take more than half a pud of salt out of the city, except for peasants belonging to junior boyars."

At the assembly called when the cossacks captured Azov the members of the council complained that governors were placed over towns in the interior, whereas previously there were elected magistrates. We have other information that in 1613, under Tsar Michael, governors and officials were placed in the towns. They were there during the boyar administration and under Shuisky but under Tsar Fedor Ivanovich and Tsar Boris, and even during the reign of the Renegade Monk,[6] no governors were sent there since there were judges, elected magistrates and municipal officials.

The number of towns which in 1613 received governors was thirty-three. During Michael's reign people had recourse to the old measures against malfeasance of officials appointed by the crown. They resurrected charters giving the community the right to be judged and administered by elected officials. In 1614 the charter was confirmed which Ivan IV granted to Ustiuzhna Zhelezopolskaia, which stated "the townsmen, elders, sworn officials, hundredmen and tithingmen and all peasants of prosperous, middling and lesser condition, are exempt from the jurisdiction of the district administrator and tax collectors. Let there be judges among these townsmen, to be chosen for the entire town quarter." Another charter issued to them by Ivan the Terrible was also confirmed, whereby they elected from their midst sworn officials, a hundredman and secretaries responsible for collecting all taxes. In 1622 the inhabitants of the Ustiuzhna rural districts petitioned that in previous years there were no chancellery officials among them, for disputes were resolved by judges elected by the community. Yet after the ruin of Moscow, chancellery officials began to appear among them, and they imposed heavy imposts and fines, while great losses were incurred through giving bribes and subsistence fees. The peasants were greatly impoverished through the exactions of chancellery officials, their violence and corruption. They had not the means to pay their taxes, and some peasants were absconding. They petitioned that there be no more chancellery officials among them, that they might have elected community judges as before. Since they were paying a higher quitrent than before they could not bear the pressure from the chancellery officials, with their bribes and fines, who should be recalled lest the townsmen perish utterly and the community dissolve. The tsar granted their request.

The inhabitants of the towns of Romanov and Borisoglebsk petitioned that, as before, they come under the jurisdiction of the secretary for the Chancellery for Foreign Affairs.[7] For a long time the revenues of the town were earmarked for the support of the Tatars settled nearby, who for this reason were called the Romanov Tatars. Just how loyally these Tatars served the Muscovite tsar is evident from the petition submitted in 1614 by the Savior monastery of Priluki, near Vologda. "After the Lithuanians devastated Vologda, the Siberian tsarevich Araslan Aleevich came to 'protect' it, accompanied by gentry, junior boyars, Tatars and cossacks. They exacted subsistence from us, and tortured people in the stocks mercilessly all day. At night they took our servants and peasants, stripped them of their shirts, put them in cellars and hung them up by their heels, extracting from us three hundred chetverts of oats, two hundred cartloads of hay, twenty-five chetverts of rye flour, and mutton and fowl to the value of a hundred and fifty rubles. They stole horses, dishes and tablecloths. Their chancellery officials extorted fifty rubles cash. From this torture one peasant died, while others were incapacitated for five or six weeks. Then in answer to the tsarevich's letter Baray-Murza came with his Tatars and cossacks, and ruined us utterly."

In 1627 the tsar ordered elected magistrates to be chosen in all the towns, honest nobles according to the list of more prosperous men, pure in spirit, who could be trusted to manage government business and the affairs of the community. In that case no investigators would be sent to the town for cases of robbery, brigandage or murder. These would be investigated by community officials, who would send written reports to the sovereign in Moscow. "If the gentry choose elected magistrates from the gentry and junior boyars of the middling or lesser categories, rather than from the senior category, we command that someone be picked from the list of the senior category, and he shall be appointed without any election, and we command the gentry and others to confirm this selection."

The towns sometimes asked that they not have governors, only elected magistrates. The tsar agreed, and the elected magistrate received the same kind of instructions as the governor. Concerning the replacement of elected magistrates and governors, a curious petition survives. "We had no governor," the inhabitants of Dmitrov petitioned, "but an elected magistrate. When he died, nobody was chosen to take his place. Previously Fedor Chaplin was in charge here, and he alone was entrusted with community affairs. He was in Dmitrov on the sovereign's business, and was diligent in all matters concerning the sovereign and the community. He protected peasants and townsmen, safeguarded them on all sides, did not inflict fines and heavy losses upon them. Command, O sovereign, that Fedor Chaplin be put in sole charge as before."

The sovereign agreed and Chaplin was appointed to Dmitrov in 1639, but in 1642 he was replaced by Shestakov as magistrate by appointment, and in 1644 Rtishchev was commanded to be governor in Dmitrov. This was at the petition of the citizens of all ranks, and the post of elected magistrate in Dmitrov was abolished *at their request.*

In 1641 the inhabitants of Uglich petitioned. "At your command the post of governor in Uglich is abolished, and we have been commanded instead to accept Pavel Rakov as our community magistrate, without any election. But this Pavel is inexperienced and of modest means, does much that is not in accordance with your sovereign decrees, and he is also quarrelsome. Order him dismissed, O sovereign, and let Ignaty Monomakhov from Bezhetsk be appointed in his stead to be in charge at Uglich."

In 1644 the inhabitants of Kashin petitioned. "According to your decree Savva Speshnev was nominated to be our community magistrate, but he is disgraceful and decrepit, he has no control over his arms and legs. Here in front of the town hall, in the town quarter and in the countryside there is much brigandage, plundering and murder, and all of it goes unpunished. Previously in Kashin there were governors and elected elders, and at that time there was not such murder, plundering and violence. Grant, O sovereign, that we have governors as before, and appoint as our governor Dementy Lazarev, one of the Moscow gentry." The tsar granted this request.

From this we can see that the towns did not share the opinions expressed by the traders at the Assembly of the Land, incessantly demanding the replacement of governors by community magistrates. On the contrary, they requested governors, but at the same time specified whom they wanted as governor so in a sense the governor became a sort of chosen or elected official.

The inhabitants of the town of Shuia carried on a running feud with successive community magistrates during Michael's reign. In 1614 they complained about their magistrate Kalachov. "In the year before last, 1612, Posnik Kalachov came to Shuia as a community magistrate, and he started lording it over the townsmen, with lies, slanders, trickery and concealment. He constantly orders us to bring him subsistence, such as bread, meat, fish, honey and wine. He drives our livestock into his own compound, he beats us, the townsmen abscond on account of his violence, and our own houses are abandoned. We did not elect this Posnik as our magistrate." This last circumstance is explained by the fact that Kalachov arrived at Shuia in 1612, still during the Time of Troubles.

In 1618 they complained about the investigator Beklemishev and the community magistrate Krotky, saying that they were using criminals to bring false accusations against townsmen, they were receiving bribes from brigands and bandits to let them out of the jail, and because of this malpractice Shuia was becoming desolate. They themselves released their peasants and then arrested them as fugitives, and incited them to make denunciations against townsmen.

In 1621 there was a quarrel between the governor and the community magistrates of Shuia. The governor asserted that through negligence of the magistrates criminals were escaping from prison. In revenge for this denun-ciation the magistrates put one of the governor's peasants in jail without cause. The magistrates complained that the governors were interfering with their work, were not delivering criminals to them, and moreover ordered one of the magistrates to be beaten with rods and canes. The clergy and townsmen when questioned declared that the governor never beat any magistrate.

Interestingly enough, the magistrate accused by his own community of perjury remained in place. In 1622 the tsar forbade him and his colleague to intervene in any case involving death caused *by a sinful act* in the town quarter. "If anyone hangs himself, or injures himself, or gets drunk, perishes in fire or drowns, or if a corpse is washed up on the riverbank by the town quarter, or if people get into a fight when drunk, the municipal magistrate and his colleague are not to intervene, because when they did so they jailed innocent townsmen or exacted excessive fines."

The inhabitants of Shuia petitioned against Kishkin in 1635 because he did not permit townsmen who brought an accusation against a bandit to come to a visual confrontation[8] with the accused, and because of his idle self-indulgence Kishkin could not be bothered to interrogate him. The inhabitants of Shuia then expressly requested that the magistrate and the investigator not have competence in matters of robbery or brigandage without the governor's supervision.

In 1627 the inhabitants of Ustiug petitioned. "Five clerks sit in the Ustiug town hall. Others when they arrived in Ustiug purchased tax-paying houses in the town quarter. Each of these clerks has a young assistant, and they have enriched themselves greatly. They have appropriated the best hamlets in the countryside, neither do they pay taxes on their houses along with the townsmen, and only half the dues from the hamlets. Some of them obtain donations by threats, and they refuse to pay many community dues. Then they take turns riding through the rural districts on government business, and they exact large cash payments, subsistence allowance, wine and beer. The clerks collect the land tax from us and send it to Moscow, but do not carry out the wishes of the community. They exact a cartage due of one altyn per ruble, take extra money in excess of the apportionment, and do not enter it in the ledger. They also demand of the whole community a salary of twenty rubles each. Perhaps the number of clerks in the town hall can be limited to three, as there were before, and without any salary, since their expenses can be defrayed out of the revenues alone. Order, O sovereign, three junior clerks to be dispatched from Moscow to Ustiug, or choose clerks from the Ustiug community, and recall these senior clerks." After the matter was investigated, the clerks were retired from service.

The towns close to Moscow, in the event of a clash between the governors and the magistrates, might appeal to the tsar. From distant regions, from Siberia, petitions could not reach Moscow rapidly, so the population of these distant places used means that the population of nearby towns also used, though not individually, but collectively. Governors and clergy were sent to the Lena with instructions that the inhabitants everywhere were to provide free transportation services. When they arrived at Fort Yeniseisk the local governor Verevkin summoned to the town hall the servicemen, townsmen, agricultural peasants, transient traders and merchants from the various towns, and demanded transportation services from them. The servicemen replied that they could not provide transportation services. "Previously we were not instructed by the treasury, nor by any previous governor appointed by the sovereign, to perform transportation duties. We did not provide oarsmen. There was no decree about this from the sovereign before, neither is there any now. If the governor requires us to mount town guard or to man the outposts, we gladly will provide transportation services for that, but if these duties are not required we will not provide transportation, since we dare not abandon the sovereign's town." "If the governor lets us off the tsar's tithe,"[9] said the agricultural peasants, "we will all perform transportation services; if not, we will not perform them."

For several days in a row the governor summoned them and urged them to perform transportation services, but each time met with the same refusal. Then the governor ordered the confinement of the more senior servicemen and townsmen, and the elected elders of the agricultural peasants, after which they were beaten in the stocks. The Yeniseisk servicemen and townsmen all went in mass with their leaders to the prison and to the stocks, saying "Why don't you imprison us all, and put us all in the stocks? God and the tsar know that we are being called upon to perform transportation services without the sovereign's decree." Refusing to perform transportation services, they all dispersed.

Golovin, governor of Yakutsk, kept his colleagues Matvey Glebov and the crown secretary Filatov in jail for two whole years. In seven prisons Golovin held more than a hundred servicemen, traders and businessmen. Grigory Kokorev, governor of Mangazeia, also was accused by his colleague Andrei Palitsyn of oppression and embezzlement. "The Samoyed came with their fur tribute, and the governor and his wife sent to them with some contraband wine. The wretched savages drank themselves naked and the tribute they brought, consisting of sables and beaver, went to the governor, while the Samoyed paid their tribute in reindeer hides. Some strip the reindeer hide clothes off themselves and their wives, and give these as tribute since everything else has been drunk away and plundered. If a trader or businessman fails to call on the governor, his wife or son, with gifts, he is thrown into jail, and also his dogs are impounded, so that he has to pay ransom both for himself and his dogs. When the governors hold a banquet, if any trader or merchant brings the governor only a small gift, the offering is thrown back in his face and he is hustled out of the house. In the market hall the governor takes goods from the traders without payment. Every day merchants visit his son to drink contraband wine. Whoever pays one grivna is given one glass, whoever pays two grivnas is given two glasses, and so on. When these men have drunk their fill, on their way out they are robbed of their crosses and girdles, while some even pawn the shirts off their backs. Traders are plagued with futile missions. Twenty or thirty prosperous men are singled out for service in the tundra, from which they never return, while others who apparently are in debt over their heads are able to bribe their way out. The tsar's decree is falsified and displayed in the town hall, while the true decree is hidden in the governor's house."

Kokorev for his part denounced Andrei Palitsyn for keeping a tavern where he corrupted others through drunkenness and himself got drunk. A certain clergyman, Palitsyn's confessor, denounced Kokorev. Another priest denounced Palitsyn and his confessor, accusing them of sodomy, criminal conspiracy and blasphemy. Palitsyn accused Kokorev of going into town and to church like a bandit chief. A two-edged sword was carried before him as it was before the Renegade Monk, and all his followers were armed with muskets and sabres like the retinue of a German elector. He gave his adherents exalted rank, calling one of his slaves a majordomo, another his treasurer and others his table attendants.

When Kokorev went to take a bath his boon companions, counselors and priests came to greet him and enquire after his health. When he gazed at them, they were so afraid that they bowed low to the ground. When Kokorev's wife came to take a bath, all women of the town quarter were required to turn out and pay their respects to her. If a child belonging to one of Kokorev's attendants died, the women of the town quarter had to come and act as mourners. Whoever was accused by Kokorev of negligence was thrown into jail or tortured in the stocks. These unfortunate people took all their possessions to Kokorev's wife, or sent them with the priest Sosna, for everyone said that whoever wished to escape harm must go to the universal intercessor, who could do as she pleased, even delivering victims from the gallows.

Matters reached such extremes that the two governors were at open war with one another. Kokorev with his henchmen and musketeers opened fire from the citadel at the town quarter where Palitsyn resided, and several were killed. Kokorev excused himself by saying this was in retaliation for an assault carried out on the citadel by Andrei Palitsyn and his adherents.

Apart from oppression by governors and chancellery officials, the inhabitants of towns suffered much from bandit raids which, as we know, were numerous even before, but must have increased after the recent Troubles and cossack rule. Brigands roved in bands. To combat them the government appointed table attendants who patrolled with armed detachments in full military equipment.

In 1618 peasants belonging to Prince Mstislavsky petitioned. "Before the Feast of the Intercession [October 1] the Cherkass came and slew many peasants in the Yaropolch district. No sooner did the Cherkass leave than the Yaropolch district was overrun by cossacks, who set up their encampment in the Voznikovsk free settlement. Then they were joined by servants and peasants of Prince Dmitry Mikhailovich Pozharsky and adherents of junior boyars from Murom and Gorokhovets, peasants and rustics from Starodub. Together with the cossacks they devastated the district of Yaropolch. Prince Dmitry Pozharsky's carters brought wine and mead to these cossacks, and traded in all kinds of articles in the marketplace. When all the wine and mead was sold out, they bought up the chattels of our peasants. Horses, cattle and all manner of clothing were taken, and livestock was driven off to the service tenures and patrimonies of their own boyars."

Overseers of small service tenures and their peasants committed brigandage, conducting petty raids, at night attacking wayfarers through the forest. Overseers of large, strong landholders operated on a much larger scale. In 1645 the inhabitants of Shuia petitioned Prince Yakov Kudenetovich Cherkassky. "We are complaining about the behavior of your overseer Beschastny Cherkasheninov, of the village of Ivanovo-Kokhma. Last year, around St. Nicholas day in the spring [May 9], at the market of Pupko, Beschastny and your peasants beat our townsmen half to death, overturned their booths and upset their wares. Bread, fancy loaves, meat and pies were thrown into the mud. We then petitioned you to order an inquiry and give redress according to the results of that investigation. Then this year, on July 24, Beschastny came to the marketplace at Shuia, accompanied by many peasants, enraged at our earlier petition against him. He wanted to assault us but we were aware what he was up to, so instead of sitting at our benches or in our booths we hid from him and remained within our houses, waiting for him to leave Shuia. But Beschastny went around the marketplace and streets with a sword, followed by peasants with clubs, canes and stakes, demanding tribute and boasting they would kill us.

Saburov, overseer of the court village of Dunilovo, petitioned against Tvorogov, overseer of the village of Vasilievskoe, also belonging to Prince Cherkassky. "Tvorogov travels to the market in Shuia and to Dunilovo accompanied by many men, up to twenty, forty or more. They call themselves cossacks, and they assault the sovereign's peasants along the roads and in the hamlets. They plunder, demand wagons and horses, defile maidens and children, shoot all kinds of game and go around demanding grain. This year they came to the market and forced their way into the home of the peasant Neverov. When the market was assembled Tvorogov emerged from the house and grabbed cloth and yarn belonging to the sovereign's peasants, whom he also assaulted. When I, Saburov, sent my men to dissuade him, he ordered that my followers be beaten to death and robbed in the middle of the marketplace. When I came out into the street to speak to him, asking why he ordered the assault on the sovereign's peasants, he abused me with all manner of unbefitting speech, and ordered his cossacks to slay me, but the inhabitants came to my rescue. I went back to my house and stayed indoors, then Tvorogov with many of his followers followed me there, fired at my house with arrows and muskets and battered down the door. I barely got away, rescued by the local people, and they plundered my house." Musketeers whenever they got the chance also resorted to brigandage. The governor of Archangel in 1630 reported that a hundred musketeers dispatched from Kholmogory and Fort Pustozersk were committing brigandage at Kedrov and along the Mezen, plundering the peasants and ravishing their wives, and their captain had lost control of them completely. It was difficult to deal with brigandage in a sparsely populated land covered with dense forest; besides, the means were not at hand. When large bands of outlaws appeared no sooner were gentry and junior boyars summoned and equipped to deal with them than suddenly the order came for them to report for frontier service, leaving the bandits to be dealt with by minor monastic servitors, townsmen and levies from the rural inhabitants. The governor wrote that these monastic servitors were unfit and untrained, only to receive from Moscow the reply "You yourselves must pursue the brigands, dispatching the community magistrate with all the remaining gentry and junior boyars." This soon turned into a laughing matter, for the gentry and junior boyars left behind were retired through old age, infirmity or sickness.

Complaints were heard that community magistrates were lenient towards criminals on account of their own idle self-indulgence, yet the magistrates of Shuia submitted the following petition against the community sworn official. "He came drunk from the tavern and released a criminal from the jail, the prostitute Asiutka whom he wanted for a bed companion, but he fell asleep in a drunken stupor. The woman Asiutka took from around his neck the keys to the jail and released seven criminals, robbers and bandits, for at that time the warder was at home at supper."

Not only townsmen suffered at the hands of magnates' officials. Gentry and junior boyars also petitioned that wherever taxpaying townsmen lived as dependents of the powerful, or were in pledge to monasteries, they did much harm to peasants belonging to the gentry in the urban settlements, around the marketplaces, in the free settlements and in the town quarters. "They plunder and kill our servants and peasants, they exact tolls on highways, ferries or causeways in excess of the sovereign's decree. In the towns the governors and chancellery officials do not bring them to justice, alleging they are forbidden to judge them within the towns." As a result of this petition a decree was issued that liquor license holders and toll collectors would be judged by the chancellery which issued their instructions. Whoever exacted at ferries and causeways tolls in excess of those stipulated by the tsar's decree would be knouted, and a fine would be exacted from the license holder at the rate of one altyn per ruble. If anyone, of whatever rank, exacted from the waters or highways running through their estates tolls at any roadblocks, ferries or fords, or established new mills which caused the waters to rise, all these mills, fords and ferries were to be dismantled.

NOVGOROD

When Great Novgorod was returned to Moscow under the terms of the Peace of Stolbovo[10] its inhabitants were given exemption from all taxes for three years. The governors appointed were Prince Ivan Andreevich Khovansky[11] and the table attendant Prince Fedor Yeletsky, with two crown secretaries. The governors were ordered to make a list of all the gentry and junior boyars ordered to serve with them in Novgorod. They were also to seek out and punish defaulters. Those who had only a small estate or none at all were each to be given an eighth share for their subsistence until they received a proper service tenure.

They were to take a survey of the artillery and stocks of munitions, make a list of the cannoneers, and of who would serve where in case of a siege, ensuring that every station would be manned. The governors and crown secretaries were responsible for assigning trustworthy men to guard the gates. For the citadel two trustworthy nobles were to be selected, to see to it that there were adequate grain supplies and all else necessary for defense, that artillery was placed at all the gates in good firing order. They were to supervise the opening and closing of the gates, and were to bring the keys to the boyar and governor Prince Khovansky in the stone citadel.

Prince Khovansky was to reside in the great stone citadel, Prince Yeletsky in another fortified place, and the secretaries were to live where previous secretaries had their quarters. For the opening and closing of the gates a special bell was to be cast, and another to signal the alert for the town garrison. Powder and all munitions were to be kept in a stone enclosure in the treasury building, or in a strong cellar. A municipal administrator was to be placed in charge of this powder magazine, and pickets were to be placed to ensure against fire.

In the event of a siege Finns, Latvians (Letts) or Russian peasants from borderland towns were not to be allowed into the citadel. They were to be kept in the town quarter, beyond the moats, but their wives and small children could be allowed into the citadel.

Junior boyars were to be appointed to close down unlicensed taverns, so that no liquor be sold anywhere except in the sovereign's taverns. These junior boyars, in order to set a good example, were not permitted to keep liquor in their own houses. Other gentry, junior boyars, merchants and traders might keep liquor in their houses for their own use, but not for sale. Should anyone engage in illegal sale of liquor, for the first offense the tavern was to be closed down and a two-ruble fine exacted. If a junior boyar committed a second such offense he was to be imprisoned for a while and double the fine exacted. A townsman, musketeer, cossack or cannoneer committing a second such offense was to be knouted, imprisoned and fined double.

Strict order must be kept, and the crier was ordered to announce several times in succession that no crime or bodily assault would be tolerated, neither any robbery or malicious deed. Cabins and bath houses were not to be heated in summer, people were not to sit around open fires in the evening, and any cooking or baking must be in ovens within enclosed spaces.

Latvians from the borderlands and Finns from the Novgorod district, as well as Germans and Finns from the borderlands, if they came with grain or on any other business, were not to be allowed into the citadel. A couple of houses were to be set aside for them in the town quarter. Two reliable junior boyars were to be appointed to watch over their movements and see that they suffered no harm from the Russians. If a dispute arose between them and the Russians the matter was to be judged in the town quarter by those captains to whom the foreign merchants' hostel was entrusted, and the governor had the final decision.

If townsmen from Muscovy proper arrived in Novgorod intending to take up residence there, and they asked for tax exemption, they were to be interrogated and ordered to live in the town quarter. They were to be assigned places outside the built-up area and beyond the outer walls. Their names were to be inscribed in a register, and information was to be sent to the sovereign concerning the taxation district from which they came, and how long ago.

Great care was to be taken that Germans and Latvians coming to Novgorod did not purchase from borderland people grain or any other commodity, or drive livestock across the border. Traders from beyond the sea were forbidden to export grain or any other kind of foodstuffs. A special hostel was to be built for the Germans within the Commercial Side, surrounded by a small enclosure.

A special place was to be designated for draymen, and as many as were needed were to be hired. They were to unload ships and take all goods to the market hall. Nobody else was to be allowed to convey these goods, and the draymen were to be paid a regular wage.

If goods from wrecked foreign ships were washed up on shore, these goods were to be salvaged and returned to the foreigner to whom they belonged, reserving a tenth share for the sovereign.

Governors were forbidden to accept gifts from foreigners or Russians in any form. If foreigners brought any such honorarium, it was not to be accepted. They might be allowed to visit Prince Khovansky in his residence, but in other towns they were to present themselves at the gates in the morning, five or six at a time, not all at once. Foreigners from overseas were not to be allowed into the stone citadel.

A market hall was to be built in Novgorod lest merchants set up shop elsewhere. In the case of the hostels for the crews of Italian or French ships storerooms were to be attached, where costly merchandise and all kinds of non-bulky goods could be kept. Food and drink must be kept for these foreigners from overseas by the doorkeepers assigned to these hostels, while a junior boyar and sworn officials were to be appointed to guarantee the security of these lodgings. Servicemen, junior boyars, cannoneers, musketeers and cossacks were not to be allowed into these quarters lest these foreign guests be cheated, robbed or suffer any other kind of criminality at their hands. Bulky merchandise such as herrings, salt, honey lead, sulfuric acid and mead were to be stored in bonded warehouses beyond the town, but foreigners could store non-bulky goods in their own storehouses. Russians also might store their goods such as flax, hemp, suet and wax in the market halls. Sables, squirrel furs and all other such precious merchandise were to be stored in town, for which purpose warehouses were to be provided.

In times of unrest the foreigners should transfer their wares from the market halls into the citadel, there to be stored in cellars or halls, whichever was more secure, but flax, wax and hemp were to be stored in stone cellars, where they would be fireproof. The streets were to be patrolled every night by two junior boyars accompanied by a detachment of ten townsmen to see that there was no robbery, and particularly to see that the area around the market hall was secure. Cannoneers, musketeers, cossacks and doorkeepers were forbidden to trade with the foreigners, and care must be taken that they committed no crimes against either foreign or Russian traders. They should be tested to see whether they could shoot, and if not they were to be replaced with those who could. Slaves of boyars, taxpayers and agricultural peasants could not be enrolled among the musketeers and cossacks, only free volunteers.

Before the catastrophe there was a mint in Novgorod. The governors were to gather together the former master coiners and find others, in order to reconstitute the mint. Dengas after the old pattern were to be minted, and also efimoks.[12] For security a reliable junior boyar was to be appointed to guard the mint, as also a leading merchant or trader, together with a sworn official to be chosen by the whole town. Election was to be by show of hands, and the oath must be administered to the successful candidate. Master coiners were to be told that the sovereign granted them their previous salaries, and great care was to be taken that the coins be minted of pure silver. No coins were to be made of copper or pewter, neither must there be any alloy of copper or tin, lest the sovereign's coinage be debased. All governors were to act according to this sovereign decree and any subsequent decrees, taking into account local conditions. Concerning weighty and important matters, they were to call upon the metropolitan and consult with him as to what would be in the sovereign's interest and be most profitable for him.

MILITARY CAPACITY

In 1626 the number of men in Novgorod capable of bearing arms was 2,752. Of these the gentry and junior boyars from all the fifths numbered 1,297; converts, Tatars and Cherkass receiving service tenures or subsistence, 36. There were 564 musketeers, with two captains and eight company commanders, 355 cossacks, 20 cannoneers and gatekeepers. Others included clerks on duty or dispatched on missions, 35, and townsmen and other taxpayers with assorted weapons, 435. As for the Novgorod bytowns, in Ladoga there were 298, Porkhov 75, Staraia Rusa 70.

In Pskov there were 4,807, of which 3,130 were townsmen, despite the fact that in 1615 three hundred families were transferred to Moscow. In Toropets there were 1,103, in Torzhok 567. In Tver there were 178, including 85 townsmen. In Kashin there were 61, in Ustiuzhna Zhelezopolskaia 335, of which 300 were townsmen, one hundred with muskets and two hundred with pikes. In Yaroslavl there were 2,480, including townsmen, all manner of palace attendants, gatekeepers and work hands, 459 with muskets and 1,669 with pikes. In addition the Savior monastery provided greater and lesser servitors, and all kinds of servants to a total of 73 armed with muskets and 51 with pikes. In Kostroma there were 1,297, including 1,200 townsmen; in Vologda 1,091, including 800 townsmen; in Vladimir 370, including 50 wage-earning truck gardeners, 128 townsmen, 62 gatekeepers, 17 peasants from the patriarch's free settlement, 31 peasants belonging to the cathedral clergy and two peasants belonging to the estates of the St. Dmitry cathedral. Suzdal could field 419, including 258 townsmen; Arzamas 650; Kolomna 558, including 287 townsmen; Aleksin 90, including five townsmen and inhabitants of crown estates; Kaluga 1,068, including 422 townsmen; Viazma 1,321, including 302 townsmen; Mozhaisk 431, including 34 townsmen; Volokolamsk 106, including 27 townsmen; Borovsk 280, of which 58 were townsmen; Bolkhov 318, of which 167 were townsmen and all manner of wage laborers; Voronezh 1,168, including 37 townsmen; in Elets 1,486, including 25 work hands.

For 1635 we have additional figures. In Vladimir, for example, instead of 128 townsmen there were now 184, and the number of gatekeepers increased from 62 to 100, but the number of truck gardeners decreased from 50 to 33. In Suzdal instead of 419 townsmen we find only 302; in Borovsk the number increased from 58 to 65. The numbers in Kaluga remained constant. In Voronezh there was a startling increase from 37 townsmen to 375. We hazard a guess that the larger figure includes 101 who were peasants belonging to the monastery and the quitrent paying settlement, who were enumerated separately in 1626 but not in 1635. In Great Novgorod also there was a large jump, from 435 townsmen to 1,097, including their children, brothers, nephews and hired hands. But in Pskov there was a sharp decrease, from 3,130 to 1,057, including children, brothers, nephews and hired hands. The sharp increase in Novgorod and the sharp decline in Pskov can be explained by the fact that the Novgorod townsmen fled from Swedish depredations primarily to Pskov, then gradually returned, while in Pskov gathered not only refugees from Novgorod but also from other ruined towns, since throughout the Troubles Pskov never was under enemy occupation.

TRADE AND COMMERCE

The insignificant number of townsmen and other urban inhabitants taking part in trade and commerce demonstrates that during Michael's reign this activity in the Muscovite realm was scarcely in a flourishing condition. The havoc caused by the Time of Troubles, the sacrifices made for the hard war against Poland, oppression by governors and strongmen, the lamentable state of the law, monopolies granted by the treasury, bad roads, lack of security on those roads by reason of banditry, lack of education and the consequent narrowness of vision, the pettiness and unscrupulousness in grubbing for profits—all these things led to Russian traders being poor and their businesses failing. Even if we assume that they were being untruthful and exaggerating their poverty in order to evade sacrifices, the motives which caused them to act this way could scarcely be conducive to the expansion of trade and commerce.

To what extent monopolies were farmed out is evident from the following petition, pertaining to the year 1639. "We are aware that in the towns ascribed to the Chancellery for Novgorod in recent times monopolies were granted for kvas, must, beer, fish and vegetable soup, hop and hay drying, soap boiling, oats, tar and other petty enterprises, through which all manner of townsmen used to make their living and pay their taxes. Previously such small enterprises were not granted out as monopolies to anyone, but now on account of them many townsmen have become impoverished. The sovereign therefore should order all these newly granted monopolies abolished."

The same situation is evident from the writing of the Pskov chronicler, who stated that in 1627 and 1628, at the instigation of the governor and crown secretary, a monopoly was granted over kvas brewers, draymen, tar manufacturers and bath house proprietors, and even over public scribes in the market place, in exchange for a quitrent. In 1629 in Moscow Ivan Nikitich Romanov's agent Khmelevsky and his companions bought up all the Pskov taverns and sold wine at four altyns a glass, and moreover gave short measure. Others bought up taverns in the rural districts.

A man of some substance must have lived in constant fear for his property and for his peace of mind, because he was incessantly the target for those wishing to live at others' expense, and such were to be found not only among the cossacks. From Moscow to Pskov there came gentry, junior boyars and all manner of traders bearing false summons, demanding that prosperous citizens appear in court in Moscow. To avoid undertaking the prohibitively expensive journey or suffer the notorious Moscow delays and corruption, they paid compensation without knowing what for, sometimes shelling out more than ten rubles. Consequently the elders representing the entire city petitioned the tsar that cases involving citizens be settled in Pskov, except for serious criminal charges. The tsar granted this request.

The inhabitants of Shuia petitioned Prince Prozorovsky concerning his servant Akinfov, alleging that he issued summons to six men of Shuia, bringing false accusations and causing great losses and damages. He also boasted ahead of time that he would cite other townsmen, causing them also great losses and damages.

The communal structure of the towns preserved the right to submit direct petitions to the tsar and magnates on behalf of the entire community without, as we have seen, raising the possibility of collective defense should the local chancellery official take it into his head to march into the town quarter uttering threats. Forms alone did not help, however good they may have been. The communal structure, on the other hand, preserved the right to complain collectively against malfeasance, though there were no safeguards against ruin and extortion when the whole community was obliged to pay taxes on derelict homesteads, which multiplied in some of the towns. In 1640 the inhabitants of Shuia petitioned that in 1631 they had, according to the cadastral surveys, 154 tax-paying households. In 1639 there were 32 abandoned homesteads, and in 1640 eighty-two homesteads were destroyed by fire. There were now another forty abandoned dwellings. When the community was surveyed stock was taken of all the businesses and partnerships, and it was discovered that all was lost in the fire. Both before and after the fire the community was being pressed for the 1639 arrears in property tax. The petition ends with the habitual refrain "Have pity on us, your orphans, lest we perish utterly or disperse."

The community availed itself of the right to complain, complaints were heard and petitions were granted, since the government did not connive at malfeasance. In 1639 the inhabitants of Shuia petitioned that Ivan Tarbeev, who was appointed to investigate illicit taverns and tobacco smuggling, was supposed to take petitions from the townsmen, who were to point out those who "drank" tobacco and those who supplied them. The townsmen said they did not know, but Ivan Tarbeev for his own profit suborned those idlers into accusing the townsmen of concealing contraband tobacco. He exacted ruinous fines from the townsmen, many of whom absconded, abandoning their wives, children and businesses. Ivan Tarbeev took these wives and children and placed them under arrest, bringing the women out of the jail into his bed for fornication, threatening them with torture and flogging in the marketplace, and ordering them to denounce other inhabitants for possessing contraband tobacco.

The government was not inattentive to this case, and dispatched Andrei Palitsyn to investigate the matter. Palitsyn was impartial towards Tarbeev, but the Shuia community again petitioned, this time not to the sovereign but to the powerful boyar Prince Ivan Borisovich Cherkassky, saying that Palitsyn tortured Tarbeev, but also was torturing some of the townsmen, some of them to death, on matters irrelevant to the investigation.

FOREIGN MERCHANTS AND TRADERS

Understandably under these circumstances Russian traders were poor and could not compete with rich foreigners. We saw that at the beginning of the reign the English received a charter granting free trade exempt from duty. The Russian traders alleged that this was because the English bribed the crown secretary Tretiakov. We cannot accept this explanation, knowing the special relationship the new Muscovite government had with England. The English were obliged to deposit in the tsar's treasury cloth and other goods in exchange for the price they would have brought in England. They were not to export silk, nor produce tobacco or other goods. Throughout the towns the governors were to see to it that the English did not receive Russians as pledge men.

In 1613 a charter was granted to a German named Buck, granting him free trade in exchange for his past and present service to the Muscovite sovereign. The same year a charter was given to a foreigner named Ivan Yuriev, giving him the right to trade freely in all Russian towns in exchange for the ruin he suffered at the hands of the Poles. In 1614 there was a charter to a consortium of Dutch merchants granting them free trade and exemption from duties, but only for three years, and that in compensation for the losses the company sustained during the Time of Troubles. At the expiry of the three years they were to pay half the normal tariffs. "On account of their being foreigners" they were to be exempt from the jurisdiction of the town governors and officials, except in major criminal matters; for civil suits they would be judged in the Chancellery for Foreign Affairs. If judgment involved the kissing of the cross, not they but their servants would take the oath. No taxes, dues or imposts would be levied on their dwellings. Finally the Dutch were permitted to keep liquor on their own premises.

In 1619 the Novgorod customs chiefs, leading merchants, elders and all the townsmen complained against a Dutchman named Samuel Leontiev, saying that he lived in the town quarter on taxable premises. Nobody knew why he kept this establishment. He did not set up in the market hall with all the other foreigners, he kept goods in his house, he did not declare his goods for the tsar's duties at the customs house, he traded retail in all manner of goods, and commissioned Russians to do business on his behalf in the trading settlements beyond the Onega. He bought up grain, fish and other commodities and exported them to German cities.

The sovereign ordered the governors to inquire of the Dutchman why he did all these things. They should exact duty from him, expel him and forbid further entry into Novgorod of any foreign merchants not possessing a charter from the tsar, except for the Swedes. The Hanseatic cities, at the request of the Dutch States-General, received the right to trade freely, but later lost it. We saw that pursuant to the Treaty of Stolbovo the Swedes were free to trade in the Russian towns. In 1629 the tsar wrote to the Novgorod governors "Traders come from across the border to our side and trade illegally in every commodity, going around the hamlets without paying duty. As long ago as 1625 Russian traders were given strict instructions that they could trade in all the Swedish towns, but not in the villages or hamlets. Likewise we command that the Swedes be told not to trade in villages or hamlets."

The Pskov chroniclers complained against foreigners in general for depressing trade. In an entry for 1632 we read "The Germans brought a trading charter from Moscow, enabling them to establish a trading post in Pskov, to enter the city and do business. Archbishop Joasaph[13] and the men of Pskov petitioned the sovereign that the Germans not be allowed to reside in Pskov, but the petition was rejected, Joasaph was deprived of his blessing and office, and many Germans entered Pskov, rode all about the town unhindered, and surveyed the site where the German trading post was to be. In 1636 they took business away from the men of Pskov. They did not trade in linen with the general public, since a leading merchant was sent from Moscow to buy it all for the sovereign at a price fixed in Moscow. The monasteries and all the people suffered great hardship thereby. The money was paid in debased coinage, the price was fixed, the transaction was not amicable, there was great grief over everything and unprecedented enmity, and the whole land was paralyzed, since nobody dared buy or sell anything."

Several times leading merchants, members of the Merchants' and Cloth Merchants' Hundred and traders from many towns[14] —Kazan, Nizhny Novgorod, Kostroma, Yaroslavl, Suzdal, Murom, Vologda, Ustiug, Romanov, Galich, Uglich, Kargopol, Beloozero, Kholmogory and many other towns—presented to the sovereign their complaint about foreigners—English, Dutch and natives of Hamburg—who used the tsar's charter to travel to Moscow and many other towns with many commodities, whereas under previous sovereigns no foreign traders other than the English did business anywhere except in the town of Archangel. Now they traveled to all the towns, bringing with them other foreigners not having charters from the sovereign, whom they call their brothers, nephews and officials. "They pass off these interlopers' goods as their own, and also smuggle goods in without paying duty. The merchants themselves travel everywhere, buying up Russian goods to sell secretly in Archangel to other foreigners without paying duty. They conspire with these other foreigners from overseas to sell these goods at a loss, so as to put us out of business, on which account Russian traders have ceased to travel to Archangel. The fairs have declined, the tsar's treasury is suffering losses, and we are utterly ruined. These same foreigners have deprived us of all the remaining shipping business. Between Vologda and Archangel, both upstream and downstream, they carry their own goods in their barges and rent cargo space to Russians and foreigners."

We noted how Astrakhan trade with the Orient suffered on account of Zarutsky, when merchants from Bukhara and Gilian[15] were forced to flee. When Astrakhan was liberated from Zarutsky trade picked up. The instructions to the Astrakhan governor read "Make a list of merchants from Bukhara and Gilian presently living in the hostel in Astrakhan and doing business on behalf of their rulers, where they came from, whether they intend to leave for their own country or reside permanently in Astrakhan, in what commodities they are dealing, and how much of their turnover goes into the sovereign's treasury." Tsar Michael gave permission for merchants from Bukhara to proceed with their wares to Kazan, Astrakhan, Archangel and other coastal towns, to hire transport and purchase vessels. Governors were not to detain them except for debt or major crimes.

Concerning Persian trade, the Muscovite merchants declared that many Russian merchants were engaged in it, from many towns. As for Persians trading in Russia, the following instructions were given to the governor of Astrakhan. "Tell merchants from Persia, Bukhara and Gilian to set up in the hostel for Bukhara and Gilian merchants, and let them trade with Russians in the marketplace and yurt Tatars in the Tatar bazaar in specified goods, except for the shah's commercial agents doing business on behalf of the tsar's household. These are permitted to buy for the shah all variety of goods: Nogay slaves, birds, hawks, falcons, gerfalcons and parrots. Apart from gerfalcons, no duty is to be levied on any of the shah's goods, but see to it that the shah's agents purchase nothing on their own behalf. If traders from the shah's towns arrive in Astrakhan the governors are to send junior boyars, customs officials and clerks, who are to record the names of those arriving, how many are accompanying them and what goods they are bringing. If these traders do business in Astrakhan, charge them the full duty; if they proceed upstream along the Volga, charge them tolls; where they do not sell their goods, charge them transit fees. Take care that when the Persians enter the sovereign's towns they do not abduct the Nogay or any other of the sovereign's subjects. Persian merchants are not to be detained in Astrakhan, so that disputes with the shah may be avoided." Turkish merchants were forbidden to trade in Astrakhan or on the Terek. Nogay and yurt Tatars were prohibited from selling horses to Russians for export to Muscovy.[16] The Tatars themselves were to drive their horses to Moscow and not dare sell them anywhere along the way. The Astrakhan governors were to promise them that when they drove their horses to Moscow the tsar would reward them and give them a personal audience.

In 1643 the governors of Astrakhan received the following document from the tsar. "Ambassadors from the khan of Khiva have petitioned us saying that Russians passed from Astrakhan through the Khiva khanate[17] but the khan would not let them pass, though if they wished to sell off their goods in Astrakhan he would provide an escort. When Khiva merchants tried to get to Astrakhan and arrived at the sea, our traders petitioned the chancellery officials not to allow the Khiva merchants to board the ships, so they were forced to sell their goods at a loss. The officials told them they could not board the ships, but must sell their goods on the spot. If they did not wish to trade, they could take their goods back home. You must allow the Khiva merchants to board the ships and proceed to Astrakhan." Thus trade was restricted, subjected to other interests and other demands, as is evident from the tsar's command to Astrakhan not to sell precious furs lest the value of the tsar's gifts to the shah be diminished.

Foreigners eagerly purchased grain in Russia, but the export of grain was a treasury monopoly. In this respect the tsar's document to the leading merchant Tarakanov and his partners, who bought grain on behalf of the treasury, is quite remarkable. "You were ordered to purchase grain on our behalf in Vologda and other towns—rye, barley, wheat, buckwheat, ground millet and linseed—and send this grain to the granaries. In spring bring these grains by boat to Archangel to be sold to the foreigners. The granaries and ships used to transport it are to be taken care of out of the treasury. Now the abbot of the St. Anthony monastery on the Sii petitions us that the monastery normally buys grain in Vologda because it cannot grow enough on its lands for its own needs. So you, in accordance with our charter, forbade him to purchase grain. You are to allow the brethren of the Sii monastery to purchase grain as they did before, only you must take care that the monastery officials, peasants and other monastic servants do not hoard grain and conspire to sell it to foreigners. If anyone does sell grain to the foreigners they are to be imprisoned and their grain confiscated."

FOREIGN EXPERTS

If Russian merchants, perceiving that they could not compete with the foreigners, wanted them banished from the interior of the realm, they had no motive for wishing the same on foreign entrepreneurs, who alone could show them the advantage of certain enterprises and teach them certain artisanal skills. More especially the government eagerly sought to attract from abroad skilled prospectors for gold, silver and other precious metals to replenish the tsar's exhausted treasury. In 1626 a safe conduct was sent to England to a squire named John Bulmer, who was skilled in prospecting for gold, silver and copper, who also knew how to find precious stones, and had sufficient knowledge where they might be found. In 1628 there were two prospectors, Fritsch and Herold, from the Holy Roman empire. In 1640 the Englishmen Cartwright with eleven master craftsmen came to search for gold and silver, but found none, and according to their agreement had to foot all expenses connected with the search. In 1642 the boyar Prince Boris Repnin went to Tver to prospect for gold, but in vain.

There was also an acute shortage of base metals and skill in their working. Steel was manufactured for some time in Moscow from crude ore from the ground near the town of Dedilov, about thirty versts from Tula, and also out of bog ore at Ustiuzhna Zhelezopolskaia.

Ever since the sixteenth century Tula was famous for its armament manufacture. In 1619 the Tula blacksmiths, gunsmiths, locksmiths and spooners, seventy-five men in all, petitioned the tsar that they were working non-stop on small arms day and night yet were expected to perform labor services alongside the rest of the townsmen. Let the sovereign order that they be required only to make weapons as before.

Despite this Tula arms production was insufficient since, as we have learned, a great quantity of weapons was ordered from abroad, and much bar iron was ordered from Sweden. For example in 1629 twenty-five thousand puds were ordered at 21 altyns and 4 dengas a pud.

The Dutch merchant Andreas Deniszoon Vinius[18] who settled in Russia with his brother Abraham and another merchant named Wilkinson presented a petition to Tsar Michael to organize a manufactory in the vicinity of Tula to mold various cast iron objects in the manner used abroad. In February 1632 Vinius received a charter from the tsar, permitting him to build mills to smelt ore into cast iron and steel, to cast cannon, shot and cauldrons, and to cast sheets and bars, so that henceforth the tsar would have a steady supply of steel, and the sovereign's treasury would profit. The sovereign's subjects also would learn steel manufacture from them, since they were not to conceal any trade secrets. In the treasury it was resolved to pay 23 altyns 2 dengas a pud for each cannon, 13 altyns 2 dengas per pud for shot. Any surplus steel the treasury did not need, as well as other objects including cannon, could be sold on the side or exported to Holland.

Vinius chose a site for his factory twelve versts from Tula on the Tulitsa stream, or rather a channel of that stream now known as the Great Tulitsa. Ore was extracted within forty versts of the factory, five versts from Dedilov. The original construction of the factories cost Vinius much money. He went into debt and in 1639 was forced into partnership with the famous Peter Gabrielsohn Marselis[19] and the Dutch merchant Thielemann Lus Akema.[20] Pursuant to their petition the court district of Solomensk with 347 peasants was assigned to the Tula factory. Marselis and Akema were not satisfied, so in 1644 the sovereign granted the foreigner Peter Marselis, a merchant from the town of Hamburg, together with his sons Gabriel and Leonty, and the trader from Holland Thielemann Akema, the privilege of establishing steel mills in three locations, on the Vaga, Kostroma and Sheksna rivers, or wherever else they found a place suitable for iron extraction in vacant lands, for a term of twenty years without quitrent or taxes. They were free to establish mills and call upon all categories of inhabitants to smelt iron.

When the factory was established and in operation they were to deliver iron according to contract, cannon at twenty altyns a pud, shot at ten altyns, musket and carbine barrels at twenty altyns. If after delivering to the treasury there was surplus steel, they could export it to foreign lands with which the tsar was in amicable relations. If they sold iron at Archangel or overseas for reichsthalers these must to be surrendered to the treasury at the current exchange rate, not sold or given away to anyone else. All labor must to be free rather than forced, no one must suffer any oppression or harm, neither should anyone be put out of business. Should the tsar command that Russians be taught iron manufacture, Peter and Thielemann must teach them, and conceal no trade secrets from the Russians.

In 1634 the interpreter Zakhar Nikolaev and the goldsmith Paul Ählrendorff were sent abroad to hire master craftsmen to extract copper from ore found in the hillsides, and other skills pertaining to copper smelting. In 1630 the master velvet manufacturer Vimbrandt was dispatched abroad to recruit craftsmen. In 1631 a safe conduct was issued to the free states of Holland and the United Provinces to hire apprentices skilled in the art of fortification. In it we read "The master diamond cutter and goldsmith Johan Martensson and the English trader Frederick Glover at our command have begun in Moscow to manufacture gold and silver ornaments, filigree, gold thread, haberdashery and all manner of small objects in gold and bronze. This business started to cost too much and the profits to our treasury were small because we did not have at hand good skilled master craftsmen in our realm. We could seek out such master craftsmen in the German lands, which would be a profitable and glorious enterprise for his majesty the tsar, cheaper in the marketplace, and the subjects of our realm could imitate them. Thus his majesty will reward them, and will allow master craftsmen to be summoned from the German land for this purpose, ten men or more to act at their own expense. They may ply their trade and trade on their own behalf for ten years, but they may not engage in any other business until the expiry of this term."

The tsar agreed to grant this privilege. In 1634 we encounter Christopher Galloway, a master watchmaker and flintlock mechanic,[21] and in 1643 Falck, a cannon and bell founder and the portrait artist Deterson. The same year the Swedish mason Kristler began construction of the stone bridge across the Moscow river. In 1634 a ten-year privilege was granted to Vimbrandt for processing elk hides. Also a fifteen-year privilege to set up a glass factory was given to someone named Coet. To the same Coet was granted a charter to set up a potash factory for ten years. In 1643 the English agent Digby received a ten-year charter to burn charcoal free of duty in the regions of Yaroslavl, Vologda and Totma. In 1644 Colonel Crawford was given a seven-year charter to burn charcoal and manufacture potash in the Murom forest.

At Tsar Michael's court there were two organ builders, Johan and Melchart Lunev, who came from Holland with parts to build their "instrument," which was assembled in Moscow. Next to this organ they fashioned a device with woodcarving adorned with red paint and gold leaf. On this instrument were carved nightingales and a cuckoo with voices; whenever the organ played, these birds sang by themselves. For this wondrous artifact the tsar ordered them to be given 2,676 rubles from the treasury, and forty sables each, and instead of being invited to the tsar's table they were sent food and drink. Melchart was dispatched abroad with a commission to recruit two master clockmakers to serve the sovereign with their skill and take on apprentices.

The influx of foreigners was so powerful that two Moscow priests, one from the church of St. Nicholas the Stylite, the other from St. Cosmas and St. Damian, presented a petition in which they complained that foreigners on their properties near their churches had established chapels.[22] They entertained Russians in their houses, and Russians suffered many insults from the foreigners.[23] Without awaiting the tsar's permission, again they were buying up houses in their parishes. German widows were operating taverns on their premises, and many parishioners were eager to sell their houses and properties to the Germans at a high price, twice or more than Russians would pay, and on account of these Germans their parishes were becoming desolate.

In response to this petition it was decreed that in the Kitay Quarter, the White City and in the free settlements around the city German men or women were not to buy or lease any homesteads. Russians who made such sales and leases would incur grave disfavor. Chapels situated on German properties close to churches were to be demolished. Longtime German military servitors, various ranks of foreigners, translators from the Chancellery for Foreign Affairs, goldsmiths and silversmiths and long-standing foreign traders were to be resettled to the area between the Frolov and Intercession gates, near the wooden structure and hall where they assembled for worship according to their own faith. According to Olearius[24] there were at that time in Moscow up to a thousand Protestant families.[25]

Foreigners were eager to buy up Russian grain. We also found that foreigners received permission to export saltpeter, which industry was fairly well developed among us at this time. Apart from those places already mentioned in connection with saltpeter production, it is also mentioned in the Severian land. Thus when enumerating the servicemen around Kursk we read "About fifty men live in the Romanov saltpeter works from spring through summer until the dismissal of the junior boyars, alternating every two months." In the listing of Belgorod servitors "they include thirty junior boyars and mounted cossacks who live around the saltpeter works belonging to Mikhalko Limarov." Various individuals, including cannoneers and day laborers were contracted by the Cannoneers' Chancellery to manufacture saltpeter in various places, in Livny and Voronezh, for a specified weight. In 1634 they received two rubles and ten altyns for every pud.

Finally to our information on commerce during Michael's reign it must be added that concerning the weight of loaves and fancy bread in 1626 chancellery officials were to go everywhere and weigh white bread and loaves made of sifted flour, plain and honeyed fancy bread. Should it be discovered anywhere that the loaves or fancy loaves were less than the specified weight, the sellers would suffer the penalty. The chancellery and sworn officials must see to it that the loaves and fancy bread were properly baked, and that the sellers added no bran or other impurities to the flour. The officials were given a detailed list of the production and preparation costs of various types of loaf or fancy bread. For example, "For fancy bread, yeast to the value of two altyns and two dengas, six dengas' worth of salt, eight dengas' worth of firewood, four dengas' worth of seed, labor ten dengas, market stall rent two altyns and two dengas, candles and brooms two dengas, and the whole product is priced at eleven altyns a chetvert."

RURAL POPULATION

With respect to rural inhabitants, the changes at the end of the preceding century were confirmed in as much as the circumstances and relationships remained the same. Gentry and junior boyars petitioned that "long-standing servants and peasants were fleeing from them to the sovereign's court and free districts and villages, or to boyars' service tenures and patrimonies, or those of the patriarch, archbishops or monasteries, in return for relief from dues. The service tenure holders, patrimonialists and monasteries were building free settlements for these runaway servants and peasants in derelict places, on account of which the petitioners' own service tenures and patrimonies were deserted. Moreover those of their fugitive servants and peasants, having lived out their free years on the estates of their new landlords, relying upon them as mighty men, come and persuade the remaining dependents to leave their former landlords, set fire to their homes and cause all manner of devastation."

Pursuant to this petition it was resolved "Whoever comes to anyone to abduct servants and peasants, and in the course of this action there is an occurrence of homicide, plundering or any other serious matter, the sovereign decrees and the boyars resolve that the matter be investigated thoroughly. Peasants abducted within the last fifteen years are to be returned, while as before those peasants and cotters who fled during the last ten years are also to be returned. If these peasants were abducted forcibly they are to be returned with all their chattels, and he who held them must pay compensation of five rubles each for every year."

To what extent small service tenure holders needed confirmation of the law enserfing peasants, to what extent they were vexed that abductions continued, is evident from the following case. In 1624 the Livny service cossack Avdey Yakovlev came up to his peasant and in the presence of bystanders said "The sovereign does not reward us, but orders that peasants be abducted from us. There are about five hundred of us banded together. If anyone abducts any of our peasants we will burn down his patrimony, kill the peasants and seek another sovereign."

The service gentry of Elets complained bitterly against the estate managers and peasants of Ivan Nikitich Romanov who, relying upon the power of their lord, permitted themselves the abduction of peasants and all manner of violence. "We cannot live," wrote the petitioners, "in neighborly relations in a borderland town with so great a boyar. We have become powerless as a result of the violence done by the servants and peasants of Boyar Ivan Nikitich! How sorely we were devastated by the Lithuanians, but our captivity by the Lithuanians was only for a time; of our present captivity at the hands of Boyar Ivan Nikitich we will know no end. Our situation has deteriorated as a result of war against the Crimeans and Nogay. In the whole of the Elets district we have not a single peasant, cotter or sharecropper." Yet in the general investigation 1,865 witnesses stated they knew nothing of such violence, neither did they hear of it from anyone else. In the new settlements erected by Ivan Nikitich there appeared not to be a single peasant belonging to anyone else. As a result the petitioners were beaten mercilessly with rods for their fraud, and were put in prison.

In 1614 the St. Joseph monastery of Volokolamsk petitioned that at the time of the Lithuanian invasion many of their peasants fled in order to serve boyars, gentry and junior boyars, and gave names concerning who was with whom. Furthermore they complained that the gentry and junior boyars were plundering and selling those they did not intend to keep for themselves, exacting sureties from others that they remain with them permanently and not go back to the monastery. Following investigation the sovereign ordered the peasants be returned to the monastery.

Complaints came from petty service tenure holders concerning the abduction or flight of long-standing peasants. Free peasantry newly entering the service of landlords either contracted not to flee from the estate, or assumed the customary obligations not to live on a portion of land subject to state taxation, to discharge all dues and imposts, to repay in full the loan advanced by the landlord, and to receive from him ten rubles in accordance with the agreement. Similar obligations are encountered concerning those taken on as cotters. There are indications that the transition of peasants from free taxpayers to proprietary peasants was harmful to their status. Thus in the petition of the English merchant Fabian Williams[26] against the peasants belonging to one Mosin in the Vologda district we find that these peasants were obliged to transport goods to Moscow, lost them and had to indenture themselves to the tune of one hundred and sixty rubles. At that time they were directly subject to the sovereign in a free tax-paying district, but now the land was given to Ivan Morin as a service tenure and there was no way they could repay the indentured sum, because they were impoverished by their landlord. The annual quitrent peasants must pay their landlord was set by the tsar's decree, as is seen in the following curious petition. "We your orphans, peasants in the village of Shiringa in the Yaroslavl district, petition through our elder Grishka Olferiev, who speaks for all of us to Tsar Michael Fedorovich of All Russia. We make petition and complain against our landlord Prince Artemy Sheidiakov. In the present year 7133 [1625], on the eve of St. Nicholas Day in the autumn [December 6], Prince Artemy came from Moscow to his estate the village of Shiringa, granted to him by the tsar. We peasants came to greet him with offerings of bread, as it is customary to greet landlords, but he beat and tortured us, and locked us up in the ice house. He took women from the unbaptized Tatars into his bed and summoned Tatar servitors to his estate. Contrary to your decree he took the annual quitrent for the year 7133 in full, without giving any receipt. When we petitioned him about this violation of your decree, he beat and tortured us, and still gave us no receipt. This same Prince Artemy during the Advent fast commanded us to provide food for his Tatar servitors—veal, mutton, goose and chicken. Having extracted the full measure of quitrent from us, he left his village for Yaroslavl, taking with him an unbaptized Tatar woman, and in Yaroslavl he took yet another woman, a Russian named Matrenka Belosheika, into his bed, and on St. Nicholas Day he heated a steam bath in the courtyard of his Yaroslavl house. Living with these women in Yaroslavl until Christmas, he played dice with them and kept these loose women for his constant amusement. The quitrent he took from us he lost at dice to these women or gave it to them, and even gambled away the clothes off his back. Having lost all, Prince Artemy once again repaired to the village of Shiringa on Christmas Eve, bringing the Tatar woman and Matrenka Belosheika to his estate. Arriving on Christmas Day, he heated a steam bath in his courtyard and extorted yet more quitrent money from us, extracting from us in excess of the tsar's decree fifty rubles and forty pails of wine. We also had to brew ten cauldrons of beer, and he extorted from us ten puds of honey. If a peasant had a serviceable horse, he took it for himself.

"We your orphans, unable to bear this excessive extortion and great torment, fled from him. Any able-bodied peasant he keeps in chains, to be ransomed for five, six or even ten rubles. The houses vacated by peasants who have fled are assigned to Tatar servitors who dishonor our women. He either confiscates or distrains our livestock. This Prince Artemy has distributed villages and estates to his former service Tatars, and to his wife Princess Fedora he also has given two hamlets as an estate. As for those peasants who petitioned your majesty concerning Prince Artemy's violence and excessive extortion, he has threatened them with death and seeks to hack them to pieces with his own hands." It is not known how this case ended since the last part of the file is missing. As far as Matrenka Belosheika is concerned, she was banished from Moscow to Yaroslavl for harlotry in connection with the Nefed Minin case.[27]

The landlord who encroached upon the sanctity of a peasant's family sometimes paid for it with his life. As far as peasants of free taxpaying districts were concerned, in a number of places they did not prosper. In 1633 there was an investigation in the Totma districts as to why the peasants fled. The answer was that the peasants dispersed because of the many imposts and great immoderate exactions, subsistence payments to the new-style soldiers, payment for provisions, dispatch of couriers, excessive barge hauling services and heavy demands for land and plow tax.

VI

EXPLORATION, RELIGION AND CULTURE

RUSSIAN EXPANSION IN NORTHERN ASIA

In European Russia the population was so sparse that landowners attracted peasants from one another by exemptions, or forcibly abducted them, regardless of the law. Meanwhile in the East, beyond the Ural mountains, empty expanses increasingly were added to the Russian domains, demanding to be populated. In the West during Michael's reign populated districts and towns were ceded to Poland and Sweden, whereas Russian possessions in the East grew to seventy thousand square miles of empty expanses. The trailblazers, the cossacks, continued to penetrate further along untamed rivers towards the eastern ocean and the Chinese borders, bringing under the sovereign's mighty hand scattered bands of savages, collecting fur tribute from them, frequently exhausting the natives' patience with their rapacity at cost of their lives.

To understand the process whereby Russian possessions expanded, how new lands were sought out, let us examine the reports of several of the leaders of various expeditions. In 1641 Vasily Vlasiev reported how he with his detachment proceeded against the Buriats, laid waste Chepchuguy's encampment, killing more than thirty, but could not take a single live prisoner because the Tungus were besieging them from their encampments. Vlasiev ordered the interpreter to tell Chepchuguy and his brother not to besiege them but to surrender to the sovereign's authority, to which Chepchuguy addressed the interpreter in a quarrelsome manner. "You do not know Chepchuguy," he said, "or what manner of men he is leading." He then opened fire from his encampment, shouting "You cossacks will not take us alive!" They wounded one man. The cossacks were wearing helmets and armor, and he pierced the helmets right through. The Russians fired around and into the encampments but achieved nothing by gunfire, so they set fire to the encampment. Chepchuguy and his son were burned to death although his wife and two other children emerged unscathed.

As soon as any servicemen brought any natives under the tsar's sovereignty they were interrogated immediately about the lands situated further on, as far as the very borders of China. Thus the same Vlasiev reported, "After concluding a treaty we plied Korshun and Adamgay with the sovereign's wine and gave them gifts, two arshins of red cloth and pewter plate weighing three pounds, and asked them, according to our instructions, about the Lama river, about the extent of the Tungus lands and about the Mugal people; what tribes lived along the Lama, and whether the Mugal princeling lived far off from them, and what was his name; along which river lay the route to the Chinese realm, and how far was it by river or overland to China; was the Shilka river far from them, or did the princeling Ladkay live on the Shilka; was there silver or copper ore near Ladkay's habitat, and what kind of grain grows on the Shilka."

The explorers even had to do without bread. "Henceforth," Postnik Ivanov reported, "there shall be on the Indiger river and in the Yukagir territory a hundred servicemen who will have to be content with fish and wild game and without bread. In the Yukagir territory there are many sables. There are many tributaries to the Indiger river, and along these rivers dwell many people who go about on foot or with the use of reindeer. There are sables and wild animals of all kinds along these rivers and in these territories. There is also silver among the Yukagir inhabitants, but I don't know from where they obtain the silver."

In the forties the tsar ordered a survey for agricultural lands along the Lena. Where found they were to be marked out to ascertain how many peasants could be set up. According to the sovereign's decree, the governor ordered a market established in the Yeniseisk fort, and he repeatedly called to all hamlets for wanderers and traders to settle crown lands along the Ilim river and receive exemption from dues for five years, after which they would render every fifth sheaf from all their harvest. Anyone wishing to take up farming along the Lena would receive an outright grant from the sovereign's treasury to buy his first horse, and for a second would receive a loan, also from the tsar's treasury, to be repaid within two years. Further, he would receive from the tsar's treasury a sickle, scythes and plowshares, and seed for the sovereign's pasture for the rest of his reign. For the first and second year he would cultivate one seventh of his land for the sovereign's benefit.

The government repeatedly stressed to the governors to be easy with newly subjected natives. "Servicemen are enjoined strictly when they go to collect fur tribute not to subject tribute payers to unwarranted harm and exactions. They are to collect fur tribute from them graciously, in a friendly manner, not with cruelty or extortion. In order profitably to collect the tsar's fur tribute, and to gather as much as possible, each must be visited by the collectors no more than once a year, not twice or three times. If the people of the newly subjected lands become disobedient, at first reason with them kindly, and if it proves impossible to persuade them, pacify them with force, but with minimum damage, in order the more easily to reconcile them. Governors, crown secretaries, clerks and servitors are not to take any natives, their women or children into their households, neither may they carry on any private correspondence with them, and they are not to be baptized. You are not to take them back with you to Moscow, neither may you send them back with anybody, in order that the Siberian land may expand and not fall into ruin. If any of the tribute payers desire to be baptized, they may do so after diligent inquiry as to whether they are coming forward of their own free will. Once they are baptized take them into the tsar's service, give them grants of money and grain, and appoint them according to their rank to positions vacated by Russian servicemen. If any women desire to be baptized, once they are baptized they are to be given in marriage either to native converts or to Russian servicemen."

Thus pushed away from the enlightened West, the Russians in the East cleared the way for European civilization in the wastes of Northern Asia. Wherever they settled there appeared a town, agriculture and the church.

In 1620 it was decided to establish an archbishopric in Tobolsk, and it was founded by Abbot Cyprian of the Khutyn monastery, already known to us from events in Novgorod.[1] There survives an instruction given to Cyprian's successor Makary[2] on how to relate to the native population, both newly baptized and unbaptized. This instruction, by reason of the uniqueness of it position, is similar to the instruction to Archbishop Gury of Kazan.[3]

THE CHURCH

Yet while concerning itself with the spread and strengthening of Christianity among the peoples of Northern Asia the Russian church during Michael's reign had to be particularly concerned with curtailing moral disorders, which were rife among the Russian populace. The source of these disorders was the profound ignorance expressed in its great outrage at the first attempt to introduce a more correct understanding of the basics of Christianity.

We learned how in the sixteenth century the opinions foreshadowing the basic beliefs of the schismatics built up and won consecration. We observed how these opinions became enmeshed in the resolutions of the so-called Hundred Chapters council (1551).[4] When service and instruction books began to be printed among us gradually there were introduced into them both the earlier and the newly emerging schismatic beliefs. In this way they became generally known and sanctified, and attempts to correct anything in them encountered stiff resistance as an arrogant, heretical attempt to violate sacred antiquity. During the interregnum, as Moscow was burned by the Poles, the printing works was destroyed by fire, all the type perished, and there remained few master printers, and even they fled to other towns. When Michael "beloved of God and chosen by the whole people" was elected, he revived the printing trade and ordered master printers be gathered together in Moscow. These were Nikita Fedorov and his companions, who were living at that time in Nizhny Novgorod.

Before the books could be printed they had to be corrected. In November 1616 Archimandrite Dionisy of the Trinity monastery, the cellarer Avraamy Palitsyn[5] and all the brethren received a letter from the tsar. "According to our decree," it read, "we have had brought to us in Moscow from the Trinity monastery the canonarch[6] Brother Arseny and the priest Ivan from the village of Klementievo to correct printed books and the missal. For the same task we also ask you to send us the librarian Brother Anthony. You wrote to us that Brother Anthony is sick, while Brother Arseny and Father Ivan petitioned us, saying 'From the time of the blessed

Prince Vladimir to the present the book of the missal in Moscow and throughout the Russian land differs in translations and through the negligence of ignorant scribes, and in many places was not corrected. In the provincial and borderland towns, close to lands of other faiths, improper customs have become consecrated through ignorance by long usage, and errors are deeply rooted. Therefore Brother Arseny and Father Ivan cannot handle the task of correcting the missal by themselves. We must correct it through consulting many opinions, and by comparison with many books.' So we," continued the tsar, "entrust correction of the missal to you, Archimandrite Dionisy, and to you, Arseny and Ivan, and to other spiritual and wise clergy, whose book learning, grammar and rhetoric is truly renowned."

Thus again we encounter the famous Dionisy in a new role. To understand Dionisy's position in this role, to understand the obstacles men like him encountered, we must turn our attention to several aspects of contemporary monastic life. Uneducated or semi-educated societies normally suffer from the malady that makes it easy for a few of some kind of superiority, usually purely superficial, to obtain immense influence and seize power. This arises in the absence of public opinion, for society is not aware of its power nor how to exercise it. The majority has insufficient education to evaluate the worthiness of its members, and by such enlightenment to imbue respect for individual members, or see through their meanness and mediocrity. In the absence of enlightenment in the majority any superiority, often only superficial, exercises fascination, and he who possesses it can do anything. Thus if in such an uneducated or semi-educated society there appears a smart, forward, dogmatic talker, what may he not permit himself? Who is there to take the measure of his worth? If he encounters an opponent, a man fully worthy, conversant with the matter and modest, with respect for his own station and that of society, the talker, who considers any means justified to defeat his adversary, starts to shout and release a flood of words. For the ignorant crowd, whoever shouts loudest is right. Impudence, quick-wittiness, unscrupulousness always prevail.

Our ancient society, by reason of lack of enlightenment, suffered greatly from such "idle chatters," as they were called at the time. Against such men Dionisy was forced to struggle within his monastic community. We have seen how in distressing times Dionisy knew how to stir up spiritual interests and transform his monastery into a consoling haven for the suffering. When the Troubles passed, material interests gained the upper hand, and the abbot's sacred zeal encountered strong opposition. The "idle chatters" did not wish him to have his way in establishing good order in the monastery and saw to it that the monastery, which thanks to Dionisy won such great renown during the Time of Troubles, attracted many enemies in peacetime. The monastery became involved in many disputes with neighbors, landlords, townsmen and peasants. Monastic officials brought many actions to court, falsely claiming money, lands and peasants. They sought them in the name of St. Sergius the Miracle Worker, but took them not for the monastery, giving the villages and hamlets to their relatives. They even aroused the anger of the sovereign, for they took townsmen from the cities and settled them on monastic free settlements. Monastic servitors committed assault and robbery on the highways. When junior boyars or servitors of magnates came complaining that the monastery was abducting peasants and slaves from them and settling them on monastic lands, they were given documents purportedly setting matters to right. In the meantime the authorities sent to have these peasants and slaves transferred to other monastic estates so that when the plaintiffs came with their charters they were shown abandoned homesteads.

Dionisy implored them to refrain from such abuses, but in vain. The "idle chatters" triumphed, as it was easy for them to do, given the current monastic arrangements. The head, the archimandrite, looked after the churches, the icons and books in the churches, the vessels and all the church treasures. The cellarer looked after the actual monastery, all the monastic fabric, the estates, finances, bequests, clothing and vestments, money for food and drink, also candles and honey, and he collected all dues. At irregular intervals, by agreement among the brethren, there were chapters at which there were elections to the offices of stablemaster, cupbearers, officers in charge of the granaries and the drying room, sub-cellarers, agents in the villages, as well as other monastic offices. At these chapters the amount of quitrent due from the peasants was fixed. All resolutions of the chapter were inscribed in a book kept in the monastic treasury. The cellarer was given the right to adjudicate disputes between the brethren, servitors, servants and peasants. Major judicial matters and lawsuits he managed in conjunction with the archimandrite, treasurer and brethren of the chapter in general. If they were unable to resolve a judicial matter it was settled by a plenary assembly of monks, in consultation with all the brethren.

Fearless in the city square amid a turbulent populace, Dionisy was surprisingly meek and mild towards those under his rule. Given the current cultural climate many of the brethren were utterly incapable of understanding the courteous forms employed by Dionisy. Thus when he needed to direct any of his monks, he said "If you will, brother, do such and such." The monk, hearing such a command, quietly went back to his place and did nothing. When the others asked why he did not fulfill the abbot's command, he replied "The archimandrite gave me a choice, so I can do it or not as I please."

Apart from those eagerly seeking the material well-being of the monastery, that is to say, of their own relatives, within the monastery were two "idle chatters," the subprecentor Login and the precentor Filaret.[7] Login amazed the brethren and visitors to the monastery with his extraordinarily pleasant voice, which was clear and loud. There was none equal to him in reading and chanting. For one verse he sang five, six or ten variations. That the verse was corrupted through these variations and lost its meaning, that instead of "seed" the word "family" was heard,[8] was of no concern to him, for he accounted skill in grammar and philosophy a mark of heresy. Arrogant by reason of his talents, of the admiration occasioned by his voice, this "idle chatterer" knew no moderation, quarreled, assaulted not only monks but even priests, and dipped his hand into the alms fund, while nobody dared say a word to him. Dionisy often addressed him with his quiet admonition, called him lord, brother, father, exalting him by name and according to his ancestry. "What advantage, my light, is it to you," said Dionisy, "that everybody complains against you, hates and curses you? For we, the leaders of the community, look at you as in a mirror. What profit is it for us to quarrel with you?" These admo-nitions were to no avail.

The other "idle chatterer," the precentor Filaret, greatly amazed the crowd, especially as he could be loud thanks to a criterion highly valued at that time, being a "good graybeard." He had lived at the Trinity monastery more than fifty years and was precentor for more than forty, an immense advantage according to contemporary ideas. All others, including the archimandrite, were "young men" in comparison. Login by his variations corrupted the sense of the verses, and Filaret went further. According to him, Christ was not born of the Father before all the ages. He considered Christ's divinity to be an invention of man.

Filaret and Login were friends, and both hated Dionisy because of his accusations. "Spare me and do not compel me to sin," Dionisy told them, "for know that this is a matter for the whole church of God, and I in charity speak to you in private, asking that the tsar's majesty and the patriarchal

authorities not hear of this lest we be humiliated and cast out of the church."
"The holy places are falling into ruin because of the fools you appoint,"
replied Login. "Everywhere you have ignorant rural priests. You teach
others, but are ignorant of what you are teaching."

Login was particularly incensed that the archimandrite, in his opinion,
was meddling in matters that did not concern him, namely that he
compelled everyone to read the teachings of the holy fathers, himself often
read them, and also frequently sang in the choir. "It is not your business to
sing or read," Login told him. "As archimandrite you need only know how
to stand dumbly in the choir stalls during office time." On one occasion at
matins Dionisy left the choir and wished to read. Login overtook him and
tore the book from his hands. The lectern and the book together clattered
to the floor, the noise and commotion distracting everyone. Dionisy
merely made the sign of the cross over his face, went back to the choir stalls
and sat in silence. Login finished the reading, approached the archimandrite
but, instead of begging his forgiveness, spat at him and uttered abuse.
Dionisy, waving his staff, said, "Stop it, Login, do not interrupt the sacred
chant, and do not distract the brethren. We can discuss this after matins."
Then Login snatched the staff from his hands, broke it into four pieces and
threw them at his knee. Dionisy glanced at the icon and said "You, Lord
God, know all. Forgive me, a sinner, for it is I who have sinned before you,
not he." Leaving his place, he wept all through matins before the icon of
the Mother of God, but after matins not even the pleas of all the brethren
could induce Login to ask the archimandrite's pardon.

In vain did Dionisy attempt to conceal the behavior of Login and Filaret
behind the monastery walls. Complaints about him were written to
Moscow and to the St. Cyril monastery. Finally the task of correcting
books, entrusted to Dionisy, provoked their even greater hatred against the
corrector, giving them the opportunity to bring him to grief. Dionisy and
his companions, while correcting the missal, among other things deleted
as an unnecessary interpolation the words "with fire" from the prayer for
the blessing of the waters, "Come, O Lord, and sanctify this water with thy
Holy Spirit and with fire!" Whereupon Filaret, Login and the vestry
deacon Markell sent a denunciation against Dionisy to Moscow, saying
that Dionisy and his companions were guilty of heresy. "They do not
believe," they alleged, "that the Holy Spirit takes the form of fire." Login
considered himself an expert on the matter because during Shuisky's reign
he printed the statutes, filling them with errors.

At that time there was no patriarch in Moscow, since everyone was waiting for Filaret Nikitich. Patriarchal affairs were handled by Metropolitan Jonas of Krutitsy, a man incompetent to judge the case between the correctors and their opponents. Dionisy and his companions were commanded to give an explanation. Four days in a row he was brought to the patriarch's palace, there to be interrogated in a humiliating and shameful fashion. Then he was interrogated in the Ascension monastery, in the cell of the tsar's mother the nun Martha Ivanovna,[9] and it was resolved that the revisers were guilty of heresy.

This decision was symptomatic, not only of ignorance, but of another of society's ills. It was indicative not only of zeal for the letter, for antiquity, against which the bold correctors raised their hands. There was also joy among his enemies that the archimandrite of the richest monastery was delivered into their hands, and they demanded that he be fined five hundred rubles. Dionisy replied that he did not have the money and would not pay and hence the dreadful vindictiveness, the shackles, beatings, blows and spitting. Dionisy, standing in chains, answered with a smile those who struck and spat upon him. "I have no money," he said, "and nothing to give it for. It is bad for a monk to throw off the habit, but to be tonsured means a crown and gladness. You threaten me with Siberia and Solovki,[10] but I am glad, as I shall have a life there." Dionisy purposely was summoned on feast or market days, when there were large crowds. He was brought on foot or on a very sorry nag, without a saddle, in chains and clad only in his shirt, amid the scorn of the crowd, some of whom threw mud and dust at him. He endured it all with a cheerful countenance, smiling when he encountered his acquaintances. He was brought sometimes before mass, sometimes after, and placed shackled in the porch of the metropolitan's courtyard. He stood there from morning to evening, not being given even a cup of water, and this was in the months of June and July, when the days were hot. Metropolitan Jonas sat after mass enthroned at the synod whilst Dionisy and his pupils were treated to blows and kicks beneath the windows of his cell, and sometimes were beaten with rods. The word "heretic" alarmed the tsar's mother Martha Ivanovna and set her against the alleged heretics. Among the people there spread the rumor that these heretics wished to take fire away from the world. Thus fear seized the simple people, especially craftsmen whose living depended on fire. They came out with filth and stones to throw at Dionisy.

Bravely enduring torment, not stooping to worry about himself, Dionisy was ever solicitous concerning his companions in misfortune, pleading for quick release from their plight. One of them, the monk Arseny Glukhoy, was not endowed with firmness of spirit and could not endure the torment. He handed the boyar Boris Mikhailovich Saltykov a petition in which, while asserting the justice of his cause and impatience at the ignorance of his accusers, also displayed a loss of morale, expressing the usual desire to shift the blame for his misfortune.

"On October 24, 1615," reads the petition, "the cellarer Avraamy Palitsyn wrote to Archimandrite Dionisy on behalf of the sovereign. He ordered that I, a wretched monk, be sent to Moscow on the sovereign's business to correct the missal book preparatory to printing. Father Ivan of Klementievo arrived in Moscow on his own initiative, not according to instructions, and when we stood before you I said on my behalf that I was not competent, being neither priest nor deacon, for the book is devoted exclusively to priestly matters. Father Ivan pushed himself forward to take part in the sovereign's service. Acting on his own initiative he pleaded that he had a wife and children in the vicinity of the Trinity monastery, and that the matter ought to be handled by Archimandrite Dionisy, and Father Ivan, Brother Anthony and I, Brother Arseny, would assist him. So you, sovereign, in accordance with Ivan's petition and our plea ordered a letter to be sent from the palace, addressed to the archimandrite."

Having justified the corrections made to the missal, Arseny continued, "There are others who have accused us of heresy, but they scarcely know the alphabet. They do not know which letters in the alphabet are vowels, consonants or dipthongs, neither can they distinguish between the eight parts of speech. They can distinguish neither gender, number, tense, persons, titles nor voice. Such things have not even entered into their heads; sacred philosophy has never passed through their hands. Without such knowledge they easily fall into error, not only over matters concerning holy scripture, but even in earthly matters, even though they may be naturally quick-witted....

"Our case has not been made public, neither has the tsar's treasury suffered any loss. If we have made a mistake, this is incidental, and we will lose our reward on account of our careless and improper work. This is no small misfortune for me, a simple monk, who have taken up such a task, occupied with the tsar's business for eighteen months, day and night. All we poor choir monks have received from the Trinity monastery for our subsistence throughout the year is thirty altyns each for clothing. We clothe and feed ourselves by the work of our hands....

"Is it not enough that our work is brought to nothing, but also that the mild and gentle heart of our pious and sovereign lady the nun Martha Ivanovna has been moved to hatred against us? If our business were done in Moscow, all would have been good and well-ordered, pleasing to the sovereign and useful to all Orthodoxy, and the great prelate Metropolitan Jonas would have been our most ardent patron.

"I spoke to Metropolitan Dionisy daily, saying 'Lord archimandrite! Refuse the tsar's project, let us not do this work in the monastery without the metropolitan's counsel, and send the draft back to Moscow lest there be unrest among the common people.' The archimandrite would not heed me or give me any support, but listened only to Father Ivan in all matters, which has brought him into dishonor and shame. At the chapter Father Ivan spat in the eyes of those who disagreed with him, which vexed many honest men. I believe that I, a wretched monk, have suffered because of Father Ivan and also because of the archimandrite, who would not heed me and did not decline the task. On the other hand Father Ivan forced his way into the tsar's project, played a large part in it, led us into misfortune while he, like a crafty fox, wriggled out of it, chasing a poor billy goat over a blind precipice while clearing the chasm himself."

Finally, the matter being decided, Dionisy was sentenced to banishment in the St. Cyril monastery of Beloozero. It was difficult to convey him there because enemy detachments were barring to road to the North. Therefore it was ordered that he be taken to the New Savior monastery, where a penance of a thousand bows was imposed upon him. He was beaten and tortured for forty days, and was made to stand in the smoke by the stove.

Dionisy's banishment did not last long. Patriarch Theophanes of Jerusalem arrived in Moscow, during whose stay, as we have seen, Filaret Nikitich returned and was installed as patriarch. According to contemporary accounts Filaret asked Theophanes "In your Greek books are the words 'with fire' added?"[11] "No," replied Theophanes, "and your version is incorrect. It would be good for you, brother, to take notice and correct it, so that you do not have 'with fire' interpolated."

Consequently a synod was convoked, at which once again there was bitter and lengthy debate. Dionisy had to appear for eight hours, succeeded in refuting all opponents and triumphantly returned to his monastery where he continued "to seek the beautification of the church and to establish good order among the brethren." Furthermore Filaret was not satisfied with Dionisy's proof or the testimony of Theophanes, to whom he said "When you return to Greece and take counsel with your brethren the ecumenical patriarchs, copy from the Greek books of ancient translations what is written there." Fulfilling this request, Theophanes and Patriarch Gerasimos of Alexandria sent letters to Moscow confirming that the interpolation "with fire" should be expunged.

Concerning the infamous Login there is fitting reference in 1633, in a letter from Patriarch Filaret, in which he ordered the suppression of the statutes printed in Shuisky's reign "because these statutes were printed by a criminal, a carouser, the Trinity-St. Sergius choir monk Login, for many of the articles contained therein were not printed according to apostolic or patristic tradition, but according to his own whim." In 1633 Archimandrite Joseph, an official of the patriarchal court of Alexandria,[12] arrived in Moscow and was detailed to translate Greek books into the Slavonic language.

Striving towards purity of dogma, the church had to make efforts to revive moral purity among its preachers. In 1636 the following missive was sent by the tsar to the Solovetsk monastery. "It has come to our attention," it read, " that hard liquor is being brought ashore near the Solovetsk monastery, together with all kinds of foreign red wines and unflavored mead, and that these liquors are being kept by the monks in their cells, not being placed in the cellars. Cellarers and treasurers are being chosen without consultation with the monks of the chapter or a general monastic assembly. Those chosen are monks addicted to strong liquor. They create disorder in the assemblies and choose those like themselves. In this way silence is kept, the guilty are not sent to do penance, and in the cellar illegal kvas is given out.

"The monks of the old tonsure, who are well versed in monastic life and preserve the traditions of the great miracle-workers Zosima and Savvaty, are dishonored and not allowed to speak in the chapter. The cellarer, treasurers and monks of the chapter maintain many disciples, but do not entrust them to priests or ordinary monks of blameless life; rather they live in the Solovetsk monastery in their cells conspiratorially. The monk covers up for his disciple and the disciple covers up for his monk. On business affairs or to the saltworks are sent only simple monks who do not know how to safeguard the monastery's interests or seek profit. They are not called to account when they return to the monastery, as a result of which the monastic treasury is depleted. Good monks are not sent to conduct business.

"Young workmen employed in the gardens are fed over the winter, maintained in the monastery along with the brethren. No separate cells are built for them outside the monastery, neither is there anyone to keep order among these monks and servants. Many other statutes within the monastery are not being observed as before. This is an unprecedented situation, which cannot be tolerated."

In 1636 the tsar sent a letter to the superior of the St. Paul monastery of Obnora. "It has come to our attention," he wrote, "that in the St. Paul monastery there is much indiscipline, drunkenness and disobedience. In the monastery strong drink and tobacco are kept; close to the monastery taverns and bath houses have been built, and home-brewed beer is sold. The monks go to the bath houses and taverns, go incessantly around the rural districts to attend peasant feasts and brotherhood banquets and drink beer. They brawl and behave in an undignified manner, committing all kinds of indiscipline." The tsar commanded the superior to bring the monks to order, and added, "Also let the peasants brew beer at the proper time, when they cannot cultivate their fields, and bring it out gradually, so that the peasants do not miss work and get drunk."

We learned how Login behaved towards Archimandrite Dionisy in the Trinity-St. Sergius monastery. It stands to reason that superiors of lesser monasteries suffered greater violence as a direct consequence of the absence of law and order. Thus in 1613 the superior of the Starodub-Riapolovsky monastery of Khotyml petitioned that the monk Hermogen came to him in the monastery, took the church keys by force, since he came with many followers, his family and relatives. He seized the monastic treasure, took possession of the monastic estates, living in violation of the monastic rule, abusing and assaulting the superior.

If the weakness of society allowed acts of violence, we must not be surprised to encounter instances of arbitrariness. In 1628 the monk Lavrenty petitioned that he was sent to Shuia by Archbishop Joseph of Suzdal to collect taxes. He sent for the porter of the Trinity monastery, the icon painter Ivan Yakovlev, on an important spiritual matter. Then the Trinity servitor Gorchakov gathered about him many unknown men, came to the archbishop's residence, abused both the archbishop and Lavrenty with unseemly words not fit to be uttered, dragged the icon painter Ivan away from Lavrenty, plundered the tax money, smashed the chest in with an axe, beat up Lavrenty and left him for dead. The night following this robbery Gorchakov again came to the archbishop's residence and fired his musket at the windows.

Gorchakov for his part petitioned that Lavrenty, having asked to see the icon painter Ivan Yakovlev on a spiritual matter, instead shackled him and clapped him in irons, and extorted two hundred rubles from him. Gorchakov went to Lavrenty with reproaches, asking him why he was doing this. Lavrenty, gathering about him many unknown men, beat, maimed and hacked away with an axe, helping himself to the monastic funds and taking a hundred and fifty rubles.

Who was innocent, who was guilty, nobody knows, only that Lavrenty was sent on behalf of Archbishop Joseph Kurtsevich, who in 1634 was banished to the monastery of St. Anthony on the Sii river for indiscipline and many other misdemeanors. To accusations of moral shortcomings some political charges also were added. It is also known that the inhabitants of Shuia were very discontented at Joseph's administration, as is evident from their petition against Father Alexis Kuzmin and his son the deacon Fedor. "The former archbishop Joseph, a *foreigner* from Suzdal, sent to us in Shuia this priest Alexis and his son Fedor in exchange for money, a bribe. Bargaining with the archbishop's deputies, foreigners from Kiev, and with the archbishop's chancellery officials, intending to trade spiritual benefits for money and to support all kinds of idle office holders, Alexis placed an impost upon us, causing much oppression and financial hardship. When Joseph was replaced by the present archbishop Serapion, the new archbishop investigated their idleness and indiscipline and expelled them from the Shuia church. Now Alexis and his son live in the Red Village of the Intercession[13] in Moscow, and issue summonses to us for all sorts of fraudulent lawsuits and bother our residents who go to Moscow on business, hiring idlers to harass us."

Filaret's successor Patriarch Joasaph was obliged to combat disorders occurring in the Moscow churches. "In the capital city of Moscow," the patriarch wrote, "in the cathedral and parish churches there is uproar, temptation and subversion of the faith. Services are rattled off in four, five, six or more voices, with all manner of negligence. Laymen stand irreverently about the churches, completely inattentive. During the sacred chant they act unseemingly, with mockery. Even priests hold conversations, act unseemingly and engage in worldly activities, seeking gratification of the flesh and devoting themselves to drunkenness, not celebrating mass at the proper hours. During Lent they recite the services very rapidly. On Sundays and feast days they chant matins late and hastily. They do not follow the precepts of the gospel, the apostles or the teachings of the church fathers. The sextons are young unmarried men. Children of priests and laymen frolic about the altar during services. During the sacred chant games of chance irreverently proceed in church, involving ten players or more, and so there is great disorder and uproar in the churches, as some fight and quarrel.

"Others, placing candles and shrouds on dishes, collect alms to build churches. Others pretend to be feeble-minded and afterwards are seen in full possession of their senses. Others pose as hermits, in black robes and in chains, with disheveled hair. Others during the sacred chant crawl around whining and cause great temptation among the common folk. Also feast days, instead of being times for holy celebration and rejoicing, become occasions for depraved sports. Performing bears and minstrels appear on the streets, in the marketplaces and at the crossroads. They play their depraved sports, beat on drums, sound their horns, clap their hands and dance. To these amusements come many folk, not just young but also old people. They stand in crowds and engage in contests of fisticuffs, sometimes resulting in fatalities. In these sports many die unshriven. All manner of unlawful deeds proliferate, pagan deceits,[14] blasphemies and other devilish sports. They eat strangled creatures[15] and sell them in the marketplace. They abuse each other shamefully, even their fathers and mothers, and with shameful impurity defile both their tongues and their souls."

Patriarch Joasaph's complaints about pugilistic contests show that this deeply rooted custom did not yield even to the stern measures undertaken against it by Patriarch Filaret, who forbade anyone to attend the pugilistic contests on the Old Vagankovo fields on pain of the knout. "Let the criers announce," Filaret also decreed, "through all the market rows, the streets, the free settlements and hundreds that there are to be no horse races, that laymen must not assemble for sports lest disorder for Orthodox Christians arise from them, neither shall there be any Yuletide revels, spring sowing or ploughing songs."[16]

The church tribunal under Filaret Nikitich also was not sparing of violators of family morals. Thus the junior boyar Semichev was sent in chains to the St. Nicholas monastery of Korela for having begotten seven children from his slave girls, and moreover these slave girls were cousins to each other. The table attendant Kolychev was punished this way for a similar offense.

Naturally moral disorders were more prevalent in distant places, on the steppe borders of the realm or beyond the Ural mountains. An instance from Voronezh may serve as an example. A junior boyar named Fedor

Pliasov submitted a petition. One evening, while sitting at his stall in the marketplace, the priest Yakov from the St. Elias church in the town quarter sent to him his son-in-law the junior boyar Ivashka Poluboiarinov to come and drink wine with him. As he came to the priest's house he saw arrived there before him the brigand Antoshka, who began to assault him. The priest tried to reconcile Antoshka with him but when it got dark the priest, Antoshka, Poluboiarinov and their hireling Ivashka bound Pliasov, tormented and tortured him, and then took him out of the town quarter towards the river, dragged him through the fort, extorted twenty rubles cash, and made him swear not to lodge a complaint against them.

Strong complaints were heard from the church authorities about the decline of morals in Siberia. Patriarch Filaret wrote to Archbishop Cyprian of Siberia. "In the Siberian towns there are many Russians and foreigners, Lithuanians and Germans, who are baptized into our Orthodox faith. They do not wear crosses or observe fast days. When they ride out to the Kalmyks or other native peoples on government business they drink, eat and do many scandalous things in company with the pagans. Some live with unbaptized Tatar women as though they were their wives, and beget children from them. Others do even worse; they marry their sisters, cousins, their own godmothers and those of their children. Others carry on liaisons simultaneously with mother and daughter. Many servitors whom the governors and chancellery officials send to Moscow or other towns on business pawn their wives to their brother servitors or someone else for a period of time. Those to whom they are pawned commit fornication indiscriminately with them until they are redeemed. If they are not redeemed on time they are sold into prostitution and made available to anyone. The buyer also commits fornication with them or gives them in marriage. Other helpless poor widows and girls are forced into prostitution. Wives are taken from poor working men and kept for prostitution, illegal indentures being taken out on them without a written contract. Those whose wives are taken from them flee, wander from homestead to homestead, and give themselves into bondage, into slavery to others who marry them off to other women, while the wives taken from them are married off to other men.

"The priests do nothing to forbid such criminal practices whilst some priests, both monastic and secular, even say the prayers and perform the marriages without documents.[17] Many, both male and female, when sick take religious vows but if they recover live in their houses as before, and many cast off the habit. In the monasteries and convents monks and nuns live together with laymen in the same house, and in no way differ from them. Siberian servitors come to Moscow and other towns and there persuade many women and girls to come to the Siberian towns to be kept as their mistresses, yet others are sold into slavery and submitted forcibly to indentures. Others are sold to work for Lithuanians, Germans, Tatars and other foreigners.

"The governors in Siberia, both now and formerly, ignore these practices. They do not turn these men away from such criminal, unlawful and shameless deeds, neither do they punish them, shielding them for their own gain. Some governors even indulge these criminals, ordering the priests to say the prayers and perform these unlawful marriages. The governors also inflict harm and losses on all the local traders and inhabitants, as well as the pagan natives in their encampments."

Thus the cause of the evil is revealed at the end of the patriarch's letter. The same cause is shown in the tsar's letter to these same Siberian governors. "In the Siberian towns servicemen and all ranks ignore the archbishop and his administrators in spiritual matters, and refuse to attend his tribunal. They urge one another to deride the archbishop, and you governors connive with them. When you send your officials to the Tatars, Voguls and Ostiaks to collect our tribute, they commit every violence against these natives and take huge bribes, to the detriment of our treasury. In drunken fits many of your people beat and stab each other to death, and you do not even bother to investigate."

The Siberians were granted a charter allowing them to bring women and girls from other towns. Filaret ordered the archbishop to withdraw this charter and send it to him in Moscow. Concerning Metropolitan[18] Cyprian's ministry in Siberia, the chronicle has this to say. "He baptized many heathen, and such weakness as unlawful marriages and other spiritual matters he corrected and strengthened, suffering from the unwise much slander, unruliness and oppression."

In 1625, during the ministry of Archbishop Makary, the following incident occurred in Tobolsk. "On Easter Sunday, at matins, some junior boyars and men of various ranks approached the boyar Prince Yury Yansheevich Suleshov to offer the customary Easter greeting. All of them embraced as was the custom, but the junior boyar Nizovtsev kissed the prince's hand.[19] Suleshov immediately, before the archbishop and in the presence of all, struck Nizovtsev and placed him under arrest. He lodged a complaint that Nizovtsev did this with criminal intent at the instigation of the Siberians." It is not known how this matter was resolved.

The government also prosecuted sorcery. In Tobolsk the quarters of a certain archpriest were searched, and there were found in a box purple grass, three roots and a clump of squirrel fur. The governor immediately informed the tsar, and the archpriest with his box were sent off to Moscow. In the possession of an ecclesiastical subdeacon Grigoriev were found horoscopes known as *rafli*. At the patriarch's behest these books were burned and the subdeacon was shackled and sent off to a monastery to perform menial work. In 1632 the tsar wrote to the governors of Pskov "Our governors have written to us from Viazma, saying they sent spies over the border, who when they reported back said that in the Lithuanian towns an old sorceress had cast a spell on hops being exported from Lithuania to our towns, to bring a pestilence upon the population." Accordingly it was forbidden, on pain of death, to import hops from Lithuania. In June 1635 there came to Moscow soliciting alms the metropolitan of Silistria, who said he had been in Constantinople where Patriarch Cyril instructed him secretly to tell the sovereign and his privy counselors that the sovereign must beware of documents and gifts coming from the Turkish sultan, as they might be injurious to his health. Something sinister should be expected in letters and gifts from the Turkish sultan, for he was vexed at the sovereign on account of his peace with the Polish king.

LEGISLATION

The means to combat crime was thought to lie in harsher punishment, the rise in crime caused by relaxation of penalties. In former times counterfeiting was punished by the offender having the molten metal poured down his throat. Tsar Michael commuted this to confiscation. "We had hoped," read the decree, "that even though we remitted the death penalty these men would desist from this crime, but these criminals took no account of our sovereign mercy, and now such criminals have multiplied, and so have their crimes. Because of malicious criminal denunciations, many innocents have suffered." As a consequence the penalty of pouring molten metal down the throat was reinstated. A nest of counterfeiters was discovered in 1634 beyond the Swedish borders in Karelia. Some Russian fugitives were taking part in this operation.

We have seen how Tsar Michael in his letter to the citizens of Novgorod declared a general amnesty. It is clearly evident that the new government did likewise in Moscow and the other provinces. While consigning to oblivion crimes committed in the fearful epoch of the Troubles the government demanded of private individuals to leave off all suits concerning wrongs suffered in the Time of Troubles. In 1622 the great sovereigns decreed that suits for theft, assault or plunder committed before or during the ruin, debt contracts and indentures signed less than fifteen years previously and concerning which there were no petitions would not be heard by the courts. To curtail litigation and procrastination, in 1635 it was ordered that criers proclaim everywhere that no loans of money or grain against clothing, horses or any equipment, no loans without indenture or promissory note be given to anyone, neither would they be valid in law.

In 1617 the tsar confirmed Ivan the Terrible's resolution not to treat with brigands. "If any plaintiff comes to an agreement with brigands or accomplices in assault in criminal cases, and reaches a settlement without awaiting verdict and brings the petition dropping the charge to the chancellery, this reconciliation will not be accepted, and the brigands will be punished for the crime of which they originally were accused, according to the sovereign's decree. The plaintiff is to be fined according to the gravity of the offense. Nobody shall treat with brigands."

Regarding homicide in the course of a quarrel, reconciliation was permitted as in the times of the Rus Justice. In 1640 the hieromonk Nikandr was reconciled to the peasants of the Tunbazh district of Beloozero, who slew his son the priest Luka. "After mass at the church of St. Nicholas the Miracle Worker there was a dispute at the house of my son the widowed priest Luka with the peasants of the Tunbazh district. One of them, Omros Semenov, stabbed my son to death. I, Brother Nikandr, tried to prevent him, but Omros wounded me also. I forgave Omros and his companions, and shall not bring any action against them. I shall not petition the tsar concerning any bloodwite or burial expenses, but will accept whatever fine the tsar imposes. I, Brother Nikandr, and my children will let God be the judge. Concerning this matter, I have given a written release to Omros and his companions."

In 1636, in Solvychegodsk, there was a curious conciliation writ. The townsmen and peasants of the rural district, exasperated at the tyranny of the governor Golovachev, drew up a "solidarity contract" not to surrender one another, went as a body to the governor's residence, saying "We are taking back the money you stole from us." They would have killed Golovachev, but Peter and Andrei Stroganov arrived at the governor's residence and reconciled Golovachev with the men of the commune. A conciliation writ was drawn up, and the commune settled for payment by the governor of three hundred rubles.

Enserfment of peasants naturally called for rulings concerning the violent death of such a peasant, which was now considered a direct tort against the landlord. In 1625 Prince Dmitry Mikhailovich Pozharsky reported to the boyars, who ruled that if a serf belonging to a boyar killed another such serf, and under investigation stated that the slaying took place during a quarrel, unintentionally or in a drunken state, "the killer shall be beaten with the knout and then awarded together with his wife and children as a slave to the boyar whose serf was killed, but the wife and children of the slain shall not be taken away from their boyar. If a junior boyar, or his son or nephew, or a boyar's official, or that of a chancellery official or junior boyar slays a peasant, and under interrogation says that he did this unintentionally, the best peasant of the slayer, together with his wife and children, without being separated, shall be taken from his estate with all his possessions and be transferred to the landlord whose peasant was killed, neither shall the landlord whose peasant was killed be deprived of that peasant's wife and children. The killer shall be put into prison, to remain there at the tsar's pleasure. If one peasant kills another but says he did it unintentionally, the killer shall be beaten with the knout and with his wife and children be handed over to the victim's landlord."

The previous legislation was confirmed, limiting the dreaded flow of oral denunciations. This confirmation demonstrates that the previous enactment was ineffective. The governor wrote from Kostroma that the brigand Shcherbak had languished in the local jail for the past five years or more. This old jailbird was uttering for the first time some oral denunciations. In previous years, when he was first caught, even under torture he did not denounce anyone. Those he now accused petitioned the sovereign, saying that this informer was slandering many. He sent to them requesting money for food, and if they did not send any he denounced them. The governor interrogated him under torture and he acknowledged that he accused them falsely, some out of malice, others because they would not give him money. The sovereign decreed that oral denunciations had no force when jailbirds after a long silence started accusing anyone against whom previously they uttered no denunciations.

In 1637 it was decreed that the provincial governors not place those held pending civil suits in the same jail as hardened criminals because they "would suffer hunger and oppression by being with these robbers, brigands and slanderers, and also die of oppression and demoralization." Those held pending civil suits were to be placed under house arrest. The same year it was forbidden to execute pregnant women because "the offspring of the accused is innocent." They were to be executed six weeks after giving birth.

The Time of Troubles taught the Russians deceit. The emergence of pretenders taught them to doubt everything, to see everywhere fraud and deceit. A Russian was told, "See, here is a tsarevich!" Thereupon he automatically replied "Is he a genuine tsarevich?" Naturally we need not pay attention to these doubts as inevitably they faded together with the memory of the dire events of the Time of Troubles. Since he could not rise above this outlook, a Russian had to pay dearly for his habitual distrust.

With all the greater esteem must the historian commemorate anyone who in this respect outdid his contemporaries. Timofey Briukhanov, the turbulent monk of the Khutyn monastery, brought a denunciation against his archimandrite Feodorit for "unseemly words." Metropolitan Affony tried to hush up the scandalous affair, but in vain. He brought Feodorit and some others in for questioning, interrogated them closely and tortured them with brands, but could obtain no information. Despite this the metropolitan solemnly in the presence of all in the Holy Wisdom cathedral delivered a stern reprimand for failure to fulfill sacred obligations.

In matters of public safety several steps were taken. In 1622 the elders of the free taxpaying districts and the tsar's free settlements presented a petition. "Between 1613 and 1622 we had thirty watchmen and three horses attached to the town office. Now, in 1622, the number of watchmen has increased to forty-five. We contribute sixty rubles a month for watchmen and their three horses. In addition, we must pay for the upkeep of the town office, for all fire-fighting equipment, tarpaulins, hooks, copper piping, hatchets, spades, pickaxes, crowbars, barrels and pails. Added to this, we have to support an additional fifteen watchmen and three horses, and we each must contribute a length of copper piping. We cannot supply this copper piping, since there is none to be purchased anywhere. The people are all poor and common and, unable to bear such a burden, they are absconding."

The sovereigns decreed that the leading merchant and cloth merchant guilds each pay for their own watchmen, and four extra horses kept for fire fighting. In winter each hundred must have four horses at the ready. The contribution of copper piping was not to be increased, but thirty lengths of pipe must kept at the town office in case of fire. The hundreds were enjoined strictly that in the event of fire they must make ready immediately with their lengths of pipe. Since the population insisted on assuming direct responsibility, no slackness in responding to the alarm was to be tolerated.

Yet the number of watchmen supported by the hundreds was insufficient. In 1629 another hundred men were added, to be paid out of the tsar's treasury through the Chancellery of Crown Revenues. Fifty tarpaulins were to be provided, measuring five by four sazhens; for shields a hundred barks were ordered, to which handles were to be affixed. Sleds and barrels were to be provided from the sovereign's treasury, twenty of each. Twenty cabmen must stand duty every night, plying their regular trade by day. In the event of fire twenty were to report to the town office. In the White Quarter, which was built of stone, and outside the town, emergency water tanks were placed along the streets, one for every ten houses, in the event of fire.

Fires as always were terrible. In 1626 the Kitay Quarter was burned at the St. Barbara intersection. The rows of market stalls and the Intercession cathedral caught fire. The blaze then spread to the Kremlin, setting alight the Miracles monastery and the Ascension convent, as well as the palaces of the sovereign and patriarch. All chancellery documents perished, forcing the tsar to send surveyors throughout the entire land. In 1629 a conflagration started at the Chertolie and spread along Tver street. Beyond the White Quarter the free settlements burned down, and the blaze spread to Neglinnaia and Intercession streets, and elsewhere.

Following this conflagration the free taxpaying peasants petitioned. "There are housed among us various lords from other countries, Germans and various foreigners, Russian visitors from Siberia, cossacks from the Don and from the Great Encampment, as well as gentry and junior boyars visiting on the sovereign's business and that of their own localities, and also provincial surveyors. During this year fires have consumed the Dmitrov, Novgorod, Rzhev, Rostov, Ustiug and Chertolie hundreds, and those rendered homeless are billeted on us, as well as various traders from the White Quarter, and this influx is causing us great hardship." The sovereign was sympathetic, and ordered the displaced housed in the court settlements.

In 1633 and 1634 again there were serious fires, after which the free taxpaying hundreds again petitioned. "Our houses and land in the burned-out hundred are heavily mortgaged to nobles and others outside the taxpaying community. We have petitioned the elders and officials of the hundred that the hundred redeem them, but they cannot find the money. In these houses live many of various ranks, and they are building on vacant lots, but do not contribute their share to taxes. The lenders from the hundreds and the settlements evade taxation, causing the hundreds and the free settlements to fall into decline, for the tax and other dues cannot be collected from anyone." The sovereign decreed that it be announced by the crier in all streets and intersections that in the free taxpaying hundreds and settlements no junior boyars or men of any other rank purchase or grant a mortgage on any house or lot owned by townsmen.

We heard at the Assembly of the Land strong complaints about the unsatisfactory state of justice. As an example of some Russians concerning the contemporary state of the administration of justice let us take the instructions of Table Attendant Kolontaev to his servant. "Get together with Peter Ilyich, and if he says you should go to the crown secretary Vasily Sychin, go to him. When you get there, don't go into his quarters, but first ascertain whether he is in a good mood. If he is, go in, present your petition and give him the document. If the crown secretary receives the document attentively, give him three rubles and promise him more but do not give chickens, beer or ham to him. Give them to his housekeeper. Concerning the Proshkin case, go to the clerk Stepka Remezov and ask him to handle it, but do not go to Kirilla Semenych. That damned Stepka has his paws in everything. Don't mention my name to Stepka, as I don't want to be beholden to him, as he is a real thief. Take him three altyns cash, dried fish and wine. That Stepka is a greedy drunkard!"

We have noted that in Michael's reign, because of the devastation and impoverishment of taxpaying townsmen, many fled heavy obligations by pledging themselves to lords. Another way for literate townsmen to evade dues was to become government clerks, a congenial occupation which also attracted many from the clerical estate. The number of taxpayers diminished, who formerly enriched the treasury by plying their trades, whereas the number of clerks expanded enormously. These men strove to enrich themselves at others' expense, harmful both to society and to the realm.

We learned that the townsmen complained at this unnecessary increase in the number of clerks, diminishing the number of taxpaying townsmen. It is not surprising therefore that at the end of 1640 Tsar Michael decreed that a memorandum be sent around the chancelleries stipulating that no sons of priest or deacons, members of the leading merchant or cloth merchant guilds, traders, members of the taxpaying hundreds or rural cultivators any longer be hired as clerks.

INTERNATIONAL LAW

In matters of international law things continued according to the old law and customs, the significant novelty being appearance of resident ambassadors. It must be noted that the straitened circumstances of the Muscovite state forced it to bribe envoys and especially influential persons at foreign courts. The ancient norms were observed in all their strictness with regard to foreign peoples and their representatives who came to Moscow. Yet the admission of more foreigners into the Muscovite heartland clearly reflected its need of them, patently acknowledging their superiority in learning. This foreshadowed a rapid revolution in the life of Russian society, a swift rapprochement with Western Europe. During the reign of Tsar Michael it was not only soldiers, master craftsmen and manufacturers who were summoned from abroad. Scholars were needed as well. In 1639 a safe conduct was issued to the famous Holstein scholar Adam Olearius to come to Moscow.[20] "It has come to our attention," the tsar said in his letter, "that you are very learned and well versed in astronomy, a geographer who knows the course of the heavens, and geometry. Such scholars are pleasing to us, the great sovereign." In accordance with the sovereign's decree the whole cosmography was translated from the Latin by John Dorn and Bogdan Lykov.

On one hand the realm needed learning to satisfy its most urgent needs, to protect its integrity and independence from foreigners who were more skilled, and therefore more powerful. On the other hand the church needed learning in order to preserve the purity of its teaching from the likes of Login and Filaret. Therefore Patriarch Filaret founded in the Miracles monastery a Greco-Latin school, which was entrusted to Arseny Glukhov, already known to us as a corrector of books.

THE KHVOROSTININ AFFAIR

The necessary acceleration of enlightenment, making inevitable rapprochement with foreigners and acknowledgment of their superiority, led some to despise the ways and people of their own land. Acknowledging foreign ways and recognizing their value, they felt their own ways a burden and sought to cast them off. We saw how the Russians sent abroad during the reign of Godunov failed to return. Even within Russia there were those who decided to give sharp expression to discontent at their own tradition, and strove to adopt the new and foreign.

About 1632 Prince Ivan Khvorostinin[21] was read the following decree from the great sovereigns. "Prince Ivan! It is known to everyone in the Russian realm that you were close to the Renegade Monk, that you fell into heresy and wavered in your faith. You derided the Orthodox faith, failed to observe fasts and Christian customs, and during the reign of Tsar Vasily Ivanovich were sent for supervision to the St. Cyril monastery. Afterwards, under Tsar Michael, you again associated with Lithuanian priests and Poles, and united with them in faith, accepted books, images and letters from them, and held them in honor. These images and pictures were confiscated from you, but you said that you venerated images of Roman origin equally with those of Greek artistry.

"Even then in our mercy we spared you, and you went unpunished, merely being given a strict warning that you no longer consort with heretics, accept any heretical beliefs or keep any Latin images or writings. But you have forgotten all this, have begun to live in an un-Christian manner and have fallen into heresy. Once again many images of Latin artistry and many Latin books have been confiscated from you. You uttered many unseemly and blasphemous words concerning the Orthodox faith and the people of the Muscovite realm, in letters written by your own hand.

"You have displayed many instances in your personal life of incorrigibility towards the Christian religion, and lack of firmness towards treason. You forbade your servants to go to church, saying that prayer is in vain and there will be no resurrection of the dead. You uttered blasphemous words concerning the Christian faith and God's faithful followers. You started to live in an un-Christian fashion, drinking incessantly. In the year 1622, throughout Holy Week you were in a continuous drunken stupor. On the eve of Easter Sunday you were drunk, and at two in the morning you ate meat and drank wine. You did not pay your respects to the sovereign on Easter Sunday, neither did you attend matins or mass.

"You also intended to flee to Lithuania, selling your house and estate. You said you would equip yourself as a hussar and meet with the ambassadors. You sent notes to Timokha Lugovskoy and Mikhail Danilov arranging that while you were performing frontier service they should correspond in order to set a meeting for you with the Lithuanian ambassadors. You also said in conversation that in Moscow there was nobody with whom you cared to live, that they are all fools, that the sovereign should give you leave to go to Rome or Lithuania.

"It is obvious that you were plotting treason and intended to flee to Lithuania. If not, why did you sell your house and estate, and why did you write while on frontier service to the Lithuanian ambassadors?

"Also in pamphlets composed by you there have been found slighting remarks about all manner of inhabitants of the Muscovite realm. You allege that the Muscovites venerate the inscriptions on the icons, not the icons themselves; that even if an icon is painted correctly, if it does not have an inscription they will not venerate it. You say that the Muscovites sow the earth with rye, but live a lie.[22] You have nothing in common with them, and you wrote many scurrilous things about them in verse.

"It is plain that you spoke and wrote these words by reason of your pride and immoderation, unrestrained by reason. Your vain opinion and pride dishonored all the inhabitants of the Muscovite realm and your kinsfolk. Also in your writings the sovereign's title is not written correctly. The sovereign is called 'the Russian despot,' but the word 'despot' is a Greek word meaning 'lord' or 'ruler,' not 'tsar and autocrat.' You, Prince Ivan, are not a foreigner, but a Muscovite born and bred, and it is improper for you to write the sovereign's style in this manner.

"For all this you deserve the most severe punishment, as this is not the first time you have offended against the faith, and many of your sins have been found out. Yet the sovereign in his mercy has ordered that you suffer no punishment. We should have ordered you, for correction in the faith, to be sent to do penance under supervision in the St. Cyril monastery. Instead we order you to give an oath and promise that henceforth you will adhere to and fulfill the precepts of the Orthodox faith, in which you were born and raised, and not accept the Latin or any other heresy, not keep any Latin images or books, nor fall into any heretical teaching. Thus according to their merciful disposition the great sovereigns have shown kindness to you, ordering you to be brought from the St. Cyril monastery to Moscow, to be admitted to the sovereigns' presence and to be received at court as before."

LAVRENTY ZIZANY AND HIS CATECHISM

As an example of the state of learning among Muscovite bookmen at this time, we may take the dispute over Lavrenty Zizany's catechism. Lavrenty Zizany Tustanovsky, an archpriest from Korela, in February 1627 brought his book *Proclamation* to Moscow, and petitioned Patriarch Filaret for it to be corrected. The patriarch first of all changed the book's title. Instead of *Proclamation* he entitled it *Dialogue,* because *Proclamation* already was the title of a book by Cyril of Jerusalem,[23] and it was not fitting for more than one book to have the same title.

Concerning other articles which did not conform to Russian and Greek translations, the patriarch ordered Abbot Ilia of the Epiphany monastery and Grishka, who was a proofreader at the Printing Office, to speak with Zizany, in charity and meekness of spirit. The conversation took place in the lower hall of the Treasury, in the presence of the sovereign's boyar Prince Ivan Borisovich Cherkassky and the conciliar secretary Fedor Likhachev.

Among other matters Ilya and Grishka said the following. "In your book you write about the celestial spheres, planets, zodiacs, solar eclipses, thunder and lightning, fearsome noises,[24] of comets and other stars. These articles are extracted from the *Astrology,* which is taken from Greek sorcerers and idolaters, and therefore is not in accordance with the Orthodox faith."

> *Zizany.* How is it not in accordance? I did not describe the wheel of fortune or the birth of men, nor allege that the stars rule our lives. I wrote only for knowledge, so that man should know that all these things are part of God's creation.

> *Ilia and Grishka.* Why did you write all this for the sake of knowledge? Why did you choose false words and name the stars, and to this add items from your own false imagination and incorrectly seek to publish them?

> *Zizany.* What did I write incorrectly? What false words and what names of the stars did I choose?

> *Ilia and Grishka.* Is it right when you say that when clouds are blown together and collide there is thunder, and when you name the stars in the heavenly firmament after wild beasts?

> *Zizany.* Then how do you propose that we write about the stars?

> *Ilia and Grishka.* We write and believe as Moses wrote. God created the two great luminaries and the stars, and placed them in the heavenly firmament to illuminate the earth and to rule the day and night. Moses did not name them after wild beasts.

> *Zizany.* How then do these luminaries move and revolve?

> *Ilia and Grishka.* By God's command. Angels serve Him and regulate all creation.

> *Zizany.* With the permission of God and the sovereign Most Holy Lord Filaret, I came and presented him my petition that he correct my intellectual shortcomings, since I know that there are many inaccuracies in my book.

Ilia and Grishka. You introduce a new interpolation into the Nicephoran Rules[25] that was not there before. It appears that this interpolation is from the Latin usage. You say that it is permissible for a simple man or anyone else to baptize an infant or anyone else.

Zizany. This is already in the Nicephoran Rules.

Ilia and Grishka. ...It is not in our Greek version of the Nicephoran Rules. Doubtless it is interpolated into your version, and we will not accept such interpolations.

Zizany. From where did you get your Greek rules?

Ilia and Grishka. Metropolitan Cyprian when he came from Constantinople to head the Russian church brought the rule books with him, containing the Christian law in the Greek language, and had them translated into Slavonic. By the grace of God they have remained uncorrupted by any tampering or new interpolations, and we also have many books in the Greek language, in the ancient translation. Now printed books are being issued in the Greek language, and we accept them with love if they correspond with the ancient translations. If on the other hand they contain any novelties we will not accept them, even though they are printed in Greek, because now the Greeks live under great hardships in lands ruled by infidels, and they cannot print according to their custom.

Zizany. Neither will we accept newly translated books in the Greek language. I thought this in fact was written in the Nicephoran Rules, but now I hear you do not have it, so I stand corrected. Forgive me, for the love of God. The reason why I came was to receive better instruction from you.

Ilia and Grishka. Tell us what you wish to discuss further concerning this book.

Zizany. I am always happy to converse with you. I have read through the book presented to me by the sovereign patriarch, and

have labored both with and without your assistance, whereby my
soul has received much enlightenment. I am amazed at the vast
wisdom of the great Orthodox sovereign patriarch. What understanding, what prescience, what divinely inspired wisdom he has
within him! It is amazing how he has composed so long a book
in such a short time. Truly God is working within him.

With that Zizany clasped the book to his breast and reverently kissed it
all over. This conversation was recorded by the proofreader Grishka.

LITERATURE

The most prolific writer of Michael's reign was Prince Semeon
Shakhovskoy.[26] He wrote chronicles, hagiographies, canons and various
missives. Having lost three wives successively he married a fourth, but
was sundered from her. For this reason he sent two "pleading letters," one
to Patriarch Filaret, the other to Archbishop Cyprian of Tobolsk, asking
that he be allowed once more to live with his wife, citing his comparative
youth and his inability to live the single life. Among the number of his
works is a lengthy letter to Shah Abbas on behalf of Patriarch Filaret, in
which he urges the shah to be baptized, but not to accept Christianity from
the Pope, since rumor had it that the shah had entertained a Catholic priest.
Intricate where it is completely unnecessary, Shakhovskoy is extremely
brief in the one work of his which, had it been very detailed, would have
been of great significance for us, namely his memoirs. Shakhovskoy was
a biblical scholar, a man of letters, having a commanding literary style, but
no external merits are evident in his works. They suffer from the same
deficiency as our entire ancient literature from the sixteenth century,
principally striving for effect, working elaborate words and phrases
devoid of meaning.

Several chronicles also suffer from this deficiency. The official chronicle
of the Time of Troubles compiled during Michael's reign and edited under
the title *The Manuscript of Filaret, Patriarch of Moscow* [27] is not free of
it. This chronicle is important for us because it is an original with
emendations from which we can see which information from the Time of
Troubles needed to be preserved in the official chronicle compiled in
Michael's reign, which needed to be suppressed, and finally which needed
to be expanded and embellished. Shuisky's election is at first described
thus. "On May 19 there came to the platform on the Red Square known as
the Place of the Skull the entire council of his majesty the tsar: the
metropolitans, archbishops, archimandrites, abbots and men of all ranks of

the Muscovite realm. All the people gathered, from the greatest to the least, and they discussed how writs must be sent to all the towns of the Muscovite realm so that delegates from all towns might gather in the capital city of Moscow, representing all the people, to elect a tsar, and then to gather in the cathedral to elect a new patriarch, whomsoever God willed. The people replied 'Before we elect a patriarch, let us elect a tsar, and then a patriarch can be elected according to the tsar's will.' The authorities, boyars and all those standing nearby spoke among themselves, saying that God had preserved Prince Vasily Ivanovich Shuisky from the blandishments and enmity of the heretic Renegade Monk, accursed by God, therefore he should be elevated to the tsar's throne. Hearing this, all the people raised their voices, saying 'Let this Prince Vasily Ivanovich rule over us.' They held fast to this counsel and proclaimed him sovereign tsar and grand prince of All Russia."

This description did not appear sufficiently lavish. It was felt necessary to put into the mouths of the crowd a more florid speech, and therefore after the words "the people replied" the original words are struck out, and another speech by the people added, so now the chronicle read "'Let an autocratic tsar be elected who can console our grief and heal the wounds inflicted on us by the plague of that apostate and perfidious heretic, that pestilent viper, that blight infesting God's vineyard. God will reveal that tsar to us, as He revealed Saul to Israel, and he in turn will bring forth a patriarch to serve as a true pastor to God's church.' This word was pleasing, and the people said 'It was the noble Prince Vasily Ivanovich Shuisky who avenged our wrongs and brought to shame Grishka Otrepiev, that infamous enemy of God. He almost suffered death at the hands of this ravening bear, not sparing his life for the deliverance of the Russian people. He is a true scion of the worthy stem of the ruling line of Russian grand princes. For this reason, as well as his great courage and nobility, let him be entrusted with the throne and scepter of the Russian realm.' When these words were heard, the crowd gathered. Some even knew not from whence the good tidings sounded, from heaven or earth, for even the rivers and the ground echoed with the cry, emanating from the crowds which gathered and gathered, all proclaiming 'Let Tsar and Grand Prince Vasily Ivanovich rule over us, for he has spared us from the snares laid for us by the cruel heretic Grishka Otrepiev.' So they with one voice elected the pious Tsar Vasily Ivanovich to rule as autocrat over the Russian realm."

After the item relating to the entry of Prince Skopin-Shuisky into Moscow, at first were included the words "Tsar Vasily was filled with envy and malice, conceiving a hatred for him on account of his victory, even as

Saul came to hate the innocent David when he killed Goliath. As it was sung that Saul slew his thousands but David his ten thousands, even so songs were sung commemorating the victory of this Prince Mikhail Vasilievich and rejoicing in his deliverance. O envy and malice, into what dishonor and ruin do you not lead noble souls, bringing them to hell and eternal torment!" This passage is deleted.

Apart from this official chronicle there have come down to us other chronicles, tales and chronographs including information concerning the Time of Troubles. Most of these chronicles were compiled in Michael's reign, so now it is time to turn our attention to them, to observe how in the first half of the seventeenth century, immediately after the Troubles, consciousness of these great and fearful events was expressed in the historical literature of the time. First of all, naturally, we must address the problem of how the causes of the Time of Troubles were represented.

Reviewing the general character of our chronicles, we have remarked that they regarded all the people's misfortunes as divine punishment for their sins. This outlook did not change during the period under consideration, especially among chroniclers belonging to the clerical estate. This is why pretenders and the ills brought in their wake appear as divine punishment for sins, consequent upon the moral decline of the inhabitants of the Muscovite realm. "Our most merciful, most wise and philanthropic God, not wishing to bring His creation to utter ruin, seeing the human propensity to sin, turning us aside in all things and leading us away from all unseemly degeneracy, sent many and various sufferings and misfortunes against us as fearful signs, wrathfully instilling us with fear and restraining us by His most merciful correction. Many sufferings were inflicted upon us; fires, enemy attacks, famine, deadly plagues and fratricidal strife. Then came the most bitter of sufferings, when God cut off our ruling stem. We sinners did not change our ways in the slightest as a result of this chastisement, and inclined more than ever to our evil ways, not abandoning our envy, pride and injustice, even more intently rushing to our ruin. God, seeing our perversity, sent on account of our sins a special punishment. As in olden times the accursed Sviatopolk was sent to punish the Land of Rus by slaying his brothers,[28] so now God sent the accursed Grishka against our Orthodox Christian faith and the Muscovite realm. God did not wish to punish us by means of tsars or kings, did not wish to avenge the innocent blood of Tsarevich Dmitry by means of the Tatar hordes; rather in the Russian land he took the dust out of the earth in the form of this accursed monk Grishka."

Here the concept of the general sinfulness of the whole land is advanced. Boris Godunov is not singled out, not represented as a sinner by reason of his dark deeds who especially brought down these sufferings upon the Russian land. Even the murder of Tsarevich Dmitry is represented as a sin committed by the whole land. Here consequently we are dealing with a concept common to all the chronicles. It does not involve the intimate connection between phenomena, does not concern itself with a review of how according to ancient law a dark deed contains its own dire consequences and carries punishment. In a society capable of tolerating such evildoing its leaders strive to attain their goals by unjust means, which in turn cause greater social degeneration. Thus in a society which tolerates injustice disorder arises, the pure mingles with the impure, blessings are mingled with curses.

Avraamy Palitsyn[29] shared this view common to all the chronicles. But for him, as well as for a people being punished for their moral decline, there stands Boris Godunov in the forefront. By his immoral means, by his decrees and innovations, he provoked general hatred, and hastened the moral decline of the people. In Palitsyn we encounter reference to one of the causes of the Troubles being the improper relationship between the classes, and we also find reference to the character of the population of Pre-Ruin Ukraine.[30] Palitsyn, while casting Godunov in the major role in the moral decline of the population as a whole, which in turn brought down the wrath of God, harmonized it with the previous chronicle consensus which contrasted Boris's might against the weapon whereby this might was shattered. "Many and various sins were committed amongst us, and when we were confident in the firmness of Boris's administration suddenly universal destruction overwhelmed us. God did not send against Boris any of those against whom he was on his guard, whose families he destroyed; neither did he send any foreign rulers. Whom then did he send? The tale is ludicrous, but the sorrow was great!"

Finally our chronograph singles out Boris's relations with the aristocrats whom he victimized as the cause of his ruin and the origin of the Troubles. Thus in the historical literature of our seventeenth century there were three contrasting views concerning the causes of the Time of Troubles. First, the view that the population was punished for its sins, without singling out any culprits who were especially sinful. Second, the same view but simultaneously pointing the finger at a specific individual. Third and last, limiting the causes of the Troubles to personal relationships between Godunov and the aristocrats.

All accounts attributed the death of Tsarevich Dmitry to Godunov. But then, when turning to the description of the Time of Troubles several chronicles, as we have seen, do not single out Godunov as the sole culprit for the catastrophe. His sin is merged with the mass of the people's sins. Only Palitsyn when speaking of the death of Tsarevich Dmitry made any attempt to mitigate Godunov's part in this general guilt by sharing his blame with others and by attributing the cause, not merely to Boris's megalomania, but to the fact that both he and others were threatened by Dmitry. "Tsarevich Dmitry as he gained in stature was stirred up by his entourage who pointed out to him how he was wronged by being banished from his brother's presence. The tsarevich was aggrieved, and frequently in his childish games he acted against those of his brother's court, and especially against Boris. Enemies, flatterers, those plotting against him magnified tenfold these tales and told them to the aristocrats, especially Boris, and on account of this many troubles were stirred up, many sins were provoked, and the most fair youth was sent violently to his eternal rest." This aspect is all the more important for us since elsewhere Palitsyn is very censorious concerning Boris, attributing to him the undermining of morals and pernicious innovations.

The fiercest attacks against Boris were by the author of the tale concerning the Time of Troubles.[31] At the same time he is distinguished as an ardent apologist for Vasily Shuisky, and so indicates the source of his hatred for Godunov, who according to him was the murderer of Tsarevich Dmitry, Tsar Fedor and many others. He obtained the tsardom by deceit and injustice. The appearance of the pretender was punishment for Boris's sins, which cried out to heaven. "Seeing with His unsleeping eye how Boris unjustly seized the scepter of the Russian realm, Christ desired to avenge the innocent blood of His new martyrs Tsarevich Dmitry and Tsar Fedor Ivanovich, as well as the other innocents slain by Boris. He wished to accuse him of his frenzy and unjust murders, and make an example to his supporters lest they rejoice in his evil cunning. He sent against him an enemy, a chieftain, a survivor from Sodom and Gomorrah, an unburied corpse disguised as a monk called Ivan Lestvichnik, who before he died prepared a grave in his cell."

This tale is distinguished by especially colorful detail. For example, there is the description of the two battles fought by Boris's commanders. Here is the description of the first. "Battle was joined. Just as two clouds coming together cause darkness and make the rain fall to earth, so also these two armies came together for the shedding of human blood. Not heavenly thunder sounded, but the roar of muskets. There was wailing and tumult from human voices and the clash of weapons, such that the earth trembled, and none could hear what the other said. The battle was as fearful as that fought on the Don by Prince Dmitry against Mamay." Obviously the writer had open before him the *Tale of the Battle with Mamay*. [32] Here is the description of the second battle. "Even as the clear-eyed falcons soar into the gray skies, and even as the snowy gerfalcons sharpen their beaks to swoop and their talons to sink into flesh, even as they spread their wings and brace their pinions to kill other birds, so did the commanders, champions of the Orthodox Christian faith, together with their Christ-loving warriors, don their armor and prepare to do battle with Satan's beloved and his demonic host."

Towards Boris several chronicles were neutral, others enthusiastically extolled his virtues, while at the same time pointing out the shortcomings causing his ruin. Some, evidently writing under the influence of factional interest, went to extremes to blacken his memory. Generally the chronicles are condescending towards Shuisky, though most regard him as someone who rushed to grasp the supreme power but proved incapable of holding on to it. Others even praise him to the skies.

Concerning False Dmitry, all accounts are unfavorable. This is understandable. Nobody sympathizes with the executioner, even when he is carrying out a just sentence upon the criminal. Our ancestors had no sympathy for the instrument whereby heaven punished either their sins or those of Godunov alone. Those concerned however superficially or timorously with the matter of imposture, who did not share the general opinion of the supernatural causes surrounding False Dmitry's appearance, perhaps failed to sympathize with his personality and deeds, without even saying that they had no such sympathy. Most people, as Palitsyn mentioned in an aside, loved False Dmitry; but "most people" do not write down their opinions, and moreover were intimidated by the fearsome words and expressions repeated by those in charge, those who were knowledgeable and wise. The majority, especially at that time, were prone to believe these expressions and be intimidated by them. Consequently they conceived a hatred for their former hero even before he was declared and confirmed to be a heretic and sorcerer.

Whence did this concept of False Dmitry as a heretic derive? Everyday experience teaches us that those who have not received, by way of enlightenment or learning, the habit of encountering new and incomprehensible phenomena, recoil against them and finally overcome them like the ancient Sphinx by guessing their riddle. Such men attribute anything emerging from the ranks of the ordinary to the action of supernatural forces. Besides, the pretender appeared as a weapon of the enemy of the human race, as the fomenter of troubles and afflictions. He also must have been a friend of heretics, an introducer of new customs, someone who did not act according to the accepted sacred standards and customs.

The word "heresy" at that time had a very broad and often corrupt meaning. The religious, eternal, unchanging, God-given meaning was attributed also to that which had nothing in common with it. It was attributed to form, the superficial and changeable. At the same time true heresy such as an incorrect, corrupt interpretation of some passage in holy scripture, incorrectly glossed by an ecclesiastical writer, passed completely unnoticed. On the other hand any violation of a generally-accepted custom sanctified by antiquity created a strong impression, upset the whole structure of life, caused perpetual unrest, broke the sacred bonds with dead ancestors and thus seemed to be a sinful rebellion against their memory, against their very existence.

In the absence of spiritual horizons, under the dominance of the superficial, of the formulaic, and given the weak development of authentic and firm bases of national consciousness, monotony, superficialities and formulae served as the sole bond of society, members of the nation. Poor development of any inner, spiritual bond in general meant that the individual who cast off the bond with his people became a permanent outcast. Thus the young men sent abroad in Godunov's reign permanently ruptured all ties with their nation.[33] Prince Khvorostinin also wanted to get away from Russia.[34] We also heard the fears expressed by Prince Ivan Golitsyn. "Russians cannot serve alongside the subjects of the king of Poland, for fear of temptation. If they serve alongside them for one summer, by the next year only half of them will be left, not only servitors of boyars, but also those who are too old or do not wish to serve. Of the poor, not one will remain."[35]

Thus it is understandable why society persecuted any violation of ancestral custom as though it were treason. Therefore external forms held religious significance, and the Russian nation in its confession of faith differed from all other European nations, separated consciously from them by insistence upon the externals of its faith. They did not see that Orthodoxy was not a matter of beards, not eating veal and so forth. Changing their external and immutable for another external and immutable was regarded as changing the basic, the substantial, the religious, and therefore a heresy and a sin. In fact, as we have seen, those who changed the externals did not confine themselves to this alone. They also could not distinguish between external and internal, between form and substance, but in their accustomed way of thinking continued to confuse them. A Russian who went abroad dressed himself in foreign garb accepted foreign customs and thus changed his ancestral faith. He did this because he had no proper understanding of that faith, it being in his consciousness inextricably bound to the customs and superficialities he renounced. Consequently by renouncing the one he could not help renouncing the other.

Therefore it is obvious why False Dmitry appeared in contemporary literary works as a heretic and a sorcerer, the instrument of dark infernal forces. He altered ancient custom, surrounded himself with foreigners, schismatics and heretics; he praised things foreign and mocked his own. He appeared too early, perhaps a century before his time. Those who could tolerate his behavior at that time could not even constitute a minority, merely exceptions. Subsequently it was discovered that he was an impostor, deceiver and seducer, thus an instrument of the spirit of falsehood and seduction. Finally, nobody knew how he appeared, how he attained the tsardom by astonishing means, which for most appeared miraculous. Even Palitsyn, indisputably the most canny of contemporary writers, said that False Dmitry was a sorcerer, even during his youth drawn to necromancy. Besides, evidence of False Dmitry's occult knowledge[36] could be accepted literally. Given the contemporary state of intellectual immaturity, arcane knowledge and the books containing it held intense fascination for curious young men, whose thoughts and imagination were over-active, who wanted to know more than could be taught by contemporary sages who were not sorcerers. It may well be that some forbidden books, some *Aristotle's Gates,*[37] at some time passed through the hands of the ardent, inquisitive Otrepiev.

If False Dmitry was a heretic and sorcerer, it follows that his wife Marina fell into the same category, perhaps even to a greater degree, for at the same time she was a heretic, a harlot, a girl of the Latin, Lutheran and Calvinist faiths. The combination of the last three applied to one person, a combination found in the writings of contemporary bookmen, nowadays completely defeats us. Yet our ancestors paid no attention to discriminating between faiths. They used the three epithets Latin, Lutheran and Calvinist as terms of abuse when speaking of anything foreign and Western. The requirement that those of other Christian confessions be baptized on converting to Orthodoxy best of all explains what a strong impression the word "foreign" produced on our ancestors. This magic word deprived them of all ability to find anything in common with someone of another Christian confession, to find a mutual basis and together define which of these confessions was closer to ours, which more distant.

Representation of other prominent actors in the Time of Troubles as expressed in contemporary literary works is very unsatisfactory and unclear. Live personalities with a sharply defined image are not found either in Skopin or in Liapunov as they are portrayed in chronicles and tales. Their external deeds were related, conventional eulogies were expressed in vague terms, as applied to any good man. Not a single word, not one line, has come down to us concerning Skopin-Shuisky either from himself or anyone close to him. Consequently to the historian his figure is shrouded from head to toe. We suspect that there is something majestic, but we do not know for sure.

Similarly lifeless is the presentation to us of the other great hero and liberator Pozharsky if we confine ourselves to the chronicles. But we have the good fortune to have the description of Novgorod's embassy to Pozharsky in Yaroslavl. There Pozharsky said a few words about himself, of his situation, about some others, and so a bright ray of light bursts through and illuminates the image! Even this consists of only a few words.

Liapunov's character was depicted more clearly by reason of his varied activities, which in their entirety prohibit generalizations or indefinite expressions. In descriptions of Minin's activities there is much that is obscure and inadequately expressed. Yet another mysterious image! It is curious that if in several accounts Minin is upstaged by Pozharsky, in the popular imagination as recorded by one of the chronographs Minin was solely responsible for the liberation of Moscow. Here there is a clear wish to contrast him with the boyar Prince Trubetskoy while Pozharsky, a figure inconsistent with the desired impression, is cast aside completely. "Calling on God for help, though unskilled in the task he was bold in action, and arrived at the capital city. At that time Prince Dmitry Trubetskoy stood there with his army. Hearing that Kuzma Minin was coming with his army, he withdrew, saying 'This peasant wants to take all the glory for himself, while my service and diligence will count for nothing.' Then Avraamy Palitsyn, cellarer of the Trinity monastery, heard that Dmitry Trubetskoy with his colleague Prokopy Liapunov (?)[38] had withdrawn, lifting the siege of the Kremlin fortress. The cellarer came to the regiments of Prince

Dmitry Trubetskoy, pleading that this peasant was coming to aid them, not to deprive them of their glory, and with difficulty he persuaded Prince Dmitry. Meanwhile Kuzma Minin and his forces laid siege to the Kremlin fortress, so Trubetskoy said 'I besieged the Kremlin for some considerable time; I captured the White Quarter and the Kitay. I can see what this peasant is up to.' So the cellarer went to the Nizhny Novgorod regiments, saying to Kuzma Minin 'I barely managed to talk Prince Dmitry Timofeevich around. Kuzma Minin, do not contradict him in anything, but fight as God shows you the way.' With that he returned to his monastery." The next day Kuzma detailed two regiments, and so the story continues. Patriarch Hermogen generally appears in a blazing light, but this very brilliance prevents us from distinguishing the individual details in the image. Only the insidious author of the chronograph whispers a few words which shatter the general impression.

TWO TALES OF ONE CITY

Among the tales whose content concerns the Time of Troubles there are two emanating from Pskov. These are remarkable because they contain expressions of the views of two opposing and hostile sides, those of the "better" and the "lesser" people. In our history, describing the struggle between these factions in Pskov, we confined ourselves to the official chronicle account because at least it was comparatively objective. Although very hostile towards the governor and the "better" people, neither did it spare the "lesser" people when they started to rally to Kudekusha. In one of the tales the events were depicted in such a way that the actions of the "better" people were shown constantly in a favorable, and those of the "lesser" people in an unfavorable light. This tale bears the title *Concerning the Confusion and Domestic Strife, and How the People of Pskov Deserted the Muscovite Realm, and How there Followed Hardships and Attacks on the City of Pskov from the Invasion of the Pagans, and How This Evil Came About at That Time.*

According to this tale, this is how the Troubles began. "There appeared in the Pskov bytowns subversive letters from the Brigand before Moscow which tempted the feeble-minded and stirred up the people, so that they began to swear allegiance to him. Soon afterwards Bishop Gennady died from grief, hearing of such waywardness. In Pskov the people were stirred up, hearing that someone or other was coming from the false tsar with a small army. The governors, seeing such unrest among the people, tried hard to fortify them, but to no avail.

"The populace seized the better people and leading merchants and cast them into prison, and the governors appealed to Novgorod for help. At that time some enemy of Christ's cross spread the rumor that the Swedes[39] were coming to Pskov. Then some rebels proclaimed among the people that the Swedes had reached the bridge across the Velikaia river. At that the insurrection became general, the governors were seized and imprisoned, and themselves sent for the Brigand's governor Pleshcheev, and swore allegiance to the Brigand. Then they began to run riot, were greatly enraged and coveted others' property.

"In the autumn there came to Pskov from the Tushino encampment various tormentors, murderers and plunderers, proclaiming to the unwise the Brigand's rule and authority, and these accursed ones gave praise to his dark dominion, boasting before them of their devotion, and slandering those pilgrims and martyrs who refused to bend the knee to Baal, namely the town officials and respectable men held in prison. The wild beasts dragged them out of the prison and slew them. Some they impaled, others they beheaded, while on the rest they inflicted various torments, confiscated their possessions, strangled the boyar Prince Peter Nikitich Sheremetev in his prison and, having taken everything from the archbishop's household, the monasteries, the town officials and leading merchants, they left to go to their false tsar outside Moscow, and there they were killed by their own people." This account of the behavior of the Tushinites is very plausible, but why does it not appear in the chronicle? The chronicler was not favorably disposed to Tushino either, and calls those insane who swore allegiance to the Tushino tsar.

Let us leave aside the causes of the popular rising against the "better" people, causes listed by the chronicler, namely the imprisonment of a courier from the cossack ataman and the flight of some of the clergy to the enemy. The author of the tale, after describing the great fire, says "The common people and musketeers began plundering the belongings of respectable people and, prompted by the devil, alleged that the boyars and leading merchants had set fire to the city. These they tried to force into the conflagration under a hail of stones, so they fled the city. The next day the mob dragged out respectable gentry and leading merchants. They tortured, executed and imprisoned respectable people, the town officials and ecclesiastical dignitaries."

Having described the triumph of the "lesser" people, the chronicler adds, "God granted that all this passed without bloodshed, for if the better people had their way there would have been much bloodshed. An inventory was taken of the possessions of those who fled Pskov territory, but of those who took refuge in Pskov, in the Caves monastery or elsewhere within Pskov territory, no inventory was taken." The account given by the author of our tale is completely different. "Those innocent Orthodox Christians whom (the victorious lesser people) sought out were brought to interrogation. There they were tortured, locked up in bare halls and cellars, and the wives of those who fled Pskov body and soul were imprisoned in cellars and later put to death. The rebels entered their houses, ate, drank and made merry, and divided up their possessions. Those who were in prison gave their last farthing to redeem themselves from torture and death. Those who had nothing either were tortured or perished in prison, and their wives and children were left to beg. There were more than two hundred such martyrs, both men and women, and they suffered until the arrival of the false tsar, the brigand Matiushka. He liberated them all, and in their place imprisoned their persecutors, and so they received a just reward for their misdeeds."

Thus the last pretender, Matiushka or Sidorka, was seen as acting in favor of the "better" against the "lesser" people. Yet in the same tale here is what is said about that pretender. "A brigand appeared at Ivangorod and various such brigands and murderers rallied around him, cossacks from Novgorod and musketeers from Pskov. The citizens of Pskov refused to receive him, but he came up to Pskov with siege engines and field artillery. The citizens stoutly resisted him, and he could do nothing against the city. The Swedes sent against him an army from Novgorod, and the accursed one lifted the siege of Pskov. Then the citizens, not knowing what to do and to whom to swear allegiance, despairing of receiving aid from anywhere, resolved to summon the false tsar. On behalf of all ranks they petitioned him and sent him their submission. The accursed one came to Pskov with all speed, and many rallied to him who rejoiced in the shedding of blood and coveted others' possessions. Besides this, he favored the pagans, Lithuanians and Germans. As a result the citizens suffered much torment on account of requisitions and numerous dues, and many were tortured. The citizens of Pskov began to complain. At that time the Lithuanians were besieged in Moscow by the Russians, and from there several respectable citizens were sent to learn the qualities of this newly proclaimed tsar. These observers, being mortally afraid, did not denounce him. Later, finding an opportune moment, when the brigand sent off some of his troops to attack Porkhov, they conspired with the citizens, arrested him and sent him to the encampment outside Moscow."

We encounter in this tale interesting details about Lisowski's sojourn in Pskov. "The citizens of Pskov, hearing that Lord Lisowski with his

Lithuanians and Russians was in the Novgorod lands, in the district of Porkhov, conveyed their respects to him, asking him to come to Pskov with his Russian troops. Having devastated the Novgorod land, he came to Pskov. He himself was admitted into the city, but the Lithuanians were stationed outside, in the musketeers' settlement. Gradually the Lithuanians infiltrated the city, spending much money on drink and clothes, for they had much in gold, silver and precious stones, having plundered the splendid cities of Rostov and Kostroma, as well as the St. Paphnutius and Kaliazin monasteries and others, where they chopped up the reliquaries of the saints, plundering the church vessels and icon settings. They also had many captives, women, girls and boys. Having plundered all they could, and gambled and drunk everything away, they threatened the citizens. 'We have laid waste and destroyed many cities, and we will do the same to Pskov, because all our means has been spent here in the taverns.' The citizens, hearing this, approached the barbarian and addressed him in flattering words, urging him to go to the relief of Ivangorod, which was being besieged by the Swedes. 'We will gather together a war chest and send it on to you,' said the citizens of Pskov. Lisowski agreed, and evacuated Pskov with all his men. By the time he realized the citizens had tricked him, it was too late."

Finally in this tale there is curious information about Pskov's relations with Livonia during the Time of Troubles. "It was a great mercy of the Immaculate Virgin of the Caves that only past her house (the Caves monastery) was the road open to the Livonian border, whence throughout all this time grain came to Pskov, for the burghers were in very peaceful relations with the citizens of Pskov. Had not the land been aided with grain, the citizens of Pskov could not have been delivered from the pagans."

Now let us turn to the tale written in the contrary spirit, from the viewpoint of the "lesser" people, in the spirit of Pskov particularism and pronounced bias against Moscow and all its works, particularly against the boyars, their conduct and their orders. If we considered ourselves justified in treating with suspicion the details included in the other tale, noting the one-sidedness of partisan views, all the more suspicious should we be of the account given by this second tale, for here we encounter blatant distortion of events. The tale carries the heading *Concerning the Tribulations, Troubles and Enemy Attacks Which Came Upon Great Russia as a Result of Divine Punishment on Account of Our Sins, Following the Days of the Eighth Epoch and at the Beginning of The Two Hundredth Year.*

"The prophecy of St. John the Theologian was fulfilled," says the author, "that the angel of the Lord poured out the vials of his wrath upon the earth, the sea and all of God's creation. All perished but a third of all living creatures.[40] I know nothing of foreign lands and do not dare say what went on there, but here in Russia everybody knows that thousands perished from these tribulations and this decimation, for where a thousand or a hundred formerly lived, barely one survived, and even then suffered greatly from insults, impositions and misfortunes inflicted by the strong in the land, so that they sold themselves into slavery and committed violence."

In the first lines we encounter the familiar refrain in the Pskov chronicles, their complaint against the governors, from which sprang all evil, all alienation of the inhabitants of Pskov from Moscow. The tale blamed Shuisky for the intensification of the Troubles since after his victory over the insurgents "the devil inflamed the tsar to concupiscence. He abandoned his army, returned to the capital, took a wife and began to eat, drink and be merry."

The tale accepted at face value the rumor that Skopin-Shuisky was poisoned by the wife of his uncle Dmitry Shuisky, here named Christina. Shuisky's overthrow is described in the following terms. "One day men of all ranks took counsel with Patriarch Hermogen, saying 'We do not want to see this Tsar Vasily on the throne. Let us go to the Polish king Sigismund and ask him to give his son Wladyslaw to rule over us.' The patriarch went to great lengths to dissuade them, saying that we were attacked frequently by the Poles in time past. They supported Grishka Otrepiev, so what now would they bring in their wake other than the utter ruin of the tsardom and the faith? Could not one of the Russian princes be chosen as tsar? 'We do not wish to obey one of our brothers,' the princes and boyars replied. 'The soldiers will not respect or obey a tsar chosen from among the Russians.'

"Then the patriarch, taking counsel with the boyars and people, sent ambassadors to the Polish king to give his son to reign over the tsardom, and the prince would be baptized according to the Greek dispensation. The pagan king, suspected treachery and said 'How can I trust you? You have a tsar sitting upon your throne, yet you ask me to send my son to rule over you. If you bring your tsar and his brothers here, I will give you my son.' Several of the boyar clans got together, traitors and destroyers of Christianity, who loved pagan customs and laws. They forced their way into the tsar's chamber, snatched the scepter from his hand, deposed him from the tsardom, tonsured him, and sent him and his brothers to the king before Smolensk.

"When the king heard that in Moscow and throughout Russia everyone was swearing allegiance to his son, the pagan king thought up this reply to the Russian ambassadors. 'Why have you come to me requesting my son? You have killed one of your tsars, you have sent another a prisoner to me, and what will you do with my son? He is not of your faith or of a Russian family, so you will deal even more harshly with him. If all of Russia will swear allegiance to me, the king, I will give my son to rule over you.'

"Then he sent his hetman Lord Zolkiewski against the Muscovite realm with many troops, ordering him to administer to everybody the oath of allegiance to the king. But in Moscow they refused, saying 'We will not swear allegiance to the Polish king.' So it was that in the capital city of Moscow the same happened as at Jerusalem, which was captured by Antiochus at the very time of the feast of Passover.[41] Some Orthodox Christians heard about this in the Lower Towns. Their leader was drawn from the common people, but he was ardent in the faith and a champion of Christianity. His name was Kuzma Minin. He collected many valuables among the population of the various towns, he recruited an army, handed it over to Prince Dmitry Pozharsky and accompanied him on campaign.

"When the pagan Poles came to attack Prince Dmitry Pozharsky, and were gaining the upper hand, the devil instilled inveterate pride in Prince Dmitry Trubetskoy, who did not come to aid his brother, as he considered himself more exalted. 'It was I who besieged the city,' he boasted. Then the Christ-loving Kuzma came to Prince Trubetskoy's regiment and implored the soldiers that in charity they must aid one another, and he promised them large gifts. Thus the cry arose like a roar of lions, and both the cavalry and infantry attacked the pagans." In this way the democratic Pskov tale took revenge on Palitsyn for having in his own tale placed Minin so much in the shadows. In the Pskov tale, Palitsyn's feat is ascribed to Minin, without mentioning a word of the famous cellarer who so loved to extol his own deeds.

Concerning Michael's election the tale says the following. "The aristocrats wanted once again to choose a tsar of a different faith, but the people and soldiers refused, and in place of the brave Mikhail Skopin, God put forward a second unexpected Michael, whom He himself chose. As in ancient times Constantinople was cleared of Latins by the Emperor Michael,[42] so now in Russia God promoted the namesake of his chief warrior Michael the Archangel. This was a meek, peaceful tsar, an imitator of Christ. The tsar was young when he ascended the throne, eighteen years of age,[43] but he was handsome, mild, meek, humble and gracious. He loved all and was merciful to everyone, like the previous pious tsar his uncle Fedor Ivanovich.

"He did not have sufficient wisdom to govern the land, but his pious mother the nun and mother superior Martha ruled under him and supported the tsardom together with her family, for his father at that time was a prisoner of the Polish king. Yet even under this pious and just tsar, on account of his humility, the devil would not leave the realm in peace. Once again he prompted those in authority to venality; once again they oppressed Orthodox Christians and enslaved them. Those who survived Polish or Swedish captivity began to gather around the towns, but these accursed ones like wolves preyed upon them, having forgotten their earlier chastisement when they were plundered by their slaves. They tried to do as before, neither did they pay any attention to or have any fear of the tsar, because he was so young. Even him they ensnared in their deceits. When he was placed on the throne of the tsardom they made him swear he would not execute anyone of aristocratic or boyar families, but only send them into exile, as those accursed ones intended.[44] If any were sent into exile, the others would petition on their behalf. They divided all of the Russian realm according to their desire. They appropriated the tsar's villages without the tsar's knowledge, for the cadastral registers perished in the ruin. On pretext of collecting for the tsar's dues and services they exacted quitrent and tribute, and from free taxpayers they collected one fifth of their possessions.

"The sovereign sent to recapture Smolensk his commanders Prince Dmitry Mamstriukovich (Cherkassky) and Prince Ivan Troekurov, who diligently fulfilled the tsar's commission and almost took the city. But the boyars recalled these commanders and sent others who did not do so well. The Lithuanians attacked and besieged them, and there was great hunger. The besieged several times sent to the sovereign requesting grain, but the boyars imprisoned these messengers, telling the tsar nothing about them. The soldiers, unable to endure hunger, withdrew from Smolensk and ravaged their own land, torturing the people in anger at the boyars. Such was the boyars' solicitude for the Russian land!

"Then the Swedish king besieged Pskov with many foreign troops and artillery. Many times did the inhabitants send to the tsar for relief, but the boyars allowed none of these messengers to appear before him. Instead they were held prisoner, whereas the boyars assured the tsar that the pagans were few and there were many defenders within the city. They said nothing about the people's suffering and hunger, and sent the messengers back with joyful news that the tsar was sending troops for their immediate relief.

"The tsar wanted to get married, and he was betrothed to Tsaritsa Anastasia[45] Khlopova. Then Satan moved certain relatives, kinsmen of the tsaritsa the sovereign's mother, by sorcery to instill hatred, and so she was banished from the tsar's presence and sent into exile. When Metropolitan Filaret arrived and was consecrated patriarch he began to administer the affairs of the land, and spoke to his son concerning marriage, saying 'Do you desire the hand of the Lithuanian king's daughter, and thereby be reconciled with him and induce him to return the towns he took from you?' Michael refused. When his mother and father sent to the Danish king to betroth his daughter to the tsar, the king refused, saying 'Earlier you brought my brother to Russia, during the reign of Tsar Boris, who wanted to marry him off to his daughter Xenia, but almost as soon as he reached Moscow he was dead, and no doubt you will do the same with my daughter.'

"Once again father and mother urged the tsar to get married, but he replied 'I pledged my word according to God's law. The tsaritsa was betrothed to me, and I want no other.' The father wished to send for her but was told that she was cursed, infertile and infirm. For a long time they tried to find out who had done this to her. It turned out to be the accursed offspring of Mikhail Saltykov, two brothers named Boris and Mikhail, who were related to the tsar's mother. They pleaded they did this for fear they would be banished from the tsar's presence and lose their rank. They were sentenced to exile, not being condemned to death by reason of their kinship with the tsar, while their father died in Lithuania. Then doctors were sent to the tsar's fiancée. The doctors healed her, and the patriarch wanted the tsar to wed her, but the mother swore vehemently that she would forsake the court if he married that girl, since she could not stand the sight of her. The tsar did not wish to be parted from his mother or to offend her, for she was his own flesh and blood. He did not marry Khlopova, although on account of this he suffered bitter reproaches from his father."

BALLADS

The foregoing tale bears clear indications that it was composed by the hundred-tongued voice of popular gossip. Popular ballads also have survived whose contents speak of the events of the Time of Troubles. Such is the *Ballad of Grishka the Renegade Monk,* which expresses the popular view of the pretender's fall. He married an accursed Lithuanian woman, a heretic and atheist, and the wedding took place on the feast of St. Nicholas, and on a Friday. While the princes and boyars were attending matins, Grishka went to take a bath with his wife. After bathing Grishka proceeded to the Red Porch and exclaimed "Hail, you my stewards and minions! Prepare various dishes, both for fasting and feasting. Tomorrow I have a dear guest, Lord Jerzy and his lady." All of a sudden the musketeers grasped what these words meant, and rushed to the dowager tsaritsa, who repudiated the False Dmitry, and so they mutinied. The atheist Marina turned into a magpie and flew out of the hall. Grishka the Renegade Monk realized what was happening, and threw himself from the gables on to the sharp-pointed spears of the musketeers, those brave lads, and so he perished.

Another ballad relates the death of Skopin-Shuisky. At a christening feast given by Prince Vorotynsky "the drunkards boasted. The strong boasted of their might, the rich of their wealth. Prince Mikhail Vasilievich did not drink of the green wine, only beer and sweet mead, without much hops. 'You foolish men,' he said, 'all your boasting is in vain. I, Prince Mikhailo Vasilievich Skopin, can boast that I liberated the Muscovite tsardom and the Great Russian realm. My praises will be sung forever, by both young and old, from my youth until the end of my days.' The boyars were humbled and immediately started to plot. They confected a deadly poison and put it in his glass, into the sweet mead, which was handed to him by his godmother, a daughter of Maliuta Skuratov."[46] The ballad here portrays an authentic action, the custom of boasting of one's own feats and belittling those of others. This ballad about Skopin represents the cause of his death being the envy of the boyars in general, not just of Dmitry Shuisky, envy provoked by Skopin's boasting.

Another ballad, also about Skopin, displays the contrast between the grief of the citizens, who hoped for an end to the Troubles, and the malicious rejoicing of the boyars. "Another event happened among us in Moscow. At midnight the bell tolled and the merchants of Moscow fell a-weeping, for now we will all perish, because our valiant commander Prince Mikhail Vasilievich is no more. All the princes and boyars opposed to him gathered together, Princes Mstislavsky and Vorotynsky, and they laughed and said 'The eagle has soared up high, but has come crashing down to his mother earth.'"

YULIANA LAZAREVSKAIA

From the period under consideration there has survived a curious tale depicting the private domestic life of Russian people of the late sixteenth and early seventeenth centuries. This is the tale of Yuliana Lazarevskaia, written by her son Kallistrat Druzhina Osoryin.[47] Yuliana was the daughter of one of the tsar's stewards. Orphaned by the death of her mother, she was raised in her aunt's household. They sought to raise her in the customary manner, trying at morning and night to make her eat and drink although from her earliest years she was more inclined to prayer and fasting. She shunned all manner of laughter and play. Her sole diversions were spinning and embroidery. Her candle did not go out all night. She made garments for all the widows, orphans and invalids in the neighborhood. The church was one or two versts from the hamlet where Yuliana lived, and so until she was married she was unable to attend church. Having married Osoryin, a rich noble of Murom, Yuliana moved into the house of her parents-in-law, who entrusted her to run the entire household. When her husband was away on the tsar's service for one, two or three years, she never slept at night and instead prayed much to God, span and embroidered. She sold her work and gave the proceeds to the poor. Everyone in the household was clothed from head to toe. She assigned everyone tasks according to their ability, and hated pride or boasting. She did not call anyone by diminutives,[48] neither did she demand that anyone bring her water to wash her hands, or pull off her boots, but did these things for herself. Perhaps of necessity, when company came, she would have her maids serve her, but after the company left she did all the chores herself, and in humility said "I am also merely a wretched individual. Why should I be waited upon by such people, who are also God's creatures?" She did not scold the serfs subject to her, on account of which frequently she was reproached by her parents-in-law. Even though she could not read, she loved to listen to the reading of sacred books. The devil tried to put all manner of harm and temptation in her way, provoking foolish quarrels between her children and her serfs, but she thoughtfully and wisely mediated their quarrels and made peace between them. Satan even provoked one of the serfs to slay her eldest son.

TRAVEL ACCOUNTS

We have encountered the name of the Moscow merchant [Rodion] Kotov and heard his answer to the question whether the English should be allowed to travel to Persia by way of the Muscovite realm.[49] In 1623 this Kotov with eight companions crossed the sea to the Persian land to do business on their own behalf as well as on behalf of the tsar's treasury. They have left us a description in their *Voyage to the Persian Empire*. From Moscow they proceeded the usual route by water, the Moscow, Oka and Volga rivers to Astrakhan. "From Astrakhan," wrote Kotov, "we went on Russian boats[50] and large rafts as far as Chern, which is a long way. Given fair weather it takes two days and nights, a week if the sea is becalmed. We proceeded overland by steppe between the cossack settlements, from the Terek to the Bystraia river, on both sides of which the cossacks operate ferries. From Tarki we went on to Derbent. Between Tarki and Derbent dwell the Lezghi. They have their own prince called Usminsky. They live in distant towns and are subject to none, and there is much brigandage committed by them. They plunder traders along the roads and hold some to ransom. Even in peaceful times they take a toll from traders, one bundle from each packload. For this stretch guides are needed. From Derbent it is three days' journey to Shirvan, through the steppe between the mountains and the sea. The journey from Astrakhan to Persia can be made on small rafts as far as the Nizova anchorage, then overland from Nizova to Shirvan, but the journey on small rafts is hard because if you must put into shore on account of adverse weather large tolls are taken from traders in Derbent and Tarki, while in open country they are attacked and plundered by the Lezghi. Brigandage is rife along the shore."

We do not need to relate the detailed description given by Kotov of the Persian towns, merely one instance. "In Isfahan the gates are lofty, and high above the gate is a clock operated by a Russian master craftsman." In Moscow the master clockmakers were German, in Persia a Russian!

In connection with the Persian trade there is also the account of the pilgrimage to the Holy Places in Palestine by Vasily Gogara. This is what the traveler says at the beginning of his narration. "I sent my servant with goods across the sea to trade in the Persian land. Through the wrath of God on account of my accursedness the boat with all my goods was wrecked, and all my possessions sank. Other hardships and misfortunes were afflicted upon me. Amid all these troubles and misfortunes I made a vow to travel to Jerusalem and other sacred places."

From Kazan, Gogara proceeded to Astrakhan, and from Astrakhan to the Georgian land. "In Georgia," he wrote, "amid the high snow-capped mountains in inaccessible places there are caves in the earth into which by the ancient law of Alexander of Macedonia the monsters Gog and Magog were chased. Many tales are related about these monsters, namely that recently they were caught by being lured out of their caves."

In Jerusalem the Greeks told him that since Trifon Korobeinikov, sent there by Tsar Ivan Vasilievich, no other Russian visitor until Gogara had arrived there. On Easter Sunday his candle was lit by a miraculous fire descending from heaven. He tried to set his beard on fire with it, but not one hair was singed. He tried a second and third time, but the beard remained whole. "After that," the traveler wrote, "I went to the metropolitan to ask forgiveness for my lack of faith, for I thought the Greeks contrived this fire by some artifice." Gogara also traveled to Egypt. "In Egypt, beyond the Nile river, there are tents as high as mountains. These were built by the Pharaohs who abused the Israelites. He built them because it was written that Egypt would be flooded."

ADAM OLEARIUS

More important for us than these descriptions of Persia and Egypt by Russian travelers is the account of the two journeys, in 1634 and 1636, of the noted Holstein scholar Adam Olearius.[51] In ancient Russian territory [on the Baltic] lately ceded to the Swedes, between Koporie and Oreshek, he was received and entertained by a Russian landholder. His host showed him wounds received at the battle near Leipzig,[52] where he was with King Gustav Adolf. Despite the fact that he was in Swedish service, he still lived according to Russian customs.[53]

As soon as he entered Muscovite territory, Olearius was amazed how cheap provisions were. A fowl cost two copecks (two shillings), ten eggs one copeck.[54] He was impressed by the Russian dance, how they danced without holding hands as the Germans did, but rather each moved independently. All along the route the travelers were tormented by mosquitoes and midges. At one place they encountered a youth of twelve, likewise a girl of eleven, both of them married.[55]

Olearius was in Moscow at Eastertide. He was told that on Easter Sunday the tsar, before going to matins, went to the prison and gave each of the prisoners an egg and a sheepskin coat, saying "Rejoice! Christ who died for our sins is now risen." On the first day of the festival, after mass, the taverns were crowded. Clergy, laymen and women fell down in the streets in a drunken stupor, and the next morning many corpses were gathered up.[56]

Adam Olearius (1644)

Herzog August Bibliothek, Wolfenbüttel

By kind permission.

While Olearius was in Moscow, fires suddenly broke out in various places, being put out by the musketeers and watchmen. They did not pour on water, but rather demolished the surrounding houses.[57] As easily as whole streets burned down, just as quickly were they reconstructed, because in Moscow there was a special market where wooden houses were sold readymade. They were dismantled, carried to the desired lot and there reassembled.[58] The streets were wide, and in the middle were placed round beams one beside the other. Without such boardwalks it would be impossible to move around in the wet weather, on account of the mud.

The land in Muscovy is especially fertile. In many places there are plenteous fruits from orchards—apples, cherries, plums and currants. There are also vegetables, especially cucumbers and melons, but in Moscow there are very few ornamental garden flowers. Tsar Michael paid much money to order plants for his own garden. Genuine double roses were unknown in Moscow until Peter Marselis brought some from the ducal gardens in Gottorp. German and Dutch merchants cultivated asparagus and lettuce. The Russians at first laughed at the Germans for eating raw grass, but later some acquired the taste for it.[59] They took to tobacco right from the start, like most peoples, and as elsewhere the wondrous weed, endowed with such addictive power, was subject to the same persecution. Olearius witnessed men and women in Moscow having their nostrils slit on account of tobacco.[60]

Olearius complained of the Russians' crudity, of their excessive inclination to sensual pleasures, some of them even unnatural.[61] He complained that their conversation consists of lewd tales.[62] He gave the Russians credit for their mental abilities and deftness in business, but complains of their mendacity.[63] The life of the common people is noted for its simplicity. Their diet consisted of several of the simplest dishes. Firewood also was especially cheap. There was no furniture in their homes. Icons were the only decoration on their bare walls.[64]

The luxury of the rich and noble was displayed by the number of their slaves (between thirty and sixty of them) and their horses. They frequently gave large banquets, where many kinds of dishes and drinks were served, but this does not cost them very much since all the supplies are brought from their country estates. Besides, guests paid handsomely for the privilege of being invited to banquets given by the famous. If a German merchant is invited to such a banquet, he knows the honor will cost him dear. Governors of market towns were renowned for such hospitality.[65]

Slaves do not receive food from their masters, instead they are given a subsistence allowance barely enough to keep them alive, on account of which there are frequent robberies and homicides in Moscow.[66]

The seclusion of maidens among respectable people means that a bridegroom cannot see his bride before the wedding. This gives rise to deceptions such as the substitution of brides, thus hindering conjugal happiness. Husbands and wives frequently live like cats and dogs.[67]

Concerning Russian customs, Olearius remarked the following. From eight days before Christmas until Epiphany some men run about the streets with special fire, burning a powder made out of club-moss, with which they scorch the beards of those passing by. Poor peasants suffer especially from this type of horseplay. He who wishes can pay protection money of one copeck. They are called Chaldeans, because they represent the servants of King Nebuchadnezzar who ignited the fire intended to consume the three Jewish youths.[68] At Epiphany they are ducked in an ice hole, and in this way they cease to be Chaldeans.[69]

NOTES

Additional information on personalities and topics found in the text and notes is available in George N. Rhyne and Joseph L. Wieczynski, eds., *The Modern Encyclopedia of Russian, Soviet and Eurasian History* (MERSH) and *Supplement*; Harry B. Weber, ed., *The Modern Encyclopedia of Russian and Soviet Literatures (Including Non-Russian and Emigre Literatures)* (MERSL); Paul D. Steeves, ed., *The Modern Encyclopedia of Religions in Russia and the Soviet Union* (MERRSU); and David R. Jones, ed., *The Military Encyclopedia of Russia and Eurasia* (formerly *The Military-Naval Encyclopedia of Russia and the Soviet Union*), all published by Academic International Press.

INTRODUCTION

1. George N. Rhyne and Joseph L. Wieczynski, eds., *Modern Encyclopedia of Russian and Soviet History* and *Supplement* (Academic International Press, 1976–) (hereafter MERSH), Vol. 22, pp. 36-39.

2. V. Berkh, *Tsarstvovanie Tsaria Mikhaila Fedorovicha* (The Reign of Michael Fedorovich), 2 vols. (St. Petersburg, 1832).

3. See E. Amburger, *Die Familie Marselis* (The Marselis Family) (Giessen, 1957).

4. See J.L.H. Keep, "Bandits and the Law in Muscovy," *Slavonic Review*, 35 (1956), pp. 201-222.

5. The relevant note by Soloviev simply reads "Collection of the Synodal Library, N° 623." The Soviet editor cites this collection as now being in the possession of the State Historical Museum, but also refers to a printed version, published in 1859, entitled "Discussion of the *Lithuanian* Archpriest Lavrenty Zizany with the Abbot Ilya and the Proofreader Grigory Concerning the Correction of the Catechism compiled by Lavrenty." (Italics mine)

6. Serge A. Zenkovsky, *Medieval Russia's Epics, Chronicles and Tales* (New York, 1963), p. 312.

7. *Sobranie gosudarstvennykh gramot i dogovorov, khraniashchikh v Gosudarstvennoi Kollegii Inostrannykh Del*. For this segment Soloviev used Part III (St. Petersburg, 1822).

8. *Pis'ma russkikh gosudarei i drugikh osob tsarskogo semeistva, izdannye Arkheograficheskoiu Kommissieiu*, Vol. I (Moscow, 1848).

9. *Akty istoricheskie, sobrannye i izdannye Arkheograficheskoiu Kommissieiu, Vol. III* (St. Petersburg, 1841); *Akty, sobrannye v bibliotekakh i arkhivakh Rossiiskoi Imperii Arkheograficheskoiu Ekspeditsieiu Akademii Nauk,* Vol. III (St. Petersburg, 1836).

10. *Dopolneniia k aktam istoricheskim, sobrannym i izdannym Arkheograficheskoiu Kommissieiu,* Vols. I-II (St. Petersburg, 1846).

11. *Dvortsovye Razriady,* Vol. I (St. Petersburg, 1850); *Knigi Razriadnye,* Vols. I-II (St. Petersburg, 1853-1855).

12. K. Wóycicky, *Pamiętniki do panowania Zygmunta III* (Memorials of the Reign of Sigismund III) Vol. I (Warsaw, 1846); E. Raczynski, *Pamiętniki Albrychta Stanisława Radziwiłła, kanclerza w. litewskiego* (Memorials of Stanislaw X. Radziwill, Chancellor of the Grand Principality of Lithuania), Vol. II (Poznan, 1839).

13. J. Hammer, *Geschichte des osmanischen Reichs,* Vol. 3 (Pest, 1835).

14. S. Kobierzycki, *Historia Vladislai Poloniae et Sueciae Principis* (Danzig, 1655).

15. V. A. Borisov, *Opisanie goroda Shui i ego okrestnosti, s prilozheniem starinnykh aktov* (Moscow, 1851).

16. Iosif Gamel', *Opisanie Tul'skogo oruzheinogo zavoda v istoricheskom i tekhnicheskom otnoshenii* (Moscow, 1826).

17. *Russkaia letopis' po Nikonovskomu spisku,* Part VIII (St. Petersburg, 1792). The more revent version is contained in *Polnoe Sobranie Russikh Letopisei* (Full Collection of Russian Chronicles, henceforth PSRL), Vol. 10, Part I (St. Petersburg, 1910).

18. See Vol. 15 of this series, Chapter I, Note 5.

19. See Vol. 15, p. xx.

20. PSRL, Vol. IV (St. Petersburg, 1848), more recently *Pskovkie letopisi* (Pskov Chronicles), Vol. 2 (Moscow, 1955); PSRL, Vol. V (St. Petersburg, 1851), more recently *Pskovskie letopisi,* Vol. 1 (Moscow and Leningrad, 1941).

21. The acts in question are gathered together in *fondy* relating to the appropriate country. Those utilized by Soloviev for this segment were 35 (England), 50 (Holland), 51 (Holstein), 53 (Denmark), 79 (Poland), 89 (Turkey), 93 (France), 96 (Sweden) and 123 (Crimea)

22. *A Course in Russian History. The Seventeenth Century,* tr. H. Duddington (Chicago, 1968); *The Rise of the Romanovs,* tr. Liliana Archibald (London, 1970).

CHAPTER I

1. Following his deposition in July 1610, Vasily Shuisky was handed over to the Poles, and died a prisoner in Warsaw in September 1612. Under the terms of the Truce of Polianovka his remains were returned to Moscow, and they were reburied in the Archangel cathedral on June 11, 1635. See Volume 16, pp. 240-242.

2. Following his death, Boris was buried in the Archangel cathedral, but after the coup which brought False Dmitry I to power he was reinterred in the St. Barsonuphius monastery alongside his murdered wife and son. During the reign of Vasily Shuisky the three were given a more honorable resting place in the forecourt of the Trinity monastery, where they were joined in 1623 by Boris's surviving daughter Xenia. There they still remain.

3. The remains of Tsarevich Dmitry were brought, from their original resting place at Uglich, to Moscow during the reign of Vasily Shuisky. See Vol. 15, p. 10. Since Boris generally was believed, even by those sympathetic to him, to have been responsible for the tsarevich's death, it was not thought fitting for the murderer to be interred alongside his victim.

4. Prince Alexis Mikhailovich Lvov (died 1654) is mentioned first in 1607, when he recaptured Arzamas for Tsar Vasily. In 1610 he was one of the three governors of Nizhny Novgorod. In 1612 he was at Yaroslavl with Pozharsky, and was one of the signatories of Michael's Confirmatory Charter, with the rank of table attendant. He was one of the delegation sent to the Trinity monastery to persuade Tsar Michael to complete his journey to Moscow, and later took part in the coronation ceremony. In 1614 Lvov and Perfily Sekerin were ordered to campaign against the Lithuanians, and were joined on campaign by Kazan princes, Tatar murzas, Chuvash and Cheremiss contingents. In 1615 Lvov was governor at Rylsk, together with Grigory Andreevich Aliabiev. In 1616 he was sent with Suleshov to Nizhny Novgorod to gather troops against the rebellious Tatars and Lowland Cheremiss. From 1618 to 1620 Lvov was governor of Astrakhan, together with Prince Andrei Andreevich Khovansky. In 1621 he was named to the Chancellery for Military Appointments, and in 1625 he received the Persian ambassador. In 1627 he petitioned the tsar, complaining that he was in Astrakhan when the rewards were handed out to the defenders of Moscow; his petition was granted, and he was promoted to the rank of lord-in-waiting. From then until 1647 he sat on the board of the Chancellery for the Tsar's Household. In 1628 he was at the reception of the Persian ambassador, and in 1630-1631 met with the Swedish ambassador Anton Monier. In 1632 he was one of the commissioners in charge of collecting supplies for the Smolensk campaign and the recruitment of military levies from the estates of those landowners who did not serve in person. He subsequently served as one of the Muscovite emissaries at the peace talks in 1634, with the title lord lieutenant of Suzdal. For his part in the successful negotiations Lvov was promoted to boyar and given additional estates. In January 1635 he was sent to Poland to receive confirmation of the peace treaty from King Wladyslaw IV, and also to secure the release of the remains of the Shuisky princes. In 1638 he was sent to Tula with the delegation greeting the Crimean khan. In 1639 he kept an all-night vigil over the bodies of the tsar's sons Ivan and Vasily, who died in January and April respectively. He was one of the ambassadors sent to Denmark to negotiate the possible marriage of Prince Valdemar to one of the tsar's daughters (see below, Chapter III). In February 1644 he once again was sent to Poland to obtain clarification about the tsar's title and rectification of the borders, and also

with secret instructions to find out about a new pretender, alleged to be a bogus son of the late Tsar Vasily. Lvov was further rewarded for his services, being greeted on his homeward journey in the tsar's name at Mozhaisk, and later given trading immunities in Yaroslavl. He continued to serve at court under Tsar Alexis and died childless. His first wife was Yevlampia Mikhailovna Nagaia, who died in 1632. The name of his second wife is unknown.

5.   The Peace, more properly the Truce, of Polianovka, was concluded in June 1634, ending the so-called War of Smolensk, a minor sideshow of the Thirty Years War. Russia returned all conquests except for the town of Serpeisk, but King Wladyslaw IV of Poland agreed to drop his claims to the Russian throne in return for an indemnity, payable to him personally, of twenty thousand rubles. See Vol. 16, pp. 229-237.

6.   Kazimierz Sapieha (1613-1655) was the son of the Lithuanian chancellor Leo Sapieha. He studied at the Wilno Academy and later at the University of Louvain in the Spanish Netherlands. In 1631 he was appointed grand notary of Lithuania, and in 1634 took part in the negotiations with Russia leading to the Truce of Polianovka. He became marshal of the Lithuanian court in 1637, and deputy chancellor in 1645. In 1648 he was an executor of Wladyslaw IV's will, and in 1649 he repulsed a cossack attack on Lithuania.

7.   Prince Semeon Ivanovich Shakhovskoy (died 1654) first is mentioned in 1606 as a commander of Tsar Vasily Shuisky's forces in the neighborhood of Elets. He was brought to Moscow on unspecified charges and then was dispatched to Novgorod. Before he reached his destination he was told to live on his country estates and await the tsar's pleasure. In 1608-1609 he was at Moscow and took part in the struggle against False Dmitry II, seeing action in the battles of Khodynka and Rakhmantsevo. Early in 1610 he defected to Tushino, and then sought service with Sigismund III, who gave him grants of land. In 1611 he was at Novgorod when it was captured by the Swedes, but he himself escaped and arrived before Moscow in the ranks of the First Militia Force commanded by Prokopy Liapunov. He was appointed by the interim boyar administration as governor of Toropets, returning to Moscow shortly after the election of Tsar Michael. He was dispatched to the Smolensk front where, in conjunction with Prince D.M. Cherkassky, he took part in the recapture of Viazma, Belaia and Dorogobuzh. He participated in the 1613-1615 campaigns against the Poles, and twice was wounded, at Velizh and Mstislavl. In 1615 Shakhovskoy was sent to combat the Polish irregulars under Aleksandr Lisowski, but complained that he was "being shunted around from service to service." For his pains he was sent, first to Unzha in the Far North, and then as governor to Yadrin, on the Volga, where he served from 1616 to 1618. At the time of Prince Wladyslaw's bid in 1618 to gain the Russian throne he was in charge of the forces guarding the Yauza river, and in 1619 he was facing the Tatars as governor of Pronsk. Shakhovskoy previous to this time was married twice. His first wife, whom he married in 1611, died in 1615. He married a second time while at Yadrin, but his second wife died late in the spring of 1619. His third wife, Tatiana, died after only a few months of marriage. In violation of canon law he

contracted a fourth union, earning the strictures of the newly-returned Patriarch Filaret, who became his life-long enemy and dissolved the marriage in 1622. Meanwhile misfortune overtook the whole Shakhovskoy family, which during a reunion staged a drunken parody of Michael's election. Prince Semeon was not even at the gathering, but suffered from guilt by association and was condemned to death along with his relatives, though these sentences later were commuted to confiscation and banishment. Shakhovskoy, stripped of his possessions and his marriage dissolved, was exiled to Tobolsk. He was permitted to return to Moscow in the early summer of 1624, and in 1625 was commissioned by the patriarch to write the famous letter to Shah Abbas (see below, Chapter VI, p. 176). Six weeks after the dispatch of the embassy Shakhovskoy was back at court while Michael was on pilgrimage to the Trinity monastery. He seems to have kept a low profile for the next few years, but nevertheless in 1628 he was appointed governor of Yeniseisk, where he remained for three years under a thinly disguised form of banishment. After this he served a two-year stint in Tobolsk, though his annual salary was raised to 39 rubles. He was permitted to return to Moscow in 1632, and his fortunes changed for the better when his old adversary Filaret died in October 1633. He was active in the War of Smolensk, advancing with the veteran Pozharsky to stem Wladyslaw's advance after the failure of the siege of Smolensk. He then served as one of the plenipotentiaries who negotiated the Truce of Polianovka in 1634. In 1637, as described here, he was sent on an ambassadorial assignment to Warsaw, and also was named governor of Yelatomsk. In 1638-1639 he was governor of Krapivna, for which service he received an estate of fifty chetverts and an annual salary of thirty rubles. In 1641 he served as Muscovite governor on the Terek. In 1643 Shakhovskoy formed a close association with the Danish prince Valdemar, brought to Moscow as a prospective bridegroom for the tsar's daughter Irina (See Chapter III, below). Once again Shakhovskoy incurred the wrath of the ecclesiastical authorities, this time for venturing the opinion that the marriage might be concluded without the prince's conversion to Orthodoxy. Shakhovskoy at first was sent as governor of Ust-Kola; then after the death of Michael and the abandonment of the marriage project, he was tried in the Chancellery for Foreign Affairs on charges of treason and heresy. He was sentenced to death, but once again the sentence was commuted to banishment, this time to Ustiug. He petitioned for pardon, but instead was banished yet further, to Solvychegodsk. He then was told to proceed to Yakutsk, but Tsar Alexis countermanded the order and bade him remain in Solvychegodsk. In 1649 he was given leave to visit his estates at Galich, but then was posted to Tomsk. He was back in Moscow by 1653, when he wrote a letter to his friend Semeon Azaryin, and died the following year. Shakhovskoy was known as a prolific writer (see below, Chapter VI). Indeed he was perhaps even more prolific than Soloviev suspected, since the *Book of Annals,* originally attributed by S.F. Platonov to Prince I.M. Katyrev-Rostovsky, appears in fact to have been written by Shakhovskoy. See G. Edward Orchard, "Chronicle in Search of an Author. The Seventeenth-Century Book of Annals," *Russian Review,* 37 (1978), pp. 197-203. It also has been argued that the initial letter in the famous epistolary exchange between Prince A.M. Kurbsky and Ivan IV was in fact written by Shakhovskoy, and therefore by implication the rest of the "correspondence" is of seventeenth-century provenance. See Edward L. Keenan, *The Kurbskii-Groznyi Apocrypha. The Seventeenth-Century Genesis of the "Correspondence" Attributed to Prince A.M. Kurbskii and Tsar Ivan IV* (Harvard, 1971).

8. The terms used, respectively, were *samoderzhavets and derzhavets.*

9. Lukasz Zolkiewski (1594-1636), nephew of the famous hetman Stanislaw, took part in the Turkish campaign of 1620 and was captured at the battle of Cecora, in which his uncle lost his life. On his return from captivity he accompanied Prince Wladyslaw on his European tour, and subsequently served on embassies to Sweden and Brandenburg-Prussia. Between 1632 and 1635 he served as governor of Pereiaslav in Ukraine, during which time he brought the Jesuits there to establish a church and a college. In 1635 he was one of the boundary commissioners to determine the Russo-Polish borders following the Truce of Polianovka. From 1636 he served as governor of Braclaw. With his death the Zolkiewski family became extinct.

10. Prince Michael of Chernigov (died 1246) was the son of Prince Vsevolod the Red. From the 1220s Michael took an active part in the political life of both Southern and Northeastern Rus. In 1223, together with the other princes, he took counsel concerning the initial appearance of the Tatars. Several times he was put in charge of Great Novgorod, and fought Princes Daniel of Galich and Yaroslav Vsevolodovich for the control of Kiev. As the Tatars approached in 1238 he fled to Hungary and then to Poland. Finding no support there, he set off to visit Khan Batu, counting on receiving investiture for the principality of Chernigov, but was killed by the Tatars for refusing to approach the khan's throne by passing between purifying fires, which was the usual procedure for foreigners seeking admission to the khan's court. He was canonized by the Orthodox church. For further details, see Volume 4 of this series, and George Vernadsky, *The Mongols and Russia* (Yale, 1953), pp. 142-145.

11. The canon (ulozhen'e) is the list of saints commemorated in the liturgy of the Russian church, adding details of their life and death.

12. In 1637 Wladyslaw IV married his first cousin Archduchess Cecilia Renata, sister of Emperor Ferdinand III. She bore him a son, Sigismund, who died in 1648, slightly before his father. Cecilia Renata died in 1645, and in 1646 Wladyslaw married Princess Marie-Louise of Gonzaga, by whom he had no issue. Marie-Louise went on to marry her late husband's brother and successor Jan Kazimierz. This union also proved childless.

13. Stepan Matveevich Proestev (died 1651) took part in the negotiations leading up to the truce of Polianovka, and in the same year (1634) was promoted to the rank of conciliar noble, and lord-in-waiting in 1635. He is last mentioned in service on March 25, 1649. Robert O. Crummey, *Aristocrats and Servitors. The Boyar Elite in Russia*, 1613-1689 (Princeton, 1983), pp. 42, 184.

14. Sables were customarily presented in multiples of forty, sometimes referred to as "timbers."

15. The term used here is *goriachee vino* ("hot wine"), which could refer to any kind of distilled spirits, though the contraband in question more likely was brandy, since presumably domestic sources of vodka were relatively plentiful and cheap.

16. It is unclear whether Nur-ed-Din, "light of the faith," is a personal name or a title. In the Crimean khanate the heir designate was styled the kalga or kalgay, while the second in succession was the nur-ed-din. When the kalga succeeded as khan, the nur-ed-din became the kalga, and a new nur-ed-din was designated.

17. Karol Ferdynand Waza (1613-1655) was the third son of King Sigismund III. He was destined at an early age for the church. At the age of twelve he became bishop of Breslau, which was in the gift of the king's brother-in-law Emperor Ferdinand II, since Breslau was under Bohemian rule since 1490, and part of the Habsburg dominions since 1526. In 1645 he became bishop of Plock. On the death of Wladyslaw IV he contested the election to the throne, waiting until the electoral Sejm to renounce his candidature in favor of his brother Jan Kazimierz. His secular honors included the principalities of Opole and Racibórz.

18. Prince Ivan Borisovich Cherkassky (died 1642) was the son of Prince Boris Kanbulatovich, first mentioned in 1598 at the election of Boris Godunov. In 1600-1601 he was implicated in the sorcery charges brought against the Romanov family. His property was confiscated and he was exiled to Siberia. While he was on his way there, the bailiff received orders to halt at Malmyzh and await the tsar's pleasure. Cherkassky and his uncle Ivan Nikitich Romanov then were ordered to serve at Nizhny Novgorod. In 1602 the sentence of banishment was lifted, and Cherkassky returned to Moscow in November. Nothing further is known about his service under Boris or False Dmitry I. Tsar Vasily appointed Cherkassky to the court office previously occupied by the pretender's favorite Prince Ivan Andreevich Khvorostinin, but was dismissed shortly afterwards. With the attack of False Dmitry II on Moscow in the fall of 1608, Cherkassky was placed in charge of one of the regiments stationed on the Khodynka. He seems to have seen little further action until 1611, when he fought under the command of Prince Ivan Semeonovich Kurakin on behalf of Prince Wladyslaw in the Vladimir region. Kurakin was defeated, and Cherkassky was taken prisoner. His fortunes changed when his kinsman Michael Romanov was elected tsar. Cherkassky was promoted boyar in 1613, two days before the coronation. The return of Filaret in 1619 improved his lot still further. Cherkassky's first active service under the Romanov regime came in September 1618, when he was sent to Yaroslavl to raise troops for the defense of Moscow. During this campaign he inflicted heavy losses on renegade cossacks operating in the environs of Yaropolch. On his return to Moscow early in 1619 he was invited to the sovereign's table, and after the banquet was awarded a sable robe and a silver goblet. In the autumn of 1624 and the spring of 1627 he was in charge of the Chancellery of Musketeers. During his long career he also served as Treasurer, and as head of the Chancellery for Service Foreigners and the Chancellery of the Apothecary. It is known that he was married, but he died without surviving issue, so his immense fortune was divided between the Sheremetev

family and his Cherkassky relatives, Princes Dmitry Mamstriukovich and Yakov Kudenetovich.

19. Prince Semeon Ivanovich Prozorovsky (died 1660) was in active service during the reign of Tsar Vasily Shuisky (1606-1610), winning a victory over the forces of False Dmitry II at Khmelniki in 1608. He was in charge of the Chancellery of Posts in 1643.

20. Ivan Petrovich Sheremetev (1586-1647) is first mentioned as a table attendant in 1606 at the court of False Dmitry I. In 1611 he swore allegiance to Prince Wladyslaw, but then appeared in Trubetskoy's army outside Moscow. In late autumn 1611 he was sent by the boyar council to be governor of Kostroma. In March 1612, when Kuzma Minin marched from Kineshma to Kostroma, he was met on the Ples river by some of the inhabitants, who warned him that Sheremetev did not wish him to enter the town. Pozharsky ordered the Militia Force to halt in the outskirts. The inhabitants of Kostroma were divided, although eventually those who supported Pozharsky gained the upper hand and would have killed Sheremetev, had not Pozharsky intervened personally to save him. Pozharsky then appointed Sheremetev to be governor of Yaroslavl and in this capacity Sheremetev greeted the newly elected Tsar Michael and his mother on their way to Moscow, and accompanied them as far as the Trinity monastery, where Michael declared he would proceed no further because of the disordered state of the land. It was Sheremetev whom the boyars sent to the tsar to urge him to continue his journey. Between 1613 and 1618 he played an important part in court ceremonial functions, and in September 1614 was sent briefly to Mtsensk to command the vanguard regiment to counter a threatened Tatar invasion. He does not appear to have been in service between 1618 and 1622, but in June of the latter year he was sent to Riazan, again to command forces on the Tatar frontier. From 1625 he was at court functions, assisted at the birth and christening of the tsar's children Irina, Pelagia and Alexis, and accompanied the tsar on pilgrimages. He disappears from the court records between 1630 and 1633. In 1634 he was appointed boyar with a salary entitlement of four hundred rubles, and named governor of Kazan, where he stayed until 1636. On March 8, 1638 he escorted the remains of Prince Johan (died 1602) to the city gates of Moscow on their way back to Denmark at the request of King Christian IV. Between April and September 1638 he was at Krapivna guarding the frontier against the Crimeans and Nogay. In 1639 he was appointed head of the Chancellery for Military Recruitment. In April 1640 he was entrusted to conduct negotiations with the Polish envoys, and was given the title Lord Lieutenant of Rostov. Between 1640 and 1647 he was in charge of the Vladimir Judicial Chancellery. In 1642 he was in a precedence dispute with Prince Andrei Vasilievich Khilkov, head of the Moscow Judicial Chancellery, which he held was inferior to the Vladimir post. He won, and Khilkov was imprisoned. On January 28 Sheremetev met with Prince Valdemar. At the end of 1644 he negotiated with the Turkish ambassador, and in January 1645 with the Polish ambassador Stempkowski. On September 28, 1645 he held the scepter at the coronation of Tsar Alexis. He

continued to head the Vladimir Judicial Chancellery until his death on July 8, 1647. Prior to his death he took the monastic tonsure under the name of Jonas.

21. Prince Ivan Andreevich Golitsyn (died 1654) was created a boyar on February 2, 1634 and is last mentioned in service in 1649 or 1650. Crummey, *Aristocrats and Servitors,* p. 184.

22. Prince Dmitry Mikhailovich Pozharsky (1586-1642) was the military commander of the Second Militia Force, which in 1612 liberated Moscow from Polish occupation. Although he was the undoubted hero of the liberation movement, he appears to have suffered a comparative eclipse during Michael's reign. This might have been because he is known to have favored the candidacy of the Swedish prince Karl Filip, or because men of greater prominence absent from the scene during the time of crisis now returned to assume their proper places. During the reign of Michael, Pozharsky seems to have been called to action whenever the skill and prestige of such a military leader was needed, but at other times was relegated to relative obscurity. See entry by Daniel B. Rowland, MERSH, Vol. 29, pp. 151-156.

23. Gustav Adolf (born 1594, reigned 1611-1632) was at war with Muscovy when he came to the throne, but after participating personally in the unsuccessful siege of Pskov in 1615 began negotiations which led to the Peace of Stolbovo (1617). Thereafter relations between Sweden and the Romanov regime were mostly amicable, and the two countries became allies in the War of Smolensk. The Russians and Swedes failed to synchronize their attacks on Poland, and in any case Gustav Adolf was killed at the battle of Lützen (November 1, 1632).

24. Kristina (born 1626, reigned 1632-1654, died 1689) grew up under the tutelage of her father's able chancellor Axel Oxenstierna (see Volume 16, Chapter II, Note 37), who admitted her to council meetings at the age of fourteen. He stayed on as chancellor when she came of age in 1644. Kristina was under constant pressure to marry, her cousin Karl Gustav being indicated as the most suitable match. Still unwilling to marry, in 1651 she appointed Karl Gustav her successor and declared her intention to abdicate. She was persuaded to reconsider for a while, but finally on June 6, 1654 the formal act of abdication took place. Shortly afterwards Kristina joined the Roman Catholic church during a visit to Innsbruck, and for the rest of her life she mostly resided at Rome, though she made two unsuccessful attempts, in 1660 and 1667, to stage a comeback, and also at various times put forward her candidacy for the Neapolitan and Polish thrones. Of Kristina it is rightly said, "It is hardly too much to say that every year or so a new biography of her is published in one language or another. Generally they are all wrong. They are based on a mass of gossip hostile to Christina, on an abundance of rumour, and on contradictory polemical writing, which began during her lifetime, and flourished especially in the eighteenth century." Sven Stolpe, *Christina of Sweden* (New York, 1966), Preface. The work cited is the most balanced and best informed account of this complex personality, based in large part on her personal papers. It is a translation by Sir Alec Randall and Ruth Mary Bethell from a German abridgement of the author's original two-volume study *Drottning Kristina* (Stockholm, 1960-1961).

25. An excellent treatment of the increasing use of "resident agents," though admittedly not pertaining to the countries here in question, is to be found in Garret Mattingly, *Renaissance Diplomacy* (New York, 1955).

26. Frantsbekov also played a part in the attempted conversion of Prince Valdemar. See below, Chapter III, pp. 63-64, and Vernadsky, *The Tsardom of Moscow 1547-1682* (New Haven, 1969), p. 381.

27. On the mission of Johan Meller, see Volume 16, pp. 176-177.

28. "...the noble, honest, highly respected, and most learned gentleman Philip Crusius of Eisleben, Licentiate in civil and canon law (now a nobleman, thanks to the special favor of the King of Sweden, who named him Philip Krusenstierne and made him royal counselor, Burgrave of Narva, and general director of commerce in Estonia and Ingermanland)...." *The Travels of Olearius in Seventeenth-Century Russia*, translated and edited by Samuel H. Baron (Stanford, 1967), p. 33.

29. "An enigmatic figure [Otto] Brüggemann gave no hint early in the journey of the irascible, imprudent, and violent nature he revealed later on. In the course of the waterborne voyage southward through Russia and the Caspian, where vigilance was certainly called for, the ambassador proved flagrantly trigger-happy. His abusive behavior not only alienated many members of the embassy, Olearius perhaps most of all, but also deeply offended their Russian and Persian escorts. In Persia, he engaged in shameless debauchery, insulted a high official by refusing to accept a gift, and wantonly had a Persian soldier thrashed and killed. A few decades ago it was discovered that he also had hatched a plan, in which he tried to interest Russia, for the seizure of Persia's silk-producing region. All in all, his conduct was as far removed from the discretion expected from an ambassador as can be imagined. Complaints pressed against Brüggemann by other members of the embassy after their return to Holstein resulted in his being tried and executed." Baron, *Travels of Olearius*, pp. 9-10. In a footnote to p. 10, Baron further comments "Incidentally, Brüggemann's irresponsible conduct in Persia perhaps stemmed from his growing realization that his scheme on which he had staked his reputation, and possibly his fortune, was in fact uneconomical; his plan for the seizure of Persia's silk-producing region was probably a desperate effort to keep alive the goals of the initial project while radically changing its form."

30. In Soloviev's text there is a detailed list of these products, which I have omitted from the body of the translation. These include *dorogi*—striped cloth, sometimes with gold or silver animal figures; *kutnia*—Asiatic half-silken cloth—of all colors; *zenden*—a silken cloth; *kindiak*—red calico or sarafan; *saf'ian*—leather made of goat hides, similar to Morocco leather; madder or pastel dyes; *mitkal'*—cotton fabric used for upholstery; *kiseia*—thin red cloth, originally made out of vegetable fibers, later out of cotton; *biaz'*—Asiatic, Persian or Bukharan cotton cloth; *kumach*—simple cotton cloth, usually reddish, sometimes blue; *byboiki*—crude cotton prints; raw cotton; *kushaki*—a type of girdle; *korni chepuchinnye*—indigo root; *pshena sorochinskogo*—millet seed; *nashivki*—printed cloth; *poiaski shelkovye*—silken girdles; *sabli, polosy*—Oriental sabres; *nozhi tulunbasov*—Turkish-style daggers; Oriental-style bows; any kind of weapons or

armor; carpets; horse blankets; large or small tents; groundsheets; gall nuts (used for the manufacture of ink or dye); incense; chandlery; and saltpeter.

31.   Here, as in many places elsewhere, Soloviev switches from indirect to direct quotation without any punctuation indicating that he is doing so. I have taken the liberty of inserting quotation marks where appropriate.

32.   *Kostël,* the term used here, usually applies to Roman Catholic churches, but it is evident from the subsequent text that only Protestants were to be allowed to participate in the venture.

33.   Friedrich III, born 1597, ruled Schleswig-Holstein from 1616 to 1659. On a small scale, he was a forerunner of the "enlightened despots." In 1658 he concluded the Peace of Roskilde with Sweden which effectively freed Schleswig from Danish suzerainty.

34.   On Vasily Shorin (died 1678), see the entry by Samuel H. Baron, MERSH, Vol. 35, pp. 28-31, and his article "Vasilii Shorin. Seventeenth-Century Russian Merchant Extraordinary," *Canadian-American Slavic Studies,* 6 (1972), pp. 503-548.

35.   Peter Marselis (died 1672), variously described as a Dane or a native of Hamburg, was a merchant and industrialist whose father Gabriel migrated to Russia during the reign of Boris Godunov (1598-1605). In 1639 Peter Marselis was a partner of the Dutch entrepreneur Adam Vinius, and afterwards sole proprietor of the first large-scale metallurgical enterprises in Russia. In partnership with the Dutchman Thielemann Akema he reconstructed the factories in Tula and built from scratch four factories in the region of Kashira. In 1644 he received a grant to construct ironworks on the Vaga, Kostroma and Sheksna rivers, and in 1645 to process copper ore in the region of Olenets. In 1642-1643 he travelled to Denmark on diplomatic business, and was involved in the negotiations over the proposed marriage between Prince Valdemar and Tsarevna Irina (see below, Chapter III, pp. 58-74). In 1662 his property was confiscated on suspicion of counterfeiting coinage, but subsequently he was restored to favor. Later he virulently opposed the trade restrictions placed on foreign merchants by the New Commercial Statute of 1667. At the behest of the diplomat Afanasy Ordin-Nashchokin he and his son Leonty organized a temporary courier service between Moscow and Wilno during the negotiations leading to the Truce of Andrusovo. See Volume 20 of this series, also S.F. Platonov, *Moscow and the West,* tr. and ed. Joseph L. Wieczynski (Academic International Press, 1972), pp. 118-119.

CHAPTER II

1.   Osman II (1603-1622) came to the throne in 1618. He undertook a military campaign against Poland, which was interfering with his vassal principalities of Moldavia and Wallachia. Despite his victory at Cecora in 1620, his forces were defeated at Chocim in 1621 largely because of the indiscipline of the janissaries. He cut down their pay and closed down their coffee shops, and was about to go

ostensibly on pilgrimage to Mecca, but in reality to Egypt to recruit an army to break the power of the janissaries, when the latter got wind of his plan. They deposed and murdered him in May 1622.

2. The Cantacuzenes were a distinguished Byzantine family, one of whom attained the imperial dignity as John VI (1347-1354). After the fall of Constantinople they sought service with the Ottoman government. Members of one branch of the family served as hospodars of Moldavia, while others in the eighteenth century migrated to Russia.

3. Ivan Gavrilovich Kondyrev (dates of birth unknown, fl. 1614-1632) was sent in 1614 to the Nogay Horde to reason with Khan Ishterek and to prevent him joining forces with Zarutsky. The next year he was sent on an embassy to King Louis XIII of France, to inform him of Michael's accession to the throne and to obtain aid against the Swedes and Poles. The king received the embassy graciously at Bordeaux, and agreed to inscribe the tsar's name as requested, but refused the proposed aid. In 1618 Kondyrev was sent to Wladyslaw's encampment near Viazma to explore peace terms, but his mission was unsuccessful. His next mission was the 1622 embassy to Turkey, related here in harrowing details. No doubt he was glad to see Moscow again in September 1623. In 1627 Kondyrev was dispatched to the Nogay Horde with gifts for the murzas. This was the end of his diplomatic career. In August 1632, during the War of Smolensk, he was given a command at Rzhev Volodimerov.

4. The term used here is komiaga, a word probably of Chuvash origin, indicating a single-hulled craft built out of a hollowed tree trunk. Evidently the boat in question was capable of carrying a considerable cargo, so I have translated it "barge."

5. Mustafa succeeded his brother Ahmed I in 1617, but was patently insane and was deposed in favor of his nephew Osman II. After the latter's violent overthrow, Mustafa was reinstated for a period of fifteen months, until the accession of Murad IV.

6. Philippe de Harlay, comte de Césy, served as French ambassador at Constantinople from 1618 to 1641. He also derived considerable profit by farming the customs duties of Aleppo. For this reason he did all he could to obstruct the mission of Louis Deshayes to Cormenin to Persia in 1626. As indicated here, he was also opposed to the official French policy of alliance with foreign Protestants against the House of Habsburg.

7. Louis XIII (born 1601, reigned 1610-1643). The policy described here especially was pursued by Cardinal Richelieu, chief minister from 1624 until shortly before the king's death.

8. Bethlen Gabor (1580-1629) was born into a leading Protestant family in Northern Hungary. As a young man he was sent to the court of his compatriot Stefan Bathory, king of Poland. Later he helped Istvan Bocksay gain the throne of Transylvania, and then supported his successor Gabor Bathory. Differences later arose, and Bethlen was forced to take refuge in Turkey. Sultan Ahmed I provided him with an army which enabled him to seize the princely throne in 1613. During

the initial stages of the Thirty Years War, Bethlen seized most of Northern Hungary, including Poszony (Bratislava), as well as the actual crown of St. Stephen which, however, he did not presume to don. He did become briefly titular king of Hungary (1620-1621), but after the defeat of the Bohemian rebels at the White Mountain he renounced his royal pretensions in return for guarantees of religious freedom previously granted by the 1606 Treaty of Vienna. He took up arms once more against Ferdinand II in 1623-1624 and in 1626, but was forced to make peace on much the same terms as in 1621.

9.   Constantine Lukaris (1570-1638) was born in Candia, Crete, at that time under Venetian sovereignty. He studied at Venice and Padua, and was ordained deacon at Constantinople by Patriarch Melitos Pegas of Alexandria. At this time he changed his baptismal name to Cyril, by which he was known for the remainder of his life. In 1594 he was sent to Poland to strengthen Orthodox resistance to Catholic proselytizing. When the synod of Brest-Litovsk proclaimed the union of the Catholic and Orthodox churches, Lukaris in a different part of town led a counter-synod which denounced the union. He remained in Poland until 1598, and then returned for a second visit in 1600-1601. Returning to Constantinople, he was ordained priest, and later in 1601 was consecrated patriarch of Alexandria in succession to Melitos. He resided for the most part in Constantinople, although he is notable for having transferred the administrative center of his eparchy from the decaying port of Alexandria to the Egyptian capital of Cairo. A staunch opponent of church union, Cyril maintained friendly relations with individual Catholics, and even wrote a letter to Pope Paul V, implying recognition of papal supremacy. At the same time he opened contacts with Dutch and English Protestants, and his *Confession of Faith,* published at Geneva in 1609, is considered to be strongly Calvinist in sentiment. In 1620 Cyril was elected patriarch of Constantinople, but was deposed and reinstated by the Ottoman authorities no less than six times. Finally he was arrested on a charge of inciting the Don Cossacks to attack Ottoman territories. He was taken out to sea in an open boat, and there he was strangled. See Steven Runciman, *The Great Church in Captivity* (Cambridge, 1968), pp. 259-288.

10.   The Cherkass, or Circassians, also known as Adyge, were a tribe of the Northern Caucasus. When the daughter of their ruler Temriuk became the second wife of Ivan IV, some members of the princely house embraced Christianity and entered Muscovite service, thus founding the Cherkassky princely family. See Vol. 10 of this series.

11.   The text reads *plennikov* (prisoners) but, given the context, the singular makes better sense.

12.   Murad IV (born 1612, reigned 1623-1640) came to the throne at the age of eleven, though for several years the regency was in the hands of his mother Kösem (see Note 15, below). Effective power lay in the hands of the *sipahiyan* (feudal cavalry) and the janissaries. Embittered by the excesses of the troops, Murad determined to re-establish order, especially since 1632 the sipahiyan invaded the palace and instigated the execution of the grand vizier and sixteen of his ministers.

Murad staged a counter-coup, ruthlessly suppressed the mutiny, banned the use of tobacco and closed down the coffee houses and wine shops. During the balance of his reign he maintained firm rule and straightened out the state finances. In foreign policy he took personal command of the continuing war against Persia, and in 1638 reconquered Baghdad after a siege that ended in the massacre of the garrison and citizenry. In spiritual affairs, Murad did not adhere strictly to the religious law, as can be seen from his execution of the Shaykh-al-Islam (the highest religious dignitary in the empire) and the fact that he drank himself to death.

13. During the period of "dual power" lasting from 1619 to 1633 Tsar Michael's father Patriarch Filaret was accorded the title of "great sovereign" which placed him on a co-equal footing with his son. Such an honor was not accorded to Filaret's successors on the patriarchal throne.

14. Ahmed I, Ottoman sultan, born 1519, reigned 1602-1617. His authority was weakened by numerous wars and rebellions, and the disadvantageous peace with Austria in 1606 was a blow to Ottoman prestige. In order to recoup his finances he was compelled to make extensive commercial concessions to the French, Venetians and Dutch.

15. The reference is to Kösem, who was the power behind the throne of three generations of sultans, being the wife of Ahmed I, the mother of Murad IV and Ibrahim I and the grandmother of Mehmed IV, whom she attempted to have assassinated, but was herself first strangled. She was apparently of Greek or Venetian origin, though I have not found any confirmation of the assertion that she was once a priest's wife. In any case Cantacuzene's assertion that Murad IV, not to mention some of his closest officials, was some kind of closet Christian must have strained even Muscovite credulity.

16. The term used is *zipunov dobyvat'*, literally "to obtain homespun coats."

17. Serdar is a Turkish word signifying a military commander or general.

18. The Truce of Altmark (September 26, 1629).

19. The term used here is *Rus'*, referring to those of the Rusyn or Orthodox religion.

20. "The Ottomans lost their supremacy at sea in the...seventeenth century, and were unable to defend even their own coasts and sea-routes. The Ottoman coasts of the Black Sea were terrorized by Cossacks, who sailed down the Dnieper in their small boats. In...1614 they burned down Sinop, while in...1625 they looted the Istanbul suburb of Yeniköy on the Bosphorus. In...1637 the Cossacks captured Azov and kept it for five years. The tsar of Muscovy did not yet dare to place them under his protection. The Ottomans and the Crimean khan tried to contain the Cossacks by building the castles of Özü and Ghazi-Kirman, and forming the new sanjaks along the western coast of the Black Sea. The Polish campaign of Osman II in...1621 was connected mainly with the Cossack question." *The Cambridge History of Islam* (Cambridge, 1970), Vol. 1, p. 350.

21. *Kapitan-Pasha.*

22. Mikhail Ivanovich Alfimov first served as a crown secretary in the Moscow Judicial Chancellery, and in this capacity travelled with Sovin on his embassy. In

1632 he was transferred to the Chancellery of Military Service Tenures, and from 1636 was inscribed in the list of Moscow nobles.

23. Following the Polish victory at Chocim (1621).

24. Meaning a Tatar living in a yurt or nomadic encampment. The term "yurt" also signified the territory to which the tribe had a proprietory right for the purpose of grazing its herds.

25. Afanasy Osipovich Pronchishchev (died 1660), is first mentioned in 1616, then is listed as a Moscow noble in the list compiled in 1625-1626. In 1632, at the start of the war with Poland he was sent to Turkey, accompanied by the crown secretary Bormosov. His brief was to persuade the sultan to enter the war against Poland and to offer Russian mediation in the ongoing struggle with Persia. The ambassadors were obliged to spend the whole winter in Constantinople, and in spring the vizier was about to proffer his good offices when news came of the cossack attacks on the shores of Asia Minor. In 1635-1636 Pronchishchev and the crown secretary Ivan Patrikeev were sent to administer the Vaga lands. There they were accused of tolerating malfeasance and bribery. In 1638 the same pair were in service at Tula, and then were listed in the entourage of Prince Alexis Mikhailovich Lvov. In August 1646 Pronchishchev accompanied Prince Dmitry Shcherbatov, one of the commissioners to rectify the disputed boundaries between Muscovy and Poland. Pronchishchev was given responsibility for the border in the neighborhood of Velikie Luki. The dispute dragged on till 1648. In 1649 Pronchishchev was sent along with B.I. Pushkin as ambassador to Sweden. In 1652, accompanied by the crown secretary Ivan Almazov, he was sent to Poland to iron out disputes concerning the tsar's title, to negotiate an offensive alliance against the Crimea and to discuss the matter of the pretender Akudinov. Nothing was accomplished, since Pronchishchev insisted before discussing any other matters that those responsible for belittling the tsar's title be executed. In 1653 he was sent to Nizhny Novgorod to receive the grandson of the Georgian tsar Teimuraz. In 1654 he was promoted to the rank of conciliar noble, and in 1655 he escorted Patriarch Makarios of Antioch, who was visiting Moscow.

26. Gustav Adolf was first cousin to Sigismund III.

27. Matvey Somov is first mentioned in 1613 in connection with the Assembly of the Land which elected Michael Romanov. In 1618 he served as escort to the Swedish ambassador, and later assisted F.V. Sheremetev in concluding the Truce of Deulino. In 1621 he was sent to the Dvina where he served first under Prince D.I. Pozharsky and later I.D. Veliaminov, with whom he returned to Moscow in 1626. In 1627 he was sent to Viazma, where he served with Prince D.P. Akhamushkov-Cherkassky. In 1628 he was appointed to the Chancellery of Crown Revenues, where he served until 1637. This period of service was interrupted only by the 1633 embassy described here.

28. Vasily Korobyin (dates of birth unknown, fl. 1619-1634) in 1619 was one of the Muscovite commissioners negotiating the exchange of prisoners under the terns of the Truce of Deulino. In 1621 he was sent along with Afanasy Kuvshinov as ambassador to Persia. The embassy was remarkable in that Shah Abbas

announced his intention of sending to Moscow Christ's seamless robe, which he captured in one of his Georgian campaigns. On the return journey in 1624 he sent news of this from Terka, and on March 11, 1625 the Persian ambassador Rusan Bek presented Michael with the relic, which was enshrined in the Dormition cathedral of the Moscow Kremlin. In 1627 Korobyin was sent to Denmark to take care of various diplomatic matters, and his mission to Constantinople in 1634, described here, is his last recorded activity.

29.   St. Peter's fast lasts from the Monday after Pentecost until June 29, the feast of St. Peter and St. Paul.

30.   See Note 24, above.

31.   Ibrahim I (born 1615, reigned 1640-1648) early in his reign was under the guidance of the grand vizier Kara Mustafa, who established peaceful relations with Persia and Austria, and recovered the Sea of Azov hinterland from the cossacks. After the fall and execution of Kara Mustafa in 1644 he started the long and costly war with Venice over Crete, which outlasted him, and though Candia fell in 1669, it was somewhat of a Pyrrhic victory. The sultan's mental instability, harem intrigues and excessive taxation led to a janissary revolt sanctioned by the religious authorities. He was deposed, and executed ten days later.

32.   These events are the subject of the celebrated epic by F. Poroshin, a military clerk and fugitive slave, entitled *Poeticheskaia povest' ob Azovskom sidenii* (Poetic Tale of the Siege of Azov). See also entry by M.Ya. Popov, MERSH, Vol. 2, p. 223.

33.   The Assembly of the Land (zemskii sobor) was an institution in which representatives of various strata of society met to discuss matters of national importance. Some historians have seen it as and abortive step towards a permanent limited monarchy, but this view is generally discounted. Ivan IV used the sobor several times to gain public approval for his fiscal and military policies, and such assemblies also met for the election of Tsars Fedor Ivanovich, Boris Godunov and Michael Romanov. The Assembly remained in more or less continuous session from the election of Michael Romanov in 1613 until the return of Filaret from Polish captivity in 1619. Thereafter the Assembly was convoked only infrequently. See entry by Richard Hellie, MERSH, Vol. 45, pp. 226-234.

34.   The Merchants' Hundred (gostinnaia sotnia) from the sixteenth to the eighteenth century was a guild of merchants inferior only to the leading merchants (gosti). Despite its name, the number of members varied greatly; for instance in 1635 there were 185 members. They were exempt from state taxation (tiaglo) and all jurisdiction of local officials. In 1613 they were given a charter similar to that granted to the leading merchants, except that they were not permitted to travel abroad. The guild usually sent two spokesmen to the Assembly of the Land. Once every two to six years, depending on the number enrolled, members were required to perform burdensome financial services for the government, and in the event of a shortfall in revenue were required to make up the difference out of their own pockets. The Cloth Merchants' Hundred (sukonnaia sotnia) was organized along similar lines, although its members were not as prosperous as those of the

Merchants' Hundred, with whom they generally served in a subordinate capacity. At the beginning of the seventeenth century there were about 250 members, but by mid-century the number declined to 116 and the government had to resort to compulsory enrollment. Contrary to specifications, not all members resided in Moscow; in fact according to a 1673 survey only about a third of them did so. In the 1720s, with the imposition of the soul tax, the merchants and townsmen were absorbed into a single merchant stratum.

35.   Presumably within the captured city of Azov the cossacks had built a chapel dedicated to St. John the Baptist.

36.   "Fifths" (piatinnye den'gi) were a tax surcharge levied seven times between 1613 and 1619, though the answer to the question "a fifth of what?" is uncertain. According to some scholars this amounted to 20 percent of an individual's net income; others consider it to have been one-fifth of available moveable property, while yet others consider it to have been levied on both moveable and immovable property. Another collection of fifths was decreed in 1632 to finance the War of Smolensk. In 1634 yet a further imposition was declared and a new chancellery was instituted to supervise its collection. See entry by V.D. Nazarov, MERSH, Vol. 28, p. 74.

37.   Ilia Danilovich Miloslavsky (died 1688) had quite an illustrious career in store for him. He became a lord-in-waiting in January 1648 and a boyar less than a month later, doubtless because of his alliance to the favorite Boris Morozov and the marriage of his daughter Maria to Tsar Alexis, January 16, 1648.

38.   Probably Parthenios II. In any case tenure of the patriarchal throne of Constantinople tended to be a high risk occupation. In the century between 1595 and 1695 there were 61 changes of occupancy, though there were only 31 individual patriarchs, since previously deposed incumbents were reinstated. Four were executed on suspicion of treason. See Runciman, p. 201.

39.   Safi (born 1611, reigned 1629-1642) was the immediate successor of Abbas I, and historians generally point to his reign as the beginning of the Safavid decline. Originally named Sam-Mirza, he was a grandson of Abbas I who named him as his successor in the absence of any other candidates, most of whom had been either blinded or assassinated. In the estimation of one historian, "...the degree of interest evinced for business of state was only peripheral in character, if not non-existent, and it seems likely that he took not the slightest part in the intellectual and cultural life of his people; for in spite of a number of efforts to begin, he had not even managed to attain a reasonable standard in reading and writing. If we add to this the fact that he indulged with increasing frequency a taste for wine and that it had been prescribed, we are told, to counteract certain effects of opium, to which he had apparently become addicted at quite an early age, we are left with a some-what grim picture of the ruler and the thirteen years he occupied the throne before death from excessive drinking carried him off." *The Cambridge History of Iran,* Vol. 6 (Cambridge, 1986), pp. 280-281.

40.   Concerning Gilian, see Chapter V, Note 15, below.

41.   An altyn was a monetary unit equivalent to six dengas or three copecks.

42. Teimuraz I (1589-1663), tsar of Kakhetia 1606-1648 and of Kartli-Kakhetia 1625-1632, together with the Georgian ruler Saakadze headed national resistance to the Persians and forced Abbas I to abandon his plan to destroy or deport the population of Eastern Georgia. Teimuraz sent five embassies to Russia between 1615 and 1649, and in 1658 went to Moscow in person to beg for help. Failing to receive any, in 1661 he retired to a monastery. He was summoned to Persia and was arrested for refusing to convert to Islam. He was imprisoned in the Astrabad fortress, where he died two years later.

43. The term used here is *protosinkel,* evidently a russified version of the Greek *protosungelos,* "first messenger." See also Chapter VI, Note 12, below.

44. Prince Fedor Fedorovich Volkonsky (died 1665) was appointed lord-in-waiting in 1634, boyar in 1650 and is last mentioned in service in 1663. Crummey, *Aristocrats and Servitors,* p. 184.

45. The Kumyks are a native tribe inhabiting the foothills and lowlands of Dagestan, on the Russian side of the border with present-day Azerbaijan.

46. See Vol. 14, p. 35.

CHAPTER III

1. Prince Johan of Denmark arrived in Moscow in 1602 as a prospective bride-groom for Tsarevna Xenia, the daughter of Tsar Boris Godunov. He died of a sudden illness while Boris was away from Moscow on pilgrimage to the Trinity monastery. See Vol. 14, pp. 27-28 and Vol. 16, Chapter III, Note 33.

2. See Chapter I, Note 35, above.

3. The Russian term used literally means "on the left hand."

4. Ivan Fomin (Johan Thomsen) was a naturalized Dane who was fluent in several languages. He was first employed by Tsar Vasily Shuisky in the translation of foreign military manuals. In 1614 he was sent to Emperor Matthias to sort out the mess left by his predecessor S.M. Ushakov (see Vol. 16, pp. 70-73). There is no further trace of him until 1640, when he was sent on the mission to Denmark related here.

5. See pp. 15-20, above.

6. Ivan Tarasievich Gramotin (died 1638) first appears at the court of False Dmitry I, but was also party to the coup which overthrew him. Instead of being appointed to high office by Shuisky, he was appointed town secretary of Pskov, where he distinguished himself for his rapacity, which played no insignificant part in provoking the subsequent disorders in that city. He fled from Pskov to Tushino in after the revolt of September 1608. In 1609 he and Mikhail Glebovich Saltykov were sent to the Trinity monastery, where Gramotin made a speech to the defenders, falsely asserting that the war was over and that Shuisky had made his submission to Tsar Dmitry. After the fall of the Tushino encampment Gramotin was one of the deputation which proceeded to Sigismund III, urging him to become the protector of Muscovy. He became the king's trusted advisor on Muscovite

affairs, and after the deposition and forcible tonsure of Shuisky was appointed keeper of the seal and conciliar secretary. From January 1611 he was assistant to the Chancellor for Foreign Affairs. He served with the High Embassy led by Filaret and Golitsyn, but when this failed and Moscow was relieved by Minin and Pozharsky, he travelled with King Sigismund back to Warsaw. While in exile he contrived to ingratiate himself with Filaret, and on his return to Moscow in 1618 he was appointed conciliar secretary. He enjoyed a distinguished career under Michael, although from 1626 to 1632 he was exiled to Alatyr, evidently having incurred the patriarch's disfavor. Restored to favor in 1634, he received the privilege of attaching the -vich (of) suffix to his patronymic. See entry in MERSH, Vol. 13, pp. 92-94.

7. ...*no kirkam ne byt'*. *Kirk or kirka* is a loan word signifying a Protestant place of worship, in the same way as kostël signifies a Roman Catholic church.

8. According to the "strand law" practiced in Baltic countries, cargoes recovered from shipwrecked vessels were placed into safekeeping and released to their owners on payment of a tenth of their value.

9. See above, Chapter I, Note 13.

10. By now, of course, Elector Friedrich V of the Palatinate (1596-1632) was long dead. In any case he was only titular king of Bohemia, having been expelled by the victory of Emperor Ferdinand II at the battle of the White Mountain (1620), and subsequently losing also his electoral lands, to part of which his son Karl Ludwig (1617-1680) was restored in 1648. There were at that time two eligible daughters, Elizabeth (born 1618) and Louise Hollandine (born 1622).

11. Prince Yury Andreevich Sitsky (died 1644) between 1618 and 1622 frequently served at ceremonial banquets. In 1619 and 1620 he was among the guard of honor for the Bukharan emissary, the Swedish ambassador and the envoy of a potentate named as "the Chinese tsar Altyn." He also greeted the Persian ambassador on behalf of the tsar. This latter duty led to several precedence disputes. In 1621 Filaret sent Prince Peter Alexandrovich Repnin to the Turkish ambassador. Repnin said he was willing to go, but complained that Sitsky boasted he was higher, because he was sent by the tsar. Michael ruled that no issue of precedence was involved, and both sovereigns would be displeased if they heard any more about the matter. Sitsky served in a ceremonial capacity at both the tsar's weddings, in 1625 and 1626. In 1620, 1633 and 1635 he was responsible for transport arrangements when the tsar went hunting or on pilgrimage. In 1628 he was present at the reception for Persian merchants. In 1635 he became court cupbearer, and a boyar in 1638. He then was sent to be governor of Nizhny Novgorod, where he gave special fishing privileges to the Trinity, Transfiguration and Ascension monasteries, and pacified the Nogay Tatars. In 1640 he was lord lieutenant of Nizhny Novgorod, and also held discussions with the Danish ambassadors. In 1642 he was governor of Venev. In 1642-1643 presided over the Criminal Affairs Chancellery and compiled the list of resident Moscow gentry. In December 1643 he was sent to meet Prince Valdemar at Pskov, and in January 1644 he was one of those boyars holding discussions with the Danish envoys. It was to Sitsky that Valdemar

admitted to slaying a musketeer in the course of his attempted escape from Moscow. Sitsky died August 3, 1644. His wife Fetinia Vladimirovna Bakhterianova-Rostovskaia afterwards became nursemaid to Tsarevna Evdokia Alexeevna (born 1658), and died in 1672, having taken religious vows under the name Feodosia.

12.   The Palace of Facets was constructed between 1487 and 1491 by the Italian architects Marco Ruffo and Pietro Antonio Solario. The name is taken from the eastern facade of the building. The interior contains an audience chamber five hundred square meters in area, with a series of vaults supported by a central column. This chamber was used for ceremonial receptions, meetings of the boyar council and sessions of the Assembly of the Land.

13.   The document alternates between the second and third person when addressing the tsar. I have rendered it throughout in the formal third person.

14.   Prince Nikita Ivanovich Odoevsky (died 1689), son of the boyar Prince Ivan Nikitich, was orphaned at an early age. He is mentioned first in 1618, taking a minor part in skirmishes with the Poles in the environs of Moscow. He was rewarded with the rank of table attendant and was given some estates. In subsequent years he was a constant companion of his near-contemporary Tsar Michael, whom he accompanied on pilgrimages to various monasteries, and served as groomsman at both his weddings. In the autumn of 1633, during the War of Smolensk, he was appointed governor of Rzhev with a commission to raise troops for the siege of that city. Recruitment was difficult, so he was ordered to join with Prince D.M. Cherkassky to march to the relief of Shein, but the column got no further than Mozhaisk when the siege was lifted and active hostilities ceased. Odoevsky was recalled to Moscow and continued to play a prominent part in court functions. In 1635 he was promoted to the rank of senior table attendant with an increase in salary, and in 1640 he was promoted boyar. He then served three years as governor of Astrakhan, and on his return in 1643 was placed in charge of the Chancellery for Kazan and Siberia. His first diplomatic mission, described here, was to head the commission to negotiate the projected Danish marriage alliance. After Michael's death he occupied a prominent place at the court of Tsar Alexis, who appointed him privy boyar. His position probably was helped by the fact that he was related to the tsar's wife by his marriage to Evdokia Fedorovna Sheremeteva, by whom he had four sons. He survived the disgrace of the Morozovs in 1648 and played a leading part in the compilation of the 1649 law code. He became a bitter opponent of Patriarch Nikon, who described him as "an excessively haughty man. He does not have the fear of God in his heart. He never has had any respect for the commands of the Apostles or the Fathers of the church and is the enemy of all truth." Odoevsky's active career continued well on into the regency of Tsarevna Sophia, though by this time, on account of his advanced age, his role was merely to add gravity to ceremonial occasions. See entry in MERSH, Vol. 51, pp. 34-36.

15.   Vasily Ivanovich Streshnev (died 1661), became a lord-in-waiting in 1634, a boyar in 1645 and is last mentioned in service in 1655. Crummey, *Aristocrats and Servitors*, p. 184.

16.   In 1609 Shuisky concluded the Treaty of Vyborg whereby, in return for territorial concessions, King Karl IX agreed to send an auxiliary force to help

defeat the forces of False Dmitry II and his Polish backers. Although this particular mission was successful and the siege of Moscow was relieved, the Swedish intervention led to an escalation of the war since Sigismund III, his hands freed by the defeat of the Zebrzydowski rebellion, embarked upon overt intervention in the Muscovite imbroglio. In the summer of 1610, having lost their war chest at Klushino and their paymaster through the deposition of Shuisky, the Swedes were forced to fend for themselves. They struck northwards and seized Novgorod. Occupying much of the adjacent territory, they proclaimed a Swedish protectorate and promoted the candidacy of a Swedish prince for the vacant tsardom. In 1615 they laid siege to Pskov, with the young King Gustav Adolf taking a personal part in the campaign. When the siege was lifted the two sides began negotiations which concluded with the Peace of Stolbovo (1617), whereby the Swedes evacuated Novgorod in return for the cession of a strip of territory on the Baltic coast. See Volumes 15 and 16 of this series.

17.   Joseph (Iosif) (died 1652) was the fifth patriarch of Moscow (evidently in enumerating the patriarchs, False Dmitry's patriarch Ignaty does not count!) A native of Vladimir, on March 20, 1642 he was chosen after a vacancy lasting almost sixteen months, by means of drawing lots among six candidates selected by the tsar. His patriarchate was largely preoccupied with the tightening of church discipline. At the beginning of Lent 1646 he issued an encyclical enjoining strict observation of the fast by clergy and laymen alike. In 1647 he secured the passing of a decree closing down the market stalls and bath houses on the eve of Sundays and major religious festivals, while all work was to cease for church services, the only exception being the feeding of livestock. Business could resume at four on Sunday afternoon. Trading also had to cease during religious processions until the cross entered the church. The 1649 visit of Patriarch Paisios of Jerusalem gave rise to the idea of comparing Slavonic texts with the Greek. Arseny Sukhanov was sent to the Orient to gather over seven hundred tomes, but returned only after Joseph's death. Ukrainian scholars also were brought to Moscow, and the boyar Rtishchev built a special monastery for them near Moscow, where they could found a school to teach Slavonic and Greek grammar, and philosophy. It seems these initiatives did not come from Joseph, but he went along with them. Under the influence of Nikon, at that time archbishop of Novgorod, the tsar raised with Joseph the issue of forbidding *mnogoglasie,* the simultaneous chanting of different liturgical texts. Joseph dragged his feet on this issue and finally opposed the abolition as being contrary to tradition. Joseph also displayed his bigotry and ignorance of canon law in a 1650 letter to Patriarch Parthenios III of Constantinople. He did not object to the establishment of the Monasteries Chancellery, which was opposed so virulently by his successor Nikon. The church historian Metropolitan Makary considers Joseph's patriarchate not to have been one of the brighter pages of Russian church history. Joseph is said to have amassed a personal fortune of 13,400 rubles, as well as leaving fifteen thousand rubles in the patriarchal treasury. Valuable gifts bestowed by the tsar were converted into cash, allegedly to buy lands. Clergy entering upon benefices were encouraged to travel as far as eight hundred versts to Moscow in

order to obtain confirmation in exchange for gifts. Many complained that this practice impoverished clergy and their families while enriching the patriarch's officials.

18.   Joasaph (Ioasaf) I (died 1640) was the fourth patriarch of Moscow, consecrated on February 6, 1634. Of gentry origin, he received the tonsure at the Solovetsk monastery at the hands of Archimandrite Isidore. When Isidore became archbishop of Novgorod, he sent for Joasaph, who supported Isidore during the Troubles. In 1621 Joasaph became abbot of the Caves monastery, and in 1627 he became archbishop of Pskov. In 1632 he supported a petition by the townsfolk complaining about the excessive privileges being given to foreign merchants. The tsar was displeased and the patriarch laid an interdict on Joasaph, but soon both he and the citizens were forgiven. In 1634 the tsar, following Filaret's designation, appointed him as patriarch. One of his contemporaries explains his election to his humble origins, which made it less likely that he would gainsay the tsar in anything. He was styled not "great sovereign" but merely "great lord." He is not mentioned alongside the tsar either in state documents or even in ecclesiastical statutes emanating from the tsar. His patriarchate was relatively uneventful, but is noted for the unprecedentedly large production of volumes by the Printing Office, largely service books and manuals of religious instruction; yet none of the staff of the Printing Office had knowledge of Greek. Joasaph also tried to reform morals and the practices of the clergy (see below, Chapter VI).

19.   Magnus (1540-1583), a Danish prince, in 1559 became administrator of the secularized bishoprics of Courland and Øsel (Saaremaa), previously purchased by his brother King Frederik II for thirty thousand reichsthalers. In 1570 he was proclaimed king of Livonia under the suzerainty of Ivan IV, and in 1573 he married Ivan's niece Maria Vladimirovna. He previously was engaged to Maria's sister Yevfimia, but she died suddenly in 1571, it was rumored of poison. See Vernadsky, *Tsardom,* pp. 99, 130. His military exploits, including repeated attempts to capture Reval, proved unsuccessful, and in 1578 he defected to the Polish king Stefan Bathory. During the conflicts between Ivan IV and his eldest son it was hinted repeatedly that the tsar wished to disinherit Ivan Ivanovich in favor of King Magnus. See R.G. Skrynnikov, *Ivan the Terrible* (Academic International Press, 1981), pp. 137, 169.

20.   Fedor Ivanovich Sheremetev (1576-1650), incorrectly entitled "Prince" in the text, was the leading figure in the interim boyar administration between the election of Tsar Michael and the return of Metropolitan Filaret (1613-1619). Although by now sixty-one years of age and no longer very active in political affairs, he was evidently a sufficiently venerable figure to impress the Danish delegation. For further details of his career, see Vol. 15, Chapter II, Note 26 and Vol. 16, Chapter I, Note 6.

21.   "Eight years later [1570] a new agreement was reached between Denmark and Ivan. Both parties, recognizing Ivan's supreme rights over Livonia, transferred the country as a whole, including the towns 'now under the Lithuanians and Swedes,' to the ownership of the Danish 'Prince,' Duke Magnus." S.F. Platonov,

Ivan the Terrible, tr. and ed. Joseph L. Wieczynski (Academic International Press, 1974), pp. 89-90

22. The alternate forms of "Bositsky" and "Basistoy" are also used in the text.

23. Basistov's arithmetic is a little off, since he stated that he brought seven puds of tobacco, but under interrogation accounted for ten!

24. The Prince Valdemar affair mercifully was cut short by Michael's death. Five days after, on July 12, 1645 Valdemar had an audience with Tsar Alexis, to whom he renewed his plea to be allowed to return home. The matter was referred to the boyar council and permission was granted on August 7. Some historians suggest that the almost indecent haste with which this matter was dealt stemmed from fears by Boris Morozov and others that certain boyar interests favored Valdemar as a possible rival to Alexis, or even that Michael had contemplated disinheriting Alexis as once Ivan the Terrible threatened to disinherit Ivan the Younger in favor of Prince Magnus. Yet according to Alexis's biographer "there is insufficient evidence to support such a view.... Although it took three weeks to answer Valdemar's petition it seems more probable that this was due to deliberations on the diplomatic consequences and financial terms of his departure rather than to attempts to keep his 'candidature' alive." Philip Longworth, *Alexis, Tsar of All the Russias* (New York, 1984), p. 254. Consult also Joseph T. Fuhrmann, *Tsar Alexis, His Reign and His Russia* (Gulf Breeze, Fla., 1981), Chapter 1.

25. See Chapter I, Note 4, above.

26. Jan Mikolaj Danilowicz (1607-1649) studied abroad in 1619 and from 1623 to 1626. He was endowed with numerous elderships and principalities and became one of the most powerful magnates. In 1627 he became the court treasurer, and in 1632 crown treasurer. In this capacity he was responsible for measures to finance the Muscovite war of 1632-1634, as well as the threatened war with Sweden. Between 1640 and 1642 he was in charge of the Cracow district.

27. The False Dmitry (reigned 1605-1606) is generally thought to have been Grishka Otrepiev, formerly a monk of the Miracles monastery in Moscow (see Note 31, below). He himself had no children, but his wife Marina Mniszech (see following note), who married the second False Dmitry, in 1610 bore a son, Ivan Dmitrievich, who was hanged at the Sepukhov gates of Moscow in 1614.

28. Marina Mniszech (1588-1614) was the daughter of Jerzy Mniszech, palatine of Sandomir. During his wanderings in Poland, False Dmitry became enamored of her, proposed marriage and was secretly converted to Roman Catholicism. Having attained the Muscovite throne in June 1605, Dmitry repeatedly sent for her, and at last she arrived in Moscow on May 2, 1606. The marriage took place shortly afterwards, and she also received an imperial coronation, but on May 17 the arrogant behavior of her Polish followers precipitated the riot which culminated in the murder of Dmitry and the enthronement of Vasily Shuisky. Marina was interned along with other Polish survivors of the massacre but on June 28, 1608 she and her father were given leave to return home. On their way to the border they were overtaken by a detachment from Tushino which overpowered the escort and brought them to the encampment of False Dmitry II. Though aware that he was a double impostor, Marina recognized him as her husband and secretly

married him in September 1608. Nevertheless she based her claim to the throne not on this marriage, but upon her own coronation as tsaritsa and the oath sworn by the population to recognize her legitimacy even in the event that her husband died without heirs. After False Dmitry fled Tushino she remained there for another two months before fleeing in male attire to Dmitrov, at that time held by Polish irregulars commanded by Jan-Piotr Sapieha. Only when Dmitrov was about to fall to Skopin and De la Gardie did Marina rejoin Dmitry in Kaluga, remaining with him until his murder in December 1610. Shortly thereafter she gave birth to a son, Ivan Dmitrievich, who thus became the heir to the pretenders' claims. When King Sigismund wrote her a letter urging her to leave while it was still possible, she haughtily refused. By this time she obtained the backing of the cossack leader Ivan Martynovich Zarutsky, who during the spring of 1613 established his base at Astrakhan. Expelled from that city, they fled to the Urals, where they were handed over to the Muscovite authorities by the Yaik Cossacks. Zarutsky was impaled and the four-year-old "Little Brigand" was hanged. Marina is said to have died of grief in her prison at Kolomna, which is still referred to as "Marina's tower." See entry by Daniel B. Rowland, MERSH, Vol. 22, pp. 241-243.

29.   Aleksandr Gasiewski (died 1636) served as ambassador to the reigning False Dmitry, after whose overthrow he was imprisoned briefly by Tsar Vasily Shuisky. Later he returned to Moscow in command of a contingent of royal troops. After the departure of Hetman Zolkiewski from Moscow he was Polish commander of the Kremlin until its capitulation in 1612. He later played a prominent part in the negotiations leading to the truce of Deulino in 1618, and was appointed palatine of Smolensk.

30.   Ivan Dmitrievich (Jan Faustin) Luba was the supposed son of False Dmitry II and Marina Mniszech. In reality he was the son of a minor Polish noble Dymitr Luba, who took his small son on campaign with him to Moscow, where he was killed. The orphan was brought by the noble Wilenski back to Poland, alleging that this was the tsarevich, whom Marina gave him for safekeeping. When the child grew up Wilenski made him known to King Sigismund and the lords of the council, who entrusted him to Leo Sapieha. Six thousand zlotys were allotted for his upkeep, so Sapieha placed him in the St. Simeon monastery of Brest-Litovsk, entrusting the abbot Afanasy to teach him Russian, Polish and Latin. Luba spent seven years in the monastery, knowing nothing of his alleged identity. Meanwhile the peace negotiations between Russia and Poland got under way, and the government lost interest in the pretender. His allowance was reduced to a hundred zlotys and then discontinued altogether. The unfortunate youth then turned to Wilenski, demanding to know who his parents really were, and why people were calling him tsarevich of Moscow. Wilenski explained the circumstances and Luba, not wishing to maintain the imposture and being without means, entered the service of Lord Osinski as a scribe and also expressed the wish to become a Roman Catholic priest. This was around 1640, when Luba was thirty years old. Rumors then reached Moscow, giving rise to the diplomatic exchanges described here. Stempkowski's negotiations with the Muscovite government were stalled because

of the illness and death of Tsar Michael. On July 26, 1645 Tsar Alexis had a personal audience with Stempkowski and honored the safe conduct granted Luba, in exchange for which the Polish government promised to discountenance both this and any other pretender. Nevertheless in January 1646 there came news that on the return journey Luba continued to call himself "tsarevich of Moscow," that the pretender was at liberty as a regimental scribe in the infantry, and that the king granted him a pension. The Poles replied that Luba was in the custody of the infantry captain Jan Osinski. Luba in fact served in the royal army. According to some accounts he was killed in battle against the Tatars in 1648; according to other versions he returned to Poland and earned his living for many years as a scribe in various magnates' households.

31. Grishka Otrepiev, a renegade monk, is generally believed to be the true identity of False Dmitry I. In secular life Yury Bogdanovich Otrepiev, he was orphaned at an early age when his father was killed in a brawl with a Lithuanian in the Foreign Settlement of Moscow. Yury then appears in the household of Prince Boris Cherkassky, where he was known for his literacy and was employed in some kind of clerical capacity. The Cherkassky princes were implicated in the Romanov sorcery trials of 1600 and Otrepiev, as one of the elite household servants of a disgraced prince, came under suspicion. He eluded the authorities by taking the tonsure under the name Grigory. He appears to have wandered from one monastery to another, until he settled in the Miracles monastery in the Moscow Kremlin. There he attracted the favorable attention of Patriarch Job who employed him as a copyist and occasional personal secretary. He was denounced by Metropolitan Jonas of Rostov for alleged treasonable utterances. Despite attempts by Patriarch Job to shield him, Tsar Boris ordered that he be sent to the St. Cyril monastery of Beloozero, there to be kept under strict surveillance. Forewarned of this action, perhaps by the Romanov interest, Otrepiev fled from Moscow to Galich, and from there to the St. Boris and St. Gleb monastery at Murom, returning thereafter to Moscow in secret. During the Lenten season of 1601 he persuaded the monk Varlaam and the chorister Misail Povadin to accompany him on pilgrimage to the Caves monastery of Kiev. From Kiev the three proceeded to Ostrog, where they spent the summer in the household of the local magnate Prince Konstantin. Thereafter Grishka parted company with his two companions, who returned to Moscow, while he threw off his monastic habit and studied for a while at the Socinian academy at Hoszcza. He next appears at Brahin, in the household of Prince Adam Wisniowiecki, who launched him on his career as Tsarevich Dmitry. See entry "Dmitrii Ivanovich," MERSH, Vol. 9, pp. 164-169

32. Marienburg (Malbork) was founded in 1274 by the Teutonic Knights on the bank of the Nogat river, and from 1309 was the residence of the grand master. Under the terms of the Treaty of Torun of 1446 it was ceded to Poland. The fortress held a number of Muscovite internees, including Metropolitan Filaret, during the second decade of the seventeenth century. The city was an important strategic point in the Polish-Swedish wars of 1626-1629 and 1665-1660. See Volume 16 of this series, Chapter I, Note 93.

33.   The date is erroneously given in the text as 1649, which of course is an impossibility, as Michael himself died in 1645.

34.   Michael Malein in the tenth century was abbot of the Kimenos hermitage on Mount Athos. He was the tsar's patron saint.

35.   Boris Ivanovich Morozov (1590-1661) was of an ancient but not particularly wealthy boyar family. He came to prominence in 1633 when he was appointed tutor of the four-year-old Tsarevich Alexis, and attained boyar rank in 1634. When Alexis came to the throne in 1645, Morozov was his chief adviser. His influence was established further through marriage to the tsar's sister-in-law Anna Ilyichina Miloslavskaia. This was his second marriage, the first having taken place in 1617. Morozov embarked on a program of ambitious fiscal reform. These measures, especially the salt tax, were very unpopular and were a major cause of the urban riots occurring in June 1648. The tsar was compelled to exile him, ostensibly for life, to the St. Cyril monastery of Beloozero, but later in the year Morozov met with the tsar at the Trinity monastery, and by October he was back in Moscow. While not enjoying his earlier prominence, he continued to be influential behind the scenes, and of course he was extremely wealthy, with an almost modern combination of landed wealth and industrial enterprises. See entry by Lindsey A.J. Hughes, MERSH, Vol. 23, pp. 71-73.

36.   Alexis (born 1629, reigned 1645-1676), Irina (1627-1679), Anna (1630-1692) and Tatiana (1636-1706). Michael's other children were Pelagaia (1628-1629), Martha (1631-1633), Ivan (1633-1639), Sophia (1634-1636), Evdokia (1637) and Vasily (1639). All were born of his second marriage.

CHAPTER IV

1.   The story that Michael agreed to certain "conditions" prior to his election is very persistent, but not generally accepted by historians. See Vernadsky, *Tsardom*, pp. 277-279.

2.   The veteran commander Mikhail Borisovich Shein was sent to recapture Smolensk in the war of 1632-1634. Instead of reducing the city, Shein himself was surrounded and forced to surrender. On his release and return to Moscow he was tried and beheaded, while his son and various relatives were sentenced to terms of banishment.

3.   *Samoderzhets* is the term used in the text.

4.   Fedor (Fedka) Andronov was a merchant who attached himself to the court of False Dmitry II, and then joined the armies of Sigismund III at Smolensk. The king appointed him to the boyar council in Moscow, where he served as treasurer. He was the foremost collaborationist, and was seized on the orders of Pozharsky before he could escape from Moscow. He was impaled outside the city in October 1612. See entry in MERSH, Vol. 1, pp. 225-226 and Volume 15 of this series, pp. 191-199.

5.   It was customary when entering the religious life for the postulant to make a donation, either in cash, land or valuables, to the monastery or convent to be entered.

6.   See Vol. 16 of this series, pp. 11-12.

7.   On the system of *mestnichestvo,* whereby commands and appointments were awaded according to pedigree rather than merit or ability, see entry by Graham, MERSH, Vol. 22, pp. 8-13. See also pp. 93-102, below.

8.   Prince Ivan Mikhailovich Vorotynsky (died 1627) is first mentioned as having been imprisoned during the reign of Ivan IV, then released on the death of his father in 1577. Under Ivan IV he served as governor of Murom, and in 1582 he was sent to Kazan to pacify the rebellious Cheremiss. In 1585 he incurred the hostility of the regent Boris Godunov by his partisanship of the Shuisky interest and was exiled to "distant places," only to return in 1592 when he was promoted boyar and appointed chief commander at Kazan. He returned to Moscow in 1598 and apparently remained faithful to Boris until the latter's death. He was one of the first to swear allegiance to False Dmitry I, and was one of the delegation sent to meet the pretender at Tula. Within a year he was in opposition to him, and was party to his overthrow. During Shuisky's reign he was loyal to the tsar, and fought against False Dmitry II and other opponents. He was also a close confidant of Patriarch Hermogen and as such suffered persecution from the interim boyar regime in Moscow. He was placed under arrest and forced to sign a document calling for the immediate surrender of Smolensk. According to some accounts he was considered briefly as a candidate for the throne, but when Michael was elected, Vorotynsky was among the deputation sent to Kostroma. He subsequently served as governor of Kazan, led the embassy to Smolensk, and when Tsar Michael was absent on pilgrimage, was left in charge of the capital. In his last years he retired from service, and on his deathbed was tonsured under the name Jonas.

9.   "Crown servitors" is the term used to translate *oprichniki,* Ivan IV's chosen band of henchmen who terrorized the land through most of the 1560s. See Vol. 10 of this series.

10.   This referred to the time when there was still a strong camaraderie between the prince and his retinue (druzhina), before the ruler began to assume trappings of autocracy which rendered him remote from even his most exalted followers.

11.   See Chapter I, Note 22, above.

12.   Prince Vasily Vasilievich Golitsyn was, along with Metropolitan Filaret, the leader of the high ambassadors interned in Poland after the collapse of talks with the Poles outside Smolensk in 1611-1612. Golitsyn therefore, although his pedigree was outstanding, was out of the running when the Assembly of the Land met in 1613 to elect a new tsar. After the Truce of Deulino at the end of 1618 he was on his way to be repatriated when he died at Grodno, and on the orders of King Sigismund was buried at the Brethren church of the Holy Spirit at Wilno. See entry in MERSH, Vol. 48, pp. 166-167.

13.   See Volume 15, pp. 198-220.

14. Tushino was the village to the northwest of Moscow where False Dmitry II established his encampment from 1606 to 1610 in anticipation of the conquest of the capital. See Vol. 15 of this series.

15. The battle of Klushino (June 24, 1610) was a decisive defeat for the Muscovite forces under the untalented leadership of the tsar's brother Prince Dmitry Ivanovich Shuisky. Much of the army defected to the Poles, while the Swedish auxiliary forces, left to their own devices, posed yet another threat to the integrity of the Muscovite realm. See Vol. 15, pp. 140-141.

16. Prokopy Fedorovich Liapunov (died 1611) came from an important landed family in the Riazan region, and was one of five brothers, of whom Zakhar was the most famous after Prokopy himself. The Riazan gentry as a whole was hostile to the regency and rule of Boris Godunov, out of envy of what they perceived to be a boyar monopoly on power. There is no indication what, if any, reward the Liapunovs received for their support of False Dmitry I, but they were certainly very active in their opposition to his successor Vasily Shuisky. Prokopy and another prominent Riazan landowner, Grigory Sunbulov led a contingent of insurgent Riazan gentry to join the Bolotnikov rebellion, but when the main force of Bolotnikov's army arrived before Moscow, composed of peasants and runaway serfs, conflict arose as to the goals of their rebellion. Prokopy then brought at least some of the Riazan gentry over to the side of Vasily Shuisky on November 15, 1606. He received conciliar rank from the tsar, and also the post of governor of Riazan, which apparently he held for the remainder of his life. Prokopy and Zakhar played a prominent part in the defeat of the rebel forces on the Vosma river, June 5-7, 1607, and were present at the siege of Tula. Apparently Prokopy was wounded in 1608 while fighting to clear his native Riazan region of the forces of False Dmitry II, and was forced for a while to retire from active service. Despite the fact that they were praised for their loyalty to the tsar and were held in high honor, the Liapunov brothers tried to get the popular hero, the tsar's kinsman Prince Mikhail Vasilievich Skopin-Shuisky, to consent to a conspiracy to seize the throne. Although Skopin refused to have anything to do with the plot, he soon afterwards died, according to the Liapunovs and many others poisoned by his jealous kinsmen. When the tsar's untalented and unpopular brothers Dmitry and Ivan suffered the disastrous defeat at Klushino, the Liapunov brothers played a leading part in the deposition of Vasily Shuisky. Although Zakhar was induced to play a part in the high embassy to support the candidature of Wladyslaw, Prokopy tended to support the second pretender. After the death of False Dmitry II at the hands of his Tatar bodyguards, Prokopy was responsive to the appeals of Patriarch Hermogen to unite all Russians in defense of the land and the Orthodox faith. Prokopy played a prominent part in the organization of the First Militia Force, but because of cossack intrigues and Polish disinformation he was murdered on July 22, 1611. See entry by John Wiita, MERSH, Vol. 19, pp. 238-241.

17. Literally "those who were their fathers' sons."

18. Prince Dmitry Timofeevich Trubetskoy (died 1625) is first mentioned as being among the defenders of Novgorod Seversk against the forces of False Dmitry

I in 1604. In 1608 he deserted the cause of Tsar Vasily Shuisky and was appointed table attendant and later boyar at the Tushino court of False Dmitry II. There he was joined by his cousin Yury Nikitich Trubetskoy, exiled by Shuisky for alleged treason during the Bolotnikov rebellion. Prince Dmitry's uncle, Andrei Vasilievich Trubetskoy, remained in Moscow, and after the overthrow of Shuisky became one of the "seven boyars" in charge of Moscow during the ensuing interregnum. At the same time Prince Dmitry obtained command of a band of cossacks and was among the besiegers of the city in the ranks of the First Militia Force. After Liapunov's murder he remained with his cossacks in the vicinity of Moscow while the Second Militia Force was forming under Minin and Pozharsky. Unlike his colleague Zarutsky he made his peace with the Second Militia Force and with them participated in the liberation of Moscow. It appears that he was considered for the vacant Moscow throne, but was bought off with lavish land grants in the Vaga region. Under the new reign he took part in the liberation of Novgorod from the Swedes, but later became involved in an embarrassing precedence dispute with V.P. Morozov, in which his compromising relations with the Poles were dragged up. He was among the delegation sent to greet Metropolitan Filaret on his return from Polish captivity in 1619. Some time later he was appointed governor of Tobolsk, where he died. See entry by Daniel B. Rowland, MERSH, Vol. 39, pp. 241-244.

19. Ivan Martynovich Zarutsky (died 1614) first took part in the Bolotnikov rebellion, and then joined forces with False Dmitry II, on whose behalf he commanded a band of Don Cossacks, and was named boyar by the pretender. After the collapse of the Tushino camp he first went to King Sigismund at Smolensk, but then returned to Dmitry in Kaluga. After the murder of the pretender he joined the First Militia Force, and after the murder of Liapunov assumed the leadership. In 1612 he attempted to organize the assassination of Pozharsky; when this failed he fled to Astrakhan, taking with him Marina and her son. With the approach of Tsar Michael's troops and a popular uprising within the city, Zarutsky fled to the Ural steppes but was handed over to the Muscovite authorities by his own cossacks, and was impaled by the Serpukhov gates of Moscow. See entry in MERSH, Vol. 45, pp. 176-182.

20. Kuzma Minin (died 1616) was described as a miasnik (butcher), but to judge from the extent of his personal fortune he must have been quite a successful retailer rather than a simple butcher. On September 1, 1611 he was elected territorial elder (zemskii starosta) and thereafter took charge of the national movement to raise forces and collect money for the liberation of Moscow. Together with Prince Dmitry Pozharsky he led the militia force and was a prominent member of the Council of the Whole Land created at Yaroslavl to discharge functions normally exercised by the central government. In 1613 he was promoted to the rank of conciliar noble, and many state documents of the early years of Michael's reign bear his signature.

21. Fedor Ivanovich Mstislavsky (died 1622) was the son of a prominent political and military figure during the reign of Ivan IV. Ivan Fedorovich was one

of the more prominent advisors of the tsar during the 1550s and then, together with Prince Ivan Dmitrievich Belsky, was head of the lands not absorbed into the tsar's crown domains (zemshchina). He was named to the council of regency on the death of Ivan the Terrible but in 1585 fell from power and entered a monastery. Fedor Ivanovich is first mentioned in court service in 1575 and became a boyar in 1576. With his father's banishment to a monastery in 1586 he became the ranking boyar in the council. In 1598 he was put forward by some as a candidate for the throne, but he himself refused to be considered. He was loyal to Boris Godunov and even on one occasion was offered the hand of the tsar's daughter, since apparently he was a widower since 1586. When he refused, the tsar refused him permission to marry at all. This prohibition was lifted by False Dmitry in 1606, but there is no evidence that he took advantage of this dispensation. His military record was not very distinguished, though after he was reputedly wounded fifteen times at Novgorod Seversk in 1604 he was given a hero's welcome in Moscow. On the other hand he was defeated soundly by Bolotnikov on the Serpukhov highway in 1606, and was forced to lift the siege of Kaluga when the relieving column under the bogus Tsarevich Peter arrived. Both in 1606 and 1610 he refused to be considered as a candidate for the throne, but was one of the "seven boyars" who formed the interim government after the deposition of Vasily Shuisky in July 1610. After the liberation of Moscow by Minin and Pozharsky he temporarily went into seclusion at Yaroslavl, but was present at the final session of the Assembly of the Land which elected Michael Romanov. It is estimated that in 1613 he was the wealthiest private landowner in Muscovy, but since his two sons predeceased him the line became extinct with his death on February 12, 1622. See entry by Emily. V. Leonard, MERSH, Vol. 23, p. 160.

22.   Concerning Boris and Mikhail Mikhailovich Saltykov, see Vol. 16, pp. 164-166.

23.   Crummey (*Aristocrats and Servitors,* p. 185) cites someone of that name who became a boyar in 1640 and died in 1670. He also states that elsewhere the date of death is given as 1642/3, which is erroneous. Obviously the latter death date refers to another Boris Alexandrovich Repnin, whose actions Soloviev is describing here, but concerning whom I have been unable to find information from any other source.

24.   Ivan Nikitich Romanov (died 1640) is first mentioned in 1591, when he was summoned to Serpukhov to participate in the campaign against the Tatars. He returned with land grants, gifts and expressions of the tsar's goodwill. In 1597 he was present at the reception for the imperial ambassador Abraham Donau, and in 1599 was ceremonial cupbearer for Tsar Boris at the reception of Prince Gustav of Sweden. When the Romanov family fell into disgrace in 1601 Ivan Nikitich was sent to Pelym, where he was joined for a while by his brother Vasily, who died February 15, 1602. The following month the terms of his exile were alleviated, and he was escorted to Ufa, and later was employed in some administrative capacity in Nizhny Novgorod. He was permitted briefly to return to Moscow, but spent the rest of Boris's reign under house arrest at his estate near Klin. In 1605 he was

bidden attend the coronation of False Dmitry I, and thereafter was promoted boyar and named to Dmitry's Polish-style Senate. During Shuisky's reign he was ordered, together with a number of other boyars and commanders, to Kozelsk. He was also one of the groomsmen at the tsar's wedding on January 17, 1608. He served as second in command at different times to Prince I.I. Shuisky and Prince M.V. Skopin-Shuisky. In 1610 Ivan Nikitich was responsible for persuading Patriarch Hermogen to withdraw his initial objection to the candidacy of Prince Wladyslaw, and his signature is prominent on the letter of the boyars to the inhabitants of Kostroma and Yaroslavl urging them to discountenance the First Militia Force commanded by Trubetskoy and Zarutsky. Yet when the Second Militia Force liberated Moscow he also signed the confirmatory charter proclaiming the election of his nephew Michael. He was also part of the family regency council, consisting of himself, Prince Ivan Borisovich Cherkassky and the boyar Fedor Ivanovich Sheremetev. The senior boyar, Prince Fedor Ivanovich Mstislavsky, also appointed as his executor Ivan Nikitich, who on his behalf distributed his fabulous wealth among various religious foundations. As related here, he became involved in a number of precedence suits in which it was generally ruled that, although the plaintiff came from a more illustrious family, Ivan Nikitich, as a relative of the tsar, must take precedence. In order to avoid more such unseemly incidents, Ivan Nikitich seems to have made himself scarce at court. In any case he was fabulously rich, although it is not known whether the estates confiscated by Boris in 1601 were restored to him. For ceremonial receptions of ambassadors he provided large contingents of armed and mounted men from his estates; in 1626 forty of the 177 members of the guard of honor were provided by Ivan Nikitich at his own expense. During the Russo-Polish war of 1632-1634 he contributed a large amount of provisions for the troops besieging the city, also at his own cost. Ivan Nikitich died July 18, 1640. His widow Uliana Fedorovna attended the first marriage of Tsar Alexis on January 16, 1648 and died October 23, 1649. Ivan Nikitich had eight children, but only two, Nikita Ivanovich and Martha, survived him. Martha married Prince Alexis Ivanovich Vorotynsky. Nikita was a lifelong bachelor, and with his death in 1654 his estates escheated to the crown.

25. Prince Boris Mikhailovich Lykov-Obolensky (died 1646) took part in various diplomatic receptions between 1593 and 1597. He was a signatory to Boris Godunov's confirmatory charter in 1598, and accompanied him on the Serpukhov campaign in the summer of that year. He was in the reception party for both of Tsarevna Xenia's suitors, Prince Gustav of Sweden and Prince Johan of Denmark. Late in 1602 he was appointed governor of Belgorod, where he remained for the rest of Boris's reign. Absence from court for several years was the result of the unsatisfactory outcome of several precedence disputes and apparent dissatisfaction with Tsar Boris. He became one of the closest followers of False Dmitry I, who sent him to the borderland towns to administer the oath of allegiance. He was appointed boyar April 13, 1606 and later married Anastasia Nikitichna Romanovna, sister to Metropolitan Filaret. Under Vasily Shuisky he took a leading part in the struggle against the Bolotnikov rebels. In 1608 he was sent to the relief of Briansk,

and then operated against False Dmitry II from his headquarters at Orel. Although he did not desert to Tushino, he was suspected of sympathies in that direction, especially as an expeditionary force under his command failed to engage Lisowski by reason of yet another precedence dispute. After Shuisky's deposition he was one of the "seven boyar" commission which acted as an interim government pending the arrival of the newly-elected Wladyslaw. He presented a petition to Wladyslaw, from whom he received two small villages in the Riazan region; the only trouble was that King Sigismund simultaneously granted the same villages to Ivan Mikhailovich Saltykov. Lykov was also one of the signatories on the letters to Shein demanding the immediate capitulation of Smolensk, and on another letter asking the ambassadors to demand the immediate dispatch of Prince Wladyslaw to Moscow. Like the other boyars held captive in the Kremlin, Lykov was absent during the initial deliberations of the 1613 Assembly of the Land, but was one of the signatories of Michael's confirmatory charter. After the coronation he brought a precedence dispute against the tsar's uncle and his own brother-in-law Ivan Nikitich Romanov, but eventually consented to take his place at table below the Romanovs. In May 1614, when Moscow was threatened with a Tatar attack, Lykov was put in charge of the defenses along the Yauza river. In September of the same year he was given the task of pacifying the southern borderlands, and defeated Zarutsky's marauding cossacks near Balakhna. He also operated against renegade cossacks and foreign mercenaries around Vologda and Beloozero in 1615. He rounded up three thousand cossacks and brought them to Moscow, where they swore allegiance to Tsar Michael. In September 1617 he was sent to Nizhny Novgorod to recruit forces in anticipation of Prince Wladyslaw's advance on Moscow, and in June 1618 he took part in the relief of Mozhaisk. In 1619 he was head of the Chancellery for Criminal Affairs, and was sent to Nizhny Novgorod to muster service cavalrymen. Between 1620 and 1622 he was senior governor of Kazan. In 1623 he headed the Chancellery for Investigations. He attended both marriages of Tsar Michael, in 1624 and 1626, and in the latter year also superintended the re-fortification of Mozhaisk. He was head of the Chancellery for Monasteries in 1628-1629, and from 1629 to 1635 headed the Chancellery of Posts. In 1632 he became involved in a precedence dispute with Prince Dmitry Mamstriukovich Cherkassky. He lost, and was forced to pay damages in the amount of twelve thousand rubles, and both litigants were removed from command of the Smolensk expedition. In view of what eventually happened to Shein and Izmailov, for Lykov this was perhaps a blessing in disguise! In 1634 Lykov was in charge of extraordinary tax levies to defray the expense of the Smolensk war, and from 1635 to 1642 he headed the Chancellery for Kazan and Siberia. When in January 1639 two of Michael's sons, Ivan and Vasily, died, Lykov kept vigil over the bodies day and night. In 1640 he was one of the commission of seven boyars left in charge of state affairs while the tsar was absent on pilgrimage. Lykov died June 2, 1646 and was buried in a stone chapel adjoining the St. Paphnutius monastery of Borovsk.

    26.   Soloviev here uses the spelling "Chepchiugov," but elsewhere it is more commonly spelled "Chepchugov."

    27.   Literally "young."

28.   Probably referring to the younger of the two brothers who were prominent conciliar secretaries. Vasily Yakovlevich Shchelkalov (died 1611) was head of the Chancellery for Crown Service and Appointments (razriadnyi prikaz) from 1577 to 1594 and of the Chancellery for Foreign Affairs from 1594 to 1601, as well as keeper of the seal from 1595 or 1596. He was disgraced and removed from office by Boris Godunov, possibly in connection with the Romanov affair. He was restored partially to favor before Boris's death in 1605, and was given the rank of lord-in-waiting by False Dmitry I, although his former estates were not fully restored, which probably accounts for the petition he submitted to King Sigismund. He appears to have enjoyed conciliar rank throughout the reign of Shuisky, although he did not enjoy his former eminence in state affairs. See entries "Shchelkalov brothers" by Graham and the separate entry on Vasily by Rowland, MERSH, Vol. 34, pp. 176-182.

29.   Boris (died 1646) is mentioned as a boyar in December 1613 and in that capacity signed the Confirmatory Charter of Tsar Michael's election. In 1625 or 1626 he was demoted to the rank of Moscow noble but in 1634, after Filaret's death, regained his boyardom. Crummey, *Aristocrats and Servitors,* pp. 180-181.

30.   Mikhail Glebovich Saltykov was employed on a number of diplomatic missions on behalf of Boris Godunov and False Dmitry I. He then threw in his lot with the second pretender, and later with the Poles, playing a prominent part in the collaborationist regime in Moscow in 1610-1611. He is mentioned in the same breath as Fedor Andronov as an arch-traitor, but managed to make good his escape from Moscow for permanent exile in Poland, where he died in 1621. See entry in MERSH, Vol. 33, pp. 45-49.

31.   Yury Ignatievich Tatishchev (dates of birth and death unknown, fl. 1598-1629) is first mentioned in the charter confirming the election of Boris Godunov. Later in 1598 he was sent to the Georgian ambassador Archimandrite Cyril with food from the tsar's table. In 1611 he was named governor of Kursk, where the next year he withstood a four-week Polish siege. In commemoration the Sign monastery was founded in Kursk, where he continued as governor until 1616. In June 1617 he served twice at banquets given to honor the English ambassador John Merrick. In June 1618 he was sent to Kaluga to convey the tsar's concern over Prince Dmitry Mikhailovich Pozharsky, who was sick. He refused the assignment on grounds of precedence, as a result of which he was beaten with the knout and forced to make his submission to Pozharsky. In 1618 he was present during the siege of Moscow by Wladyslaw, and was rewarded for his services with a patrimony. In 1619 he was sent with the rank of lord lieutenant to survey boundaries around Toropets and Velizh. A precedence complaint by his subordinate Glebov was left unanswered. On April 17, 1621 he was sent to invite the Persian ambassador to the tsar's table. In 1622 he was sent with the lord-in-waiting Golovin to round up gentry and review their service grants. He brought a precedence dispute against Golovin and lost, and spent three days in prison. In 1625 he took part in the re-fortification of Serpukhov, and in 1626 he was governor of Viazma. In 1627 he was promoted from table attendant to Moscow resident noble. On July 12, 1627, the feast day of St. Michael

the Archangel (one of the tsar's name days) he dined at the sovereign's table in the Golden Pavilion. He was present at a reception for the Persian ambassador in September 1628. Early in 1629 he was given additional estates, an entitlement of a thousand chetverts and a salary of ninety rubles; a few months later his entitlement was increased by another two hundred chetverts.

32.   Prince Fedor Fedorovich Volkonsky (died 1665), lord-in-waiting 1634, boyar 1650. Prince Peter Fedorovich Volkonsky (died 1649 or 1650), lord-in-waiting 1645. Crummey, *Aristocrats and Servitors,* pp. 184, 186.

33.   Gavrila Pushkin (died 1638) first appears in 1581 as a musketeer captain in the campaign sent to Reval with the tsar's document for the local commanders. In 1592 he saw service at Borisov. In 1598 he commanded the Kasimov Tatars in the great regiment during the Serpukhov campaign. Under Boris Godunov he suffered disfavor and was posted as a musketeer captain to Pelym. In 1605, in company with Naum Pleshcheev he brought the proclamation of False Dmitry I to Moscow and read it aloud to the assembled populace. He was in attendance in 1606 at Dmitry's marriage to Marina Mniszech. After Dmitry's death he opposed the Tushino forces. In 1608 he intercepted enemy messages at Pogoreloe Gorodishche and sent them on to Tver. In February 1611 he signed the document sent by the boyars to Wilno to ask for the immediate dispatch of Prince Wladyslaw. He was sent in 1612 by Prince Dmitry Timofeevich Trubetskoy to the Trinity monastery to work out an agreement with the Second Militia Force under Pozharsky. At the 1613 coronation of Tsar Michael he was asked to present Pozharsky to the boyar council, but begged off on grounds of precedence. Michael responded by calling off considerations of precedence for the duration of the coronation celebrations. Pushkin continued as a conciliar noble, and in 1614-1615 served as governor of Viazma. In 1618 he attended the assembly called to consider means to counteract Wladyslaw's renewed bid for the Muscovite throne. During the defense of Moscow he was put in charge of the stretch from the Presentation to the Frolov gates. In 1619 he was in the party sent to Viazma to greet Filaret on his return from captivity. In the same year he was appointed as a colleague of Prince B.M. Lykov as head of the Criminal Affairs chancellery. In 1626 for some reason he was banished to the country with his two sons, but in 1629 he was once again in the list of conciliar nobles. He took monastic vows some time before his death.

34.   Boris Ivanovich Pushkin (died 1659) was the son of Ivan Mikhailovich "the Greater," who was a conciliar noble during the Interregnum. With the rank of table attendant Boris was sent on the high embassy with Filaret and Golitsyn, and shared their captivity in Poland. Returning to Muscovy in 1619, on the way he was ordered to Viazma, where he was rewarded by the tsar for his sufferings in captivity, and received a fur robe and a goblet with a lid. In 1623-1624, in company with Ivan Fedorovich Somov, he was sent to Astrakhan to investigate the malfeasance of the town secretary Mark Pozdeev. In 1625 he returned with the rank of "Moscow noble" and took a prominent part in court life. He was especially close to Filaret, having been his companion in misfortune. In March 1630 he became deputy head of the Criminal Affairs chancellery. In October 1632 Pushkin was sent with G.I.

Gorikhvostov and the secretary M. Neverov on an embassy to Sweden to conclude the proposed anti-Polish alliance. When they reached Pskov they heard that King Gustav Adolf was dead and received a new decree to convey the tsar's condolences to the widowed Queen Maria Eleonora and her daughter Queen Kristina. They returned from documents confirming that Queen Kristina's government would continue to observe the terms of the Stolbovo treaty, but that hostilities with Poland would have to be suspended. In 1635 Pushkin was appointed governor of Mangazeia, where he remained until 1639. In 1640 he was governor of Yablonov, returning to Moscow to resume his responsibilities at the Criminal Affairs Chancellery. In 1644 he escorted the Danish embassy and Prince Valdemar from Pskov to Moscow, and while they were in Moscow he was appointed their bailiff. In 1646 he was promoted to lord-in-waiting and was placed in sole charge of Criminal Affairs. In 1648 he attended the marriage of Tsar Alexis to Maria Miloslavskaia, clearing the path for the bride. In 1648 again he was named to the embassy to Sweden, but only set out the following year, with the title of lord lieutenant of Briansk. This time the embassy concerned those who fled across the border to Russia out of fear of religious persecution; besides Russians, these included a number of Karelians and Letts. It was agreed that those who migrated between 1617 and 1648 should remain Russian subjects, and Sweden accepted twenty thousand rubles indemnity. Those fleeing after 1648 were to be returned to Sweden. Part of the indemnity was paid in cash to the Swedish agent in Moscow, the remainder to be paid in kind from the tsar's granaries in Pskov. The scarcity thus created sparked off the so-called "Pskov bread riots." In 1651 Pushkin was appointed governor of the Dvina lands, where he remained until 1656, considerably extending the wooden town at Kholmogory. At his death he left a son Nikita, who later became the monk Nifont at the Trinity monastery. With the death of Boris's grandson Afanasy Nikitich, this branch of the Pushkin family became extinct.

35.   Prince Yury Yansheevich Suleshov (1584-1643) was the son of a prominent emigrant from the Crimean Horde. He held the rank of table attendant under Boris Godunov, by whom he was sent early in 1605 to Novgorod Seversk to reward Prince Yury Nikitich Trubetskoy with gold. He remained as table attendant, presumably third in that rank, under Tsar Vasily Shuisky. In 1610 he married Martha Mikhailovna Saltykova, a cousin of Michael's mother. He took part in both Militia Forces and in January 1611 his name appears on the charter granting the Vaga lands to Prince Dmitry Timofeevich Trubetskoy. He played a prominent role in Michael's coronation in July 1613. He was involved in a number of precedence disputes and won all of them, but not all the losers appeared in an inferior position to him throughout Michael's reign. In 1614 he was on active service against Zarutsky, along with Prince Ivan Nikitich Odoevsky "the Younger." In 1615-1616 he was sent to Kazan to deal with the Cheremiss rebellion, but got no further than collecting levies in Nizhny Novgorod. Early in 1617 there occurred his most important military feat, when he beat off the Poles trying to capture Dorogobuzh. His last military campaign was in 1618, when he was one of the commission of

boyars entrusted with the defense of the capital. During the siege of Moscow he was joined by his brother Mahmet-Shah-Murza, who received the baptismal name Vasily. In 1619 both brothers were awarded estates in the Murom and Nizhny Novgorod regions. Prince Yury in 1621 served in the Chancellery of Investigations, conducting a review of service tenures in the Riazan and Meshchera regions. He was appointed governor of Tobolsk in 1623, apparently an honorific exile, since he alienated too many during his tenure at the Chancellery of Investigations. Nevertheless Filaret showed considerable favor to his brother Vasily, and he himself was given considerable freedom by Prince Dmitry Mamstriukovich Cherkassky, who as head of the Chancellery for Kazan was his immediate superior. In many ways Suleshov's governorship was a turning point in the history of Western Siberia. He handed over to his successor Prince Dmitry Timofeevich Trubetskoy on May 29, 1625, and was rewarded richly for his services, once again taking his place in the boyar council. In 1626 he was present at the tsar's marriage to Evdokia Streshneva and became one of the most long-serving judges in the Chancellery of Investigations, from 1626 also heading the Office of Chancellery Affairs. Between 1628 and 1630, in addition, he served on the Chancellery for Criminal Affairs. In 1630 he was appointed governor of Novgorod, and his brother also disappears for seven months from the service lists, giving rise to the speculation that this was yet another honorific exile. He was recalled in 1632 and once again served on the Chancellery for Criminal Affairs for three and a half years. He also led the donkey at the consecration of Patriarch Joasaph I in 1634. (On Palm Sunday and other ceremonial occasions the patriarch was mounted on a donkey, of which the tsar held the bridle. Since the tsar was too infirm to perform this ceremony, Suleshov presumably was deputizing for him). In 1635 he was one of the boyars receiving the remains of the former tsar Vasily Shuisky at the Arbat gate. After retiring from the Chancellery for Criminal Affairs, Suleshov was inactive for eighteen months. Early in 1638 he again was appointed governor of Novgorod after which, in 1640, he retired from active service but remained in attendance at court and on the tsar's pilgrimages. He died February 7, 1643, and his funeral was conducted by Patriarch Joseph. He was buried in the Simonov monastery.

36.   Prince Grigory Petrovich Romodanovsky (dates of birth and death unknown, fl. 1586-1626). His first recorded service is as commander at Mikhailov under the vicegerent Vasily Verderevsky. He was senior governor at Voronezh 1590-1591, then held a field command at Kashira as second in command of the left flank. He then was ordered to assume command in the Novgorod territories, which gave rise to precedence disputes, first with Mikhail Glebovich Saltykov, then as a defendant against Prince Alexander Fedorovich Zhirov-Zasekin. In 1597 he served a bailiff to the Austrian ambassador Abraham Donau, replacing Peter Nikitich Sheremetev, again as the result of a precedence dispute. In the same year he served in the frontier defense forces, third in command of the left wing. In 1598 he was sent as governor to Belgorod, where he remained until 1602. In that year he was sent to receive Prince Johan, prospective bridegroom for Tsarevna Xenia. Romodanovsky then was sent to Orel, and from there was dispatched to the

Mountain Cherkess, where he established the fortress on the Terek. Next he is seen in Moscow as part of the conspiracy against False Dmitry I, after which he was sent by Shuisky to ensure the safety of the Polish ambassadors Olesnicki and Gasiewski. Later in 1606 Romodanovsky was appointed lord-in-waiting. On January 17, 1608, the occasion of the tsar's marriage, he was entrusted with the security of the city. He also served with distinction at the battle on the Khodynka. He was dispatched under Prince Ivan Ivanovich Shuisky to attack Sapieha at the Trinity monastery and fought at Rakhmantsevo, in which engagement his brother Andrei was killed, but Grigory fought on valiantly in a losing cause. In 1609 he was appointed governor of Kashira. After Klushino a letter went out from Kolomna to the towns urging them to submit to Dmitry; one of these letters came to Kashira, but Romodanovsky refused to comply, and nearly was lynched by the inhabitants, but he managed to talk them around. After the deposition of Shuisky, Romodanovsky went along with the boyar administration and swore allegiance to Prince Wladyslaw. During the Polish occupation he was second in charge to Prince F.I. Mstislavsky, who administered the treasury. He was also appointed to the mixed commission to adjudicate disputes between Russians and Poles. In 1613 he was a signatory to Michael Romanov's confirmatory charter. The next year he was dispatched to Livny to confer with the Crimean emissaries and to escort the ambassadors Volkonsky and Yevdokimov. At Christmas 1615 he was promoted boyar, and in 1616 was sent to Kazan to investigate breaches of the peace by the Cheremiss. His colleagues were Kuzma Minin and Mark Pozdeev. In 1618, in anticipation of Wladyslaw's advance on Moscow, Romodanovsky was placed in command of the sector between the Nikita and Tver gates. As soon as the siege was lifted he was dispatched to Mozhaisk to recruit gentry and junior boyars. With him was sent Artemy Izmailov, with whom later he would get into a precedence dispute. In February 1619 he was appointed to the Moscow Judicial Chancellery. He was sent on a recruiting drive in 1622 among the various towns. In January 1623 he was appointed governor of Novgorod, where he remained until April 1626. In relations with Sweden he was ordered to adopt the historical title of vicegerent or lord lieutenant. He met with the Turkish ambassador Thomas Cantacuzene in December 1626. Amid these various appointments he took an active part in the life of the court, and was present on many ceremonial occasions.

37.   Nikita Vasilievich Godunov, lord-in-waiting 1598, died 1622. Crummey, *Aristocrats and Servitors,* p. 179.

38.   Vasily Petrovich Morozov (died 1630) was lord-in-waiting since 1600 or 1601, and became a boyar in 1608. He was second in command of the Pskov garrison which held out against the four-month Swedish siege in 1615.

39.   Kromy was a small fortress besieged by Boris Godunov's army in the spring of 1605. The defection of the commander Peter Fedorovich Basmanov to Dmitry's side was a decisive turning point in the pretender's career. See Vol. 14, pp. 92-93.

40.   Prince Ivan Semeonovich Kurakin (died 1632) was governor and lord lieutenant of Smolensk in 1606 and was also prominent in the plot to overthrow False Dmitry I. In late 1607 and early 1608 he operated successfully against the

second pretender, coming to the relief of the Briansk levies. His efforts were undone by his replacement, the tsar's brother Prince Dmitry Ivanovich Shuisky. In the spring of 1608 he inflicted a reverse on the Polish irregulars under Lisowski, advancing on Moscow from Kolomna after defeating Prokopy Liapunov. In the winter of 1609-1610 he was among the boyars under the overall command of Skopin who cleared the area around Moscow of marauding bands. The inability of Vasily Shuisky to keep control led Kurakin, together with F.I. Mstislavsky, to consider the idea of choosing a new tsar outside the circle of Moscow boyardom. He initially favored Wladyslaw's election, but when the "seven boyars" failed to agree on conditions, he openly espoused the king's cause. This was a particularly inglorious period of his career, as he was under the command of Gasiewski, and was considered only slightly less a traitor than Saltykov and Andronov. In 1615 he was sent into honorific exile as governor of Tobolsk, where he remained for five years. After his return he appears no longer to have taken any active part in affairs.

41.   Prince Yury Nikitich Trubetskoy (dates of birth and death unknown) was cousin to the more famous Prince Dmitry Timofeevich. He was at first loyal to Tsar Vasily Shuisky, but changed sides after being accused unfairly of treasonable dealings during the campaign against the Bolotnikov rebels. Unlike his cousin, who eventually sided with the liberation forces, he remained loyal to False Dmitry II. After the death of the pretender it was Prince Yury who came to Kaluga to urge the inhabitants to swear allegiance to Wladyslaw, while it was Prince Dmitry who successfully urged them to temporize.

42.   Fedor Levontievich Buturlin, surnamed Voron (died 1640), was governor of Riazan in 1603, and chief commander of the Pskov garrison in 1615, at the time of the Swedish siege. In 1616, in anticipation of a Nogay invasion, he was put in charge of the Alexis tower in Moscow. In 1617 as commander of Mozhaisk he foiled an attempt by Prince Wladyslaw to capture the town. In June 1619 he was promoted lord-in-waiting and was dispatched to Zvenigorod to greet Metropolitan Filaret on his journey to Moscow while returning from Polish captivity. In 1620 he was appointed a judge in the Chancellery for Petitions, and until 1629 was constantly in attendance on the tsar, taking part in court ceremonies. In 1629 he was sent to Valuiki to supervise the exchange of Muscovite and Crimean ambassadors. In 1630 he was appointed governor of Kazan, and in 1633 he was back in Moscow to supervise the construction of fortifications between Tver street and the Yauza river. For the remainder of his life he remained in attendance at court.

43.   Ivan Vasilievich Golitsyn was a boyar since 1605. He was exiled in 1624 as a result of the precedence dispute described here, and died in May 1626. Crummey, *Aristocrats and Servitors,* p. 178.

44.   Prince Ivan Ivanovich Shuisky (died 1638) began his career in the household of Tsar Fedor Ivanovich. Although the date of his birth is unknown, he was probably much younger than his brothers Vasily and Dmitry, since he outlived them both by twenty-six years. He was named boyar in 1596, but there is no record that he saw active service during the reign of Boris. After his brother's accession he was sent to the relief of Kaluga, which was being besieged by Bolotnikov, but

without success. He was similarly unsuccessful in his mission to interdict the progress of Jan-Piotr Sapieha towards the siege of the Trinity monastery, being defeated at Rakhmantsevo. After this poor record he does not seem to have been called to active duty again, but he became jealous of his successful kinsman Skopin, whom he slandered to the tsar. The chief blame for the poisoning of the popular hero fell on his brother Dmitry, but the hatred Ivan felt for Skopin was well known, and so he shared the fate of his two brothers in being handed over to the Poles. Vasily and Dmitry died in Polish captivity. Ivan was allowed rather more freedom, but was left to fend for himself in dire poverty, at times being placed under the guard of a troop of hussars. When the Truce of Deulino was concluded he refused to return to Moscow until Wladyslaw released him of his oath of allegiance. He finally appeared at Michael's court in 1630, thereafter taking part in diplomatic receptions as well as presiding over the Moscow Judicial Chancellery and, after 1634, heading the Chancellery for Investigations. He died without heirs, and with him the Muscovite branch of the Shuisky family became extinct.

45. Prince Dmitry Mamstriukovich Cherkassky (died 1651) could claim kinship to the ruling house through the marriage of his aunt Maria Temriukovna to Ivan IV (his second marriage). In 1601 Prince Dmitry fled his native Kabardia and was taken into Muscovite service. After Vasily Shuisky's defeat on the Khodynka river (July 25, 1608) he deserted to Tushino, where he was awarded the title of boyar, and he and Prince Yury Trubetskoy were the last two boyars to remain with False Dmitry II at Kaluga. After the murder of the pretender he swore allegiance to Wladyslaw along with the other inhabitants of Kaluga, and on January 24, 1611 arrived at Sapieha's encampment. Forsaking the Poles he joined the First Militia Force, and was dispatched against Hetman Chodkiewicz in 1612. He established his base at the Antonov monastery, from whence he cleared Uglich of roving cossack bands. For these deeds he was given a hero's welcome at Yaroslavl. He remained with the Second Militia Force, and was with it at the liberation of Moscow. His name appears on the charter granting the Vaga lands to Prince Dmitry Timofeevich Trubetskoy, and he took part in the early deliberations of the Assembly of the Land in 1613. After the initial rejection of Trubetskoy and Michael Romanov, the cossacks convoked a "circle" and proposed Cherkassky as a compromise candidate. Cherkassky, although a foreigner, was in Muscovite service and he had exalted connections in Muscovy. His most recent feats raised his stock with the Second Militia Force, and indeed he had an illustrious career under Michael Romanov, becoming a table attendant in 1613, and then in 1619 being given a boyar rank more legitimate than his Tushino title. He served as head of the Chancellery for Kazan from 1624 to 1636.

46. Temriuk, ruler of Kabardia, was reputed to have been fabulously wealthy. His second son Mikhail accompanied his sister Maria to Moscow and served in Ivan IV's personal corps until he fell into disgrace and was executed in 1571. Temriuk's eldest son Mamstriuk remained in Kabardia, where he inherited much of his father's wealth. He was murdered in 1601, and his son Dmitry fled to Russia.

47. The Russian term in the text is *sotennye i podezdnye spiski.*

48. Grigory Andreevich Aliabiev was governor of Putivl (1622), Viazma (1624) and Pelym (1627). In 1631 he was ambassador to the Netherlands. In 1633 together with Buturlin he campaigned against the Poles in the Severian region.

49. Prince Semeon Ivanovich Prozorovsky (died 1660) was in active service during the reign of Tsar Vasily Shuisky, winning a victory over the forces of False Dmitry II at Khmelniki in 1608. He was in charge of the Chancellery for Posts in 1643.

50. Prince Fedor Mikhailovich Lykov (died 1628) became a lord-in-waiting in 1622, and is last mentioned in active service in 1626. Crummey, *Aristocrats and Servitors*, p. 182

51. Flor Yudich Lugovskoy (sobriquet Tomila, dates of birth and death unknown, fl. 1607-1637). Lugovskoy first appears as a crown secretary in May 1607, when he took part in Tsar Vasily Shuisky's campaign against Tula. In 1608 he was one of the negotiators with the Polish-Lithuanian ambassadors over the renewal of the truce and the release of Polish internees. In 1610 he was employed in the Chancellery for Novgorod and later in the same year participated in the negotiations concerning the election of Prince Wladyslaw. Later he was included in the high embassy sent to the king's encampment outside Smolensk. The negotiations dragged on but, despite Sapieha's blandishments, Lugovskoy refused either to accept rewards from the king or abandon the embassy. Consequently he was interned in Poland along with Filaret and Golitsyn (see Vol. 15, pp. 188-190). He was released in June 1619. Between then and 1628 he rose steadily in rank. From conciliar secretary he was promoted to Moscow noble and eventually to conciliar noble. He conveyed proclamations concerning promotion to boyar or lord-in-waiting and acted as judge in a number of precedence disputes. In March 1628 he was appointed deputy governor of Kazan, where he served for two years. At the time of the Smolensk campaign of 1632 he contributed a hundred quarters of grain for the provisioning of the troops. At Easter 1634 he received a personal audience with the tsar and at Easter 1635 he was a table guest of the tsar and Patriarch Joasaph. Later the same year he was sent to Putivl to survey the land boundaries, and he is last mentioned in 1637 when he attended a reception for the Lithuanian embassy. He then entered the monastic life, but the date of his death is unknown.

52. Prince Peter Alexandrovich Repnin (died 1643) first appears in 1611 as a table attendant serving at Nizhny Novgorod. He was in Moscow in 1618-1619 while it was besieged by Prince Wladyslaw, and served wine at the tsar's table. In 1625 he was posted to Pereiaslavl, the rallying point in the event of a Tatar invasion. In 1625 and 1626 he was among the mounted escorts at both of Tsar Michael's weddings. In the years 1627 to 1629 he dined frequently at the tsar's table. In 1628 he received the Persian ambassador, and in 1631 the Swedish ambassador Anton Monier. In the same year he assumed a field command at Velikie Luki and obtained the surrender of Nevel. In 1635 he was promoted boyar. Prince Ivan Andreevich Golitsyn was supposed to present him, but refused and was imprisoned. Repnin was presented instead by Fedor Stepanovich Streshnev. Repnin was governor of

Novgorod from 1636 to 1638, largely to guard against Swedish infiltrators into Novgorod territories. He also refurbished the fortifications at a cost of 170 rubles in building materials. When he returned to Moscow he was put in charge of the Ustiug tax district, with the task of seeking out tax-paying townsmen who fled during the Moscow disorders. In 1639 he stood vigil over the corpse of Tsarevich Ivan Mikhailovich. Later that year he was in command of troops at Pereiaslavl-in-Riazan. In 1640 according to the tsar's decree he dismissed the troops and returned to Moscow. He died January 27, 1643 and was buried in the St. Paphnutius monastery of Borovsk.

53.   Larion (or Ilarion) Dmitrievich Lopukhin (died 1677) came from a minor provincial gentry family. He himself was enrolled among the resident Moscow gentry, but then according to his petition to Tsar Michael "lost status by becoming a chancellery secretary." He wanted to be dismissed from the bureaucracy, but apparently was satisfied with the tsar's ruling that such an occupation did not demean his family, and spent the rest of his career as a functionary in the various Moscow chancelleries. In 1652 he was promoted to conciliar secretary, and in 1653 headed the Foreign Affairs chancellery while the Moscow government was carrying on negotiations with Bohdan Khmelnitsky. In 1654 he accompanied the tsar on campaign and set up a mobile chancellery in a tent where he gathered copies of all the documents from the field. When preliminaries to peace negotiations began Lopukhin, along with Semeon Romanovich Pozharsky, was the leading Muscovite spokesman. In 1656 talks reopened with the mediation of Emperor Ferdinand III. Lopukhin held discussions with the emperor's special envoy Allegretti, but refused to accept documents or discuss substantive matters until the tsar's title was inscribed correctly. He returned to Moscow in December, and the Austrian embassy which arrived shortly thereafter was referred to him. In 1659 he was sent along with Prince A.N. Trubetskoy to the New Jerusalem monastery to reason with the fallen Patriarch Nikon; although they did not persuade Nikon to return, they did prevail on him to ask the tsar's forgiveness and to give his blessing to the metropolitan of Krutitsy to carry on the affairs of the church. In 1672 Lopukhin, this time on his own, was sent to interview the former patriarch at the Ferapont monastery. In 1667 Lopukhin was promoted to conciliar noble.

54.   Xenia Borisovna Godunova (1582-1622) was the only daughter of Tsar Boris Godunov. During her father's reign she was betrothed twice, first to Prince Gustav of Sweden and secondly to Prince Johan of Denmark. Gustav proved unsuitable and Johan died suddenly a few weeks after his arrival in Moscow. After Boris's death her mother and brother were killed in the coup which brought False Dmitry I to power. According to some accounts she was forced to become Dmitry's mistress; in any case she was banished to a convent, where she took the veil under the name Olga. In 1608 she accompanied the remains of her parents and brother to the Trinity monastery, where she was trapped by the Polish siege. After the lifting of the siege she retired again to her convent.

55.   For information on Prokopy Liapunov, see Note 16, above.

56.   Zakhar Petrovich Liapunov first came to the attention of the Muscovite authorities in 1603 for sending contraband materials to the Don Cossacks. In 1607-1608 he led a detachment of gentry from Riazan against rebellious peasants and supporters of False Dmitry II. In July 1610 he took the initiative in the movement which led to the dethronement of Vasily Shuisky. Then he was a member of the embassy sent to conclude an agreement with King Sigismund III in his encampment outside Smolensk with regard to the accession of Prince Wladyslaw to the Muscovite throne. Before negotiations turned really sour Zakhar returned to Moscow, where his brother Prokopy had been murdered and the First Militia force had collapsed. He fought in the Second Militia Force and witnessed the liberation of Moscow.

57.   Prince Vasily Grigorievich Romodanovsky "the Elder" (dates of birth and death unknown, fl. 1613-1644). Romodanovsky was sent in 1613 with Larion Sumin to Pskov to survey the boundary with Lithuania. Sumin quarreled with Romodanovsky in the town office, accusing Romodanovsky's cousin Pozharsky of buying the throne for twenty thousand rubles. Sumin retracted his words, but witnesses confirmed them. Romodanovsky therefore petitioned the sovereign. Later the same year Romodanovsky was in the guard of honor to greet the Persian ambassador. This gave rise to the precedence dispute with Chepchugov mentioned in this chapter. In 1616, in anticipation of a Tatar attack. Romodanovsky was given a field command at Elets. replacing Ivan Ivanovich Saltykov. In the same year the Lithuanians approached Bolkhov. Romodanovsky was told to stay at Elets and join up with the army of the chief commander I.F. Khovansky. He was replaced in 1617, and in 1618 once again attended a reception for the Persian ambassador. In 1619 he was based on Mtsensk in anticipation of a Crimean and Nogay invasion. In December 1619 he attended the patriarch's table. In 1620 he was once again on frontier guard duties, this time based on Dedilov. Here he came into conflict with Pozharsky, who based his claim "not on genealogy but on service." The tsar did not give a ruling, but ordered that the current campaign be "without precedence." Romodanovsky was also successful in a dispute with Yury Ivanovich "Kosoy" Shakhovskoy, who was imprisoned for three days. In the years 1621 to 1623 he served at court ceremonials of the tsar and the patriarch. In 1623 he was governor of Putivl, and at Toropets from 1625 to 1628, when he accompanied the tsar on pilgrimage to the Trinity monastery. In 1630 he was appointed to attend the Hungarian ambassador, but was replaced because of illness. At the end of 1630 he was appointed governor of Briansk, and at the time of the Smolensk War he was ordered to capture Pochep, where he left a siege commander. He also secured Trubchevsk, and as a result received a message from the tsar inquiring after his health. In 1634 he took part in the reception of the Turkish ambassador Ali-Aga. After conclusion of peace he served as a boundary commissioner in the areas of Pskov and Velikie Luki. This gave rise to the dispute with Prince A.M. Lvov, which Romodanovsky lost and as a result suffered brief imprisonment. In 1635 he met the ambassadors Pesoczynski and Sapieha outside the city of Moscow, and later that

year also received the Persian ambassadors. In 1637 he was a field commander on the southern frontier near Venev, and in 1640 and 1641 was governor of Viazma. In 1644 he took part in the reception of Prince Valdemar.

58.   Yakov Kudenetovich Cherkassky (died 1666) was from the ruling family of Kabardian princes. He arrived in Russia and was baptized in 1624. Between 1641 and 1645 he was a commander on the southern borders, and at the end of this tour of duty received boyar rank. In 1648 he headed a boyar group hostile to the Morozovs, but after the return of Boris Morozov to Moscow he was relieved of all duties. He took an active part in the wars against Poland (1654-1667) and Sweden (1656-1658). He was one of the richest landowners, according to an incomplete survey holding 44,000 desiatinas of land and fifty thousand dependent peasants.

59.   Concerning Maria Khlopova, see Vol. 16, pp. 161-166 and Chapter IV, Note 1 of the same volume.

60.   Prince Ivan Borisovich Cherkassky (died 1642), the son of Prince Boris Kanbulatovich, was first mentioned in 1598 at the election of Boris Godunov. In 1600-1601 he was implicated in the sorcery charges brought against the Romanovs. His property was confiscated and he was exiled to Siberia. While he was on his way there, the bailiff received orders to halt at Malmyzh, there to await the tsar's pleasure. Cherkassky and his uncle Ivan Nikitich Romanov then were ordered to serve at Nizhny Novgorod. In September 1602 the sentence of banishment was lifted and Cherkassky returned to the capital in October. Nothing further is known of his service under Boris or False Dmitry I. Tsar Vasily appointed Cherkassky to the court office previously held by the pretender's favorite Prince Khvorostinin, but he was dismissed shortly afterwards. With the attack on Moscow by False Dmitry II in the fall of 1608, Cherkassky was placed in charge of one of the regiments stationed on the Khodynka. He seems to have seen little further action until 1611, when he fought under the command of Prince Ivan Semeonovich Kurakin on behalf of Prince Wladyslaw in the Vladimir region. Kurakin was defeated, and Cherkassky taken prisoner. His fortunes changed for the better when his kinsman Michael Romanov was elected tsar. Cherkassky was promoted boyar in July 1613, two days before the coronation. The return of Filaret in 1619 improved his lot still further. His first active service under the Romanov regime came in September 1618 when he was sent to Yaroslavl to raise troops for the defense of Moscow. During this campaign he inflicted heavy losses on renegade cossacks operating in the region of Yaropolch. On his return to Moscow early in 1619 he was invited to the sovereign's table, and after the banquet was awarded a sable robe and a silver goblet. Between the autumn of 1624 and the spring of 1627 he was in charge of the Chancellery of Musketeers. During his long career he also served as Treasurer, as head of the Chancellery for Service Foreigners and the Chancellery of the Apothecary. It is known that he was married, but he died without any surviving issue, so his immense fortune was divided between the Sheremetev family and his Cherkassky relatives, Princes Dmitry Mamstriukovich and Yakov Kudenetovich.

61.   See Note 51, above.

62.   See Chapter III, Note 6, above.
63.   By this time the most common form of slavery was through *kabala,* or indenture. There was repeated legislation against servicemen indenturing themselves to others in order to evade obligations. For a comprehensive study of the practice, see Richard Hellie, *Slavery in Russia 1450-1725* (Chicago, 1982).
64.   According to Russian law a man who married a female slave himself became unfree.
65.   Sir Arthur Aston during the Time of Troubles was a mercenary in Russian service, but was accused of plotting with the Poles. As a result of the intercession of the English agent John Merrick he was given leave to depart from Russia, but immediately left for Poland and later appeared in England recruiting mercenaries for Polish service. At the insistence of the Russian ambassador Pogozhy he was confined for a while to the Marshalsea prison, but was released a few days after the ambassador's departure.
66.   John Merrick (1559-1638) was the son of a founding member of the Muscovy Company and began his apprenticeship while accompanying his father on a visit to Russia in the years 1573-1575. He became the Company's agent in Yaroslavl in 1584, and chief agent in Russia in 1594. In 1596 he was admitted to full membership of the Company. He also served as a diplomatic conduit for messages between the governments of Tsar Fedor and Boris Godunov and that of Elizabeth I. Merrick resigned his post in 1601 but resumed it in 1603, and proved indispensable to the embassy of Sir Thomas Smith in 1604-1605. He remained in Russia throughout the Time of Troubles, preserving the interests of the Company through bewildering changes of regime, returning home for only brief periods of home leave. In 1612 he acted as intermediary for a proposal to establish an English protectorate over parts of Northern Russia but when he returned to Russia Tsar Michael had been elected, so Merrick confined himself to the conventional courtesies from King James I. Michael requested English mediation in peace negotiations with Sweden, for which James appointed Merrick, conferring a knighthood on him before his departure. On this occasion Merrick stayed three years in Russia (1614-1617). His attempts to obtain further concessions for English merchants achieved only limited success, whereas from the Russian side proposals for a military alliance against Poland were totally unsuccessful, although a small monetary loan was advanced and delivered in 1618. Merrick's last visit to Russia occurred in 1620-1621, when he obtained repayment of the 1618 loan and a new charter for the Muscovy Company. In 1627 he became governor of the Company, as well as the English government's chief advisor on Russian affairs. See Geraldine M. Phipps, *Sir John Merrick. Merchant-Diplomat in Seventeenth-Century Russia* (Newtonville, Mass., 1980), and her entry in MERSH, Vol. 21, pp. 237-239.
67.   Jacques Margeret (died 1619) was a French Huguenot soldier of fortune whose *Estat de l'Empire de Russie* (Paris, 1607) was dedicated to Henri IV after Margeret's first sojourn in Russia as a mercenary soldier, successively, of Boris Godunov, False Dmitry I and Vasily Shuisky. He later returned to Russia, this time in the service of False Dmitry II, and was among the mercenaries in Polish service

occupying the Kremlin 1610-1612. His memoirs are available in English translation by Chester P. Dunning, *The Russian Empire and Grand Duchy of Moscow* (Pittsburgh, 1985). Unfortunately Margeret left no memoir of his second period in Moscow. After the liberation of Moscow, Margeret and his colleagues, now out of work, requested employment of Pozharsky, who could hardly be blamed for thinking that Margeret had a colossal nerve! Pozharsky declined his application and sent troops to Archangel to prevent his re-entry into Russia. Later Margeret was active in Hamburg, still trying to recruit mercenaries for service in the Polish-Russian wars. See Dunning's entry in MERSH, Vol. 21, pp. 96-99.

68.   See Vol. 16, pp. 116, 146.

69.   Not to be confused with his namesake Alexander Leslie, first earl of Leven, who also served in foreign wars, but returned to Scotland in 1629 to take part in the Bishops' War and the subsequent conflicts between Charles I and his subjects. Roberts refers to him as "Alexander Leslie the Younger." "On 21 June [1631] he [Gustav Adolf] wrote to the Tsar giving leave for Alexander Leslie to raise 5,000 men in North Germany for Russian service." Michael Roberts, *Gustavus Adolphus. A History of Sweden 1611-1632,* Vol. 2 (London, 1958), p. 563. Roberts does not state whether the younger Leslie was related to the future earl of Leven. It appears that he left Russia after the Smolensk War, but returned in 1647 and was given an estate in the Volga region. "Before long the Russian tenants on Leslie's estates and the Russian servants employed in his home began complaining to the local authorities of the cruelty of their new lord, and especially of his lady, as well as the offenses they committed against the Orthodox religion. In one complaint it was stated that Lady Leslie compelled her servants to eat dog meat, and that in Lent. It was reported also that she threw an icon into the fire, and that the colonel and his guest, Lieutenant Thomson, amused themselves by shooting at the cross on the local church. The Leslies were arrested." Vernadsky, *Tsardom,* p. 422. Despite this incident, rather than be herded into the newly instituted Foreign Quarter, Leslie and his family converted to Orthodoxy in 1652. Vernadsky, *Tsardom,* p. 567.

70.   "Colonel Leslie, the most senior of the foreigners, urged striking at the enemy. Colonel Sanderson, an Englishman, gave the opposite opinion. Leslie began to argue, calling Sanderson a traitor, and Shein was barely able to separate them. But on December 2 the Russians, who were suffering from the cold, went out into the forest for wood. The Poles attacked, and five hundred were left on the field. When news of this misfortune reached the blockhouse, Leslie persuaded Shein to go out and reckon for himself how many Russians had fallen. Sanderson accompanied Shein and Leslie. Leslie suddenly turned on him and pointed to the corpses, saying 'This is your doing. You told the king that our men were going into the forest.' 'You lie!' exclaimed the Englishman. Then Leslie, without a word, pulled out his pistol and shot Sanderson dead right in front of Shein." Vol. 16, pp. 218-219.

71.   It was common practice at this time to name artillery pieces in much the same way as is customary with ships.

72.   Literally "Rare Oak."

CHAPTER V

1. See Chapter I, Note 18, above.
2. Prince Daniel Ivanovich Mezetsky (died 1625) was a favorite of Boris Godunov. In 1608, under Shuisky, he was appointed lord-in-waiting. He was one of the signatories of the armistice concluded with Hetman Zolkiewski at Tsarevo-Zaimishche in 1610. He later was one of the plenipotentiaries at the Deulino peace talks in 1618, after which he was promoted boyar. He headed the Chancellery of Artillery from 1626 to 1628, then retired to a monastery, taking the monastic name David.
3. See Chapter II, Note 34, above.
4. Prince Ivan Fedorovich Troekurov, boyar, died 1621.
5. The Russian term is *chetvertyi snop*. The meaning is unclear; probably it meant that a quarter of the crops was taken for the upkeep of the local garrison.
6. False Dmitry I (reigned 1605-1606) most commonly is assumed to have been Grigory (Grishka) Otrepiev, a former monk who cast off the habit after fleeing to Poland. Hence he was referred to frequently as *Rasstriga,* the "untonsured" or renegade monk. See Chapter III, Note 31, above.
7. The town of Romanov was founded in the fourteenth century. In the reign of Ivan IV, together with the settlement of Borisoglebsk across the river, it was given to subject Tatar murzas to form a Muslim enclave similar to that at Kasimov. The enclave was abolished upon building the Resurrection monastery in 1652. In 1882 the two communities were brought together under a single municipality called Romanovo-Borisoglebsk. In 1921 it was renamed Tutaev in honor of a Red Army commander who fell in combat against the Whites in 1918.
8. The process in Russian law is known as *ochnaia stavka.*
9. The "tsar's tithe" (desiatinnaia gosudareva pashnia) was an impost levied from free peasants on court or crown land, principally in Siberia, but also on crown lands in Southern Russia. Though theoretically the amount of land the peasant was to cultivate for the government was equivalent to one-tenth of his holding, in practice it was set by the local administration at between one-seventh and one-fifth. The grain harvested from these lands was used by the government to support servicemen, to subsidize cossack atamans or to be used in the state distilling monopoly. This arrangement first appeared towards the end of the sixteenth century, but about a century later the "tsar's tithe" was commuted to a fixed rent in kind, and in 1769 to a cash payment.
10. Swedish forces occupied Novgorod and much of its territories in 1611. Under the terms of the 1617 Peace of Stolbovo, the Swedes evacuated Novgorod in exchange for the cession of most of the Karelian isthmus. See Vol. 16 of this series.
11. Prince Ivan Andreevich Khovansky (died 1621) fought in 1607 on behalf of Tsar Vasily against the forces of False Dmitry II and the Poles, and then with the

First Militia Force. In 1611 he was defeated by Lisowski near Zaraisk. Later he recaptured Rzhev and Staritsa from the invading Swedes and laid siege to Belaia. During the absence of Prince Dmitry Pozharsky on pilgrimage, in connection with Kuzma Minin he led the Second Militia Force from Yaroslavl to Rostov. In 1615 he was sent to command the Muscovite forces besieging Smolensk. Subsequently he commanded the forces opposing the Lithuanians in the province of Severia, but when he allowed the enemy to break through near Belgorod, he was recalled to Moscow. In 1616 he was appointed head of the Vladimir Judicial Chancellery, and was governor of Novgorod from 1617 to 1619, immediately after it was evacuated by the Swedes.

12. The "dengas after the old pattern" probably refers to the Novgorod denga with the spearman (kopeika) on the reverse, which became the copeck accepted as common currency for all of Muscovy at the rate of one hundred to the ruble. The efimok was an imitation of the Joachimsthaler, overstamped with the Russian emblem, and circulating at the equivalent value of one ruble.

13. See Chapter III, Note 18, above.

14. All these terms are in the diminutive, to emphasize the abject nature of the ensuing petition.

15. Gilian was a region of Northern Persia adjoining the Caspian Sea. In the ninth and tenth centuries it was subject to the Arab caliphate, but between the tenth and fourteenth centuries enjoyed virtual independence. Gilian was under Mongol rule from 1310 to 1370, then in the late sixteenth century came under Persian domination, though between 1570 and 1629 there were several revolts against Safavid rule.

16. The term used here is the archaic *Rus'*. Of course by this time the environs of Astrakhan were under Muscovite sovereignty, but the conquest was sufficiently recent for Astrakhan to be regarded as not part of Russia proper.

17. Soloviev uses the term *Iurgenskoe tsarstvo,* though he explains parenthetically that this signifies the khanate of Khiva.

18. Andreas Deniszoon Vinius (died 1662) came to Russia from Holland in 1627 and initially was engaged in the grain trade at Archangel. In 1632 he was granted a government subsidy and received an exemption from duties for twenty years. He then built iron foundries in the vicinity of Tula. Later he performed various diplomatic missions, travelling to Holland and Denmark to obtain military equipment for the Russian armed forces. He also held a number of administrative positions in the various Muscovite chancelleries. His son Andreas Anderszoon (1641-1717) continued in Russian service, and was a close adviser to Peter the Great during his formative years. See Platonov, *Moscow and the West*, pp. 118-119.

19. See Chapter I, Note 35, above.

20. Thielemann Lus (in Russian Filimon Filimonyich) Akema (died 1675) first came to Russia in 1631 as a commercial agent in Archangel and Moscow. In 1633 he received a charter from Tsar Michael to trade in Russia, and in 1639 joined in partnership with Andreas Vinius, Peter Marselis and Boris Morozov to operate the

Tula ironworks. Although this partnership dissolved in acrimony, Akema and Marselis retained the Tula ironworks and received permission to build another on the Vaga river. The Russian government confiscated these enterprises in 1647, but Akema and Marselis mobilized sufficient political and economic pressure from abroad to have them returned the following year. In 1653 the partners established four additional manufactories in the Kashira district, acquired an ironworks from Ilia Miloslavsky on the Porotva river in 1656 and built a new enterprise on the Ugodka river in 1659. When Peter Marselis fell into disgrace in 1662 his share of the enterprises was confiscated by the Russian government, which thus became Akema's partner. Akema was dissatisfied with this situation, so an accommodation was reached in 1663 which gave him full ownership of the Porotva and Ugodka enterprises, with compensation of five thousand rubles for the remainder. He then took on two additional partners, his nephew Thielemann and his brother-in-law Richard Andrews. A new charter was received from Tsar Alexis in 1665. Three years after his death Akema's widow Anna (née Dekroo) married another expatriate, Werner Müller, who further expanded the business. See entry by Joseph T. Fuhrmann, MERSH, Vol. 1, pp. 70-71.

21.   Christopher Galloway designed the upper part of the Kremlin Savior tower and installed the clock.

22.   Soloviev here uses the term *ropata,* denoting a non-Orthodox, not necessarily Christian, place of worship. The more common word for a Protestant church was kirk or kirka.

23.   Here and elsewhere the term *nemtsy* (literally "Germans") is applied to foreigners in general, especially those of North European origin.

24.   Adam Ölschläger (1599-1671), best known by the Latinized version of his surname, Olearius, was born at Aschersleben in the principality of Anhalt. Though of humble birth—both his father and grandfather were tailors—he completed grammar school and matriculated at the University of Leipzig, receiving his bachelor's degree in 1624 and his master's in 1627. For the next few years he taught in various schools, and in 1632 he was appointed to the university faculty. The Thirty Years War forced Olearius to abandon academic pursuits, and he readily accepted an invitation to enter the service of Duke Friedrich of Holstein. He was assigned as secretary to the embassy for its initial journey in 1633, and was attached to subsequent missions as an accompanying scholar. He so impressed his hosts that in 1639 and 1643 Tsar Michael tried to recruit Olearius into his own service. His travel account originally appeared in 1647 under the title *Offt begehrte Beschreibung der newen Reise so durch Gelegenheit einer Holsteinischer Legation an den König in Persien geschehen* (Oft-desired Description of the Recent Oriental Journey which a Holstein Legation Had the Opportunity to Make to the King of Persia), and an augmented version was published in 1656, entitled *Expanded New Description of the Muscovite and Persian Empires.* Both editions were published in Schleswig. The success of his book won Olearius an honored place in Holstein, where he served as court mathematician and philosopher, becoming known as the "Holstein Pliny." During his travels he acquired a unique knowledge of the Persian language

and on his return to Europe did pioneering work in Oriental studies. See entry by Samuel H. Baron, MERSH, Vol. 25, pp. 240-243. Soloviev apparently used the 1647 edition, though most translations are based on that of 1656. See Chapter VI, Note 51, below.

25. Actually he estimated only about a thousand individual Protestants, *bey tausend Häupter.* Platonov, *Moscow and the West,* p. 57.

26. In Russian "Ulianov."

27. See p. 106, above.

CHAPTER VI

1. On Cyprian's role as abbot of the Khutyn monastery, see Vol. 16, pp. 90-95. He served as archbishop of Tobolsk from 1620 to 1624. While in Siberia he founded monasteries and convents in Turinsk and Tara. He also started new settlements and the compilation of the first Siberian chronicles. On his return to Russia proper he became metropolitan of Krutitsy, in other words coadjutor to the patriarch, from 1624 to 1627, and then until his death in 1635 served as metropolitan of Novgorod.

2. Unfortunately there is little or no information available on this important missionary prelate.

3. Gury was the first archbishop of Kazan, sent there almost immediately after the conquest. The situation of Cyprian and Makary was almost identical, being missionary archbishops in recently conquered territory, and providing a classical example of how settlers and missionaries quickly come to cross-purposes. For information on Gury, see Vol. 12, Chapter IV, Note 7; also in the same volume the initial segment, entitled "Expansion of Orthodoxy," of Chapter VI.

4. The Hundred Chapters (Stoglav) council met in January-February 1551 and completed its work in May. It received its name from the collection of resolutions which were divided into a hundred "chapters." It was summoned on the initiative of the Muscovite government to combat heresy and to bring the church under the jurisdiction of the secular authorities. The government was not able to obtain assent to the secularization of monastic properties or the subjection of the clergy to the secular courts, but managed to obtain a prohibition against further monastic franchises within the towns. The council adopted measures aimed at standardizing church ritual and improving the education and morals of the clergy, and also placed scribed and inconographers under ecclesiastical control. See Vols. 10 and 12 of this series.

5. Avraamy Palitsyn (died 1626), cellarer of the Trinity monastery, was one of the heroes of the liberation movement, as well as being one of its leading chroniclers. He also played a leading part in the defense of the Trinity monastery against Prince Wladyslaw in 1618, but in 1619 fell into disfavor and spent the remaining years of his life at the Solovetsk monastery. See entry in MERSH, Vol. 26, pp. 195-197.

6.   The canonarch was responsible for directing the choral singing in the monastic choir.

7.   The choir was divided into two sections. The canonarch (kanonarkhist) was responsible for the overall direction of the choir. The precentor (ustavshchik or ustavnik) led the right-hand choir which sang the versicles; the left-hand choir, led by the subprecentor (golovshchik), sang the responses.

8.   In Russian *semia* and *sem'ia* respectively.

9.   The nun Martha, in secular life Xenia Ivanovna Romanovna, was married to Filaret Nikitich Romanov. When the Romanovs were disgraced in 1601 she was forced to take the veil and was banished to a distant convent. She returned to Moscow during the reign of False Dmitry, and at the time of her son's election in 1613 she was with him at the Hypatian monastery in Kostroma. During the earlier years of his reign she exercised some control over affairs, and even vetoed one of Michael's proposed marriages. When her husband Filaret returned from Polish captivity in 1619 Martha retired to the Ascension convent within the Kremlin, where she spent the rest of her days. She died January 27, 1637.

10.   Solovki is the site of the Solovetsk monastery, a place of harsh northern confinement.

11.   See p. 155, above.

12.   Archimandrite Joseph is described as a *protosingel,* which the lexicographer Sreznevsky describes as "an ecclesiastical dignitary at the court of Byzantine patriarchs," but he does not indicate the functions of this office. See also Chapter II, Note 43, above.

13.   *Pokrovskoe Krasnoe Selo.*

14.   *...ellinskie bliadosloviia.* "Greek" here is in the sense of "pagan."

15.   In some respects the Russians followed the Jewish dietary laws. Already referred to was the prohibition against eating veal. According to Jewish law, animals slaughtered for food must have their throats slit and their blood drained. This law also applied to gentiles living among the Jews. See Leviticus 17:10-14.

16.   *...koledny b, ovseniia i plugi.* The Koliada was a form of pagan revelry, only superficially christianized, celebrating the winter solstice. Similarly the spring sowing and ploughing songs, in the mind of the clergy, constituted vestigial pagan fertility rites.

17.   Evidently when performing a normal marriage the officiant issued a certificate (znamia). Since these marriages were irregular, no official record was kept.

18.   Although subsequently Cyprian became a metropolitan, first of Krutitsy and then of Novgorod, in Tobolsk he only ranked as an archbishop. Soloviev here is promoting him somewhat prematurely.

19.   This reflects a nicety of protocol which Soloviev here does not find it necessary to decode, but which might prove puzzling to modern readers. Suleshov was a recent Crimean Tatar convert. Nizovtsev, by kissing his hand rather than giving him a proper embrace, apparently was casting aspersions on the sincerity of Suleshov's new-found Christianity.

20.   See below, section "Adam Olearius," also Chapter I, Note 35, above.

21.   Prince Ivan Andreevich Khvorostinin (died 1625) began his career at the court of False Dmitry I, apparently as the pretender's homosexual favorite. During

the reign of Vasily Shuisky he was exiled to the monastery of St. Joseph of Volokolamsk, from which he returned to Moscow in 1610 or 1611. During the reign
of Michael he received a series of arduous assignments but, under constant suspicion, was banished for a second period of monastic confinement on charges of
heresy, drunkenness and "lack of firmness towards treasonable activity." He was
released in 1624, but shortly afterwards voluntarily became a monk and died at the
Trinity monastery during the following year. See entry in MERSH, Vol. 16, pp.
204-206.

22.   ...*moskovskie zhe liudi seiut zemliu rozh'iu, a zhivut vse lozh'iu.*

23.   Cyril (315-386) was ordained presbyter in 345, and in 350 became bishop
of Jerusalem. His metropolitan Bishop Acacius of Antioch inclined to Arianism,
while Cyril maintained the Nicene position. As a result Cyril was deposed until the
accession of Theodosius I in 379 permitted him to return. He attended the Second
Council of Constantinople in 381, and was welcomed for his defense of Orthodoxy.
His one important work is the *Catacheses,* a series of twenty-three lectures to cat-
echumens delivered in 348. This is doubtless the work referred to here by the title
of *Proclamation.*

24.   ...*tresnovenii, shibanii i perune.*

25.   The *Nicephoran Rules* was a compilation of canon law brought by Metropolitan Cyprian in the late fourteenth century from his native Balkans. Evidently
they were in the original Greek, of which he commissioned a Slavonic translation.

26.   See Chapter I, Note 7, above. As indicated in that note, Shakhovskoy may
have been even more prolific a writer than Soloviev imagined.

27.   The *Manuscript of Filaret* was composed between 1626 and 1623 at the
patriarchal court, very likely with Filaret's personal participation. In the opinion
of some scholars, portions of it are in the patriarch's own handwriting. It is based
on the *Book of Annals,* attributed variously to Sergei Kubasov, Prince Ivan
Mikhailovich Katyrev-Rostovsky, but now most likely to Shakhovskoy (see
preceding note), with entries to bring the chronicle up to date. It was available to
Soloviev in printed form under the title *Rukopis' Filareta, patriarkha Moskovskogo
i vseia Rossii,* ed. P.A. Mukhanov (Moscow, 1837). A second edition was
published in 1866. See Platonov, *Drevnerusskie skazaniia i povesti o smutnom
vremeni XVII veka kak istoricheskii istochnik* (Ancient Russian Stories and Tales
Concerning the Seventeenth-Century Time of Troubles as a Historical Source),
2nd ed. (St. Petersburg, 1913), pp. 281-291.

28.   Sviatopolk "the Damned" (960-1019) became prince of Turov in 968 and
grand prince of Kiev in 1015. He was married to a daughter of the Polish king
Boleslaw the Brave, with whose help he conspired against his father Grand Prince
Vladimir Sviatoslavich, after whose death he seized the grand-princely throne,
having ordered the slaying of his brothers Boris, Gleb and Sviatoslav. Another
brother, Yaroslav of Novgorod, came in arms against him and defeated him at
Liubech. In 1018 he returned with Polish help, defeated Yaroslav on the Bug river
and expelled him from Kiev, but his Polish supporters were driven out of the
country through a popular uprising. In 1019 Yaroslav made another bid for the

grand-princely throne, and Yaroslav fled to the Pechenegs. He was defeated on the Alta river, after which he fled to Poland, and then Bohemia, and was never heard of again. See Vol. 1 of this series.

29.   See Note 5, above.

30.   "In Ukrainian history the period following the Union of Pereiaslav, Bogdan Khmelnitsky's death in 1657, and the Treaty of Andrusovo is vividly described as 'the Ruin,' and its complexities rival those of the Russian Time of Troubles. Divided both physically and in orientation and allegiance, the Ukrainians followed a number of competing leaders who usually, in one way or another, played off Poland against Moscow; Hetman Peter Doroshenko even paid allegiance to Turkey. Constant and frequently fratricidal warfare decimated the people and exhausted the land." Nicholas V. Riasanovsky, *A History of Russia,* 5th ed. (New York, 1993), p. 181. See also Vol. 20 of this series.

31.   Soloviev here refers to the *So-called Other Tale* (Tak nazyvaemoe Inoe Skazanie), of which the author is unknown, but which was written as a rebuttal to the version given by Avraamy Palitsyn (see Note 5, above). There is less detail about earlier events or the siege of the Trinity monastery, but a much more circumstantial account of the Bolotnikov rebellion, and is almost unique among chronicles in praising Vasily Shuisky, who gets a rather negative press from most other writers. The narrative incorporates such literary compositions as the *Tale of How Boris Godunov Unjustly Seized the Throne,* the *Life of Tsarevich Dmitry,* and documents issued by False Dmitry I and Vasily Shuisky. Also included is the account by Archpriest Terenty of the Annunciation cathedral of the vision seen by a certain clergyman in the Dormition cathedral (see Vol. 15, p. 32). Platonov, *Drevnerusskie skazaniia,* pp. 1-103.

32.   *Skazanie o Mamaevom poboishche* (Tale of the Battle with Mamay) is an early fifteenth-century poem commemorating the battle of Kulikovo Field (1380). According to the late nineteenth-century scholar A.A. Shakhmatov, it was based on a lost account of the battle composed at the court of Prince Vladimir Andreevich of Serpukhov. For a summary in English, see A. Pronin, *History of Old Russian Literature* (Frankfurt, 1968), pp. 309-311.

33.   "During Boris' time the Muscovite government first had recourse to an enlightened measure that later became customary. It sent abroad to 'learn various languages and reading and writing' several Russian boys, young noblemen. They were to learn 'strictly how to read and write the language of the country to which they were sent.' We know from the records that five were sent to Lübeck and four to England. According to private accounts, eighteen were sent in all, six each to England, France and Germany. Interestingly, none of those sent returned with the desired results of study. Several died. Others proved to be 'refractory and did not listen to the lessons,' and even 'ran away' from the teachers 'for some unknown reason.' Some of them accepted the 'lessons' but remained abroad forever. One of these, Nikifor Alferievich Grigoriev, became a priest in England, 'a noble member of the Episcopalian clergy,' and lived to old age. In 1643 during the Puritan movement he even suffered for his steadfastness in his new belief and lost his parish in

Huntingdonshire." Platonov, *Moscow and the West,* pp. 32-33. See also Vol. 16 of this series, pp. 121, 184, and Vol. 14, p. 48.

34. See pp. 171-173, above.

35. See Chapter I, pp. 10-11, above.

36. *Chernoknizhiia,* literally knowledge of "black books." The nuance of the following sentence is impossible to render adequately into English.

37. *Aristotle's Gates* (Aristotel'skie vrata) was a work of cabalistic literature known to have been somewhat of an underground classic in a number of monastic institutions.

38. Soloviev queries here the mention of Prokopy Liapunov at the Kremlin siege of 1612 because, of course, he was murdered by the cossacks in June 1611, thus causing the collapse of the First Militia Force.

39. The text actually reads *nemtsy* (Germans), but the foreigners in question were Swedes, present in Novgorod since 1609, when Shuisky invoked the aid of Karl IX to fight the Polish intervention of King Sigismund III. See Volume 15 of this series.

40. Probably a garbled reference to Revelation 8:7-8 and 9:18.

41. In 198 B.C. the Jews opened the gates of Jerusalem to Antiochus the Great, being disenchanted with Ptolemaic rule based on Egypt. See Josephus, *Antiquities* 12:3. There is no indication that the event took place at Passover, though the Russian chronicler might have added this detail in order to heighten the analogy with Holy Week.

42. Michael VIII Paleologus recaptured Constantinople 1261, putting an end to more than half a century of Latin rule.

43. In fact Michael was only sixteen years of age at his accession.

44. See Chapter IV, Note 1, above.

45. Her name actually was Maria.

46. Grigory Lukianovich Belsky (died 1573), generally known as Maliuta Skuratov, was one of the chief henchmen in Ivan the Terrible's oprichnina. He had two daughters, one of whom, Maria, was married to Boris Godunov, while the other, Catherine, was married to Prince Dmitry Ivanovich Shuisky.

47. A translation of Osoryin's biography of his mother is contained in Zenkovsky, pp. 312-320.

48. Servants or others of inferior social status usually were addressed by diminutive forms of their Christian names.

49. See Vol. 16 of this series, pp. 119-120, 183; also Chapter IV, Note 27 of the same volume.

50. The term used is *bus,* probably a Russian variant of the Dutch *buis,* a two-masted craft generally used in the herring fisheries.

51. See Chapter V, Note 24, above. Olearius's account is best accessible in the abridged English translation *The Travels of Olearius in Seventeenth-Century Russia,* translated and edited by Samuel H. Baron (Stanford, 1967). All citations are from this version.

52. Probably referring to the battle of Breitenfeld, September 17, 1631.

53. "From Capurga [Koporie] the way went across the estate of a boyar named Nikita Vasil'evich, but since the estate was seven leagues away and we had departed late, we were obliged to travel through the night until we reached the house. At 3 o'clock in the morning, the boyar received us kindly and feasted us with various foods and drinks in silver vessels. He had two trumpeters who played gaily while we were at table, and especially when we drank toasts, a practice he had probably learned from the Germans. It was abundantly evident that he was a gay and brave fellow. He had participated in the battle before Leipzig in 1631 and showed us the scars of the wounds he had received." Olearius, p. 42.

54. "In Russia generally, as a result of the fertility of the soil, produce is very inexpensive; for example, for a chicken, two kopeks (which is equal to two schillings of Meissen money); for nine eggs, one kopeck. We daily received two rubles and five kopeks (that is four reichsthalers and five schillings). Each person was allotted a share proportionate to his rank." Olearius, p. 48.

55. "In this village [Vyshny Volochek] we met a 12-year-old boy who had been married several weeks before. A marriage of the kind was contracted in Tver for an 11-year-old girl. In Russia, as in Finland, children 12 years old, and even younger, are permitted to marry. Usually these weddings are between widows and boys whose parents have died. In this manner, they can keep their property, and do not have to depend on friends and guardians." Olearius, pp. 94-95. In a footnote to this passage, Baron points out that the Hundred Chapters Council of 1551 stipulated the minimum age for marriage as twelve.

56. "On April 17, Holy Easter Day, there was great rejoicing among the Russians, partly because of the Resurrection of Christ, partly because it was the end of their long fast. That day, and for fourteen days thereafter, practically everyone—notables and commoners, young and old—carries colored eggs. In every street a multitude of egg vendors sit, hawking boiled eggs decorated in various colors. When they meet on the street, they greet each other with kisses on the mouth. One says 'Khristos voskrese,' that is, *'Christ is risen'; and the other answers, 'Voistinu voskrese,'* which means 'Indeed He has risen.' And no one, neither man or woman, neither magnate nor commoner, refuses to another a kiss and greeting and an egg. The Grand Prince himself distributes Easter eggs to his courtiers and servants. It is also his custom, the night before Easter, before he went to morning prayer, to visit the prison, open the cells, and give each prisoner (there were always many) an egg and a sheepskin coat, saying: 'Let them be happy. For Christ, who died for their sins, has indeed arisen.' Then he ordered the prison shut again and went off to church. All during Holy Easter not only did good friends visit [each other] in private homes, but everyone—lay and ecclesiastical people, men and women—avidly patronized simple *kabaki,* that is beer, mead, and vodka houses. They drank so much that frequently people were seen lying here and there in the streets, and some of them had to be thrown onto wagons or sleighs by their relatives and taken home. Under the circumstances, it may be understood why many people, murdered and stripped of their clothing, were found in the morning lying in the streets. Now, thanks to the Patriarch, these great excesses from visits to taverns or pothouses have abated somewhat." Olearius, pp. 100-101.

57. "Not a month, nor even a week, goes by without some homes—or, if the wind is strong, whole streets—going up in smoke. Several nights while we were there we saw flames rising in three or four places at once. Shortly before our arrival, a third of the city burned down, and we were told that the same thing happened four years earlier. When such disasters occur, the streltsi and special guards are supposed to fight the fires. They never use water, but instead quickly tear down the houses nearest the fire, so that it will lose its force and go out. For that purpose every soldier and guard is obliged to carry an axe with him at night." Olearius, p. 112.

58. "Those whose houses are destroyed in a fire can quickly obtain new ones. Outside the white wall is a special market with partly assembled houses. One can buy one of these and have it moved to his site and set up at little expense…. In this district is located the wood market and the house market mentioned above, where one may purchase a house that can be built in another part of the city in just two days." Olearius, pp. 112, 116. He also calls this part of the city, later known as the Earthen City, "Skorodom" ("quick house").

59. "They also have all sorts of kitchen vegetables, notably asparagus as thick as a thumb, which I myself sampled in Moscow at the home of a good friend of mine, a Dutch merchant. Besides, they grow good cucumbers, onions, and garlic, in great quantities. The Russians have never planted lettuce or other salad greens; they paid them no attention and not only did not eat them but even laughed at the Germans who did, saying they ate grass. Now some of them are beginning to try salad." Olearius, p. 121.

60. "The Russians also greatly love tobacco, and formerly everyone carried some with him. The poor man gave his kopek as readily for tobacco as for bread. However, it was presently remarked that people got no good whatever from it, but, on the contrary, appreciable ill. Servants and slaves lost much time from their work; many houses went up in smoke because of carelessness with flame and sparks; and before the ikons, which were supposed to be honored during church services with reverence and pleasant-scented things, the worshippers emitted an evil odor. Therefore, in 1634, at the suggestion of the Patriarch, the Grand Prince banned the sale and use of tobacco along with the sale by private taverns of vodka and beer. Offenders were punished very severely—by slitting of the nostrils, and the knout. We saw the marks of such punishment on both men and women…." Olearius, p. 146. In a note to this passage, Baron points out that this prohibition was reiterated in the 1649 Law Code, and that both it and the 1634 decree even prescribed the death penalty. In practice enforcement of the ban became very lax, until Peter the Great repealed it altogether and sold the monopoly of the tobacco trade with Russia to an English nobleman. As we have seen earlier, tobacco features prominently among contraband items allegedly smuggled and illicitly sold by foreign merchants and diplomats.

61. "So given are they to lusts of the flesh and fornication that some are addicted to the vile depravity we call sodomy; and not only with boys…but also with men and horses. Such antics provide matter for conversation in their carouses. People caught in such obscene acts are not severely punished. Tavern musicians

often sing of such loathsome things, too, in the open streets, while some show them to young people in puppet shows." Olearius, p. 142.

62.   "Most of their conversation is directed to the side of things toward which their nature and base way of life incline: they speak of debauchery, of vile depravity, of lasciviousness, and of immoral conduct committed by themselves and others. They tell all sorts of shameless fables, and he who can relate the coarsest obscenities and indecencies, accompanied by the most wanton mimicry, is accounted the best companion and is the most sought after." Olearius, pp. 141-142.

63.   "With regard to intelligence, the Russians are indeed distinguished by cleverness and shrewdness. However, they use these qualities not to strive for virtue and glory, but to seek advantage and profit and to indulge their appetites." Olearius, p. 133.

64.   "Their houses are shoddy and cheap, and the interiors have few furnishings and utensils. Most have not more than three or four earthen pots and as many clay and wooden dishes.... None of the houses, whether rich or poor, display vessels as ornaments; the walls are bare, except in the houses of the wealthy, where they are hung with mats and some icons." Olearius, p. 155.

65.   "However, when the magnates have feasts and invite people beneath them in rank, it is certain that they are seeking something other than their good company. Their largess serves as a baited hook, with which they gain more than they expend. For, according to their custom, guests are supposed to bring the host valuable gifts. Formerly, when a German merchant received such attentions and an invitation, he was already sensible of what this honor would cost him. It is said that the voevodas in the cities, especially those where a lively trade is carried on, show their liberality once, twice or three times a year, by inviting the rich merchants to banquets of this sort." Olearius, p. 158.

66.   "The slaves and servants of magnates are countless. Many have more than fifty, and some even more than a hundred, on their estates and in their households. Most of those in Moscow, instead of being fed in the households, are given a subsistence allowance, though it is so small as hardly to sustain life. That is why there are so many thieves and murderers in Moscow." Olearius, p. 149.

67.   "Generally, even the lesser notables raise their daughters in closed-off rooms, hidden from other people, and the groom does not see the bride before he receives her in the marriage bedroom. Thus some are deceived, and instead of a beautiful bride are given an ugly and sickly one; sometimes, instead of the daughter, some friend, or even a maidservant is substituted. Such cases are known [even] among high-ranking personages. Under the circumstances, one should not be surprised that husbands and wives live together like cats and dogs, and that wife-beating is so common in Russia." Olearius, pp. 164-165.

68.   Daniel 2:2 and 3:13-27.

69.   "Chaldeans was the name given, when we were there, to certain dissolute people who received the Patriarch's permission, for a period of eight days before Christmas to the Day of the Three Saintly Kings [Epiphany], to run about the streets with special fireworks. They often burned the beards of passersby, especially the

peasants. While we were there, they burned up a load of peasant's hay, and when he began to resist them, they burned his beard and the hair on his head. Whoever wanted to be spared had to pay a kopek. They were dressed as carnival revelers, wearing on their heads painted wooden hats, and their beards were smeared with honey to prevent their being burned by the fire they were casting about. They were called Chaldeans in memory of those servants in King Nebuchadnezzar's time who, as legend has it, started a fire in an oven wherein they intended to burn Shadrach, Meshach, and Abednego. Perhaps, in former times, they also meant to commemorate a miracle that was supposed to have occurred at their conversion. They make the fire with a special powder which they pound out of a plant or herb that they call plaun'. These flames are marvelous and enjoyable to watch, especially when they are thrown at night or in the dark, and one can get much amusement from it. During their escapades the Chaldeans were considered pagans, and impure. It was even thought that if they should die during these days they would be damned. Therefore, on the Day of the Three Saintly Kings, a day of great general confession, they were all baptized anew, to cleanse them of their godless impurity and join them once again to the church. After receiving baptism they were again [considered] as pure and holy as the others. Some of these people had been baptized ten times and more. Since these hoodlums committed many grievances and much mischief against the peasants and common people, as well as against pregnant women, and since their playing with fire had caused no little danger besides, the Patriarch has entirely abolished their ridiculous games and masked running about." Olearius, pp. 241-242.

INDEX

THE EDITOR AND TRANSLATOR

George Edward Orchard was born in London, England in 1935 and grew up in Hampshire, where he received his primary and secondary education. At the age of eighteen he was conscripted into the British armed forces, where he learned Russian in the Joint Services' School for Linguists, Bodmin, Cornwall, and then served with the 755 Signals Unit in the British Army of the Rhine. Having completed his military service, he read Modern History at St. John's College, Oxford, receiving his Bachelor of Arts degree in 1959. After several years of school teaching in England, Nigeria and Canada, he studied at McGill University, Montreal, Canada from 1964 to 1966, receiving his Ph.D in history in 1967. From 1966 until his retirement in 1990 he taught at the University of Lethbridge, Alberta. He has also taught summer courses at Nipissing University, North Bay, Ontario, and in 1991 was a visiting professor at the Université Canadienne en France, Villefranche-sur mer. He visited the Soviet Union three times, and was one of the first participants in the Canada-USSR Academic Exchange. He has also conducted research in England, the Netherlands and Germany. His publications include scholarly translations of Isaac Massa's *Short History of the Muscovite Wars* and Conrad Bussow's *Disturbed State of the Muscovite Realm,* as well as three volumes in the Soloviev series. Work is also in progress on scholarly translations of Sigismund von Herberstein's *Notes on Moscow* and Hans Georg Peyerle's *Journey to Moscow.* In 1991 he assumed responsibility as General Editor of the Soloviev project for Academic International Press. Professor Orchard lives with his wife Ellen and his daughter Catherine in Lethbridge, Alberta.

FROM ACADEMIC INTERNATIONAL PRESS*

THE RUSSIAN SERIES Volumes in Print

THE CENTRAL AND EAST EUROPEAN SERIES

THE ACADEMIC INTERNATIONAL REFERENCE SERIES

The Modern Encyclopedia of Russian and Soviet History 58 vols.

The Modern Encyclopedia of Russian and Soviet Literatures 50 vols.

The Modern Encyclopedia of Religions in Russia and the Soviet Union 30 vols

Soviet Armed Forces Review Annual

Russia & Eurasia Facts & Figures Annual

Russia & Eurasia Documents Annual

USSR Calendar of Events (1987- 1991) 5 vol. set

USSR Congress of Peoples's Deputies 1989. The Stenographic Record

Documents of Soviet History 12 vols.

Documents of Soviet-American Relations

Gorbachev's Reforms. An Annotated Bibliography of Soviet Writings. Part 1 1985–1987

Military Encyclopedia of Russia and Eurasia 50 vols.

China Facts & Figures Annual

China Documents Annual

Sino-Soviet Documents Annual

Encyclopedia USA. The Encyclopedia of the United States of America Past & Present 50 vols.

Sports Encyclopedia North America 50 vols.

Sports in North America. A Documentary History

Religious Documents North America Annual

The International Military Encyclopedia 50 vols.

SPECIAL WORKS
S.M. Soloviev History of Russia 50 vols.
SAFRA Papers 1985-

*Request catalogs